Language Policy

Volume 22

The last half century has witnessed an explosive shift in language diversity not unlike the Biblical story of the Tower of Babel, but involving now a rapid spread of global languages and an associated threat to small languages. The diffusion of global languages, the stampede towards English, the counter-pressures in the form of ethnic efforts to reverse or slow the process, the continued determination of nation-states to assert national identity through language, and, in an opposite direction, the greater tolerance shown to multilingualism and the increasing concern for language rights, all these are working to make the study of the nature and possibilities of language policy and planning a field of swift growth.

The series will publish empirical studies of general language policy or of language education policy, or monographs dealing with the theory and general nature of the field. We welcome detailed accounts of language policy-making - who is involved, what is done, how it develops, why it is attempted. We will publish research dealing with the development of policy under different conditions and the effect of implementation. We will be interested in accounts of policy development by governments and governmental agencies, by large international companies, foundations, and organizations, as well as the efforts of groups attempting to resist or modify governmental policies. We will also consider empirical studies that are relevant to policy of a general nature, e.g. the local effects of the developing European policy of starting language teaching earlier, the numbers of hours of instruction needed to achieve competence, selection and training of language teachers, the language effects of the Internet. Other possible topics include the legal basis for language policy, the role of social identity in policy development, the influence of political ideology on language policy, the role of economic factors, policy as a reflection of social change.

The series is intended for scholars in the field of language policy and others interested in the topic, including sociolinguists, educational and applied linguists, language planners, language educators, sociologists, political scientists, and comparative educationalists.

More information about this series at http://www.springer.com/series/6209

Richard Powell

Language Choice in Postcolonial Law

Lessons from Malaysia's Bilingual Legal System

Springer

Richard Powell
Nihon University
Tokyo, Japan

ISSN 1571-5361 ISSN 2452-1027 (electronic)
Language Policy
ISBN 978-981-15-1172-1 ISBN 978-981-15-1173-8 (eBook)
https://doi.org/10.1007/978-981-15-1173-8

This Springer imprint is published by the registered company Springer Nature Singapore Pte Ltd.
The registered company address is: 152 Beach Road, #21-01/04 Gateway East, Singapore 189721, Singapore

Preface

On one of my first visits to a Malaysian courthouse, I sat fascinated even before the hearing began by the mix of languages being bandied around among lawyers and clerks. Malay, English, Cantonese and Tamil flowed under a sign reading *Gunakan bahasa kebangsaan* (*Use the national language*). With the bailiff's order to rise for the judge's entry, these multilingual exchanges gave way to bilingual ones. A clerk announced the first case in Malay. Prosecuting counsel introduced himself in Malay and the defence followed in English. Preliminaries proceeded partly in English and partly in Malay peppered with "mention", "deferral", "ex parte application" and other terms heard in courtrooms throughout the common law world.

Just as I was settling down for the case, the judge glanced up at the public gallery, set his gaze on me and asked who I was, triggering memories of my days as a solicitor's clerk when to be addressed by a judge generally meant trouble. After I stammered something about my interest in legal language, *Yang Arif* (His Honour) warned me that proceedings would be in Malay and seemed about to get on with matters when he looked up again and invited me to sit right behind the lawyers so as to hear better. And after another moment's reflection, he instructed the counsel to "feel free to use whatever language you feel most comfortable in, in view of our international guest". From that point, nearly everything was English.

A classic example of an observer's presence contaminating their data collection, this shift from bilingualism to monolingualism was initially disappointing, but there was compensation in the string of questions it put into my head. How did an "international guest" warrant the use of a language other than the national language? Why was the alternative readily understood to be English and willingly and capably taken up? Was it only for my benefit or also a concession to the legal professionals?

In coming to know Malaysia better, I've learnt that language choice is rarely straightforward in a country where the word *keadilan* (justice) was ruled out after it was decided the Palace of Justice needed a Malay name, as it featured in the title of an opposition party (Hafiz 2012.9.19); where a deputy prime minister's fumbling English in a speech at the UN divided those for whom the language is a basic educational marker from those for whom it is an emblem of colonialism (Kee 2016.10.04); where authorities may remove Chinese signs if they are bigger than those in Malay (*Malaysiakini* 2018.9.06); and where a new snack failed to get halal certification, not because of its ingredients but because of being marketed as a "pretzel dog" (*Malaysiakini* 2016.10.17). Controversy is never keener than when the languages jockeying for position are Malay and English, and the stakes are never higher than when the arena is the judicial system.

A poignant example of this can be found in an appeal filed in a suit against Mahathir Mohamad, prime minister between 1981 and 2003 and now back in power at the age of 92, by Anwar Ibrahim, the deputy he fired. It was dismissed on the grounds that Anwar submitted documents in English – even though the judges used that very same language when condemning this "injustice to the respondent" (*Dato' Seri Anwar Ibrahim* 2010). More recently, years of debate over the Malay translation of "parent" in constitutional Article 12 culminated in a ruling that the word was intended to cover both parents (*Indira Gandhi* 2018.1.29), thus appearing to vindicate those claiming a change in the Malay version of the Article from *ibubapa* (mother-father) to *ibu atau bapa* (mother or father) had been a ploy to allow fathers to change their children's religion without the consent of mothers.

Depending on the judge, case, judicial level, stage of proceedings and other factors, Malay (the national language and official legal medium), English (the medium of colonial administration and international common law) or a mix of the two may be heard in any court hearing in West Malaysia, but never any other language unless it is interpreted. In East Malaysia, the law is still mainly in English, but Malay is heard more and more, both officially and unofficially. There is some kind of choice, then, but it is not a free choice. There are written rules, but there are also unwritten ones. And there are endless debates about the relation between language proficiency and legal acumen. While many lawyers switch effortlessly between two languages in court (and to yet another outside), there are younger advocates whose English is halting and older ones whose Malay is non-existent.

A Japanese Supreme Court judge once told me bluntly that law was quite complicated enough without letting in the uncertainties of bilingualism. This view, shared by many legal professionals, is premised on the assumption that monolingualism is more practical than bilingualism; but it implies a formalist conception of law that overlooks the fluid, socially situated reality of legal practice. Malaysian society is highly multilingual. Malay, Mandarin, Tamil and English are all used as media of instruction in state schools, and the elephant of multiculturalism is always in the courtroom. The initial impetus for this study may have arisen from observations of professional discourse in micro settings, but motivation to pursue it grew with interest in macro-level vernacularisation policies that bring sociopolitical tensions to professional practice.

Today's bilingual Malaysian law is the product of five decades of promises and compromises attending the introduction of Malay into a domain previously monopolised by English. This process may culminate in language displacement, but for the foreseeable future, both languages will be used in ways informed by a range of collaborative and competitive positions that go beyond the local orientations of participants in any given proceeding. When deciding between Malay and English, Malaysian lawyers do not merely calculate which medium better serves their client;

they also engage, often unconsciously, with issues that exercise and divide Malaysians in all walks of life.

Officially, Malay unites a multilingual and multicultural people in postcolonial independence. Less officially, English is acknowledged as the key to individual success and a link to the world of international business and science. Its importance as a global, regional and local lingua franca offering economic and educational opportunity is hard to dispute. Moreover, it is overwhelmingly the language of global common law. But it is hard to argue with the view that law ought to function in the language best understood by the majority, and in many of the societies surrounding common law jurisdictions, English is an elite language. Access to judicial procedures means access to power.

Bilingual policies seem an obvious way out of this communicative dilemma. Yet when we look for examples around the world, shifts toward vernaculars have not necessarily enhanced transparency or fairness. It would be a stretch to label trials in Indonesia, conducted in a language understood by almost everyone, as fairer than trials in Hong Kong, where many lower court cases and most higher court cases still proceed in English. Myanmar's thoroughly vernacularised proceedings are hardly a model of judicial transparency. Understanding the language of the law is a necessary but insufficient condition for legal impartiality, with professional independence and competence also playing an indispensable part. And while facility with language is more important in law than in most professions, eloquence rarely decides outcomes: Chooi Mun Sou, one of Malaysia's longest-serving lawyers, remembers a High Court judge regularly heaping praise on his youthful advocacy skills – before sentencing his clients to hang.

While disconnects between linguistic reform and equitable communication are partly the result of flawed implementation, they also reflect the reality of language policies that serve various functions other than ease of understanding. Vested interests and nationalist agendas may come before the needs of individual legal participants. Nor is justice a purely domestic concern. Globalisation has increased the role of locally enforceable cross-border agreements. Jurisdictions inheriting common law are interconnected particularly closely – and exclusively through English.

Throughout the world, people alternate and mix languages with little deliberation, but it is a less casual matter for professionals to do so under the scrutiny of judges and public galleries when their reputations ride on their ability to persuade. If language were merely about communicating propositional meanings, the use of different languages under the constraints of a legal system would be complex enough. Formal rules about language choice must be integrated with judicial constraints on who may address who, when and how and interwoven with covert rules and customs. Effective bilingual legal communication depends on a corps of professionals proficient in various registers of admissible languages, as well as interpreters to assist those with language disadvantages. Differences of judicial interpretation are likely to increase when a bilingual dimension is added to the ambivalence inherent in any linguistic interaction.

However, language does not merely communicate ideas but rhetorically constructs meaning, conveys symbolic associations, carries identity markers and influences interpersonal relations. It delimits access to economic and political capital not merely as a means of communicating intent but as a way of negotiating institutionalised and unconscious barriers to social acceptance. These complexities affect law more deeply than almost any other domain. Parents may bypass state education, teachers may subvert rules about how they teach, and students may learn things that were never actually taught, but lawyers, still less witnesses or defendants, enjoy less agency. Legal communication proceeds cautiously, much of it under the public gaze, and all of it that counts is preserved in writing. It is this level of complexity against which the pros and cons of language change must be evaluated.

This study aims primarily to shed light on two questions: how a highly formal institution such as Malaysian law came to support bilingual proceedings and how practising and aspiring lawyers manage the burdens and exploit the benefits of bilingualism. Answering them involves a number of far-reaching issues. How does language intervention in legal domains come about? Is it motivated primarily by legal concerns, such as transparency, accessibility and efficiency, or more by sociopolitical and cultural concerns such as postcolonial unity? What particular challenges do legal domains present for language planning? What are the extralinguistic implications of language change? And what might we find in the Malaysian experience that could be of value to other postcolonial common law jurisdictions in multilingual societies?

Malaysia is now entering a fascinating period in its history following the 2018 defeat of a coalition that had ruled ever since independence through a combination of patronage, media control, manipulation of electoral boundaries, populist policies in rural areas and growth-producing economic management. It is possible that the legal domain's somewhat messy but relatively stable bilingualism will be affected by recent political changes, but this seems unlikely given that language policy is one of the few issues not neatly polarised along party lines.

While I've been interested in Malaysian law for a decade, the key information for this study comes from fieldwork done in 2013–2014 for a thesis at the University of Melbourne. Too many people generously helped me before, during and subsequent to that research for me to mention them all, but the least I can do is express my gratitude here to those whose support was crucial: Joseph Lo Bianco and Amanda Whiting (my supervisors in linguistics and in law at the University of Melbourne); Vijay Bhatia (Chinese University of Hong Kong); Robert Kaplan (University of Southern California); Maya Khemlani David, Azirah Hashim, Dato' Johan Shamsuddin Hj Sabaruddin and Nurjannah Chew Li Hua (University of Malaya); John Gibbons (Monash University); Ikuko Nakane and Michelle Hall (University of Melbourne); Chin Oy Sim (Malaysian Bar Council); and Amanda Castillo (freelance interpreter, London). Their kindness and patience in challenging my ideas, helping me track down informants and materials or checking my prose will not be forgotten. I am also grateful to Lawrence Liu at Springer for taking on this publication and to Ramabrabha Selvaraj for overseeing it and allowing the references to reflect the various cultural backgrounds and publishing preferences of the large number of academics and journalists cited. If there are any errors, I take full responsibility and extend my apologies to the writers concerned. I am particularly indebted to Lay-Peng Ang at Springer for her remarkable understanding throughout the many delays I caused in struggling to balance this project with others.

Having named some names, I must also acknowledge the huge debt I owe the many lawyers, lecturers, students and administrators who, for a number of reasons, spoke to me anonymously, thereby giving me insights not only into Malaysian law but also into the multilingual and multicultural qualities of the dedicated and open-minded individuals who support it.

Dato' Seri Anwar Ibrahim v Tun Dr Mahathir Mohamad [2010] 3CLJ 444 CA.
Indira Gandhi A/P Mutho v Pengarah Jabatan Agama Islam Perak [2018] 1LNS 86.

Hafiz Yatim. (2012, September 19). Dr M does not expect BN to win big. *Malaysiakini,* accessed 20 Sept 2012 from http://www.malaysiakini.com/news/209346

Kee Thuan Chye. (2016, October 4). Embattled Zahid turns language into a political issue. *Malaysiakini*, accessed 5 Oct 2016 from http://www.malaysiakini.com/columns/357750

Malaysiakini. (2016, October 17). Exec: Auntie Anne's halal application rejected over 'Pretzel Dog', accessed 5 Oct 2016 from http://www.malaysiakini.com/news/359365

Malaysiakini. (2018, September 06). Sayed Saddiq against 'forceful removal' of Chinese signage in Muar. Accessed 08 Sept 2018.9.08 from http://www.malaysiakini.com/news/441927

Tokyo, Japan Richard Powell

Contents

List of Abbreviations, Malay Words, Malaysian Terms

Adat	Customary law of Malay and other *bumiputera* communities
AGC	Attorney-General's Chambers
Amanah	Parti Amanah Negara ("National Trust Party") formed mainly of PAS defectors, currently in ruling Pakatan Harapan coalition
Asasi	Preuniversity degree foundation course
Bar Council (of Malaysia)	Body regulating the bar and coordinating the state-level Bar Committees (see also *Majlis Peguam*)
Bersatu	Party formed by UMNO defectors, currently in ruling Pakatan Harapan coalition
BM	*Bahasa Malaysia* (also *bahasa*, *Bahasa Melayu*, *Bahasa Kebangsaan, Malay*, national language)
BN	*Barisan Nasional* (National Front): long-ruling coalition currently in opposition
Bumiputera	Malays and indigenous East Malaysian groups recognised in Constitution; excludes Chinese and Indians by default (West Malaysian *Orang Asli* groups are not mentioned, except as "aboriginal"); frequently written *bumiputra* or abbreviated as *bumi*
CA	(1) Conversation Analysis (2) Court of Appeal/Mahkamah Rayuan
CDA	Critical Discourse Analysis.
CJ	Chief Justice of Malaysia (not to be confused with Chief Judge of Malaya or Chief Judge of Sabah and Sarawak); known before 1994 as Lord President
CLP	Certificate of Legal Practice
DAP	Democratic Action Party; currently in ruling coalition
DBP	*Dewan Bahasa dan Pustaka*/Dewan Bahasa (Institute of Language and Literature)

EIC	(British) East India Company
FC	Federal Court/Mahkamah Persekutuan (Malaysia's supreme/apex court)
FMS	Federated Malay States (Negeri Sembilan, Pahang, Perak and Selangor, where British colonial administration was more influential than in the Unfederated States of Johor, Kedah, Kelantan and Terengganu)
Istilah Undang-undang	Malay-English legal terminology published by Dewan Bahasa
J	(after name) = judge
JLS	Judicial and Legal Service
Kadi	Syariah judge; also written *qadi*
Klang Valley	Metropolitan area including Kuala Lumpur
LAB	Government Legal Aid Bureau/*Biro Bantuan Guaman*
LAC	Bar Council Legal Aid Centre/*Pusat Bantuan Guaman*
LOTE	Languages other than English
LPQB	Legal and Professional Qualifying Board of Malaysia
LPP	Language Policy and Planning
Majlis Peguam	Body regulating the Malaysian bar and coordinating the state-level Bar Committees (see also Bar Council)
Malaya	This may refer to the colonial and precolonial territories associated with the Malay people, to the federation created in 1948 and achieving independence from Britain in 1957, or to the Malayan Peninsular, which forms the western and more populous part of the federal constitutional monarchy of Malaysia that united Malaya with Sabah, Sarawak and Singapore in 1963, Singapore leaving the federation in 1965
Matrikulasi	Matriculation/preuniversity degree course
MCA	Malaysia Chinese Association: BN component party currently in opposition
MIC	Malaysian Indian Congress: BN component party currently in opposition
MMU	Multimedia University (Melaka)
MOI	Medium/media of instruction
Orang Asli	Collective term for indigenous ethnic groups of West Malaysia
Pakatan Harapan	"Pact of Hope" (PH) coalition of Amanah, Bersatu DAP and PKR
Pakatan Rakyat	People's Pact, linking DAP, PAS and PKR when in opposition, superseded by Pakatan Harapan
PAS	*Parti Islam se-Malaysia*, currently in opposition
PKR	*Parti Keadilan Rakyat* (People's Justice Party), currently in ruling Pakatan Harapan coalition.

PPSMI	*Pengajaran dan Pembelajaran Sains dan Matematik dalam Bahasa Inggeris* (English-medium science and maths schooling)
SFG	Systemic Functional Grammar
SPM	*Sijil Pelajaran Malaysia* (exam usually sat at age 17)
State	Depending on context this may refer either to an entire polity (i.e. Malaysia) or to one of the 13 administrative divisions that, in addition to three federal territories, make up the federation of Malaysia
STPM	*Sijil Tinggi Persekolahan Malaysia* (exam usually sat at age 18 or 19)
Tunku	Royal title of Abdul Rahman Putra, first prime minister of Malaya/Malaysia
UIA	Universiti Islam Antarabangsa (International Islamic University of Malaysia/IIUM) (Selangor)
UiTM	Universiti Institut Teknologi MARA. (Selangor and provincial campuses)
UKM	Universiti Kebangsaan Malaysia (Malaysian National University) (Selangor)
UM	Universiti Malaya/University of Malaya (Kuala Lumpur)
UMNO	United Malays National Organisation (Main BN component party, currently in opposition)
UniSZA	Universiti Sultan Zainal Abidin (Kuala Terengganu)
UUM	Universiti Utara Malaysia (Kedah)
Vernacularisation	Shift from an elite to a more widely spoken medium, which in the case of Malaysian law indicates the Malay language (although in the context of Malaysian elementary schooling "vernacular" refers to Mandarin or Tamil since Malay is the "national language")

List of Figures

Chapter 1
Conceptualising and Contextualising Malaysian Bilingual Law

For the individual bilingual, languages co-exist in his/her repertoire, but for the multilingual society, languages do in fact compete for registers, for power, for acceptability, for social status.
Kaplan and Baldauf (1997:236)

Ultimately, language policy is a conversation; a conversation about the communicative abilities, rights and opportunities of a society. Developing such a conversation will be easier and more effective if the aim is to develop explicit, comprehensive and public national language statements in a collaborative and democratic endeavour.
Joseph Lo Bianco (2010:62)

1.1 Approach to Study

Malaysia is among a dozen or so common law-based jurisdictions that use a language other than English. Common law, much the largest legal system but cohabiting with *Syariah* and customary law, functions in two languages. In more populous West Malaysia the official legal medium is the national language, Malay (or Bahasa Melayu, sometimes also referred to as Bahasa Malaysia). English is also admissible in 'the interests of justice'. In East Malaysia English remains the official medium, but the courts are increasingly open to the use of Malay.

This study investigates why and how bilingual law has been implemented in Malaysia by adopting a language planning perspective that unfurls from an expectation of large-scale linguistic reforms being motivated more by extralinguistic factors such as politics and socioeconomics than by linguistic factors such as communicative need. The manipulation of language status, corpus, acquisition and discourse have been targeted as key components of language planning, with interviews with lawyers, law lecturers, law students and administrators employed to shed light on these interrelated processes, in addition to documentary analysis of laws, judgments, and educational and news reports.

R. Powell, *Language Choice in Postcolonial Law*, Language Policy 22,
https://doi.org/10.1007/978-981-15-1173-8_1

As well as investigating language planning this study explores how lawyers and future lawyers orientate to language policies. Interviews were conducted with solicitor-advocates, lecturers in law or language for law, and administrators involved with legal affairs. These interviews were supplemented with questionnaire data from nearly 500 law students and follow-up interviews with some 100 of them. Drawing on structuration theory's emphasis on the recursive relationship between individual behaviour and inherited rules and resources, the study explores how individual agency, while highly constrained by the politicised character of language planning and the authoritarian nature of legal institutions, is immanent in tensions in the language policy itself between idealism and pragmatism, sociopolitical stability and economic growth, and national unity and international engagement. The extent to which agency is contingent on individual bilingual proficiency is also considered.

A third strand of the study is comparison with other common law jurisdictions that have attempted vernacularisation. Few of these currently employ a vernacular in higher courts or in jurisprudence as extensively as Malaysia, which makes Malaysian bilingual law unusual, interesting, and a potential model for other multilingual postcolonial societies seeking to enhance access to justice without undermining legal stability and integrity. Malaysian law is also worthy of attention as an ongoing example of conflict and compromise between languages in postcolonial contexts.

I started out with the principle that where there is a vernacular understood by most citizens it is reasonable and desirable for the legal system to use it. This approach differs somewhat from the one taken by Ng Kwai Hang (2009) in his fascinating study of Hong Kong law, where he concludes that the language of a stable legal institution tends to be so entrenched, even when it is the preserve of a social elite, that unusual sociopolitical pressures are required to erode it. Given that over a dozen polities have implemented a shift from English toward a vernacular within relative sociopolitical continuity my own interest is less in how this has happened than in why it has not gone further.

Taking on board Bourdieu's (1991:45) conception of official language as bound up with state formation and Heller's (2008:253) positioning of bilingual policymaking at the heart of national discourse-formation, the trajectory of this study prioritises top-down policy-formation. Such an approach is justified by the centralised and hierarchical nature of national legal systems. While seminal to any study of language planning, political power is a crucial factor when analysing law, where individual action is constrained more than in most professions by national-level concerns. Legal systems are sites of struggle in which most of the weapons are linguistic, but the agency attached to individual eloquence is limited by underlying power hierarchies that are more readily reconstituted by language than overturned by it. Ng (2009:197) found agentive, individualised models to be inadequate for understanding legal practice, and it is also worth remembering that Marx's (1852/1960:117) axiom about men making their own history under inherited circumstances foregrounds a claim, later reworked by Bakhtin (1981), that current action depends on language borrowed from the past.

This stance by no means dismisses the role legal practitioners play in refining policy through daily orientation to it in a variety of professional circumstances. Legal practice does accommodate individual spontaneity and flexibility. The duality in human behaviour, individual and social, spontaneous yet historical, unconscious as often as deliberate, persistently exercises social theorists interested in language. Gramsci saw individual worldviews as contingent on language communities (1971:324–5), language as personal and particular at the same time as collective and historical (ibid:349), and power as inculcated through civil society practices as much as the overt actions of political society (ibid:268). Foucault, in positing power as ebbing and flowing through participatory micro-behaviour (1980:97–99), threw attention upon "subtle tactics of domination" (ibid:102). Bourdieu (1982, 1991) highlighted the role of language-based habituses in shaping the perceptions and choices of actors in civil society and professional activity; yet he scorned the idea (Bourdieu 2000:10) that linguistic resistance can change social inequality in the absence of state intervention. I find it significant that lawyers interviewed for this study, from chambering students to experienced barristers, spoke of *enduring*, *tolerating*, *managing* or *accepting* language policy rather than *co-constructing* it.

In addition to structural constraints, I would further argue that when it comes to language policy, the leverage of agency is attenuated by individual variation in linguistic performance. While official policies are organised at macro level, countless personal histories show the ability to use more than one language effectively to be uneven and unpredictable, even after accounting for factors such as educational opportunities and the age at which they arise. Some people pull off bilingualism with little effort; others struggle with it throughout their careers.

In exploring how Malaysian lawyers and law students negotiate language policy I have borne in mind Giddens' (1979) concept of agency and structure as dynamically related rather than contradictory. This idea borrows from structuralism's view of societies as virtual systems whose members cannot escape pre-existing conscious and unconscious constraints (ibid:47), but it also seeks to account for change by positing mutual dependence between structure and agency (ibid:69), linked by the recursive character of social action in general and language in particular: "[E]very process of action is a process of something new, a fresh act, but at the same time all action exists in a continuity with the past, which supplies the means of its initiation" (ibid:18).

The Bakhtinian idea of interdiscursivity has been especially influential in studies seeking to clarify the relationship between individual actions and institutionalised practice in professional contexts. Bhatia (2011a, b) has explored how lawyers' multiple professional and social identities produce hybrid practices and texts. Viewing legal practice as interdiscursive activity helps illuminate the power dynamics within legal systems that, according to Giddens (1979:109) intersect even in their most formalised aspects with more diffuse, normative elements in society. Evasion, innovation, resistance and subversion are all possible, but always circumscribed. Thus solicitors may draft contracts that depart from the usual formats while preserving essential legal components, but their employers and clients are likely to resist innovation for fear they may not stand up to challenge. Advocates may bend the rules of speaking in court, but those wanting to win their cases gauge the attitudes of judges before doing so. In short, Malaysian lawyers' capacity to affect language policy and invent language practices is heavily compromised.

1.2 Researching Legal Vernacularisation

For the purposes of this study, legal vernacularisation means shifting the language of a legal system from an elite medium (such as Latin in late medieval Europe or Portuguese in postcolonial Macau) to one better understood by the majority – though it may still lack accessibility in its more legalistic registers. There have been few studies and there is no default research paradigm.

Legal vernacularisation might be framed principally as a legal rights problem, with language evaluated according to how it delivers legal information and shapes decisions. However, relegating language to a tool of justice may overlook crucial linguistic factors such as how to prepare languages hitherto absent from legal domains for complex jurisprudence. Alternatively it could be framed as a legal translation problem on a grand scale, encompassing equivalence between legal corpora in addition to the more usual concerns with lexical and text-level equivalence. While macro-level analysis does interest many in the field (Šarćević 1997:70–71, discusses the need to translate entire legal systems in order to understand the legal effect of a text), a translation framework might overlook the political factors behind macro-level change and the cultural implications of language choice, including how language change alters social practices even where semantic equivalence is achieved. Another framework could be pedagogical, given that vernacularisation inevitably requires a corps of bilingual lawyers and administrators to carry the process. But legal educators answer to a range of potentially incompatible stakeholders, including policymakers, the judiciary, legal professional bodies and the corporate and individual clients of legal services, implying a need for investigation outside the classroom and with lawyers and administrators as much as inside the classroom with educators and students.

Evidence going into this investigation of the crucial role of state-level policymaking is the main reason language policy and planning (LPP) was chosen as the main research frame. Although much recent work in the field has taken a local turn, with Albury and Aye (2016:73) warning of a risk of underestimating centralised planning, LPP typically highlights the crucial role of the state. As De Schutter, Helder and Robichaud (2016:3) argue in their critique of recent attempts to develop a theory of linguistic justice, while governments might adopt a laissez-faire stance on civil society issues such as religion, when it comes to language they cannot avoid some role. In the legal domain, a good example of the unavoidable involvement of the state in language-related decisions comes from Kymlicka (1995:111):

> The state can (and should) replace religious oaths in courts with secular oaths, but it cannot replace the use of English in courts with no language.

Another advantage of LPP is its tendency to prioritise description over theorisation. LPP researchers tend to ask questions about particular issues that are better viewed as "domains of enquiry" than as theories (Ricento 2006:12), an cautious approach that is particularly appropriate for complex and dynamic ecologies in which languages, dialects and ways of speaking are co-dependent (Kaplan and Baldauf 2008:44). Large-scale planned language shift LPP's main preoccupation (although it also addresses more spontaneous and localised dimensions of language choice) and is typically applied to the problems multilingualism poses for developing countries like Malaysia that seek to balance *nationism*, or national development (Fishman et al. 1968) with *nationalism*, or national identity and integration (Fishman 1968:39–51). Malaysian law may be characterised as a particularly intractable aspect of the struggle to construct an independent postcolonial identity and national unity while maintaining legal standards and international recognition.

1.2.1 Language Policy and Planning

LPP offers four analytical categories for breaking down the complex dynamics of legal vernacularisation into manageable components: status planning, corpus planning, acquisition planning and discourse planning. While these constantly intertwine, they afford an opportunity to separate out the administrative rules that regulate language choice, the reforms that enable languages to be introduced into new domains, the education of those required to use these languages, and the ways in which proponents and opponents of language policy enlist support. While LPP has been accused of being too uncritical (Nekvapil 2006:2) and too accepting of monolingual nationalism (Rubdy 2008:212), in the case of a complex authoritarian national institution like law a measure of large-scale descriptive analysis is inevitable and useful, but I have tried to add colour to the study with institutional-level observations and individual interviews. LPP has always emphasised the political dimensions of language. Jernudd and Das Gupta's (1971:211) characterisation of planning as a political means for solving language problems was turned on its head by Cooper (1989:34), who saw it essentially as a linguistic tool to achieve political goals. Postcolonial national unity has long been invoked in calls to promote legal Malay (Malayan Malay 1962.11.02).

Language rights discourse is a critically orientated spin-off from LPP that offers valuable contextualisation for postcolonial law. A Malaysian Chief Justice once described the judiciary as English's "strongest bastion" (*Utusan Malaysia* 1989.12.05), while a director of the Legal Aid Bureau has called the courtroom its "bunker" (Wan Adnan Muhamad 1991:2). English is the prime suspect for many writing in the paradigm of linguistic imperialism. Phillipson (1992) and Pennycook (1994) pay comparatively little attention to other expanding languages such as Mandarin, Hindi, Indonesian or Portuguese. Tupas (2008:54) references Bourdieu's idea of the forgetting of history to show how power imbalances inherent in the adoption of English are camouflaged by misconceptions of its spread as a disinterested process. The idea that language choice is bound up with neo-colonial dominance is of undeniable relevance to postcolonial polities like Malaysia where English persists in higher echelons of administration (Mohamad Azim Fitri Abd Aziz 2011.10.15). Wee (2005:65), however, questions the validity of transferring the rights paradigm, which has evolved around individuals, to languages, which are community-based. His observation is germane to language reform in Malaysian law because discourses supporting the rights of the nation or its Malay majority are more prominent than those focusing on individual participants in the legal system. A further complication in applying rights theory to Malaysia is the approach's association with minorities, given that legal vernacularisation there promotes the majority language. Numbers may be less important than status in the formation of majority-minority perceptions, however (Spolsky 2004:113). Even in Malaysia Malay is arguably a minority medium in internationally oriented domains like law and business.

A few Malaysian studies have looked at the discrete components of language policy relevant to law, such as legal terminology (e.g. Zaiton and Ramlah 1994) and courtroom code-switching (David 1993, 2003), without linking them systematically to national language planning or politics. Zubaidah (2002), on the other hand, specifically connected the daily problems of the country's court-based interpreter-clerks to national language planning. While this investigation focuses on bilingual practices that are not mediated by interpreting, and addresses legal translation primarily as a component of corpus planning and legal education, it acknowledges the considerable overlap between the practice of interpreting and attitudes toward unmediated bilingual discourse that Angermeyer (2008, 2015), among others, has exposed.

Although considered the most productive analytical framework here, and indeed chosen as the paradigm in which the earliest study of Malaysian language-in-law reforms was written (Mead 1988:3), LPP lacks examples of research in legal language, being more usually applied to educational and administrative domains. To address this gap the investigation has drawn on two other research fields. Studies of bilingualism in professional settings in general, and legal settings in particular, sheds light on the constraints that work practices place on individual language choice and helped shape the courtroom observations and interviews undertaken here. Research on legal language was especially helpful in the sections on corpus and acquisition planning for its insights into the complexity, conservatism, formality and appearance of neutrality that legal reformers have to grapple with.

1.2.2 Bilingualism in Professional Settings

Intersecting at many points with language planning, research on bilingualism has implications for vernacularisation at societal and especially institutional level. For Ng and Wigglesworth (2007:127) "there is no doubt that dominant ideologies expressed in official language policies influence bilingual communication". Heller

(2008.259) goes further: "Bilingualism is always somewhere about power, if we understand power to be the control over the production and distribution of resources, and the ability to attribute value to them". Short of radical legal transplant, effective legal vernacularisation cannot occur without processes such as documentary translation and bilingual discourse.

Most studies of bilingual legal discourse remain inside the courtroom, presumably because this is more accessible than the office and involves fewer confidentiality issues. Angermeyer (2003) attributed bilingual dialogue in New York small-claims courts to a relaxation of the stigmas commonly attached to code-switching in more formal proceedings. His study considers interdiscursivity – between speakers and texts and among speakers of differential language ability – as a motivation for courtroom language alternation. Another bilingual site on the periphery of US common law is the Hopi courts, where Richland (2008) found witnesses preferring their heritage language to engender a sense of sincerity and community (ibid:105). His findings served as a reminder for this study that cultural and identity issues interact with proficiency considerations in language choice.

Turning to more formal sites, Thekiso (2001) mined different Botswanan magistrates proceedings to show how lawyers and judges divert pragmatically from an English-only policy to accommodate Setswana speakers at various trial stages. But studies of the introduction of Chinese into Hong Kong's courts indicate that official and systematic bilingualism is rather more challenging. Cheung (1997) highlighted the lack of bilingual judicial personnel and the complexity of translating English case law, with Poon (2011) noted the consequent resilience of English a decade after bilingualism was brought in. Ng (2009) referred to Weber's concept of legal formalism (ibid:33–37) in arguing that the elite and isolated status of English in Hong Kong helps English-medium law project itself as rule-based and rational. While English-medium trials proceed rather as in England (ibid:5), Cantonese, as the medium of everyday life, produces colourful, Bakhtinian exchanges and struggles to control witness discourse. Ng's interest is not so much in which language is better for law but in what Hong Kong lawyers perceive each language to be capable of (2009:29). This investigation is similarly less interested in the respective merits of English or Malay as legal media than in what lawyers feel about them.

The accelerated use of courtroom Malay in the 1990s generated a number of local studies, although only one, Ahmad et al's (1993) survey of language practice in 1123 firms, attempted to evaluate the whole language policy. Mhd Ariff Yusof (1993) and Faiza (1993) found deficiencies in practitioners' Malay, while Nik Safiah and Faiza's (1994) collation of language reports revealed slower than anticipated vernacularisation. Nik Ramlah (1993) emphasised the continued importance of English for lawyers and voiced fears of language shift leading to declining standards in legal education. David (1993) hinted at the importance of external factors on advocates' language choices in court, with Powell (2008), on courtroom dialogue, and Powell and Azirah (2009), on arbitral discourse, also linking local discursive practices to national and institutional orientations. Studies of legal language in Malaysia have since tailed off, possibly reflecting general acceptance that a pragmatic and relatively stable bilingual status quo has emerged.

1.2.3 Legal Language and Discourse

To understand the challenges and implications of shifting the language of the law we need to have a good idea of what legal language is. The field of language and law (also referred to as forensic linguistics, a term sometimes applied more narrowly to communication evidence), has generated descriptions of legal registers (Maley 1994; Gibbons 1999, 2003; Tiersma 2001), exposed the ideologies that shape legal discourse (Eades 2008), and shed light on power structures framing courtroom interactions (Atkinson and Drew 1979; Conley and O'Barr 1998).

Legalese emerges not as a monolith but as a network of linked registers, some too lexically dense and complex to be understood unless read, others on the level of everyday discourse. Employing genre analysis to highlight the communicative purposes of written and oral practices, Bhatia (1993, 2001) found extensive interdiscursivity within this diversity, with the drafting of documents recursively linked to lexical choice at one end of the professional spectrum and institutional-level culture at the other. Legal practitioners mix identities in daily practice as they accommodate different jurisdictional (e.g. common/civil law), professional (legal/corporate) or cultural (national/individual) loyalties. MacLean (2010:187) showed how trainee lawyers struggle to reconcile tensions between roles, going as far as to argue (ibid:173) that orientation to both legal and client needs teaches them to hold incompatible perspectives simultaneously. In the case of Malaysia it should be noted that a profession that was compact, elitist, anglophone and mostly non-Malay only two decades ago has expanded ten-fold and now draws entrants from a wide socioeconomic and ethnic base (*Majlis Peguam* 2013).

This study thus set out with the assumption that individual lawyers combine a number of roles and that the profession encompasses a range of sociocultural influences. Some legal discourses are specialised, obscure to lay people and resistant to change; others lend themselves better to plain language and vernacularisation. All professions employ language in the service of efficiency, integrity and gatekeeping. While elitism surely plays its part, we should not dismiss legal professionals as elitist simply for resisting language change as they may have genuine concerns about the law itself changing if the language in which it is practised changes.

Straddling a pivotal point between legal and lay culture are the schools and offices where future lawyers study and train. The extent to which law courses should include vocational as well as academic education is as vigorously debated in Malaysia as elsewhere. Lecturers are further divided over whether legal education should continue to focus on writing with its emphasis on lexicogrammatical accuracy, prioritise legal content over language, or employ a range of oral and written skills in the service of problem-solving. The choice between English and Malay adds a fascinating dimension to this debate, given the different sociocultural roles associated with the two languages.

1.3 Malaysia's Common Law Legacy

The relationship between common law and English is so intimate that many legal practitioners have difficulty uncoupling them. Some lean toward linguistic relativism: financial lawyer Nik Ramlah (1993:175) questioned Malay's capacity to express concepts imported from England; Hong Kong barristers and judges often scorn legal discussion in Cantonese (Ng 2009:214, 230). Others adopt a culturalist standpoint. Karpal Singh warned of alien legal concepts creeping in with vernacularisation (in Mead 1988:45). Some Hong Kong lawyers expect comprehensive shift to Chinese to lead to complete abandonment of common law (Ng 2009:268). Such positioning may help explain why most common law jurisdictions remain wary of accommodating other languages.

Yet common law grew historically out of a trilingual ecology in which English was for centuries a junior partner. Narrowly, common law describes the judge-made law emerging from the practice of the *Curia Regis* (royal courts), Court of Exchequer and Court of Common Pleas in the twelfth–fourteenth centuries of dispatching justices throughout England and Wales to try cases along common principles (Cantor 1991:72). The emphasis on *stare decisis* (precedent) differentiated it from admiralty, mercantile, ecclesiastical and Star Chamber law, as well as from statute and the Court of Chancery's rules of equity. Hence the Malaysian legal dictionary *Kamus Undang-undang Bahasa Inggeris Melayu* (1995:103) defines common law as a part of English law rather than the whole. More broadly, however, common law is taken to include statute and also equity, with which it merged formally in England in 1873–75 and in Malaysia on the eve of independence.

Among the earliest global institutions of knowledge (Ng 2009:252), common law has been labelled "one of the world's great legal systems – but one maddeningly hard to know" (Friedman 1985:21). Legal historian Frederic Maitland emphasised its historical continuity and ability to systematise while adapting to new circumstances (Hudson 2007:16–17). Samuel (2012:170–173) highlights its resistance to abstract scholarship, focus on oral hearings, and conception of law as a nexus of cases. After nearly a millennium of evolution in England, centuries of expansion in British colonies and decades of interaction with European civil law and other legal traditions, common law is less a unitary system than a family of jurisdictions sharing historical roots, ways of reasoning and procedural preferences. As legal families are "always on the move" (Husa 2012:502), formal macro-comparisons are giving way to emphasis on local sociocultures (ibid:491–493), and indeed the United States and England have been referred to as two countries separated by common law (Gilpin 2000:49). However, emphasis on precedent, adversarial trials and cross-border referencing remain distinguishing features.

Common law's global web of reported judgments pursues what Komárek (2012:14) calls the "ideal of authority based on coordination, whereby the shared experience of legal officials, their attachment to 'real-life' situations and 'common sense' is important". Whereas legislators look to broad principles when drafting statutes, judges rule according to circumstances (Friedman 1985:22), comparing and contrasting precedents and producing "legal argots and terms of art that eventually allowed the case law method to develop a self-referential system of formal rationality" (Ng 2009:38). *Stare decisis* is not marginal to civil law, and it is not unfettered in common law (Komárek 2012:14), where statutes are increasingly important (Samuel 2012:178) and legal interpretation increasingly 'statutorified' (Tiersma 2007:1188). But beyond Myanmar, the historical and international dimensions of case law place particular constraints upon linguistic and cultural reform in common law. The fact that subordinate courts are not normally considered courts of record may explain why they seem better disposed than higher courts to departure from English.

A preference for testing evidence in oral proceedings also marks common law out from civil law (Ng 2009:31). Indeed Gibbons (1994:4) argues that the hypothetical language of cross-examination typified by the phrase 'I put it to you' is hard to translate into inquisitorial contexts. Arbitration, initially influenced by civil law (Bhatia 2011b) and touted in Malaysia and elsewhere as less confrontational than litigation (Powell and Azirah 2011:96), tends to be more adversarial where participation by common law advocates increases (Bhatia: 2011b). This adversariality has been criticised as alien to Malaysian 'consensual' norms (Faridah 2004.10.13). Yet Powell (2008:50) found no shortage of discursive tools of conflict in the Malay language.

A third defining feature, cross-border linkage, presents another obstacle for the indigenisation of common law. London's Judicial Committee of the Privy Council may be the final court of appeal for just a handful of small polities nowadays (Privy Council 2012), but Commonwealth collaboration continues through institutions such as the Legal and Constitutional Affairs Divisions of the Commonwealth Secretariat. There is widespread movement of judges, lawyers, legal scholars and students: Guyanan Cecil Miller was Kenya's fourth expatriate Chief Justice (Mazrui and Mazrui 1998:109) and eight expatriates currently sit on Botswana's Court of Appeal (Botswana Administration of Justice 2012). A director of Sri Lanka Law College was recently posted to Fiji. Wealthy litigants in Hong Kong routinely hire London QCs. Malaysians called to the bar in England are admissible back home without taking further exams, while foreign advocates have standing where there is a lack of local expertise. Reliance on expatriate teachers in Malaysian law faculties has even been used as grounds for keeping university courses in English (Nik Ramlah 1993:136).

Despite variations in procedure and practice among jurisdictions, then, the idea of an "international common law family" (Hong Kong Chief Justice Andrew Li, 1998, in Ng 2009:267) has ideological, procedural and institutional underpinning that goes beyond the common use of English.

1.4 Language Reform and Legal Culture

Decades after the official demise of Anglo-American colonialism, English persists in every common law system and remains the sole medium of most, even where another language is used more widely in society. This resilience of legal English demands problematisation, If vernacular law is thought of as the default position for equitable justice, just as vernacular instruction remains the ideal for effective education, what is it about common law that keeps English in pole position?

If authorities aiming to change the medium of law are to understand what is at stake, the idea that lawyers are more dependent on language than most professionals needs to be addressed. To what extent does the evolution of law in one language constrain its adaptation to others? Is common law, with its reliance on cases as well as legislation, more resistant to translation than civil law? And perhaps the most crucial question for prospective language reformers is this: if we change the language of law, how does legal practice itself change?

At my own law school in London, the two top students, from Malaysia and Hong Kong, impressed me by their grasp of tomes of case law (unfortunately for us this was before electronic databases) written in an archaic form of what for them was a second language and situated in distant sociocultural contexts. To understand the principle of nuisance we analysed *Aldred* (1610), a complaint by a Norfolk farmer about his neighbour's pigsty. The mischief rule (against literal interpretations riding roughshod over a text's underlying purpose) emerged from *Heydon's Case* in the wake of Henry VIII's dissolution of the monasteries. Trust law revolved around Elizabethan poor laws, Georgian peers and Victorian widows. Despite my advantages as an English native speaker with some Latin and French and a degree in history, I rarely grasped legal principles as quickly as these two classmates. While they undoubtedly had better legal minds and studied harder, I also wonder if cultural and historical familiarity actually got in the way of legal reasoning. Cases that have retained authority over the years contain principles applicable to different historical contexts, and if they have validity over time perhaps they also have validity across sociocultural and linguistic contexts.

All professions rely on specialised lexis, registers and discourses. In 2002 Malaysia attempted a rapid shift from three vernaculars to English for maths and science education, assuming numerical and physical demonstration would compensate for verbal intricacies, but it turned out that maths and science teachers use a lot of language, and 8 years later the government announced that the policy would be shelved (*Malaysiakini*, 2013b.11.14). In the case of law, there is hardly anything but language. Physical aspects, such as arrests and confiscations, depend on the performative force of statements by those invested with judicial authority. Forensic evidence depends on the ability of experts to explain and the capacity of advocates to persuade. In few other domains are people forced to answer questions in specific ways or incarcerated for making the wrong utterance at the wrong time. In few other professions are documents rendered non-existent if written in the wrong language.

And language is not only the main vehicle of judicial power but also the dominant element in all the mini-dramas that constitute everyday legal practice (Conley and O'Barr 1998:2).

A further layer of complexity lurks in the multiple functions of modern legal systems. As well as defining and punishing criminal behavior and regulating civil disputes, cases may involve foreign citizens and corporations and challenges over jurisdictional rights. The legitimacy of legal decisions is adjudicated by the local legal system, but the jurisprudence that results has implications for other countries and future generations.

In other words there is a lot resting on legal language, and even where there is no intention of changing procedures, the introduction of another language into the legal domain implies a risk of administrative or cultural shift that for many jurisdictions may outweigh the benefits of any increased accessibility.

1.5 Multilingualism and Multijuralism

Bilingualism occurs in various guises in a number of jurisdictions, and many face dilemmas all too familiar to Malaysian planners: how to balance national stability with international dynamism, cultural identity with economic development, the religious and cultural preferences of the majority with those of well-established and economically influential minorities.

Bangladesh, Canada, Hong Kong, Kenya, Myanmar, Pakistan, Sri Lanka, Tanzania, Tonga and several Indian states admit two or more languages to some extent in common law, as do the mixed common-civil law systems of the Philippines and South Africa and the civil law systems of Macau and Timor Leste, while Botswana tolerates bilingualism unofficially. Bilingualism is also a central component of legal transition, best exemplified by the common law of England itself, which shifted from trilingualism to monolingualism between the thirteenth and eighteenth centuries. This makes Malaysian legal bilingualism rare enough to be interesting without it being so isolated as to obviate comparisons.

Myanmar, with a postcolonial history of political and economic isolation, has come furthest among common law sites in restricting English, with Burmese used up to Supreme Court level, yet English texts are still taught in law school. Canada's apex court judgments are bilingual and Bangladesh and Malaysia have produced apex rulings partly in their national languages. But elsewhere, higher courts are dominated or monopolised by English. Colonial languages also monopolise several civil law systems, notably in former French and Portuguese colonies: indeed legal Portuguese has staged a comeback in Timor Leste law after decades of absence. Nevertheless English is conspicuously embedded in postcolonial common law.

The bilingualism of Malaysian common law functions within a society that is highly multilingual. The national census no longer collects language data but a survey of 237 polities (Ethnologue 2019) ranks it at 50 for linguistic diversity, with 134 living languages, the largest being Malay (13.5 m first-language speakers); Min

Dong (including Hokkien, 2.6 m); Iban (1.4 m); Tamil (1.3 m); Mandarin (1.2 m); Cantonese (1 m); Hakka (1 m); English (380,000 with perhaps 7 m second-language speakers); Kadazan Dusun (250,000); Min Dong (including Fuzhou, 250,000); and Bidayuh (150,000).

A blend of educational policies (with Malay, Mandarin, English and Tamil all used as media of instruction), social engineering (affirmative action on behalf of Malays and other groups deemed indigenous) and communalist politics (most parties being dominated by one ethnicity) makes Malaysia unusual. Partly the result of continuous immigration, this multilingualism is sustained by multicultural policies that restrict assimilation. Constitutionally, to be Malay is to speak Malay, practise Malay customs and profess Islam. Leaving Islam is seldom permitted, and non-Muslims must convert before marrying Muslims. On the other hand *masuk Melayu* or 'entering Malayness' (Milner 2008:200) is implicitly available under Constitutional Article 160(1) to anyone following the prescribed religion, language and customs (Asmah 2007:345).

Malaysia is not only multilingual and multicultural but also multijural, with three distinct and long-established legal traditions.

Common law, phased in under British colonialism and reinforced by extensive incorporation of English law prior to independence (Wu 1999:25–30), is the largest. It has been practised bilingually for over 30 years, during which time the size of the bar has outgrown the intimate profession of English-educated Chinese, Indians and expatriates of old. With this expansion come complaints from older members about the poor English of their juniors and doubts among younger members about the Malay of their seniors.

There is also a comprehensive and well-funded system of *Syariah* courts dealing with family, inheritance and Islamic criminal matters for the majority Muslim population. Administered by individual states, *Syariah* operates mostly in Malay but has remodeled many of its institutional and procedural structures on common law (Peletz 2013a, b) and produces enactments in English as well as Malay. Universiti Antarabangsa (UIA, aka International Islamic University or IIUM), teaches both *Syariah* and common law in English. There are perennial discussions about whether *Syariah* could take over matters currently monopolised by common law and whether its jurisdiction should extend to non-Muslims. In 2001, when UMNO was losing support to PAS (Parti and PKR, Mahathir sparked heated debate by labelling Malaysia an Islamic state rather than a country with Islam as the state religion (Netto 2010.6.24). His successor, Abdullah Badawi, promoted *Islam Hadari* (Civilisational Islam adaptable to modern capitalism). However, Islamic banking is regulated nationally by statute and the common law courts and marketed internationally in English.

A smaller but older system is *adat*, the customary law of Malay and other indigenous communities that shares many traditions with neighbouring Indonesia. Its jurisdiction in West Malaysia is almost extinct but in East Malaysia regularly comes to prominence during land disputes, especially those involving logging companies and rain forest communities. *Adat* lacks a written tradition and is practised mostly in Malay and other Austronesian languages, but its legitimacy and functions are recognised in the English and Malay drafts of national and state legislation.

The East Malaysian states of Sabah and Sarawak, with 60% of the nation's territory but under 20% of its population, joined the Federation in 1963 and share a British administrative heritage with West Malaysia (Malaya), comprise a distinct legal jurisdiction under the overarching authority of the Federal (Supreme) Court. While also common law in origin, with its lawyers largely educated in West Malaysia and many of them having practised there, East Malaysian law operates under a separate language policy that prioritises English. This study focuses mainly on more populous and economically developed West Malaysia because it is a valuable site of contact between Malaysia's national language and its 'strong second language' (Government of Malaysia 1976), whereas East Malaysian law is still mostly monolingual. However, there is analysis of reports by law students from East Malaysia, and reference to interviews conducted with lawyers there, especially where its separate language policy raises discussions about the future of legal Malayanisation.

Although not a separate legal system as such, alternative dispute resolution (ADR) is worth mentioning for its promotion by the government as a speedier alternative to the courts. Mediation may occur in any language, but arbitration is nearly always in English (Azirah and Powell 2011:143), even where all parties are Malaysian, and the country is trying to position itself as a regional ADR hub through the Kuala Lumpur Regional Centre for Arbitration.

Two decades ago a head of a consumers' association condemned the adversarial nature of common law as inimical to local conciliatory traditions (in Mead 1988:53). In 2004 then Chief Justice Ahmad Fairuz, hinted at a preference for inquisitorial legal systems: following the government's defeat in an appeal involving Anwar Ibrahim he claimed Malaysia needed "a system whereby the truth prevailed and not one where the side with the more persuasive legal mind triumphed" (Faridah 2004.10.13). There have also been observations (Whiting 2008) of Malaysian common law being Islamicised through the increasing use of religious references, marking a departure not only from its own secular traditions but also from the multiculturalism of civil society. Meanwhile a recent exchange of judges between West and East Malaysia raised fears about the erosion of the latter's judicial independence and comments about plans to introduce more Malay into the courts there (*Malaysiakini* 2013a.10.17).

The courts are increasingly sites of politicised conflict. When it was decided to replace 'Palace of Justice' as the name of the Federal Court building with Malay, *Istana Keadilan* ('palace of justice') was rejected in favour of *Istana Kehakiman* ('palace of the judiciary') since *Keadilan* is the name of the opposition party founded by Anwar Ibrahim (Hafiz Yatim 2012.9.19). Anwar, in prison at the time of 2018 elections for a highly controversial sodomy conviction, has been involved in a string of lawsuits as well as prosecutions, including for participating in Bersih 3.0, a mass rally for clean elections that was declared illegal (Kow 2012.7.02). Rally organiser and former bar president Ambiga Sreenevasan was sued for property damage occurring at the same protest (Aw 2012.5.23). Online discussions frequently include comments about the preference of many leading Bar Council members, including Ambiga, for using English in public statements and debates.

1.6 Aims, Scope and Implementation of Study

This monograph sets out firstly to identify structural influences on vernacularisation in Malaysian law by reviewing historical, political, sociolinguistic and legal contexts, and goes on to describe the implementation of vernacularisation through the lenses of status, corpus, acquisition and discourse planning. It then explores the orientations of the lawyers, lecturers and students who are most affected by the bilingualism that has resulted from vernacularisation. Following this, Malaysian bilingual law is evaluated from the perspective of global postcolonial law by drawing comparisons with other polities seeking to balance local languages with English, nation-building with economic development, and access to justice with legal stability. In conclusion, the implications of the Malaysian model for other jurisdictions are discussed.

Except where specifically referred to, *Syariah* and *adat* are excluded from the inquiry, and although some observations and interviews were conducted for East Malaysia, most data is from West. Ethnographical enquiry focused on Malaysian lawyers and future lawyers, with additional information from law lecturers, all groups that can be identified with reasonable clarity as those admitted to the bar. I did not target the judiciary, partly because of time and access constraints but also because of doubts about the likelihood of obtaining candid on-record opinions, but evidence of the stances on language policy by members of the judiciary have been garnered from the accounts of other legal professionals.

Like Ng (2009:31) in his study of Hong Kong, I have mostly sidestepped the issue of how language choice affects the outcome of legal cases, even though this might appear to be the million-dollar question for legal language planners and was sometimes raised by lawyers wondering why I wanted to interview them about language at all. While there may be cases where a difference in the wording of bilingual texts suggests different decisions, as in *Tam Yuk-ha* (1996) in Hong Kong, and potentially in Malaysia's constitutional Article 12(4) on religious conversion, language and law generally interact more subtly. The law exhibits "extravagant vagueness" about how cases differ (Endicott 2011:182) and direct comparison of proceedings differing only in their choice of language would require some kind of elaborate and replicable experiment. The general matter of linkage among language, transparency, accessibility and impartiality is, however, referred to throughout the book.

Six main documentary sources were analysed: legislation and orders with legal force, including the Rules of Court in which the practical implications of language policy for courtroom procedure are laid out; judgments that either rule on language matters or demonstrate the stance of the judiciary in the way they are written; circulars and directions issued within the profession; professional publications such as the bar's *Praxis* and its predecessor, *Insaf*; media reports, from the print press, which is strongly constrained to follow government lines but sometimes shows diversity on language issues, and also the more independent and online press; the online portals of law-related bodies such as the AGC, DBP, Malaysian Courts, and overseas bars judiciaries; and law student reports resulting from Universiti Malaya's *Program Sangkutan*, whereby third-year students spend 6 weeks attached to government offices, courtrooms and private firms of various sizes. The 117 reports that were read covered the whole country: 55 in the Klang Valley (the conurbation centred on Kuala Lumpur), 37 in other parts of Malaya, and 10 in East Malaysia. Worksites included 55 private firms, 24 regional legal aid bureaus (LABs) or legal aid centres (LACs), the legal departments of two corporations, and the Attorney-General's Chambers.

Four categories of informant were targeted for interviews and/or questionnaires: legal practitioners; other professionals involved with the legal domain; law lecturers; and law students. Although the views of the judiciary would have been fascinating, after initial approaches I found that even after assuring them they could remain anonymous most preferred to talk off the record. Their comments nevertheless helped me frame questions for lawyers, with whom the attitude and role of the judiciary were frequently raised. Some of the lawyer informants had also served as justices.

When I approached my main batch of lawyer interviews in 2013 there were some 15,000 practitioners in Malaysia.[1] I did not conduct randomised stratified sampling when seeking informants (through snowballing methods that occasionally decelerated instead of accelerating) as, like Ng (2009), I saw the value of interviews less in representativeness than in their capacity to produce a range of positions on language policy and practice. I nevertheless came close to the reported age range (*Majlis Peguam* 2013) with 30% in their 20s, 25% in their 30s, 25% in their 40s, 8% in their 50s and 9% over 60, and reasonably close to reported ethnicity: 35% Malay (against the reported figure of 41%), 40% Chinese (39%), 20% Indian (19%) and 3% 'other' (1%). At the time there was an even gender balance but my sample was 55% male (in the most recent figures it is females who comprise 55%).

I initially thought I might manage to speak with 150 (1% of the profession then) but had to settle for 60. Although this compares unfavourably with Ng's (2009) 40 interviews in less populous Hong Kong, his enquiry did not extend to lecturers, students or administrators. While I would have preferred more interviews if I'd had more time (and more success in persuading busy lawyers to give up their own time), when stories started to sound familiar I felt able to start hazarding conclusions about common perceptions and experiences, while remaining on the lookout for novelty and disagreement.

Nearly half the lawyer informants worked in the Klang Valley, where roughly 50% of the profession is based. The two main provincial sites were Melaka, a former Straits Settlement on the west coast, and Kuala Terengganu on the east coast, with additional interviews in Ipoh and Penang in the northwest, Kota Bharu in the northeast, and Johor Bahru in the south, covering nine of West Malaysia's 13 states and territories. Interview data on East Malaysia came from just three Sarawak- and

---

[1] This has since risen to 17,000 according to the Bar Council's 2016/017 *Annual Report*.

two Sabah-based lawyers but was enriched by the reports of law students on attachment there and from a focus group discussion held with members of the Sibu bar in Sarawak. Beyond Malaysia, limited observations were supplemented by interviews with 24 legal practitioners, 14 conducted in person in Colombo, Dhaka, Kuala Lumpur and Nuku'alofa, and others by email.

In addition to soliciting individual experiences I had three broad questions to cover in lawyer interviews (all of which were taped except for a handful where this was impractical): how language policy influences educational or professional choices; how professionals choose among languages when performing specific legal tasks; and what attitudes they hold or associate with particular languages.

In addition to lawyers, a number of professionals involved in law were interviewed, including a legal translator and administrators at the Attorney General's Chambers (AGC), the Legal Profession Qualifying Board (LPQB), the Bar Council and Dewan Bahasa dan Pustaka (DBP – the Institute of Language and Literature).

Seventeen lecturers were interviewed at three law-teaching institutions: Universiti Malaya (UM), one of five public universities whose law graduates are directly eligible for bar admission; Multimedia University (MMU), the only private university whose graduates are similarly eligible; and Universiti Sultan Zainal Abidin (UniSZA), a public institution with a law programme less than 7 years that did obtain full Qualifying Board approval until after my visits, meaning its graduates, like those of private colleges and most overseas institutions, had to pass the Certificate of Legal Practice (CLP) before bar admission. UM is in KL, MMU in Melaka and UniSZA in Kuala Terengganu, but faculty and students at all three come from throughout Malaysia.

A small number of law students were interviewed in person but most were engaged through questionnaires. A general survey about educational background, language choice in legal study and career plans was completed by 490 students and information about language practices experienced or observed during attachment to law offices was collected from reports written by 102 students after their attachments in 2012 and a further 20 from 2013, covering private firms, government law offices, courtrooms and police stations all over Peninsular and East Malaysia. It was anticipated that these reports would be more productive than sending questionnaires cold to law offices around the country. A short questionnaire was also collected from the 2013 attachment students with specific items about language at work.

There were two sets of observations: law classrooms and courtrooms. Classes were observed at UM, MMU and UniSZA. The primary aim was to witness medium of instruction (MOI) choice and evaluate it against interview data from students and lecturers. These observations also enabled me to collect examples of code-switching and code-mixing in legal education and consider the efficacy of corpus planning for legal Malay.

Courtrooms are where language-in-law policy is most evident. The policy is largely silent about office practice, but legislation and court rules affect courtroom practice directly. Furthermore, most Malaysian solicitor-advocates spend some of their career advocating in or preparing documents for court. Again, the three main sites were Klang Valley, Melaka and Terengganu, supplemented by less extensive observations at a court in Pahang, central Malaya (Fig. 9.2). For comparison with other common law jurisdictions I also attended hearings (from 3 to 5 days) in Bangladesh, Fiji, Sri Lanka and Tonga.

1.7 Structure of Book

Political and historical factors are paramount in any language planning perspective, and many complex aspects of Malaysian society, including affirmative action, communalist politics, multilingual education and multijuralism, are implicated in what has been planned for the legal domain. The following chapter (Chap. 2) thus analyses the historical, sociopolitical, educational and legal contexts from which Malaysian language-in-law policy has evolved. Extensive use was made of *Malaysiakini*, Malaysia's most popular media portal (*Malaysiakini* 2018.6.07) for events unfolding during the main period of fieldwork.

Chapters 3, 4, 5 and 6 describe Malaysian legal vernacularisation in terms of status, corpus, acquisition and discourse planning, explaining its evolution with reference to political events, the modernisation of Malay in general and its use in legal education, and the role of public debate. Concerns about how bilingualism influences day-to-day legal practices are adumbrated in references to practitioners' and students' opinions on policy, with their practical engagement reserved for the following chapter.

Chapters 7, 8 and 9 then turn to the daily orientation of the professionals tasked with interpreting and applying language policy in legal education, office practice and courtroom advocacy.

In considering the possibilities for identifying dynamics between language and law that may applicable beyond Malaysia the study then takes up the role of language in the colonial expansion of common law and summarises various patterns of bilingualism to be found in postcolonial law in Asia and further afield (Chap. 10). The wider implications to be drawn from Malaysian bilingual policy and practice are expanded upon in the concluding chapter (Chap. 11), which discusses the extent to which bilingual law, even if flawed and inadequately supported in its Malaysian form, may be a valid and viable means of ameliorating complex legal communication problems in multilingual societies.

As the book covers a range of related topics, Malaysian and non-Malaysian, contemporary and historical, each chapter has a separate list of references for readers with more interest in some parts of the books that others.

Cases Cited

R. v Tam Yuk-ha MA1385/1996 [Hong Kong].

References

Ahmad Mhd Yusof, Mansor Jusoh, Juneidah Ibrahim, & Abd. Kahar Yaakob (1993) *Laporan Kaji Selidik Penggunaan Bahasa Melayu dalam Bidang Kehakiman dan Undang-Undang.* [Investigative report on the use of Malay in judicial and legal sectors.] Kuala Lumpur: Dewan Bahasa dan Pustaka. Accessed 31 July 2005 from http://www.geocities.com/CapitolHill/Congress/5544/law1207.htm

Albury, Nathan John, & Khin Khin Aye. (2016). Malaysia's national language policy in international theoretical context. *Journal of Nusantara Studies, 1*(1), 71–84.

Angermeyer, Philipp Sebastian. (2003). Lexical cohesion as a motivation for codeswitching: Evidence from Spanish-English bilingual speech in court testimonies. In L. Sayahi (Ed.), *Selected proceedings of the first workshop on Spanish sociolinguistics* (pp. 112–122). Somerville: Cascadilla Proceedings Project. Accessed 10 Jan 2005 from www.lingref.com. document#1014.

Angermeyer, Philipp Sebastian. (2008). Creating monolingualism in the multilingual courtroom. *Sociolinguistic Studies, 2*(3), 385–403.

Angermeyer, Philipp Sebastian. (2015). *Speak English or what? Codeswitching and interpreter use in New York City courts.* New York: Oxford University Press.

Asmah Haji Omar. (2007). Malaysia and Brunei. In A. Simpson (Ed.), *Language and national identity in Asia* (pp. 337–359). Oxford: Oxford University Press.

Atkinson, J., & Drew, P. (1979). *Order in court. The organization of verbal interaction in judicial settings.* London, Macmillan.

Azirah Hashim & Powell, Richard. (2011). Exploring language choice in Malaysian trials and arbitrations: Common aims, complementary methods. In M. Petersen & J. Engberg (Eds.), *Current trends in LSP research: Aims and methods* (pp. 129–161). Bern: Peter Lang.

Aw, Nigel. (2012, May 23). Gov't sues Ambiga, 9 others for Bersih 3.0 damage. *Malaysiakini.* Accessed 24 May 2012 from: http://www.malaysiakini.com/news/198817

Bakhtin, M. M. (1981). *The dialogic imagination: Four essays by M.M. Bakhtin* (M. Holquist, Ed., C. Emerson & M. Holquist, Trans.). Austin: University of Texas Press.

Bhatia, Vijay. (1993). *Analysing genre. Language use in professional settings.* London/New York, Longman.

Bhatia, Vijay. (2001). The power and politics of genre. In Burns & Coffin (Eds.), *Analysing English in a global context* (pp. 65–77). London: Routledge.

Bhatia, Vijay. (2011a). Interdiscursive colonisation of arbitration practice. *World Englishes, 30*(1), 76–80.

Bhatia, Vijay. (2011b, August 25). Contested identities. Symposium on 'Interdiscursive colonization of arbitration practices: Key perspectives'. *AILA conference*, Beijing.

Botswana Administration of Justice. (2012). Official portal accessed 12 Dec 2012 from http://www.gov.bw/en/Ministries%2D%2DAuthorities/Ministries/Administration-of-Justice-AOJ/

Bourdieu, Pierre. (1982). *Ce que parler veut dire. L'économie des échanges linguistiques* [What speech means. The economics of linguistic exchange]. Paris: Arthème Fayard.

Bourdieu, Pierre. (1991). *Language and symbolic power.* Cambridge, MA: Harvard University Press.

Bourdieu, Pierre. (2000). *Pascalian meditations.* Cambridge: Polity Press.

Cantor, Norman F. (1991). *Inventing the middle ages: The lives, works and ideas of the great medievalists of the twentieth century.* New York: Morrow.

Cheung, Anne S. Y. (1997). Towards a bilingual legal system – the development of Chinese legal language. *Loyola of Los Angeles International and Comparative Law Review, 19*(2), 315–336.

Conley, John, & O'Barr, William. (1998). *Just words. Law, language and power*. Chicago: University of Chicago Press.

Cooper, Robert L. (1989). *Language planning and social change*. Cambridge: CUP.

David, Maya Khemlani. (1993). Language and law: Communicative strategies in a court of law a Malaysian experience. In K. L. Tee (Ed.), *Legal education in Malaysia Quo Vadis?* Kuala Lumpur: University of Malaya.

David, Maya Khemlani. (2003). Role and functions of code-switching in Malaysian courtrooms. *Multilingua 22*. Accessed 01 Nov 2003 from http://www.degruyter.de/journals/multilin/2003/pdf/22_5.pdf

De Schutter, Helder., & Robichaud, David. (2016). Van Parijsen linguistic justice – context, analysis and critiques. In De Schutter & Robichaud (Eds.), *Linguistic justice. Van Parijs and his critics* (pp. 1–26). London/New York: Routledge.

Eades, Diana. (2008). *Courtroom talk and neocolonial control*. Berlin: Mouton de Gruyter.

Endicott, Timothy. (2011). Vagueness and law. In G. Ronzitti (Ed.), *Vagueness: A guide* (Logic, Epistemology and the Unit of Science 19, pp. 171–191). Accessed 26 Aug 2014 from https://doi.org/10.1007/978-94-007-0357-9

Ethnologue. (2019). Periodically accessed 2011.10.1~2019.1.22, from http://www.ethnologue.com/

Faiza Tamby Chik. (1993). Language and the law: The role of Malay and English in legal education and the practice of law. In K. L. Tee (Ed.), *Legal education in Malaysia Quo Vadis?* (pp. 103–107). Kuala Lumpur: University of Malaya.

Faridah Begum. (2004, October 13). CJ plans to review justice system. *The Star Online*. Accessed 14 Oct 2004 from http://www.thestar.com.my/services/printerfriendly.asp?file=/2004/10/13/nation/9114874.asp&sec=nation

Fishman, Joshua. (1968). Nationality-nationalisms and nation-nationism. In Fishman, Ferguson, & Dasgupta (Eds.), *Language problems of developing nations* (pp. 39–51). New York: Wiley.

Fishman, Joshua., Ferguson, Charles., & Das Gupta, Jyotirindra. (Eds.). (1968). *Language problems of developing nations*. New York: Wiley.

Foucault, Michel. (1980). *Power/knowledge: Selected interviews and other writings 1972–1977*. (Gordon, Ed., Gordon, Marshall, Mepham, & Soper Trans.). New York: Vintage.

Friedman, Lawrence. (1985). *A history of American law*. New York: Touchstone.

Gibbons, John. (Ed.). (1994). *Language and the law*. London: Longman.

Gibbons, John. (1999). Language and the law. *Annual Review of Applied Linguistics, 1999*, 156–173.

Gibbons, John. (2003). *Forensic linguistics*. Oxford: Blackwell.

Giddens, Anthony. (1979). *Central problems in social theory. Action, structure and contradiction in social analysis*. London: Macmillan.

Gilpin, Alan. (2000). *Dictionary of environmental law*. Cheltenham: Edward Elgar.

Government of Malaysia. (1976). *Third Malaysia plan, 1976–1980*. Kuala Lumpur: Government Press.

Gramsci, Antonio. (1971). *Selections from the Prison notebooks*. (Quintin Hoare and Geoffrey Nowell-Smith, Trans./Eds.). New York: International Publishers.

Hafiz Yatim. (2012, September 19). Dr M does not expect BN to win big. *Malaysiakini*. Accessed 20 Sept 2012 from http://www.malaysiakini.com/news/209346

Heller, Monica. (2008). Doing ethnography. In L. Wei & M. Moyer (Eds.), *The Blackwell guide to research methods in bilingualism and multilingualism* (pp. 249–262). Malden: Blackwell.

Hudson, J. G. H. (2007). *F. W. Maitland and the Englishness of English law*. Selden society lecture delivered at Lincoln's inn, London, July 5th, 2006. London: Selden society.

Husa, Jaakko. (2012). Legal families. In J. M. Smits (Ed.), *Elgar encyclopedia of comparative law* (pp. 491–504). Cheltenham: Edward Elgar.

Jernudd, B. H., & Das Gupta, J. (1971). Towards a theory of language planning. In J. Rubin & B. H. Jernudd (Eds.), *Can language be planned?* (pp. 195–215). Honolulu: University of Hawaii Press.

Lo Bianco, Joseph. (2010). The importance of language policies and multilingualism for cultural diversity. *International Social Science Journal, 199*, 37–67. Oxford: Blackwell.

Kaplan, Robert., & Baldauf, Richard. (1997). *Language planning from practice to theory.* Clevedon: Multilingual Matters.

Kaplan, Robert., & Baldauf, Richard. (2008). An ecology perspective on language planning. In A. Creese, P. Martin, & N. H. Hornberger (Eds.), *Encyclopedia of language and education* (2nd ed., Vol. 9, pp. 41–52).

Kow Gah Chie. (2012, July 02). Bersih 3.0: Anwar, Azmin slapped with new charge. *Malaysiakini.* Accessed 24 May 2012 from http://www.malaysiakini.com/news/202450

Komárek, Jan. (2012). Reasoning with previous decisions. Beyond the doctrine of precedent. *LSE law, society and economy working paper 8/2012.* Accessed 20 Nov 2012 from http://www.lse.ac.uk/collections/law/wps/WPS2012-08_Komarek.pdf

Kymlicka, Will. (1995). *Multicultural citizenship: A liberal theory of minority rights.* Oxford: Oxford University Press.

Maclean, Rod. (2010). First-year law students' construction of professional identity through writing. *Discourse Studies, 2010*(12), 177–194.

Majlis Peguam. (2013). *Bar Council Annual Report 2012/13.* Accessed 30 Nov 2013 from http://www.malaysianbar.org.my/general_notices/bc_general_statistics_2013.html

Malayan Malay. (1962, November 02). Replacing English with Malay in our courts. *The Straits Times* (Letters to the editor) p. 16.

Malaysiakini. (2013a, October 17). MP questions 'replacement' of Sabah judges. Accessed 19 Sept 2013 from http://www.malaysiakini.com/news/244097

Malaysiakini. (2013b, November 14). Group: PPSMI will cause Malays to lose identity. Accessed 30 Aug 2014 from http://www.malaysiakini.com/news/246612

Malaysiakini. (2018, June 27). Malaysiakini is top news portal, Reuters study shows. Accessed 30 June 2018 from http://www.malaysiakini.com/news/431574

Maley, Yon. (1994). The language of the law. In Gibbons (Ed.), *Language and the law* (pp. 11–50). London: Longman.

Marx, Karl (1852/1960) *Der achtzehnte Brumaire des Louis Napoleon* [The 18th Brumaire of Louis-Napoléon]. *Karl Marx Friedrich Engels – Werke*, Vol. 8, pp. 115–207. Berlin: Dietz. (First published in Weydemeyer (Ed.), *Die Revolution*: New York: Deutsche Vereinsbuchhandlung.)

Mazrui, Ali A., & Mazrui, Alamin M. (1998). *The power of babel: Language and governance in the African experience.* Nairobi: EAEP.

Mead, Richard. (1988). *Malaysia's national language policy and the legal system.* New Haven: Yale.

Mhd. Ariff Yusof. (1993). Language and the law: the role of Bahasa Malaysia and English in legal education and the practice of law. In K. L. Tee (Ed.), *Legal education in Malaysia Quo Vadis?* (pp. 117–125). Kuala Lumpur: University of Malaya.

Milner, Anthony. (2008). *The Malays.* Chichester: Wiley-Blackwell.

Mohamad Azim Fitri Abd Aziz. (2011, October 15).

Nekvapil, Jiří. (2006). From language planning to language management. *Sociolinguistica, 20*, 92–104. Accessed 4 Apr 2012 from http://uk-online.uni-koeln.de/remarks/d5134/rm2169329.pdf.

Netto, Terence. (2010, June 24). Dr M – an unlikely minority rights defender. *Malaysiakini.* Accessed 10 July 2012 from http://malaysiakini.com/news/135453

Ng Bee Chin & Wigglesworth, Gillian. (2007). *Bilingualism. An advanced resource book.* Abingdon: Routledge.

Ng Kwai Hang. (2009). *The common law in two voices. Language, law and the postcolonial dilemma in Hong Kong.* Stanford: Stanford University Press.

Nik Ramlah Mahmood. (1993). Language and legal education in Malaysia –past and emerging trends. In K. L. Tee (Ed.), *Legal education in Malaysia quo Vadis?* (pp. 134–146). Kuala Lumpur: Universiti Malaya.
Nik Safiah Karim & Faiza Tamby Chik . (Eds.) (1994). *Bahasa dan Undang-Undang*. [Language and the law.] Kuala Lumpur: Dewan Bahasa dan Pustaka.
Peletz, Michael. (2013a). Malaysia's Syariah judiciary as global assemblage: Islamization, corporatization, and other transformations in context. *Comparative Studies in Society and History, 55*(3), 603–633.
Peletz, Michael. (2013b, October 10). A Tale of two courts: *Shari'ah* Transformations in Anthropological and Historical Perspective. Paper presented at Institute of Advanced Islamic Studies (IAIS) Law Department, Academy of Islamic Studies, University of Malaya.
Pennycook, Alastair. (1994). *The cultural politics of English as an international language*. Harlow: Longman.
Phillipson, Robert. (Ed.). (1992). *Rights to language: Equity, power and education*. Mahwah: Erlbaum.
Poon, Anita Y.K. (2011). Language use, and language policy and planning in Hong Kong. In Kaplan & Baldauf (Eds.), *Language planning in the Asia Pacific* (pp. 26–91). London: Routledge.
Powell, Richard. (2008). *Motivations for language choice in Malaysian courtrooms and implications for language planning*. Kuala Lumpur: Universiti Malaya.
Powell, Richard & Azirah Hashim. (2009, July 6–9). Language policy, language choice and language alternation in conflict resolution: Comparing adversarial and arbitral discourse in multilingual Malaysia. Paper presented at *9th International Forensic Linguistics Conference*, Vrije Universiteit, Amsterdam.
Powell, Richard, & Azirah Hashim. (2011). Language disadvantage in Malaysian litigation and arbitration. *World Englishes, 30*(1), 92–105.
Privy Council. (2012). *Website of the judicial committee of the Privy Council*. Accessed 2012.10.26 from http://www.jcpc.gov.uk/about/index.html
Ricento, Thomas. (2006). Language policy: Theory and practice – An introduction. In T. Ricento (Ed.), *An introduction to language policy. Theory and method* (pp. 10–23). Malden: Blackwell.
Richland, Justin. (2008). *Arguing with tradition. The language of law in Hopi Tribal Court*. Chicago: University of Chicago Press.
Rubdy, Rani. (2008). Language planning ideologies, communicative practices and their consequences. In M. Martin-Jones, A. M. de Mejia, & N. H. Hornberger (Eds.), *Encyclopedia of language and education, 2nd edition, volume 3: Discourse and education* (pp. 211–223). New York: Springer.
Samuel, Geoffrey. (2012). Common law (United States). In J. M. Smits (Ed.), *Elgar encyclopedia of comparative law* (pp. 169–190). Cheltenham: Edward Elgar.
Šarćevič, Susan. (1997). *New approach to legal translation*. The Hague: Kluwer Law International.
Spolsky, Bernard. (2004). *Language policy*. Cambridge: Cambridge University Press.
Thekiso, Elma. (2001). *A sociolinguistic analysis of communication processes in a bilingual court of law in Gaborone, Botswana*. Unpublished PhD thesis, University of Warwick.
Tiersma, Peter (2001). Textualising the law. *Forensic Linguistics, 8*(2), 73–92.
Tiersma, Peter. (2007). The Textualization of precedent. *Notre Dame Law Review, 82*, 1187–1278.
Tupas, T. Ruanni. (2008). Bourdieu, historical forgetting and the problem of English in the Philippines. *Philippines Studies, 56*(1), 47–67.
Utusan Malaysia. (1989, December 05). *Semua kes sivil akan guna bahasa Malaysia tahun depan – Hashim* [Hashim – All civil cases will be in Malay from next year] p. 3.
Wan Adnan bin Muhamad. (1991). *Peranan Bahagian Penyelidikan dan Sekretariat Bahasa Mahkamah Agung dalam Usaha Meningkatkan Penggunaan Bahasa Malaysia dalam Bidang Kehakiman* [Role of the Research Department and Secretariat for legal language in efforts to increase use of Malay in field of justice]. Paper presented at Seminar Bahasa dan Undang-undang [Seminar on Language and Law], Dewan Bahasa, 1991.12.3–4.

Wee, Lionel. (2005). Intra-language discrimination and linguistic human rights: The case of Singlish. *Applied Linguistics, 26*(1), 48–69.

Whiting, Amanda. (2008). Desecularising Malaysian law? In P. Nicholson & S. Biddulph (Eds.), *Examining practice, interrogating theory: Comparative legal studies in Asia* (pp. 223–266). Leiden: Martinus Nijhoff.

Wu Min Aun. (1999). *The Malaysian legal system*. Petaling Jaya: Pearson Malaysia.

Zaiton Ab. Rahman, & Ramlah Muhamad. (1994). *Penterjemahan karya undang-undang* [Translating the law]. In Nik Safiah Karim & Faiza Tamby Chik (Eds.), *Bahasa dan Undang-Undang* (pp. 113–121). Kuala Lumpur: Dewan Bahasa dan Pustaka.

Zubaidah, Ibrahim. (2002). *Court interpreting in Malaysia in relation to language planning and policy*. Unpublished, doctoral thesis, Universiti Malaya. [Viewed Universiti Malaya 2005.5.1].

Chapter 2
Political and Economic Influences on Multilingualism and Multijuralism

The position of language in Malaysian law has little to do with the legal system itself but reflects its position in other domains.
Multimedia University Law Lecturer (2013.3.14)

I love Malay, but legal language is something different and there still aren't enough texts or materials. We need to focus on practicalities more than politics.
Hendon Mohamed (former Bar President) (2013.12.19)

2.1 Language and Law in Precolonial and Colonial Malaya

The importance of contextualising language practices historically and politically is emphasised by key figures throughout the field of language planning, including Fishman (1968), Kaplan and Baldauf (1997:13), and Lo Bianco (2004). The current language policy for Malaysian law is a response to complex sociopolitical tensions that were already at play in the colonial era. This chapter begins (2.1) with an account of how colonial administrative, educational and legal policy privileged English by restriction rather than propagation, positioned Malay as an integrative medium while failing to accord it sufficient instrumentality to extend it beyond its traditional user- and use-based speech communities, and sowed the seeds of postcolonial communalist politics and multijural law. The subsequent section (Sect. 2.2) describes how language was at the centre of differential conceptions of postcolonial nationhood that led to a communalist model of development privileging Malay ethnicity. The final section (Sect. 2.3) describes how language issues and communalist politics have influenced the main institutional components of Malaysian law.

R. Powell, *Language Choice in Postcolonial Law*, Language Policy 22,
https://doi.org/10.1007/978-981-15-1173-8_2

2.1.1 Precolonial Malaya

The earliest record of law in Malaya is multilingual and bijural. *Batu Bersurat*, the inscribed Terengganu Stone rediscovered in 1902, is engraved in Arabic, Sanskrit and *Jawi* (Malay in Arabic script) and has been dated to 1303 (Hooker 1976:127). This was a period of Islamic encroachment upon Indo-Javanese traditions, although references to *Syariah* are richer in polemic than specifics (ibid:130). According to Abdul Monir (2013.12.10), neither *Batu Bersurat* nor similar inscribed tombstones from Pekan alter the established view that Islamic law did not began in the peninsula until the fifteenth century, when *Undang-undang Melaka* (the 1424 Malacca Codes) appeared.

Frequently cited in arguments about the importance of pre-colonial legal traditions, the Malacca Codes' blend of Hindu (Winstedt 1961/1981:100), Muslim and Minang (Newbold 1839:217) and Chinese (Tan 1997:267) practices list penalties for offences ranging from livestock theft to beating other citizens' slaves (Newbold 1839:231–314) and are rich in detail on rank and etiquette (ibid:220). Similar compilations of Islamic, Malay and Hindu traditions were in use in Kedah, Johor (Andaya and Andaya 1982:224) and Pahang and Perak (Abdul Monir 2013.12.10). The *Sejarah Melayu* annals glorifying Melaka's early rulers provide evidence of complex ceremonial rules and procedures (Brown 1953/1970:190–191). Andaya and Andaya (1982:42) argue that many of the provisions found there, such as standardised weights and measures, brought predictability for traders. But there are no records of judicial processes (Farid Sufian 2008:1; 2013), which seems to support Wu's (1999:18) view that political and legal authority were fused. Opinion is divided about whether there was even a common Malay identity prior to colonisation. Wu (1999:20) sees loyalty to the local sultan as the only significant identity marker until the early twentieth century, but Andaya and Andaya (1982:93) find a long heritage of shared language and customs.

Although Melaka's fall to Portugal in 1511 brought new legal institutions, local laws also continued, with the jurisdiction of the *Ouvidor* (Chief Justice) and magistrates limited to the city-state (Kennedy 1993:33), and despite the present-day survival of a small community claiming knowledge of Kristang creole (David and Faridah Noor 1999) it seems unlikely the Portuguese language penetrated very deeply. The Dutch, who took over Melaka in 1641, codified and preserved the matrilineal laws (*adat perpatih*) brought by the Minang while largely leaving Chinese settlements to regulate themselves (Andaya and Andaya 1982:94–5). Far fewer Dutch loanwords survive in Malaya than Java – and even in the latter, the use of Dutch hardly spread beyond the colonisers (Kartini 1903/2005:121).

2.1.2 British Colonial Administrative Policies

The British were similarly parsimonious with their language, seeing it as a potential vehicle of subversive ideas and destabilising socioeconomic mobility (Powell 2002:232). They were consequently open to administrative and legal use of vernaculars in India (Mir 2006). Other than the desire to maximise profit at minimal expense, the second empire built on Asian adventurism following the loss of America lacked a defining ideological framework, even after the Crown assumed administration from the East India Company (EIC) in the mid-nineteenth-century (Powell 2002:216). Said (1993:240) called it a mass of competing interests. In his history of the colonial civil service, Kirk-Greene (1999:6) sees no rationalisation behind the empire's conception and little coherence in its growth.

From literature, however, we find centuries-old evidence of triumphalist attitudes toward English:

> *And who in time knows wither we may vent The treasure of our tongue, to what strange shores This gain of our best glory shall be sent. T'enrich unknowing nations without store?*
> *Musophilus*, Samuel Daniel (1599, in Lamson and Smith 1956:640)

This suggests that Thomas Macaulay was hardly a maverick when, in a widely circulated Minute on Education by (1835) he extolled English as a civilising force and dismissed the admiration of his orientalist EIC colleagues for the Subcontinent's ancient languages (Pennycook 1994:82). Racial arrogance this may have been (Bhabha 1994:87), but it hardly constitutes evidence of foisting English on Indians, and in any case Macaulay's influence on EIC policy was limited. Rahman (1998:42) points to an 1847 Governor-General minute recommending English schools be limited to one per province. Loh (1975:2) recounts bureaucratic sabotage of plans to divert funds to English schooling and reminds us that vernacular teaching continued in Indian primary schools (ibid:3).

A stronger case for English being promoted as a colonial tool can be made for the dying decades of empire. With retreat into protectionism during the interwar recession, imperial trade became increasingly vital for Britain and undoubtedly influenced the creation of a unified Colonial Administration in the 1930s, while decolonisation after the Second World War brought compensatory strategies of cultural imperialism (Reynolds 1991:189). However, the need for coordinated educational policies as a part of colonial welfare was being voiced as early as 1925 (Mair 1944:24). Consistent with their prioritisation of the financial rationale behind empire, Cain and Hopkins (1993:13) see the rise of US-led global capitalism as more significant than British cultural politics for administrative reform.

English law in Malaya had most impact in the Straits Settlements of Dinding, Penang, Melaka and Singapore, occupied from the late eighteenth century and under EIC control from 1824. It had less importance in the FMS (Federated Malay

States of Negeri Sembilan, Pahang, Perak and Selangor) established in 1895, or the states of Johor, Kedah, Kelantan and Terengganu (known by default as the Unfederated States). After a general education in classics, mathematics, law and politics at the EIC's Halleybury College, officers bound for the Settlements were sent to Bombay, Madras or Calcutta for instruction in Oriental languages and law, but this rarely included Malay, the lingua franca of the Straits (Mills 1960:111–112), as they were expected to learn it on their own initiative (ibid:112). The unified administration of the Settlements in 1826 brought allowances for Malay lessons and bonuses for passing exams in it, but remuneration was less than for Chinese or Siamese and ended when the Penang Presidency was abolished in 1830 (ibid:113). According to the Straits Government Gazette of November 4th, 1859, candidates for government employment had to have "a fair colloquial knowledge" of Hindustani, Tamil, Bengali, Chinese or Telugu and pass a Malay exam within 12 months. An 1864 report claimed all Straits officials knew Malay (ibid:113). Yet in Singapore lack of Malay speakers remained problematic until a Straits Civil Service was established in 1867 (Andaya and Andaya 1982:161).

Pennycook (1994:89) describes Malaya as a place attracting romantic and paternalistic colonial servants who combined uneasiness about the cultural disruptions of mercantilism with a condescending idea of Malay docility. Again, financial motives may have underlain such a mindset: to develop tin and rubber with minimal economic and sociopolitical upheaval entailed importing Chinese and Indian workers and discouraging Malays from abandoning rurality. Chinese communities in Malaya and Borneo long predated British colonisation (Nomura 1989:39–64), but the twentieth-century expansion of the tin industry brought unprecedented economic immigration and this continued mid-century because sustained growth in Asia compensated for falling demand for raw materials when the western economies went into recession (Godemont 1997:37). By 1930, Indians (20%) and the increasingly diversified and settled Chinese (40%) together outnumbered the Malays (ibid:33).

Four economically and linguistically distinct Indian migrant groups can be identified: Tamil and other South Indian plantation workers and railway labourers; Sikhs employed in the security forces; literate Ceylonese and South Indian administrators; and lawyers and other professionals (Appudurai and Dass 2008:4–5). While the labourers often failed to earn enough to pay off their bonds (Tate 2008:28), many among the English-speaking middle class became estate managers or government servants (ibid, 2008:32) and numerous professionals leveraged their English into positions of commercial and political influence (ibid, 2008:31).

Ethnically separate development was by no means exclusive to Malaya. Throughout the British Empire, importing labourers with a proven record in railway-building, rubber-tapping or tea-production was preferred to the financial cost and social disruption of training locals. When Winstedt, Settlements Director of Malay Education from 1916 to 1931, cautioned against encouraging the "unattainable aspirations" of Malays (in Andaya and Andaya 1982:232) he joined a line of cultural separatists, including Indian Viceroy George Curzon, who opposed native involvement in politics and favoured vernacular over English education (Krishnamurti 1990:17), and Nigerian High Commissioner Frederick Lugard

(1922), who promoted administration through existing social and cultural structures and believed English education led to "utter disrespect for British and native ideals alike" (in Mazrui and Mazrui 1998:21).

Dualist administration in Malaya became "an idiom of official and everyday discourse when a host of legal codes and enactments…were introduced by the colonial government based on census-constructed ethnic categories" (Shamsul 1998:137). The 1913 Malay Reservations Enactment prevented non-Malays from extending their landholdings (Cheah 1983:5). When recruitment started for a native Civil Service in 1910 in recognition of the need for bigger but cheaper government, eligibility was restricted to Malays (ibid:5), "…the stable element in the population…" (Mair 1944:17). Efforts to preserve notions of traditional Malay culture even spread to Malay-minority Borneo, where the Brookes dynasty encoded the first laws for Sarawak in Malay (Gunn 1997:36). Like Cham (1975:446), Kua (2005:9) relates current marginalisation of non-Malays to colonial divide-and-rule strategies.

2.1.3 Colonial Education Policies

2.1.3.1 Malay-Medium Schools

Precolonial education appears to have been entirely religious and provided few economic opportunities (Loh 1975:12). Some form of Malay may have been taught in the Dutch Indies, but there is no evidence of formal schooling in Malaya before the Penang Free School[1] was established in 1821 (Gunn 1997:67). The East India Company opened a small number of vernacular schools (ibid:67) and the Crown added to these in the 1860s after taking over administration of the Settlements, but many were abandoned (Andaya and Andaya 1982:231). Opinions differ over the effect of a requirement introduced in the 1880s that teachers have competence in Qur'anic studies. Andaya and Andaya (1982:231) claim Malays remained reluctant to send their children to school but Gunn (1997:69) notes an increase from 16 schools/598 pupils in 1872 to 189 schools/7218 pupils in 1892. While Kua (2012.6.22) claims the British were as neglectful of education in Malay as in other vernaculars, it was hardly better supported in areas further from British control: apart from the religious *pondok* schools, Malay schooling did not begin until 1897 in Kedah, 1903 in Kelantan, 1915 in Terengganu (Mohamed Nor 1983:7) and 1883 in Sarawak (Gunn 1997:69).

Winstedt produced a report in 1910 prioritising vocational and practical training for Malays (Pennycook 1994:89) and in 1922 introduced the first unified curriculum for Malay at the Sultan Idris Teachers College, where *rumi* (romanised) literature was taught alongside agriculture (Andaya and Andaya 1982:232). The 1923 Imperial Education Conference prioritised the "language best known and understood by the

[1] 'Free' meant open to all rather than gratis, though schooling gradually became fully assisted (Abdul Rahman (2007:131).

child on his entry into school life" (Mair 1944:40), but English was indispensable for secondary education because of a paucity of vernacular literature (ibid:40). A Translation Bureau established under Zainal Abidin bin Ahmad in 1924 produced textbooks, promoted literature and translated government publications (Adelaar 1996:729), thus reducing reliance on materials imported from the Dutch Indies (Rustam 2008:58). By 1920 the 757 Malay schools received the bulk of educational funding (Kua 2011:24). Kua (ibid:24) and Rustam (2008:45) see these initiatives as seminal to the evolution of a vernacular intelligentsia; the latter further links them to the rise of a Malay press.

2.1.3.2 Chinese-Medium Schools

Not foreseeing permanent settlement, the British left Chinese schools in the hands of clan associations, financial patrons and private tutors (Andaya and Andaya 1982:223–224). However, the import of teachers and texts from China (ibid: 224) accelerated under the renewed interest in Mandarin that the 1911 revolution spurred among diverse language communities, and as this coincided with a shift from mining to more permanent agricultural and commercial employment the authorities grew wary of Chinese nationalism (ibid:224–225). From 1929 textbooks were censored and the import of teachers restricted, yet the federal grants offered in return for greater administrative control were often rejected, especially by schools supported by the *Guomindang* (KMT) (ibid:226). Pennycook (1994:92) describes attempts to limit Chinese schooling and encourage enrolment in Malay schools in the 1930s, but Andaya and Andaya (1982:226) note an enduring preference for Chinese education and Loh (1975:92) reports a move away from English- to Chinese-medium schools, with only 17.6% enrolled in the former by 1937.

2.1.3.3 Tamil Schools

Dating back to the early nineteenth-century (Tate 2008:160), Tamil education had spread by 1900 throughout the Straits Settlements, Johor, Perak and Seremban, with some government support (ibid:161), but the bulk was on plantations and of poor quality (ibid:162). Required by a 1923 Federal Malay States Labour Ordinance as an instrument of social welfare in every estate (Andaya and Andaya 1982:223) and, uniquely in the empire (Mair 1944:40), demanded by the Indian government as a condition for labour export (Tate 2008:161), vernacular teaching was grudgingly funded by plantation owners (ibid:162) who often employed unqualified instructors (Andaya and Andaya 1982:222) and offered children greater incentives to work than study (ibid:222).

2.1.3.4 English-Medium Schools

English education started with the Free Schools (Penang, 1816, Singapore, 1824 and Melaka, 1826), together with missionary schools attended mostly by Chinese (Pennycook 1994:82), but in 1882 there were just 19 schools teaching 1761 pupils (Gunn 1997:69). Neither these, nor schools set up in Perak in 1878 and 1883, attracted the Malay elite (Andaya and Andaya 1982:227). However, in 1888 the Perak sultan initiated a Raja Class at Kuala Kangsar under a British tutor, and 2 years later the heir to Selangor set up similar classes for local princes under a British clergyman (Andaya and Andaya 1982:227). The Victoria Institute in Selangor, Taiping Central School in Perak and St. Paul's School in Negeri Sembilan soon followed (ibid:227). Interest from Malay royalty met an increasingly positive response from the British once they realised the need for a local civil service. At the 1903 Conference of Rulers it was reported that only 2636 of the 310,000 Malays in the FMS had government jobs (Stevenson 1975:175), despite recruitment as police (ibid:175), magistrates and judges (Andaya and Andaya 1982:226). While FMS Schools Inspector Frank Swettenham had seen 'safety' in restricting Malays to rural-focused education (Loh 1975:15), his successor, Richard Wilkinson, favoured the recruitment of Malay civil servants and in 1905 established the Malay College at Kuala Kangsar. This 'Eton of the East' included Qur'anic classes (Andaya and Andaya 1982:229).

With a shift toward cash-crop agriculture and rising demand for commercial clerks, English education gradually attracted more Malays (Loh 1975), but there was official resistance. In 1895 Perak's Inspector of Schools declared: "It is the mere smattering of English and English ideas that is harmful, and which in India causes the country to swarm with half-starved, discontented men who consider manual labour beneath them" (in Kua 1999:19). The Chief Secretary of the FMS closed English classes in Klang and in 1919 rejected a petition for free English education (Loh 1975:56). But there were scholarships to English schools for Malay village boys from the 1890s (Abdul Rahman 2007:139), with top performers eligible to take civil service exams (Loh 1975:79). The percentage of Malays in FMS English schools rose from 9% to 15% between 1919 and 1936 (Andaya and Andaya 1982:229). For Rustam (2008:43–44), English was a marker of socioeconomic polarisation among the Malays rather than a vehicle of social mobility.

An influential minority of Chinese had been educated in English for generations, especially in the Straits Settlements, and Chinese were largely behind the 1906 establishment of English-medium King Edward VI Medical College in Singapore, the forerunner of the University of Malaya (Cheah 1983:8). By the 1920s there were also 13 government, 23 missionary and 69 private schools providing English education to Indians aiming for the civil service (Nagalingam 1987:12). The overall picture of British education policy is one of English for the elites of each main ethnic community and vernaculars for the rest. Yet an enduring tendency to associate English more closely with the non-Malays can also be traced to colonial practices. That Malays are underrepresented in the legal profession even today may therefore add to its image as an 'English' institution.

2.1.3.5 Japanese Administrative and Educational Policy

During their 4-year occupation Japanese forces drastically restricted English education, but the resulting shift was as much toward Malay as Japanese. Military authorities were as "blatantly communal" as their British predecessors (Kua 2011:27), coming to see the advantage of preserving the Malay rulers' formal authority of (Akashi 2008:5) and favouring Malays for administrative appointments (ibid:6), thus adding to Chinese resentment (ibid:7). Tamil instruction was tolerated but English and Chinese schools were closed pending or reorganised as Japanese MOI institutions (Kratoska 1998:124). Pahang teachers were offered accelerated promotion for studying Japanese (ibid:128). Children were taught *katakana* and Japanese songs (Ahmad Mustapha 2007:112). Wartime newspapers such as *The Syonan Times*[2] (e.g.1942d.6.12) carried study tips and announced salary incentives for learning Japanese. However, admonition of the slow progress of Japanese persists throughout the war in *The Syonan Shimbun* (1942b.12.23), while daily *Nippongo* columns remained rudimentary. Malay appears to have taken up the slack. It became an important medium of administration and propaganda (Kratoska 1998:124). A Malay radio network was launched throughout Malaya and Indonesia (Gunn 1997:102). Malay became a common language of military command (Kua 2011:28) and was promoted as a regional lingua franca (*The Syonan Shimbun* 1942a.12.12). Anglophone citizens were instructed to use it (Kathigasu, 1954/2006:34). English was nevertheless retained in many domains for its value for propaganda and maintaining law and order.

2.1.4 Introduction and Expansion of English Law

Dezalay and Garth (2010:65) contend that colonial expansion into Asia, less readily deemed *terra nullius* than more sparsely populated regions, involved concern for good governance and sound legal practices, not least to establish legitimacy in the face of domestic criticism. A perennial question for administrations in Malaya as elsewhere was the extent to which good governance should involve existing laws and customs.

After 20 years of vague regulations, rough and ready judgments and petty trials conducted by local communities in their own languages (Mills 1960:55–56), the 1807 Royal Charter of Justice established a Recorder's Court and formally introduced the laws of England into Penang. Europeans were largely exempt from prosecution except for serious crimes, which were tried in Bengal (ibid:57). In keeping with common law principles, the Charter required consultation with native customs compatible with the spirit of English law (ibid:57). But for Farid Sufian (2011:2) it

[2] Later *Syonan Shimbun*, perused at the National Diet Library, Tokyo, and on microfiche at the National Library of Singapore.

marked the beginning of an "onslaught of English law" that bypassed Islamic practices when inconvenient. Chinese subjects of the Crown were tried under English law (Wu 1999:24).

Singapore was administered under a compromise with the Johor *Temenggong* (fiefdom chief) that applied English laws while taking account of local practices (Mills 1960:79–80). *Penghulu* (headmen) remained in charge of law and order (Kennedy 1993:144). A provisional code of English-based law devised by Raffles in 1822 appointed merchants as magistrates and police officers and an enforcement committee drawn from multiple communities (ibid:112–113) and heeding native customs (Mills 1960:84). A second Charter extended English law throughout the Settlements in 1826, but only magistrates' courts remained in Penang after Singapore assumed the Settlements presidency in 1832 (ibid:106). Subject to "such modifications as are necessary to prevent it from operating unjustly", it acknowledged practices such as polygamy and matrilineal inheritance (Tan 1997:268). In a study of Singapore's Grand Juries, Lee (1973:58) found lay administrators to have been fair, pragmatic and cost-effective. When the Settlements came under India's Governor-General in 1851, those of the "native community" with sufficient English became eligible for jury service (ibid:67), a development *The Straits Times* hoped would improve understanding of local customs (ibid:93).

Notwithstanding legal pluralism and the cooption of local elites, English law expanded, culminating in an 1878 Civil Law Ordinance incorporating English precedents and statutes, notably in commercial law (Wu 1999:17), that survived the 1946 dissolution of the Settlements (Woon 1997:337). The rest of Malaya stayed formally under the administration of local sovereigns (Wu 1999:23) and London remained wary of the political and financial risks of further encroachment until the late nineteenth century (Andaya and Andaya 1982:154). However, the installation of British advisors through a series of treaties with the sultanates opened up possibilities for intervention.

Under the 1874 Treaty of Pangkor, for example, Britain recognised the sovereignty of the Perak sultanate in return for acceptance of a Resident whose advice "must be asked and acted upon on all questions other than those touching on Malay religion and custom" (in Andaya and Andaya 1982:155). Such arrangements inevitably came up against culturally differential conceptions of the parameters of religion and custom. James Birch, a Resident with limited Malay (ibid:162), believed he was authorised to centralise Perak's laws and modernise its finances (Kennedy 1993:195) and was infamously punished for his views by assassination in 1875. There was also resistance to attempts by Clifford, the Pahang Resident, to set up courts of justice and centralised policing (Andaya and Andaya 1982:173). Some rulers accepted intervention in order to maintain political and fiscal control, however (Loh 1975:5) In turn the Colonial Office came to view Malay rulers as a buffer against democracy (ibid:71). Although the constitutional autonomy of the Malay states remained intact, Abdul Aziz (2008:5) comments: "But of course we know that the British went beyond what was agreed in the treaties". Farid Sufian (2008:2) sees the import of English laws, both directly and via colonial instruments such as the Indian Penal Code, as marginalising Islamic law and indigenous dispute resolution, with British judges bypassing local laws and *kadi* courts relegated to subordinate status in the judicial hierarchy (Farid Sufian 2013.12.10). On the other hand Abdul Monir (2013.12.10) finds Terengganu's *Syariah* courts to have been active in criminal law through the First World War, even as the role of *adat* declined. Winstedt (1961/1981:114) cites a 1878 finding by the Perak State Council that most local law was "unwritten yet generally understood", adding examples where the Council favoured *adat* custom over Muslim law to protect women's property rights (ibid:116), although Mills (1960:136) describes Melaka's land and revenue law as dysfunctional.

While leaving legislation to individual State Councils (Kennedy 1993:275), the 1896 Federation facilitated greater centralisation across states and paved the way for the introduction of Criminal Procedure (1902) and Penal (1905) Codes modeled on India's (Wu 1999:22). A 1927 agreement exempted the sultans from Federal Council sessions, effectively putting Federated States legislation in the hands of the Residents (Andaya and Andaya 1982:242). English statutes were introduced there under the Civil Law Enactment of 1937 and in the Unfederated States under the 1951 Civil Law (Extension) Order (Wu 1999:23), with the formal incorporation of English law throughout Malaya coming with the 1956 Civil Law Ordinance. English law had already been received in Borneo under the 1928 Law of Sarawak and 1938 Civil Law Ordinance (ibid:30). Both bar and bench were largely educated in England and "at times English law was treated as if it were the only law" (ibid:24). With only documents to go on, we have little knowledge of the extent to which Malay or other languages were used orally in courts, but newspaper notices and advertisements show interpreting in urgent demand as early as the 1840s (*The Singapore Free Press and Mercantile Advertiser* 1849.3.29) at all court levels and for Malay – often undertaken by British residents (*The Straits Times* 1896.6.20) – as well as Chinese and Tamil.

2.1.5 Law and Language Under the Japanese Occupation

Although Japanese administration was brief its tolerance for English in the courts highlights the entrenched position of the language in the legal system. For all the political and economic disruptions, anti-British propaganda and attempts to impose Japanese (and subsequent shift to Malay), there was considerable formal judicial continuity, with the courts reopening – under new names – within 4 months of invasion using pre-war officers and conducting proceedings in English (*The Syonan Times* 1942b.5.26).

Notwithstanding the brutal summary justice meted out to those seen as threats to the new order, use of established institutions was advised in administrative principles (*Nanpō Sakusen Senryōjitōchi Yōkō An*, in Akashi 2008:3–5) to hasten restoration of law and order and also vaunted in propaganda (*The Syonan Shimbun* 1943.1.11). Just 4 weeks after the invasion of Singapore, all "non-British" lawyers were summoned to the Supreme Court (*The Syonan Times* 1942a.3.03) and in May the Criminal District, Police and Coroner's and Supreme Courts were reopened under Eurasian, Indian and Chinese justices and prosecutors (*The Syonan Times* 1942b.5.26), with the former system and laws to apply "in so far as they do not interfere with the authority of the Military Administration (*The Syonan Times* 1942c.5.28). While Spanish was permitted to continue in the Manila courts (*The Syonan Times* 1942e.9.04), documents from Penang, including a 1943 subpoena, a 1944 Registrar application and a handwritten summons from the same year,[3] evince continued use of English in Malaya. From Kathigasu (1954/2006:157), a Eurasian detained under torture in Perak, we hear of a charge sheet drafted in Japanese and translated into English. Yasuda Toshiaki, author of a comprehensive study (1997) of Japanese wartime language policy, finds no documentation of the use of Malay in the courts and concludes that English, supported by Japanese, was retained as in other administrative domains.[4] Judging by the names of court officers appearing in news articles and notices before and during the war it may be hypothesised that one impediment to Malay was a paucity of legally trained Malays.

2.2 Ethnicity and Politics

2.2.1 Emergence of Communalist Politics

Brown (2000) theorises three approaches to nation building. Primordialist construction appeals to feelings of innate attachment reinforced by ethnic essentialism (ibid:6). Situationalist construction is also collectivist but regards ethnicity as framed by self-interest (ibid:13). Constructivist nation-building rests on an ideological solidarity built on economic incentives (ibid:20) and thus resembles a model proposed by Lo Bianco (2005:120) of nationhood as political membership.

While Shamsul (1996:17) points out persistent failures on the part of policymakers and their critics to problematise ethnic constructs, Malaysian nation-builders have evolved an enduring blend of primordialism and situationalism through pragmatic collaboration among the elites of essentialised ethnic groups in the guise of a social contract. Four decades ago Cham (1975:449–451) saw weaknesses in cultural nation-building, but failed to predict the success with which Malaysia's leaders would reinforce it through steady, if unevenly distributed, economic growth. While increasingly polarising, elite collaboration and politically strategic handouts have become entrenched. Their roots go back to the pre-independence struggle between the Malayan Union and the communalist federal model that supplanted it.

The Malayan Union of April 1946 excluded Singapore, confirmed the Crown's postwar usurpation of sultan authority, and proposed common citizenship for all

---

[3] Kindly loaned by Peter O'Connor, author of (2011) *The English-language Press Networks of East Asia, 1918–1945*. Leiden:Brill.

[4] Yasuda, p.c. 2005.2.25.

Malayan-born, regardless of race, with residency conditions for others (Carnell 1952: 507). Within a month, the United Malays National Organisation (UMNO) was formed to oppose equality for non-Malays and it continues to draw much of its strength from this stance. Kua (2011:6) notes that it did not oppose British colonialism at the time, whereas the Council of Joint Action under Tan Cheng Lock, the founder of the Malayan Chinese Association, demanded self-government in addition to citizenship for all races (Wade 2009). The Colonial Office was alarmed by the Council's plan to include Singapore, not only because of the island's economic and strategic importance to the Crown but because its large Chinese population would make the Malays a minority (ibid: 2009). The following year, a People's Constitution published by Pusat Tenaga Ra'ayat and the All Malaya Council of Joint Action proposed equal citizenship (PUTERA-AMJCA 1947, s.2), with Malay as the language of a new Assembly and Council of Races but political debate in other languages to be permitted on the grounds that colonial policy had failed to spread Malay proficiency (s.34). There were no language provisions for the courts (s.28).

1947 was a year of economic and security crises as well as political conflict. Strikes by estate and factory workers and violent activity by the Chinese-dominated Malayan Communist Party (MCP) led in June 1948 to a State of Emergency, which for Kua (2011:5) was "as much a crackdown on the workers' movement as it was a war against anti-colonial insurrection". Seeing Malay support as paramount, in February 1948 Britain replaced the Union with a Federation of Malaya Agreement that restored the sultans' rights and restricted citizenship to subjects of State rulers, resident British subjects, non-Malays born in the territory and foreign-born residents with adequate knowledge of Malay or English (Carnell 1952: 508). The Crown justified limitations on Chinese and Indians and the exclusion of Singapore by regarding Malays as "peculiarly the people of the country [with] no other homeland, no other loyalty" (Wade 2009). However, with less than a third of Chinese acquiring citizenship, and a need to shore up national unity in the face of the Emergency, a Federal Ordinance was enacted in 1952 to facilitate citizenship for those with Malay or English proficiency (Carnell 1952:511–513). The durability of this linkage between language and loyalty was reaffirmed recently in a call by Malay-rights body Permas to banish Chinese and Indian Malaysians lacking fluency in Malay (*Malaysiakini* 2014c.2.06).

With 75% of the population registered by 1953, Malay citizens outnumbered Chinese by over 2:1 (Chai 1977:9) and the decade down to independence, set against a communist insurgency that continued into the 1960s, saw growth in UMNO's influence along with accommodation toward it by the Malayan Chinese Association (MCA), formed in 1949 in the wake of concerns over the resettlement of Chinese in insurgent areas (He and Yang 2012:82), and by the Malayan Indian Congress (MIC), founded in 1946 by anglophone Indian professionals (Tate 2008:83). While lacking a united position (ibid:78), most Indians had supported the Malayan Union for its promise of citizenship (ibid: 74–75), but the MIC's initial radicalism in reaction to the Union's collapse gave way to conservatism during the Emergency (ibid:87). In 1954 it allied itself with UMNO and the MCA (ibid:91). The Alliance Party (rebranded Barisan Nasional in 1974) won by a landslide in the 1955 general election, demonstrating the effectiveness of communalist politics (ibid:76) – the only kind to survive in West Malaysia according to Rustam (2008:1). UMNO founder Onn Jaafar, struggled to achieve an impact after relinquishing the presidency to Tunku Abdul Rahman in protest at the party's refusal to accept non-Malays (Mead 1988:9). Despite its non-communalist founding charter in 1965, the opposition Democratic Action Party (DAP) soon came to be viewed as a Chinese party (Wade 2009).

2.2.2 Linguistic, Political and Economic Construction of Ethnicity

Despite rising popular support for the Malay language in the 1950s, the Malay political elite remained equivocal, with some of them criticised for favouring English (Harper 1999:299). It may be significant that the first three prime ministers (the Tunku, Abdul Razak and Hussein Onn) were London-educated barristers. Even Mahathir, the Malay nationalist and Singapore-trained doctor who succeeded them with "a totally different style of administering" (Ahmad Mustapha 2007:63), had described Malay as "hopelessly inadequate" for modern life (Det 1949.4.24). Indian politics was once dominated by the anglophone elite that founded the MIC but has since been steadily Tamilised (Tate 2008:92). As for Chinese language politics, the MCA's long record of championing Mandarin is framed within rhetoric acknowledging the importance of the national language, although it has sometimes defended English against government-sponsored expansion of Malay while also resisting the encroachment of English on Mandarin (Samuel et al. 2012).

The Reid Commission drafting the postcolonial constitution recommended Malay as the national language, with English to continue for official purposes until parliamentary review 10 years later (Reid Report, para. 170, in *Merdeka University v Government* 1982). The 1957 Constitution incorporated its recommendations (Art.152) and made "elementary knowledge" of Malay a condition for registration of citizenship by birth (Art.16). There seems to have been little objection to the status of Malay (Asmah 1979:13, Mead 1988:9).

Senior lawyer Chooi Mun Sou[5] remembers great controversy surrounding a provision in Art.153 to safeguard the "special position of the Malays" by reserving a proportion of public service positions, scholarships and trade permits for them. Wade (2009) argues that in mentioning "great opposition in some quarters" to prolonged preferential treatment the Commission intended the provision to be transitional, yet in 1963 it was extended to "natives of Sabah and Sarawak" when the Bornean states were incorporated into a Malaysian Federation along with Singapore. The same year saw the First Bumiputera Economic Conference, a term thereafter

[5] Interviewed in Kuala Lumpur, 2013.9.

officially promoted for Malays and indigenous East Malaysians (Shamsul 2006:364). Asmah (2007:347) describes Malay privileges as compensation for conceding citizenship rights to others – for whom entry into the privileged group remains open under the constitution if they profess Islam, speak Malay and conform to Malay customs (ibid:345). She fails to mention, however, the constitution's omission of West Malaysia's indigenous *Orang Asli*, whose 178,000 people speak several languages (Yayasan Orang Asli 2012) that, according to one Universiti Malay law student from the community, hold decreasing instrumental value. One law lecturer from the same institution notes that many *Orang Asli* still lack proficiency in the national language, yet increased reliance on Malay as a link language has been documented as a key factor exacerbating language attrition because of the tendency of authorities to lump together different language communities when resettling forest dwellers (Vengadesan 2019.4.14).

Concern for *bumiputera* rights, fueled by robust Chinese economic and educational achievement, has been used to justify decades of affirmative action. The most far-reaching initiative was the New Economic Policy (NEP), implemented in 1971 after the Tunku stood down for Abdul Razak in the wake of racial rioting following the 1969 elections. The riots' immediate cause was Malay outrage at the lacklustre showing of UMNO and its allies against the DAP and a new Chinese-based party, Gerakan, both of which had campaigned against Malay privileges and, according to Wade (2009), gained votes from disaffected English-educated MCA members. But an underlying reason was widespread Malay discontent with their economic position vis-à-vis the Chinese (Abdul Rahman 2007:176). Only 4 years after questioning the value of quotas in the House (*Malaysiakini* 2013d.12.12b), Mahathir, who lost his seat in 1969, attributed social unrest to concessions made by the Tunku to the Chinese (Wade 2009). In guises such as the National Development Policy and National Vision Policy, quotas for government contracts, educational places and equity holdings have survived the official expiry of the NEP (Wain 2009:103). The government justifies the ethnic categories that appear on most official forms as an instrument of social justice (Koh 2015.11.23), and periodic talk of removing them draws mixed reactions from a public brought up on them (Muzaffar 2014).

Although Vaillancourt and Leblanc (1993:50) found an increase in business ownership among the francophone majority in the years following Quebec's 1974 and 1977 pro-French reforms, neither linguistic nor cultural Malayanisation seems to have broken Chinese dominance of Malaysian business. While the figures are hotly debated, Malays do appear to have gained ground in equity ownership (*Malaysiakini* 2012.4.23) but remain underrepresented (*The Malaysian Insider* 2013.10.06). The key question is whether government ethnic quotas have continued primarily for economic or for political reasons.

Fisk (1982:14) found economic polarisation already beginning to transcend racial polarisation three decades ago. If quotas are meant primarily to target economic disparity then many in the Indian community have reason to question why the considerable socioeconomic and educational deprivation in their subaltern ranks (Appudurai and Dass 2008:47–49) fails to attract the affirmative action available to

Malays, rather than sporadic largesse whenever Indians are seen as holding the balance in tight elections (Boo 2014.5.30). The group's relative demographic decline, from 11.3% of the population in 1957 to a projected 6.4% in 2021 (Appudurai and Dass 2008:7) adds to despondency, with middle class Indians fearing they are losing ground to Malays and Chinese in English-dominated professions they used to do excel in such as law (Tate 2008:105).

Despite hints from BN in its last years in power about moving away from ethnic to poverty-targeted policies (Aw 2013.9.14), affirmative action continued to be practised in the name of closing ethnic wealth gaps (*The Star* 2013.9.20). But while ethnic quotas have long been associated with a brain drain (Roasa 2011.4.22) that affects Chinese and Indians disproportionately (Lim and Boo 2013.8.08), increasing number of Malays have joined them to study and work overseas (Mariam Mohktar 2013.12.09). Kua (2005:10) views decades of preferential university entrance and public employment as ineffective. But Wain (2009:111) points out that by 2000 Malays constituted a third of dentists, doctors and lawyers. They now comprise 40% of the bar (Majlis Peguam 2013). From the accounts of lawyers and law students, ethnicity emerged in this investigation as a strong influence on educational and career choices but a weaker indicator of professional language choice (see Chaps. 7, 8 and 9).

Despite economic shifts, ethnicity rather than income has remained the paramount identity marker that Cham (1975:458) found it to be back in the tense years following the 1969 riots. While Canagarajah (2005:419) contends that globalisation has turned people away from essentialist concepts of culture and identity, seeing this as propelling a surge behind English around the world, Rappa and Wee (2006:5) find the concept of ethnicity remarkably durable in postmodernist Southeast Asia. A 2006 poll showed ethnic boundaries to be a dominant defining characteristic among Malaysian youth (Merdeka Center 2006) and a more recent survey (Merdeka Center 2012) found only 25% of Chinese agreeing that the country was going in the right direction, compared with 53% of Indians and 69% of Malays. An enquiry funded by a large banking group (Ananthi et al. 2017) revealed a marked preference for in-group friendships, especially among Malays, with two-thirds of non-Malays feeling economically discriminated against (but half of the Malays feeling the same) and 49% of Chinese and 37% of Indians considering emigration, as against 16% of Malays. In East Malaysia there is some evidence of communalist voting increasing (Mahavera and Davidson 2014.7.11). A BN government minister went as far as to propose weighting the electoral system according to racial composition (Yuen and Carvalho 2014.4.01), and the last redelineation of electoral boundaries by the BN regime, condemned by the bar as rushed and secretive (Varughese 2018.4.03) and widely thought to have been an attempt to push marginal constituencies into government hands, had the effect of increasing ethnic divisions (*Malaysiakini* 2018b.3.29). Many older informants for this study commented that society used to be better integrated, although back in the 1950s students already seemed to be averse to mixing (Ahmad Mustapha 2007:132).

2.2.3 Economic and Political Pressures on Policymakers

Needing strong economic growth to maintain financial assistance programmes condemned by the opposition as vote-buying (*The Star Online* 2012.1.21), BN engaged with globalisation and propagated an image of modern secularism through a business culture open to foreign investment, desire for internationally transparent law, and promotion of English proficiency. Yet it also depended increasingly on rural Malay voters, many of whom feel marginalised by economic change, fearful of the erosion of Muslim values and frustrated that English, to them a foreign rather than a second language, remains economically dominant.

Hence language policies have been shaped by a political culture that melds ideological nationalism with pragmatic nationism, and overseen by a political hegemony that for six decades was remarkably resilient yet increasingly polarising. The UMNO-dominated BN coalition holding power uninterrupted until 2018 combined centrally controlled economic policies delivering high growth and competitiveness[6] with political policies purporting to balance majority and minority interests. But it rarely shrank from prioritising the Malay majority when feeling threatened. As a consequence, multilingual policies that include Chinese and Tamil schooling and English in the more prestigious strata of education and law are generally able to coexist with expansionist policies for Malay, but whenever languages fight for territory the dispute becomes highly politicised. In the case of the legal domain there is room for pragmatic use of both Malay and English (but no official role for any other language) provided that the symbolic preeminence of the former is acknowledged. But legal Malay is not *merely* symbolic. The functional legitimacy it has acquired as a court medium reinforces the enduring power of Malay-centric identity politics and means that lawyers need to pay more than lip service to the language.

The key to Barisan Nasional's political longevity was the economy. Although Malaysians are wont to measure themselves ruefully against their former compatriots in Singapore, which boasts GDP per capita of $53,000 (World Bank 2018), by many measures their nation has done well, its GDP p.c. of $9500 ranking third in ASEAN after Singapore and Brunei and dwarfing Ghana's $1500, a country gaining independence in the same year as Malaya at a similar economic level (Bolt and van Zanden 2013). Annual GDP growth consistently exceeds 6%, falling below 5% only ten times since independence (extrapolated from World Bank 2018). In the run-up to the 2018 election the Youth and Sports Minister said he expected the World Bank to recognise Malaysia as a developed country by 2020, in keeping with government targets (*Malaysiakini* 2018a.03.06). The new government estimates this will be achieved by 2024 (*Malaysiakini* 2018i.10.18). Economic security remained BN's strongest electoral card, exemplified by the director-general of the Public Service Department warning civil servants not to "jeopardise the good things that we have

[6] Malaysia ranks 23/138 in the World Economic Forum's Global Competitiveness Report 2017–2018 (http://www3.weforum.org/docs/GCR2017-2018/05FullReport/TheGlobalCompetitivenessReport2017-2018.pdf)

now just because you want to try a new one (administration)" (Fairuz and Irwan 2018.2.25). But no economy can sustain high growth indefinitely, as stagnation in Japan, once the focus of Mahathir's Look East Policy, has shown, and preparing for slower expansion is of particular concern for one as heavily dependent on finite natural resources as Malaysia has been.

While most regimes draw on economic performance for legitimacy, this was crucial for BN since the raison d'être of UMNO, progressively dominant as the fortunes of its MCA (A. Jalil Hamid 2014.2.16) and MIC (Loone 2015.4.28) allies waned, was to remove the historical weaknesses of the Malays and show that they could compete not only with other groups domestically but also in the global economy. However, national economic growth has been at the expense of equality, and there has been fierce debate over whether the key fissures remain ethnic. Some attempts to show Malays closing the wealth gap entailed questionable accounting methods (Lee Hwok Aun 2015.10.16), and there were also political advantages in claiming that the gap between Chinese and *bumiputera* remained the most significant economic fissure (*Malaysiakini* 2015a.10.21). Yet measures to raise the relative position of the Malays have been criticised for benefitting only the selected few and failing rural inhabitants. *Bumiputera* are now the largest ethnic group among the highest earners (*Malaysiakini* 2015d.11.26), but there are high levels of inequality within the group, and indeed within all the main ethnic groups (*Malaysiakini* 2013a.9.20). With a Gini coefficient of 46.3 Malaysia has one of the largest wealth gaps in Asia (World Bank 2018).

Hence in its latter years the BN coalition was increasingly tempted to augment economic arguments with communalist scaremongering. This was especially the case when opponents focused on its financial weaknesses, such as rising national debt and unpopular proposals to plug it with a goods and services tax (Lim 2013.3.15). A few months after the coalition won the 2013 election, despite losing the popular vote (*The Economist* 2013.5.06) and most of its non-Malay support, Malay rights group Perkasa warned of fresh riots if affirmative action programmes were abandoned (*The Malaysian Insider* 2013.10.06). In the lead up to the 2018 elections the Communications and Multimedia Minister invoked the 1969 riots when accusing the opposition of racialising issues (Arfa Yunus 2017.12.31).

In addition to falling back on ethnocentricism following the collapse of support for the MIC and MCA, UMNO has been drawn to it as a way to rebuild bridges with Parti Islam Se-Malaysia (PAS) (*Malaysiakini* 2015e.12.10), an Islamic UMNO breakaway dependent on Malay voters (although sometimes backed by Chinese electors when no other anti-BN candidate is standing). After PAS joined the Pakatan Rakyat opposition pact in 2008, the government missed few chances to emphasise differences between it and its allies, Parti Keadilan Rakyat (PKR), popular with urban Malay supporters of Anwar after his rift with UMNO, and the largely Chinese DAP, especially on the question of introducing *hudud* Qur'anic penal law. PKR's capacity to bridge the gulf between PAS and DAP was weakened after Anwar's imprisonment on sodomy charges (Kim Quek 2014.4.23), his second conviction following a similarly controversial and politicised case in 1999. Tensions came to a head in 2015 when Pakatan Rakyat regrouped as Pakatan Harapan (PH), continuing collaboration between PKR and DAP but dropping PAS as a partner in favour of Amanah, a less conservative PAS splinter group (Nazari 2015.9.22). UMNO also faced the dilemma of preventing rural supporters from defecting to PAS without pursuing policies so conservative as to push urban Malays toward PKR, but in the 2018 election, PAS tended to split the opposition vote in UMNO's favour (Koh 2018.5.13). UMNO appears to be courting PAS more openly since its electoral defeat, with its Youth Chief in Kelantan, long a PAS-controlled state, recently pointing out that prospects for instating Qur'anic law had dimmed now that Pakatan was in power (*Malaysiakini* 2018f.7.24).

Such evidence as there is of a weakening of communalism is very much on the non-BN side (Hafiz 2013.9.16). The DAP which has had Indian leaders such as Karpal Singh prominent in its ranks and now fields more non-Chinese candidates (Lam 2014.6.02), and although abandoned by PAS in 2015, within Pakatan Harapan cooperates not only with Malay-dominant PKR and Amanah (a PAS splinter-group) but also with Bersatu, a party of UMNO defectors. Indeed after PH won the 2018 election *Malaysiakini* (2018c.5.10) drew attention to the fact that PKR won more seats than DAP, thereby undermining UMNO claims that PH was a largely Chinese movement.

Barisan Nasional's defeat in 2018 was unexpected (*Utusan Online* 2018.4.10). Its strength in overrepresented and subsidised rural areas (Koh 2013.3.05) saw it through the setback of the 2013 election and appeared to hold up despite a global financial scandal surrounding Prime Minister Najib Razak's management of the 1MDB (1 Malaysia Development Berhad) fund. But signs of pre-election jitters were evident from BN's endorsement of a chain of administrative measures likely to hamstring the opposition. Two months before polls the Electoral Commission redrew constituency boundaries in a way slammed by many as unusually skewed (*The Economist* 2018.3.10), even for a country where strategic redelineations have been commonplace (*Malaysiakini* 2013c.11.25) ever since the government took advantage of a large parliamentary majority in 1973 to overturn constitutional caps on unequal electoral districts (Chin Abdullah 2014.8.06; Wade 2009). Then less than a month before the vote the Registrar of Societies suspended Bersatu and refused to register Pakatan Harapan on technical grounds, forcing the coalition to campaign under the PKR logo (*The Straits Times* 2018.4.16). Such practices have helped drag Malaysia toward the bottom of international electoral integrity indices, despite the fact that, unlike most polities with similar rankings, it has regularly held elections (*Malaysiakini* 2017.12.01).

It was Pakatan Harapan's ability to secure 56% of seats in the face of gerrymandering, rather than its 48% of the popular vote (compared with 34% for BN), that thwarted BN's staying in power through an alliance with PAS (17%). But markets initially reacted negatively to the overthrow of a decades-long set-up (*Business Insider* 2018.5.10).

2.2.4 Outlook for Language Policy

While the first change of regime in six decades is a significant political event, there are few reasons to expect a marked change in language policy in the foreseeable future as there is broad agreement across Pakatan Harapan on the importance of both Malay and English. However, the details of specific proposals could open up differences, particularly in educational policy. With a prime minister known for promoting English in education back in power and willing to install non-Malays in key positions there could be greater resistance to Malay language nationalism than before, but any shift toward English is likely to be limited if the premiership passes to Anwar, who was president of the Malay Language Society as a student at UM and Minister of Education when Malayanisation programmes were gathering momentum in the late '80s. Indeed Mahathir's own party, Bersatu, includes many Malay nationalists.

With the DAP now in the ruling coalition, calls to abolish Mandarin and Tamil schools (see Chap. 5) may subside, but many Malay nationalists are currently on the alert for evidence of a slide in official language policy. In June, 2018, DAP Secretary-General and new Finance Minister Lim Guan Eng was accused of violating the constitution by issuing a policy statement in Malay, English and Chinese. The Malay Consultative Council commented that while any language might do for the "coffee shop", official communications should be in the national language, although protesters apparently carried "Love Bahasa" as well as "Bahasa Jiwa Bangsa" (Malay is the soul of the nation) placards (Shakira 2018.6.29).[7] Similar complaints have been raised against officials who added English and Chinese attachments to official documents drafted in Malay (Ben Tan 2018.9.25).

PKR's former Communications Director Nik Nazmi[8] sees families of various ethnicities continuing to be drawn to Chinese schools, as well as the English-dominated private sector, until Malay-medium national schools improve. Many urban PKR supporters would like a greater role for English, but at policy level the national language is prioritised, and like Amanah and Bersatu, the other Malay-majority components of the coalition, it will be keenly aware of the electoral weight of rural and conservative Malays after PAS's 2018 gains on the East Coast. Advocates for Malay have struggled to position it as the embodiment of both Malay identity and also the aspirations of multiethnic Malaysia, and with PH needing to concern itself with the views of non-Malays more than UMNO did, frictions may emerge. One trigger could be the reintroduction of PPSMI (*Pengajaran dan Pembelajaran Sains dan Matematik dalam Bahasa Inggeris*, or English-medium science and maths schooling), which was proposed controversially by Mahathir in 2002, abandoned no less controversially under Najib in 2012, and put back on the table by

[7] In a protest against the Attorney-General's use of English protesters similarly wielded signs in English, and also in Chinese (https://www.malaysiakini.com/news/432651), implying awareness of a gap between that the status of the national language and its communicative impact on target audiences.

[8] Interviewed Shah Alam, 2013.10

Mahathir before he returned to power in 2018 (Astroawani 2018.2.28). Mahathir has already warned senior civil servants (*Malaysiakini* 2018.6.06) and police officers (*Malaysiakini* 2018.8.13) that they will be required improve their English proficiency.

English is not without ethnic and regional associations, being less used on the East Coast while enjoying higher vehicularity in urbanised West Coast areas as well as higher status in East Malaysia, where Adenan Satem, the late Chief Minister of Sarawak, resisted the expansion of Malay (*Malaysiakini* 2016b.10.17). But its main association is economic, rather than ethnic or political. *The Star* reported the BN Education Minister's celebration of Malay as the language of unity on the same page as Mahathir's criticism of graduates' English as inadequate for employment (Macintyre and Embun Said 2013.10.09). Alongside promises to defend the language of the Malay race (*Malay Mail Online* 2016.3.25) and even to promote it as a medium for ASEAN (Azura and Fairuz 2017.7.26), Najib Razak, who was educated partly in England like his father, prime minister Abdul Razak, emphasised the economic importance of English (Koh 2015.11.11). The nation's nine leading local-born CEOs obtained their first degree abroad in anglophone countries (Easyunit 2014.7.30). Three decades ago Chitravelu (1985:iii) already saw government-driven employment expansion for Malay-speakers being outpaced by globalisation's demand for English speakers. Malay linguist Asmah Omar (1996:530) called English "essential to Malaysia's rise to become a developing and industrial nation". For Nair-Venugopal (2001:21) "nowhere is the use of English more entrenched in Malaysia than in the private domains of corporate business, and industry, banking and finance". Delfolie (2012:19) claims governments remain bent on showing their former colonisers that Malays, the ethnic group most excluded from commerce under colonialism, can succeed economically and notes (ibid:9) that 50% of those funded for overseas study (80% of whom are *bumiputera*) go to Australia, Britain or the US.

Business expansion also creates work for lawyers and, as the personal accounts of lawyers and students confirm (Chaps. 5, 7 and 8), underlines traditional ties between English and law. The new government, under a leader best known for his management of economic growth, is certain to prioritise policies that gain the confidence of international business over domestic cultural agendas. Moreover the bar, which became increasingly critical of BN, is likely to feel freer to operate now, and its upper echelons favour English. Already there have been calls to the judiciary to recruit more from the bar (Ganesan Kasinathan 2018.5.19). This will not change the fact that a whole generation of judges and lawyers alike has grown up stronger in Malay than English. In other words, bilingual law will continue.

2.3 Language, Communalism and Multijural Law

2.3.1 Indigenisation of Common Law

Malaysian common law maintains close links with the rest of the Commonwealth. The rights of citizens to criticise authorities were defined recently by reference to UK case law (Hafiz 2018a.3.5). Malaysians admitted to the English bar are also admissible in Malaysia if they have sufficient knowledge of Malay (see Chap. 5). One KL advocate who had practised in both jurisdictions described Malaysian legal culture as "very English".

Yet distinct features began emerging even before independence. A 1948 Ordinance restructuring the judiciary into Supreme, Appeal, High, Sessions and Magistrates Courts also provided for Penghulu's Courts, empowering village headmen to hear minor civil complaints among parties "of an Asian race speaking and understanding the Malay language" (Art 94). The 1956 Civil Law Ordinance (Art.3), which applied the common law of England, rules of equity and statutes of general application, and extended the English commercial law already used in Penang and Melaka (Art.5), specifically excluded English land law (Art.6), although common law and equitable principles may be referenced when interpreting the Torrens land registration system that is in place.

According to Abdul Aziz (2008:3), even those academics who value pre-English law tend to underestimate its impact or the continued importance of local influences. However his claim about the constitution having indigenous roots over-relies on provisions in support of the historical (though hardly indigenous) institutions of Islam and the sultans, together with the Malay language. Few would agree with him that Art. 4(1)'s requirement that legislation be consistent with the Constitution makes the judiciary more independent from the executive than in Britain – especially since the clause can be circumvented (Art.150(6)) during states of emergency.[9] Indeed allegations that judges were made to attend 'national transformation' training sessions just before the last election (*Malaysiakini* 2018g.7.28) has strengthened the belief that executive interference has been considerable. Recent allegations that senior judiciary attempted to influence religious conversion (*Malaysiakini* 2019.1.18) and constituency redelineation (Hafiz 2018.8.06) cases hint at a high degree of politicisation. One Court of Appeal judge reported (*Malaysiakini* 2019b.2.14) relief among top judges upon learning the new Harapan government was not about to launch a clean-up, but in February, 2019 decided to open a Royal Commission of Enquiry into judicial interference (Varughese 2019a.2.22).

[9] States of emergency, provided for under constitutional Art. 150, are a perennial feature of Malaysian politics. In a 2011 article in *The Star* written shortly before the lifting of an emergency that had remained on the books since 1964, UiTM law professor Shad Saleem Faruqi suggested the ordinary legal system had been eclipsed for 47 years by parliament's capacity to suspend a range of constitutional provisions. (http://www.thestar.com.my/story.aspx/?file=%2f2011%2f9%2f16%2fnation%2f9514472&sec=nation)

Postcolonial English cases have persuasive authority but are not binding unless specifically incorporated.[10] The right of appeal to the Privy Council ended in 1985 under the reforms of the 1983 Constitution Amendment Act, although its previous decisions remain persuasive (Abdul Hamid Omar 1994:28). Since independence a body of local case law has evolved that sometimes departs from English principles, including raised negligence thresholds for local authorities and wider interpretation of contempt laws (Farid Sufian 2011). Abdul Aziz (2008) emphasises the influence of Commonwealth jurisdictions other than Britain, citing Indian case law and Australian land registration. Wu (1999:xvii) observed a tendency to move away from Britain's legislative models after its entry into the EU. English barristers no longer have local standing but may be heard if their expertise is required. When Cherie Blair Q.C. was barred from appearing on the grounds that sufficient local expertise existed, a judicial panel clarified that foreign lawyers were not disqualified merely for inability to speak Malay (Arfa'eza and Wong 2006.6.15).

2.3.2 *Multijuralism*

While legal pluralism does not appear to be a strong predictor of vernacular common law around the world (see Chap. 10), contact between legal English and Malay to some extent reflects influences from *adat* and *Syariah*, in addition to planned bilingualisation. There is also some evidence of Malay encroaching informally upon English's formal monopoly of East Malaysian law.

2.3.2.1 Adat

A number of provisions in the Constitution refer to the customs of the Malays and natives of Sabah and Sarawak. Articles 76(2) and 150(6A), for example, restrict parliament's capacity to rule on customary matters in parallel to restrictions regarding Islamic law. In West Malaysia, however, the power of Penghulu's Courts to hear minor criminal and civil cases was abolished in 2013 by an amendment to the Subordinate Courts Act that transferred jurisdiction to the Magistrates courts. *Adat* customary rights are sometimes invoked in civil litigations (for example, when claims of continuous occupation were made in opposition to land seizures proposed to build Kuala Lumpur's airport expressway) but they have been subjected to strict standards of proof (Lee and Tan 2008). Bulan (2008) nevertheless finds the courts becoming more receptive to oral histories as evidence. Although the oldest inhabitants of the Peninsula, the Orang Asli are mentioned only indirectly in the constitution in a reference in Art.8 (5)(c) to the "the protection, well-being or advancement of the aboriginal people of the Malay Peninsula", but the Bar Council (Varughese

[10] Senior solicitor-advocate David Dass, interviewed Kuala Lumpur, 2013.6.

2019b.2.26) argues that their customary rights over land they have used for generation have been acknowledged under common law in cases such as *Kerajaan Negeri Johor v Adong bin Kuwau* (1998).

Adat has retained a stronger presence in East Malaysia, with separate customary courts remaining active in both Sabah and Sarawak. It lacks a written tradition but its legitimacy and functions are recognised in national and state legislation and regulated by the *Majlis Adat Istiadat Sarawak* (a Council for Customs and Traditions set up under a 1977 Ordinance) and the 1992 Native Courts Ordinance. In July, 2018 there were 19 fulltime magistrates to deal with native land and customs disputes in Sarawak, assisted by 52 ex-officio magistrates, with nearly 6000 cases still pending (*Malaysiakini* 2018e.7.10).

However, offences already covered by the Penal Code must now be heard in the Magistrates courts (Edward 2008). Constitutional Article 161(3) admits the use of native languages for proceedings and codes and hearings are conducted mostly in Malay or East Malaysian Austronesian languages. *Majlis Adat Istiadat Sarawak* also has a bilingual (Malay-English) portal[11] with information about marriage and inheritance rules.

2.3.2.2 Syariah

If *adat* is increasingly being absorbed or marginalised, Islamic law is well-supported and thriving. Peletz (2013b) reported a transformation in a Negeri Sembilan court he revisited 25 years after doing fieldwork there. Informal dispute resolution in the village head's house in the local Malay dialect had been replaced by modern courtrooms, computers, tight schedules and lawyers speaking standard Malay laced with Qur'anic references. On enquiring about the business suits worn by *kadi* (now referred to as *hakim,* the same term as for common law judges), he was told "Itu *rebranding* lah". With respect to institutions and procedures, common law's influence over *Syariah* is more evident than *Syariah*'s impact on common law.

Syariah is important for the question of language in Malaysian common law as it functions mostly in Malay and is the legal model most often cited by those who criticise common law as an exonormative imposition. In 2007 Chief Justice Ahmad Fairuz told an Islamic conference that *Syariah* should replace common law to rescue Malaysia from the "clutches of colonialism" (Bell 2007.9.01). Further, increased use of Malay in common law coincides with the growing dominance of Malays – all constitutionally Muslim – in the judiciary, currently exceeding 84% in the Federal Court (Hafiz Yatim 2018b.8.15). It has also been suggested that common law courts are being desecularised. Whiting (2008:252–254) reports several instances of civil court justices referring both didactically and instrumentally to Islam in order to add rhetorical weight to their judgments.

[11] http://www.nativecustoms.sarawak.gov.my

Legal, linguistic and religious conflicts are at the forefront of ongoing controversy over Malaysian Christians' use of words such as 'Allah' in their worship. When Selangor's Islamic Affairs Department claimed Peninsular Christians had no reason for "a language largely used by Malays who are Muslims", the irony was not lost on non-Malay commentators after decades of being criticised for tepid espousal of the national language (*Malaysiakini* 2014a.1.06). Following a spate of similar comments, novelist Faisal Tehrani (Mahavera 2014.5.18) pointed out the contradiction between attempts to tie language to ethnicity and religion and the official policy of making Malay a language for everyone. Some lawyers nevertheless feel Muslim Malays' absence from civil family courts tends to favour the use of English for proceedings there.

Constitutional Amendment 121(A), 1988, separates the jurisdictions of civil and *Syariah* courts. The latter are administered at the level of each state and handle cases where all parties are Muslim – typically family and property disputes but also Islamic offences such as drinking and gambling – with powers to incarcerate, fine or impose corporal punishment (Powell and Azirah 2011). State provisions (e.g. Selangor's 2003 Syariah Civil Procedure Enactment, s.232) prescribe Malay for proceedings and documents. Well-funded federal agencies such as JAKIM (Jabatan Kemajuan Islam Malaysia/Islamic Development Office) have helped harmonise the state jurisdictions (Whiting 2012:3) through a series of reforms modelled consciously on common law, with the court hierarchy restructured into five levels (*Malaysiakini* 2013b.11.13). Comments from a UniSZA lecturer about the active role of judges and propensity to give out advice were confirmed by two UM students on attachment to *Syariah* courts. Hence procedure is not entirely adversarial, but it follows common law stages such as examination-in-chief, cross-examination and re-examination (Powell and Azirah 2011). According to Mukhtar Abdullah, a former head of the Terengganu bar who practises in both systems, English legal principles may be quoted to fill lacunae in Islamic law.[12] For this study, 20% of UM students reported involvement in *Syariah* cases during their professional attachments. A diploma from JAKIM is required for *Syariah* practice (Whiting 2012) and another Terengganu lawyer noted increasing numbers of common law students studying for this immediately after getting their LLB. Perusal of judgments (e.g. *Ramli bin Sulaiman* 2009) reveals generic textual organisation into *fakta kes* (facts of the case) and *alasan penghakiman* (grounds of judgment) supported by legislative (as well as Qur'anic) referencing.

Farid Sufian (2013.12.10) justifies innovations in *Syariah* insofar as they preserve traditions of justice. Former Chief Justice Abdul Hamid Mohamad (2012) defends the adoption of English criminal procedure in the absence of authentic *Syariah* alternatives. While stressing (Abdul 2011:4) that financial products must be cleared by the National Bank's *Syariah* Advisory Council (SAC) and every Islamic financial institution have an SAC-approved *Syariah* committee, and further noting (Abdul Hamid Mohamad 2011:10) that most of the lawyers specialising in Islamic

[12] Interviewed in Kuala Terengganu, 2014.2.

finance are Muslims, Abdul (2011:7) points out that most documents related to Islamic banking are in English and drafted by common law lawyers who don't appear in the Islamic courts. Indeed the AGC experienced difficulties understanding Arabic terms when embedding Islamic banking in statute (Abdul Monir 2013.12.10). Hence Malaysia's drive to become a world leader in Islamic finance by no means implies an expansion of *Syariah*. Rather, this strategy supports Delfolie's (2012:4) contention that national positioning toward the wider Muslim world, although not devoid of ideological elements such as opposition to western neo-colonialism, is primarily pragmatic and puts economics and politics before religion.

Peletz suggests *Syariah* hankers after the prestige and legitimacy of common law (ibid:610–613). Abdul Hamid Mohamad (2011:10) even claims that the Malaysian *Syariah* courts' adoption of procedures such as precedent and the testing of oral evidence give it a transparency and consistency that may be lacking in Muslim societies where Roman law models apply. There is certainly linguistic evidence for this orientation toward common law. Asmah (1998:68) remarked on the introduction of litigious terms such as *membawa ke mahkamah* (take to court) and *mengambil tindakan undang-undang* (take legal action). Peletz (2013a:616) found habitual use of English terms such as *afidavit, bailif, klien, litigan.* Mukhtar Abdullah noted Latin phrases such as *inter vivos.*[13] We should nonetheless resist reading too much into lexical borrowing in an endemically multilingual society. During 20 hours of observations at *Syariah* courts in urbanised Shah Alam, Powell and Azirah (2011) found lexical transfer from English and Latin and code-switching with English, as well as judges using Arabic. They point out that the provision for bilingual drafting of post-1966 enactments also applies to *Syariah*, with English and Latin loans found in Malay texts and Malay and Latin in English. Oral and written code-switching featured heavily at a seminar on Islamic law held at UM's Akademi Pengajian Islam in December, 2013.[14]

While Abdul Hamid Mohamad (2012) concedes that Islamic principles have shaped several tort rulings (e.g. *Nepline Sdn Bhd* 1965), most claims of religious encroachment into common law are limited to conversion cases. In *Lina Joy* (2006), the Federal Court held that constitutional freedom of religion (Art.11) did not entail the right to leave Islam for an appellant prevented from doing so under *Syariah*. Civil court judges have been reluctant to rule on matters passing through Islamic courts, even where non-Muslims are involved, and the National Syarie Lawyers Association asked the Chief Justice to direct them not to hear such cases after one justice granted custody to a Hindu mother despite a *Syariah* court ruling for the father (*Malaysiakini* 2014d.4.18). Declaring the two systems to be of equal standing, one Inspector General of Police refused to carry out civil court orders that appeared to conflict with *Syariah* rulings (*Malaysiakini* 2014.6.25b). In February 2016, however, the Federal Court affirmed the principle that custody in non-Muslim marriages was within the civil courts' purview (Hafiz 2016a.2.19). Two years later

[13] Mukhtar, op. cit., 2014.2.

[14] Personal observation, 2013.12.12.

the Federal Court asserted its right to rule on a custody case involving a non-Muslim, while commenting that civil law and *Syariah* "co-exist in their respective spheres" (*Indira Gandhi* 2018). Peletz (2013c) stresses that despite the publicity they garner, custody and conversion cases play a minor part in either system.

2.3.2.3 East Malaysian Law

In addition to greater use of *adat*, East Malaysia's distinct history brings distinct features to its administration and common law. 59% of Sarawakians have said they want more autonomy in economic affairs and 42% favour a more independent education system, though few desire an independent language policy (Merdeka Center 2016). Sabah and Sarawak have border controls with Malaya and politicians from the Peninsula – generally from the opposition – are frequently denied entry on the grounds of 'disrupting unity' (Kow 2016.3.24). There are separate High Courts and subordinate courts under a unified Federal Court. This study focuses mainly on West Malaysian law because of its bilingualism, but thinly populated East Malaysia is of interest because of having resisted Malay, despite most of its lawyers training in Malaya (there are no LLB programmes in the East) and enjoying unreciprocated rights of audience there if they complete local chambering.

Since East Malaysia carries disproportionate electoral weight and has a large Christian electorate, BN governments conceded that rulings restricting Christian activities in Malaya should not apply to Sarawak and Sabah (Davidson 2013.10.14), and a Kuching High Court went as far as to rule that *Syariah* court agreement is unnecessary to convert to Christianity (*Malaysiakini* 2016a.3.24). One news forum commenter connected the Inspector-General of Police's announcement of his willingness to execute a court order against a Sarawak Muslim convert to forthcoming elections there (Hafiz 2016b.4.29).

Under the 18-point and 20-point memoranda signed respectively by Sarawak and Sabah in 1963 (Bong and Pilo 2011.9.16), English was to continue for official purposes without limitation of time. Constitutional Amendment 161 requires the passing of an enactment in each state before English may be restricted in the courts or state legislatures (Suulok Tawie 2012.2.20). In 2015 Chong Chieng Jen, head of the Sarawak division of the DAP, insisted on his constitutional right under the agreement with Malaya to speak English in the federal parliament (*Malaysiakini* 2015b.11.17), sparking criticism from cabinet minister Ismail Sabri Yaakob that this violated the constitutional position of Malay as the federation's official language (Anne Muhammad 2015.11.24). Parliamentary Standing Order 8 attempts to bridge the gap between the two positions by allowing English if the Speaker gives permission. Around the same time Sarawak's Chief Minister announced that English was co-official with Malay there, drawing flack from the government's Social and Current Affairs Adviser for 'sowing seeds of discord' (*Malaysiakini* 2015c.11.23).

The Rules of the High Court (1980 O.92 R.1) direct that documents filed to East Malaysian courts be in English, although a Malay translation may accompany them, a contrast with West Malaysia that was reaffirmed following *Dato' Seri Anwar*

Ibrahim (*The Star Online* 2009.12.11). Powell (2011) found lower court cases in Sibu, Sarawak conducted entirely in English but was informed by local lawyers that advance permission had been obtained to use Malay in cases in the Kuching High Court. For this study one UM student on attachment to the Magistrates' courts in Sarawak's state capital reported that all proceedings were in English, but another, posted to more remote Sandakan in Sabah, found Malay being used without translation.

Sabah and Sarawak are even more linguistically diverse than Malaya, which can pose particular difficulties for the legal system. Rodziah (2004), for example, has warned of the potential risks of relay interpreting, where Malay if often positioned as an intermediate language between the English of the court and the language of witnesses and defendants.

2.4 Implications for Legal Vernacularisation

To summarise, impetuses for and constraints on legal vernacularisation in modern Malaysia have evolved from a long history of political and economic tension. Written law in Malaya predates British colonialism by nearly four centuries, and unwritten customary law by considerably longer, with some areas beyond direct British administration law relying on a blend of *Syariah*, *adat* and sultanate authority into the twentieth century. But the English-based practices introduced by colonial authorities in the Straits Settlements steadily spread to other states with the extension of political control and expansion of commercial practices. Colonial economic policy accelerated Chinese and promoted Indian immigration while administrative and educational polices sought to stave off social instability through communal separation. English education was available only to the few, the Chinese supported their own vernacular schools, and Malay and Tamil education were at the bottom of the pile, it was the sole medium of common law, with little evidence of even the limited use of vernaculars introduced into India.

The main change in the decades preceding independence was the cultural and political coopting of the Malay elite. After the Malayan Union failed because of opposition from Malays fearing political, economic and even demographic marginalisation in their heritage homeland, a postcolonial regime emerged leaving Malays with political power and Chinese with economic power. English remained the language of administration and law despite the symbolic importance accorded to Malay. Non-Malay lawyers outnumbered Malays, most were educated in England and all in English.[15]

In this situation, vernacularisation of law might have remained a matter of symbolic respect for the national language and pragmatic accommodation of witnesses unable to speak English, if not for politically-calculated initiatives after the 1970s to

[15] Chooi Mun Sou, 2013.9 (See note 5).

reinforce the position of the Malays through affirmative action in economic and educational domains. Status and corpus planning were accelerated to open the way for more use of Malay in law. However, the ambivalent outlook of the political elite, seeking national unity under Malay hegemony and national development through international economic engagement, inhibited comprehensive vernacularisation. How these constraints shape bilingual law is the focus of the next four chapters.

Cases Cited

Dato' Seri Anwar Ibrahim v Tun Dr Mahathir Mohamad (2010) 3CLJ 444 CA.
Indira Gandhi A/P Mutho v Pengarah Jabatan Agama Islam Perak (2018) 1LNS 86.
Kerajaan Negeri Johor v Adong bin Kuwau (1998) 2 MLJ 158.
Merdeka University v Government (1982) 2 MLJ 243.
Lina Joy v Majlis Agama Islam Wilayah Persekutuan, Kerejaan Malaysia Rayuan Sivil no. 01-2-2006(W).
Nepline Sdn Bhd v. Jones Lang Wooten (1965) 1 CLJ 865.
Ramli bin Sulaiman lawan *Rohani binti Ab Hamid* [Kes Rayuan Mal bil: 04500-054-0001-2009] [Malaysian Syariah Courts].

References

Abdul Aziz Bari. (2008). The indigenous roots of the Malaysian constitution. The provisions and the implications. *CLJ Legal Network* [2008] 6 CLJ xxxiii. Accessed 30 Aug 2012 from www.cljlaw.com/

Abdul Hamid Mohamad. (2011). Malaysia as an Islamic finance hub: Malaysia law as the law of reference and Malaysian law as the forum for settlement of disputes. *12th Emeritus Professor Ahmad Ibrahim Memorial lecture*. Accessed 10 Apr 2014 from http://www.tunabdulhamid.my/index.php/speech-papers-lectures/item/135-malaysia-as-an-islamic-finance-hub

Abdul Hamid Mohamad. (2012). Harmonisation of Shari'ah and common law in Malaysia:the way forward. *2nd international seminar on Shari'ah and Common Law* 2012, Universiti Sains Islam Malaysia, 2012.3.06. Accessed 30 Mar 2013 from http://www.tunabdulhamid.my/index.php/speech-papers-lectures/items/317-harmonisation-of-shariah-and-common-law-in-malaysia-the-way-forward

Abdul Hamid Omar. (1994). *The Judiciary in Malaysia*. Kuala Lumpur: Asia Pacific Publications.

Abdul Monir Yaacob. (2013, December 10). *Undang-undang Islam kini dari teori kepada polisi dan implementasi dalam konteks perundangan dan kehakiman Negara* [Islamic law today from theory to policy and implementation in a national legal and judicial context]. Paper presented at *Seminar on Islamic law in practice with global perspective*, Akademi Pengajian Islam, Universiti Malaya, 2013.12.10.

Abdul Rahman Arshad. (2007). *Unity and education in Malaysia*. Kuala Lumpur: Dewan Bahasa dan Pustaka.

Adelaar, Alexander K. (1996). Malay: Its role and spread. In Wurm, Mühlhäusler, & Tyron (Eds.), *Atlas of languages of intercultural communication in the Pacific, Asia, and the Americas* (pp. 673–693).

Ahmad Mustapha Hassan. (2007). *The unmaking of Malaysia. Insider's reminiscences of UMNO, Razak and Mahathir*. Petaling Jaya: SIRD.

Akashi Yoji. (2008). Introduction. In Akashi & Yoshimura (Eds.), *New perspectives on the Japanese occupation in Malaya and Singapore, 1941–1945* (pp. 1–20). Singapore: NUS Press.

Ananthi Al Ramiah, Hewstone, Miles, & Wölfer, Ralph. (2017). *Meeting the challenge and maximizing the promise of multicultural Malaysia*. Final report of CIMB foundation survey and recommendations. Accessed 12 Dec 2017 from https://www.cimbfoundation.com/clients/CIMB_Foundation_D894EB94-B114-4E11-8175-EB426BB876F0/contentms/img/pdf/attitudes-and-%20ethnoreligious-integration-survey-and-recommendations.pdf

Andaya Watson, Barbara, & Andaya, Leonard. (1982). *A History of Malaysia*. London: Macmillan.

Anne Muhammad. (2015, November 24). Minister: DAP MP 'biadap' for wanting to debate in English. *Malaysiakini*. Accessed 20 Jan 2016 from http://www.malaysiakini.com.new/320802

Appudurai, Jayanath, & Dass, David G. A. (2008). *Malaysian Indians: Looking forward*. Petaling Jaya: Strategic Information and Research Centre.

Arfa Yunus. (2017, December 31). Opposition playing up racial, religious issues: Salleh Said Keruak *New Straits Times*. Accessed 10 Jan 2018 from https://www.nst.com.my/news/politics/2017/12/319982/opposition-playing-racial-religious-issues-salleh-said-keruak

Arfa'eza A. Aziz & Wong Yeen Fern. (2006, June 15). It's a 'no go' for Cherie Blair. *Malaysiakini*. Accessed 22 Mar 2011 from http://www.malaysiakini.com/news/52586

Asmah Haji Omar. (1979). *Language planning for unity efficiency: A study of the language status and corpus planning of Malaysia*. Singapore: RELC.

Asmah Haji Omar. (1996). Post-imperial English in Malaysia. In C. Fishman & Rubal-Lopez (Eds.), *Post-imperial English. Status change in former British and American colonies, 1940–1990* (pp. 373–399). Berlin/New York: Mouton de Gruyter.

Asmah Haji Omar. (1998). *Concepts of conflict, war and peace in the Malay language*. Kuala Lumpur: Akademi Pengajian Melayu, Universiti Malaya.

Asmah Haji Omar. (2007). Malaysia and Brunei. In A. Simpson (Ed.), *Language and national identity in Asia* (pp. 337–359). Oxford: Oxford University Press.

Astroawani. (2018, February 28). *PPSMI mungkin dikembalikan jika PH memerintah* [PPSMI may be reinstated if PH takes over]. Accessed 02 Mar 2018 from http://www.astroawani.com/berita-malaysia/ppsmi-mungkin-dikembalikan-jika-ph-memerintah-169277

Aw, Nigel. (2013, September 14). PM reassures non-bumis amid race-based measures. *Malaysiakini*. Accessed 16 Sept 2013 from http://www.malaysiakini.com/news/241117

Azura Abas, & Fairuz Mohd Shahar. (2017, July 26). 'Let's strive towards making Bahasa Melayu the language of Asean'. *New Straits Times*. Accessed 28 July 2017 from https://www.nst.com.my/news/nation/2017/07/261094/lets-strive-towards-making-bahasa-melayu-main-language-asean

Bell, Thomas. (2007, September 01). Malaysia considers switch to Islamic law. *The Telegraph*. Accessed 12 Dec 2013 from http://www.telegraph.co.uk/news/worldnews/1561896/Malaysia-considers-switch-to-Islamic-law.html

Ben Tan. (2018, September 25). *The Malay Mail*. Accessed 27 Sept 2018 from https://www.malaymail.com/s/1676303/johor-exco-clears-air-on-language-used-in-vexing-council-letter

Bhabha, Homi. (1994). *The location of culture*. New York: Routledge.

Bolt, J., & Van Zanden, J. L. (2013). *The first update of the Maddison Project*. Accessed 30 Mar 2014 from http://www.ggdc.net/maddison/maddison-project/data.htm

Bong, Karen & Pilo, William. (2011, September 16). An agreement forged and forgotten. *Borneo Post Online*. Accessed 20 May 2013 from http://www.theborneopost.com/2011/09/16/an-agreement-forged-and-forgotten/

Boo Su-lyn. (2014, May 30). As clock ticks, BN looks to Teluk Intan Indians for crucial votes. *Malay Mail Online*. Accessed 01 June 2014 from http://www.themalaymailonline.com/malaysia/article/as-clock-ticks-bn-looks-to-teluk-intan-indians-for-crucial-votes

Brown, C. C. (Ed./Trans.). (1953/1970). *Sejarah Melayu/Malay Annals*. Oxford: Oxford University Press.

Brown, David. (2000). *Contemporary nationalism: civic, ethnocultural and multicultural politics*. London: Routledge.

Bulan, Ramy. (2008, May 06). Customary law and the federal constitution. *3rd international conference on multiculturalism and law,* University of Malaya.

Business Insider. (2018, May 10). *Malaysia's Mahathir, 92, to be sworn in as prime minister after historic poll win.* Accessed 10 May 2018 from http://www.businessinsider.com/r-malaysias-mahathir-92-to-be-sworn-in-as-prime-minister-after-historic-poll-win-2018-5?yptr=yahoo&r=UK&IR=T

Cain, P. J., & Hopkins, A. G. (1993). *British imperialism. Vol. 2: Crisis and deconstruction.* Harlow: Longman.

Canagarajah, A. Suresh. (2005). Dilemmas in planning English/vernacular relations in post- colonial communities. *Journal of SocioLinguistics, 9/3*, 418–447.

Carnell, F. G. (1952). Malayan citizenship legislation. *The International and Comparative law Quarterly, 1*(4), 504–518. Accessed 20 Mar 2014 from http://www.jstor.org.stable/755175.

Chai, Hon Chan. (1977). *Education and nation-building in pluralistic societies: The West Malaysian experience*. Canberra: ANU.

Cham, B. N. (1975). Class & communal conflict in Malaysia. *Journal of Contemporary Asia, 5*(4), 446–461. Accessed 16 June 2014 from https://doi.org/10.1080/00472337508566973.

Cheah Boon Kheng . (1983). *Red star over Malaya. Resistance and social conflict during and after the Japanese occupation of Malaya.* Singapore: NUS Press.

Chin Abdullah, Maria. (2014, August 06). Delineation and seats increase (Part I) *Malaysiakini.* Accessed 07 Aug 2014 from http://www.malaysiakini.com/columns/270722

Chitravelu, N. (1985). *The status and role of English in Malaysia. US Information Agency Report.* Singapore: RELC.

David, Maya Khemlani and Faridah Noor Mhd Noor. (1999). Language maintenance or language shift in the Portuguese settlement of Malacca in Malaysia? *Migracijske Teme: A Journal for Migration and Ethnic Studies, 15*(4), 465–481.

Davidson, Desmond. (2013, October 14). It's worship as usual, Sarawak Christians will continue to use "Allah" – state Minister. *The Malaysian Insider.* Accessed 14 Oct 2013 from http://www.themalaysianinsider.com/malaysia/article/its-worship-as-usual-sarawak-christians-will-continue-use-allah-state-minis

Delfolie, David. (2012). Malaysian extraversion towards the Muslim World: Ideological positioning for a "Mirror Effect". *Journal of Current Southeast Asian Affairs, 31*(4), 3–29.

Det, C. H. E. (1949, April 24). Malay – "modern" and standard. *The Straits Times*, p. 6.

Dezalay, Yves., & Garth, Bryant. (2010). *Asian legal revivals – Lawyers in the shadow of Empire.* Chicago: University of Chicago Press.

Easyunit. (2014, July 30). Educational background of nation's top 10 CEOs. *Malaysiakini.* Accessed 31 July 2014 from http://www.malaysiakini.com/news/270137

Edward, Ronnie [Chief Registrar Native Court of Sarawak] (2008, May 06). Contemporary relevance of customary laws and the native courts within the plural legal system in Sarawak. *3rd international conference on multiculturalism and law.* University of Malaya.

Fairuz Mohd Shahar & Irwan Shafrizan Ismail. (2018, February 25). Thinking ahead for the people. *New Straits Times.* Accessed 26 Feb 2018 from https://www.nst.com.my/news/nation/2018/02/338731/thinking-ahead-people

Farid Sufian Shuaib. (2008). Development of Syariah Courts in Malaysia: Waves of reformation. *CLJ Legal Network* [2008] 9 CLJ xli. Accessed 30 Aug 2012 from www.cljlaw.com/

Farid Sufian Shuaib (2011). Towards Malaysian common law: convergence between indigenous norms and common law methods. *CLJ Legal Network* [2011] 1 LNS(A)ix. Accessed 2012.8.30 from www.cljlaw.com/

Farid Sufian Shuaib (2013). Transformation of the Syariah courts: tradition, constitution, law and practice. Paper presented at *Seminar on Islamic law in practice with global perspective*, Akademi Pengajian Islam, Universiti Malaya, 2013.12.10.

Fishman, Joshua. (1968). Nationality-nationalism and nation-nationism. In F. Fishman & Dasgupta (Eds.), *Language problems of developing nations* (pp. 39–51). New York: Wiley.

Fisk, E. K. (1982). Development in Malaysia. In E. K. Fisk & H. Osman-Rani (Eds.), *The political economy of Malaysia* (pp. 1–23). Kuala Lumpur: Oxford University Press.

G.K. Ganesan Kasinathan. (2018, May 19). Time to rebuild the Malaysian Judiciary. *Malaysiakini*. Accessed 20 May 2018 from https://www.malaysiakini.com/news/425809

Godemont, François. (1997). *The new Asian renaissance*. New York: Routledge.

Gunn, Geoffrey. (1997). *Language, power and ideology in Brunei Darussalam*. Ohio University Press.

Hafiz Yatim. (2013, September 16). 'New affirmative action policies could create divide'. *Malaysiakini*. Accessed 17 Sept 2013 from http://www.malaysiakini.com/news/241249

Hafiz Yatim. (2016a, February 19). Father granted custody of son, Deepa gets daughter. *Malaysiakini*. Accessed 20 Feb 2016 from https://www.malaysiakini.com/news/329917

Hafiz Yatim. (2016b, April 29). IGP cannot refuse to order officers to arrest Ridhuan. *Malaysiakini*. Accessed 30 Apr 2016 from http://www.malaysiakini.com/news/339681

Hafiz Yatim. (2018a, March 5). Appellate court explains why public officials can be criticised. *Malaysiakini*. Accessed 5 Mar 2018 from https://www.malaysiakini.com/news/414464

Hafiz Yatim. (2018b, August 15). 'More judicial activism today but winter of 88 lingers'. *Malaysiakini*. Accessed 15 Aug 2018 from https://www.malaysiakini.com/news/439074

Hafiz Yatim. (2018c, August 16). COA Judge: I was reprimanded for dissenting in Indira Gandhi's case. *Malaysiakini*. Accessed 17 Aug 2018 from https://www.malaysiakini.com/news/439151

Harper, T. N. (1999). *The end of empire and the making of Malaya*. Cambridge: Cambridge University Press.

He Jia Xun, & Yang Pei Gen. (2012). 爱国者与冒牌者 [*Patriots and Imitators*]. Petaling Jaya: Suaram Komunikasi.

Hooker, M. B. (1976) The Trengganu inscription in Malayan legal history. In *Malaysian branch royal Asiatic society reprint No.4: A centenary volume* (MBRAS, Vol. 49.2, pp. 127–131). Singapore: MBRAS.

A. Jalil Hamid (2014, February 16). Crucial test ahead for MCA. *New Sunday Times*, p. 16.

Kaplan, Robert, & Baldauf, Richard. (1997). *Language planning from practice to theory*. Clevedon: Multilingual Matters.

Kartini, Radeng Adjeng. (1903/2005). *On feminism and nationalism. Kartini's letters to Stella Zeehandelaar, 1899–1903*. (Joost Coté, Trans.). Melbourne: Monash Asia Institute.

Kathigasu, Sybil. (1954/2006). *No dram of Mercy*. Kuala Lumpur: Prometheus.

Kennedy, J. (1993). *History of Malaya*. Kuala Lumpur: Majid & Co. (Reprinted 2007 by Synergy Media).

Kim Quek. (2014, April 23). Justice down the drain in Sodomy II, what next? *Malaysiakini*. Accessed 24 Apr 2014 from https://www.malaysiakini.com/news/260777

Kirk-Greene, A. (1999). *On crown service: A history of HM colonial and overseas services, 1837–1997*. Taurus: London/New York.

Koh Gah Chie. (2015, November 23). *Race column still needed in 198 official forms, says Entulu*. Accessed 24 Nov 2015 from http://www.malaysiakini.com/news/320667

Koh Jun Lin. (2015, November 11). English prerequisite in job market, says Najib. *Malaysiakini*. Accessed 12 Nov 2015 from http://www.malaysiakini.com/news/319147

Koh Jun Lin. (2013, July 23). Terengganu MB defends practice of cronyism. *Malaysiakini*. Accessed 25 July 2013 from www.malaysiakini.com/news/236508

Koh Jun Lin. (2018, May 13). GE14: Umno won just 13 of its 54 seats with a simple majority. *Malaysiakini*. Accessed 25 July 2013 from www.malaysiakini.com/news/424362

Kow Gah Chie. (2016, March 24). Opposition MPS barred to safeguard unity, says Krupp. *Malaysiakini*. Accessed 26 Mar 2016 from www.malayskiakini.com/news/335177

Kratoska, Paul H. (1998). *The Japanese occupation of Malaya, 1941–1945*. St. Leonards: Allen and Unwin.

Krishnamurti, B. H. (1990). The regional language vis-a-vis English as the medium of instruction in higher education: the Indian dilemma. In D. P. Pattanayak (Ed.), *Multilingualism in India* (pp. 15–36). Clevedon: Multilingual Matters.

Kua Kia Soong. (1999). *A protean saga. The Chinese schools of Malaysia*. Kajang: Dong Jiao Zong Higher Learning Centre.

Kua Kia Soong. (2005). *The Malaysian civil rights movement*. Petaling Jaya: SIRD.

Kua Kia Soong. (2011). *Patriots and pretenders. The Malayan people's independence struggle*. Petaling Jaya: SUARAM.

Kua Kia Soong. (2012, June 22). Mother tongue schools: Blueprint for integration. *Malaysiakini*. Accessed 22 June 2012 from http://www.malaysiakini.com/news/201586

Lam Choong Wah. (2014, June 02). 'Malaysian seats' are the future of DAP and Pakatan. *Malaysiakini*. Accessed 12 June 2014 from http://www.malaysiakini.com/news/201586

Lamson, Roy, & Smith, Hallet. (Eds.). (1956). *Renaissance England: Prose and poetry from the reformation to the restoration*. New York: Norton.

Lee, Y.K. (1973) The grand jury in early Singapore 1819–1873. Journal of the Malaysian Branch of the Royal Asiatic Society vol. XLVI Part 2, 55–150.

Lee Yin Harn, & Petrina Tan Tjin Yi. (2008, May 06). The interface between culture and law. Paper presented at *3rd international University of Malaya law conference,* University of Malaya.

Lee Hwok Aun. (2015, October 16). Malaysia's spectacular drop in inequality – for real? Accessed 17 Oct 2015 from http://www.malaysiakini.com/news/315933

Lim Kit Siang. (2013, March 15). Economy in for hard times, warns IMF report card. *Malaysiakini*. Accessed 20 Mar 2013 from http://www.malaysiakini.com/news/223959

Lim, Ida. & Boo Su-Lyn. (2013). *The Malay Mail* (online edition) Racial policies enforced Malaysia's brain drain, admit BN leaders. Accessed 2013.8.21 from http://www.themalaymailonline.com/malaysia/article/racial-policies-enforced-malaysias-brain-drain-admit-bn-leaders

Lo Bianco, Joseph. (2004). Language planning as applied linguistics. In A. Davies & C. Elder (Eds.), *The handbook of applied linguistics* (pp. 738–763). London: Blackwell.

Lo Bianco, Joseph. (2005). Globalisation and national communities of communication. *Language Problems and Language Planning, 29*(2), 109–133.

Loh, Philip Fook Seng (1975). *Seeds of Separatism: Educational Policy in Malaysia* (pp. 1874–1940). Kuala Lumpur: Oxford University Press.

Loone, Susan. (2015, April 28). DAP: MIC's daydreaming on Indian votes. *Malaysiakini*. Accessed 30 Apr 2015 from http://www.malaysiakini.com/news/296682

Macaulay, Thomas Babington. (1835). *Minute on Indian education, february 2nd*. Viewed at British Library, London, 2001.9.10.

MacIntyre, Ian, & Embun Said. (2013, October 09). DPM: BM the language of unity. *The Star*, p. 16.

Mahavera, Sheridan. (2014, May 18). Malay language policy dividing communities instead of uniting them, forum told. *The Malaysian Insider*. Accessed 20 May 2014 from http://www.the-malaysianinsider.com/malaysia/article/malay-language-policy-dividing-communities-instead-of-uniting-them-forum-to

Mahavera, Sheridan, & Davidson, Desmond. (2014, July 11). Is a racial divide breaking out in Sarawak after GE13? Accessed 12 July 2014 from http://www.themalaysianinsider.com/malaysia/article/is-a-racial-divide-breaking-out-in-sarawak-after-ge13

Mair, L. P. (1944). *Welfare in the British colonies*. New York: Royal Institute of International Affairs.

Majlis Peguam. (2013). *Bar Council Annual Report 2012/13*. Accessed 30 Nov 2013 from http://www.malaysianbar.org.my/general_notices/bc_general_statistics_2013.html

Malaysiakini. (2012, April 23). *PM: Bumi equity ownership rose to 23.09pct*. Accessed 24 Apr 2012 from http://www.malaysiakini.com/news/195809

Malaysiakini. (2013a, September 20). *Analysts say M'sia has most unequal society in SE Asia*. Accessed 21 Sept 2013 from http://www.malaysiakini.com/news/241603

Malaysiakini. (2013b, November 13). *Efforts to enhance syariah law in the final stage*. Accessed 13 Nov 2013 from http://www.malaysiakini.com/news/246326

Malaysiakini. (2013c, November 25). *Ex-EC chief admits to gerrymandering?* Accessed 26 Nov 2013 from http://www.malaysiakini.com/news/247598

Malaysiakini. (2013d, December 12). *Umno and Dr M culpable, not new media, Hanif told*. Accessed 12 Dec 2013 from http://www.malaysiakini.com/news/249183

Malaysiakini. (2014a, January 06). *'Sure the Bahasa Bible only for Christians?'* Accessed 07 Jan 2014 from http://www.malaysiakini.com/letters/251176

Malaysiakini. (2014b, February 04). *Home Ministry bans 12 books*. Accessed 5 Feb 2014 from http://www.malaysiakini.com/news/253493

Malaysiakini. (2014c, February 06). *Chickens slaughtered, blood smeared on banner*. Accessed 07 Feb 2014 from http://www.malaysiakini.com/news/253660

Malaysiakini. (2014d, April 18). *Lawyers: Syariah Court must decide on custody*. Accessed 19 Apr 2014 from: http://www.malaysiakini.com/news/260423

Malaysiakini. (2015a, October 21). *Gov't: Chinese and bumiputera income gap the largest*. Accessed 22 Oct 2015 from http://www.malaysiakini.com/news/316531

Malaysiakini. (2015b, November 17). *'English' row in the House, Azizah told to make a stand*. Accessed 20 Nov 2015 from http://www.malaysiakini.com/news/319921

Malaysiakini. (2015c, November 23). *S'wak asked to reconsider English official language decision*. Accessed 24 Nov 2015 from http://www.malaysiakini.com/news/320741

Malaysiakini. (2015d, November 26). *Bumi majority of top earners*. Accessed 26 Nov 2015 from http://www.malaysiakini.com/news/321081

Malaysiakini. (2015e, December 10). *Najib: Umno offers olive branch to PAS*. Accessed 14 Dec 2015 from https://www.malaysiakini.com/news/322891

Malaysiakini. (2016a, March 24). *High Court allows Sarawakian to renounce Islam*. Accessed 26 Mar 2016 from: http://www.malaysiakini.com/news/335170

Malaysiakini. (2016b, October 17). *Stupid! S'wak CM censures past education policy*. Accessed 20 Oct 2016 from http://www.malaysiakini.com/news/359331

Malaysiakini. (2017, December 01). M'sia one rank above Zimbabwe at bottom of electoral integrity index. Accessed 02 Dec 2017 from https://www.malaysiakini.com/news/404006

Malaysiakini. (2018a, March 06). *TN50 not 'extra time' for Vision 2020 – Khairy*. Accessed 07 Mar 2018 from https://www.malaysiakini.com/news/414621

Malaysiakini. (2018b, March 29). *Pusat Komas: Redelineation exercise a racial tragedy waiting to happen*. Accessed 30 Mar 2018 from https://www.malaysiakini.com/news/417666

Malaysiakini. (2018c, May 10). *Kiniguide: G14 numbers – What it means for BN, Harapan and PAS?* Accessed 10 Jan 2018 from https://www.malaysiakini.com/news/424038

Malaysiakini. (2018d, June 09). *English test, allowance cut for top civil servants*. Accessed 10 June 2018 from https://www.malaysiakini.com/news/428541

Malaysiakini. (2018e, July 10). *Over 11,000 NCR cases handled by Sarawak native courts this year*. Accessed 10 July 2018 from https://www.malaysiakini.com/news/433563

Malaysiakini. (2018f, July 24). *Road to Act 355 more difficult with Harapan in power – UMNO leader*. Accessed 25 July 2018 from https://www.malaysiakini.com/news/435751

Malaysiakini. (2018g, July 28). *LFL: Sessions court judges made to attend BTN course pre GE-14*. Accessed 28 July 2018 from https://www.malaysiakini.com/news/436284

Malaysiakini. (2018h, August 03). *Senior cops to undergo English course*. Accessed 05 Aug 2018 from https://www.malaysiakini.com/news/438660

Malaysiakini. (2018i, October 18). *Highlights of RMK11 midterm review*. Accessed 18 Oct 2018 from https://www.malaysiakini.com/news/447931

Malaysiakini. (2019a, February 18). *Possible judicial meddling in redelineation challenges – Bersih*. Accessed 18 Feb 2012 from https://www.malaysiakini.com/news/464446

Malaysiakini. (2019b, February 14). *Senior judge: Harapan win rattled judges, but now 'business as usual'*. Accessed 15 Feb 2019 from https://www.malaysiakini.com/news/464045

Mariam Mohktar. (2013, December 09). *Umno Baru running scared*. Accessed 11 Dec 2013 from http://www.malaysiakini.com/columns/248855

Mazrui, Ali & Mazrui, Alamin M. (1998). *The power of Babel: Language and governance in the African experience*. Nairobi: EAEP.
Mead, Richard. (1988). *Malaysia's national language policy and the legal system*. New Haven: Yale.
Merdeka Center for Opinion Research. (2006). *Merdeka Center Youth Survey 2006*. Accessed 20 Feb 2012 from http://www.merdeka.org/
Merdeka Center for Opinion Research. (2012). *National Public Opinion Survey*. Accessed 20 Jan 2013 from http://www.merdeka.org/
Merdeka Center for Opinion Research. (2016). *Merdeka Sarawak Survey*. Accessed 30 Jan 2017 from http://www.merdeka.org/
Mills, L. A. (1960). British Malaya, 1824–1867. *Journal of the Malayan Branch of the Royal Asiatic Society,* vol XXXIII (3). Reprinted 2003 by MBRAS, Singapore.
Mir, Farina. (2006). Imperial policy, provincial practices: Colonial language policy in nineteenth-century India. *Indian Economic Social History Review*, (43.4), 395–427..
Mohamed Nor Abdul Samat. (1983). *Planning the role of Bahasa Malaysia in the Malaysian educational system: An historical perspective*. Unpublished Diploma Thesis, SEAMEO Regional Language Centre. Singapore. [Viewed at RELC, 2002.4.30.]
Muzaffar, Chandra. (2014, February 28). Mixed reaction found to ethnicity in forms. *Malaysiakini.* Accessed 01 Mar 2014 from http://www.malaysiakini.com/letters/255697
Nagalingam, Mahaletchemy. (1987). *Status planning and language choice: A case study*. Unpublished diploma thesis. SEAMEO Regional Language Centre. Singapore.
Nair-Venugopal, Shanta (2001). The sociolinguistics of choice in Malaysian business settings. *International Journal of the Sociology of Language, 152*, 21–52.
Nazari, K. C. (2015, September 22). Pakatan Harapan is new opposition pact, supports Anwar for PM. *The Malaysian Insider*. Accessed 22 Sept 2015 from http://www.themalaysianinsider.com/malaysia/article/pakatan-harapan-is-new-opposition-pact-supports-anwar-for-pm#sthash.WqrOsCha.dpuf
Newbold, T. J. (1839). Political and statistical account of the British Settlements in the Straits of Malacca, viz Pinang, Malacca and Singapore, with a history of the Malayan States on the Peninsula of Malacca, Vol 2. London: John Murray.
Nomura Tōru. (1989) Sejarah Melaka Dilihat dari Sumber-sumber Cina [A history of Melaka seen from Chinese sources]. In Omar Farouk Bajunid (Ed.), *Esei-esei Budaya dan Sejarah Melaka*, 39–64. Kuala Lumpur: Asrama Za'ba Universiti Malaya.
Peletz, Michael. (2013a). Malaysia's Syariah Judiciary as Global Assemblage: Islamization, Corporatization, and other Transformations in Context. *Comparative Studies in Society and History, 55*(3), 603–633.
Peletz, Michael. (2013b, October 10). *A tale of two courts: Shari'ah transformations in anthropological and historical perspective*. Paper presented at Institute of Advanced Islamic Studies (IAIS) Law Department, Academy of Islamic Studies, University of Malaya.
Peletz, Michael. (2013c, December 10). *Transformation of the Syariah courts: Tradition, constitution, law and practice*. Paper presented at Seminar on Islamic law in practice with global perspective, Akademi Pengajian Islam, Universiti Malaya.
Pennycook, Alastair. (1994). *The cultural politics of English as an international language*. Harlow: Longman.
Powell, Richard. (2002). Language planning and the British empire: Comparing Pakistan, Malaysia and Kenya. *Current Issues in Language Planning, 3*(3), 205–279.
Powell, Richard. (2011, December 8–11). English or Malay or both? Comparing language policy and practice in the courts of East and West Malaysia. Paper presented at *16th ESEA (English in Southeast Asia) conference,* Yogyakarta.
Powell, Richard, & Azirah Hashim. (2011, September 30). *Comparing language policy and discourse management in Malaysian Syariah and common law courts*. Paper presented at East Asian Law and Society Conference, Seoul.

PUTERA-AMCJA. (1947/2005). *The people's constitutional proposals for Malaya,* 1947. Great Britain Colonial Office/Kajang, Selangor: Ban Ah Kam.

Rahman, Tariq. (1998). *Language and politics in Pakistan.* Karachi: Oxford University Press.

Rappa, Antonio., & Wee, Lionel. (2006). *Language policy and modernity in Southeast Asia. Malaysia, the Philippines, Singapore and Thailand.* New York: Springer.

Reynolds, David. (1991). *Britannia overruled: British policy and world power in the 20th century.* Harlow: Longman.

Roasa, Dustin. (2011, April 22). Malaysia at economic crossroads as it fights the great brain drain. *The Guardian* (online edition). Accessed 2011.4.23 from https://www.theguardian.com/world/2011/apr/21/malaysia-fights-brain-drain

Rodziah Matled. (2004). Rape and constitutional law on trial. In Zubaidah, Fauziah, & Rajesway (Eds.), *Language, linguistics and the real world, vol II: Language practice in the workplace. Selected papers from the first international conference on language, linguistics and the real world, Kuala Lumpur, 2002.* Kuala Lumpur: University of Malaya.

Rustam, A. Sani. (2008). *Social roots of the Malay left.* Petaling Jaya: SIRD.

Said, Edward. (1993). *Culture and imperialism.* New York: Random House.

Samuel, Moses, Mahmud Hasan Khan, Lee Luan Ng, & Kin Wai Cheang. (2012). Articulation of medium of instruction politics in the Malaysian Chinese press. *Discourse: Studies in the cultural politics of education.* Accessed 10 Aug 2013 from https://doi.org/10.1080/01596306.2012.745731

Shakira Buang. (2018, June 29). Ex-IGP and two 'Tan Sri' in protest against Guan Eng. *Malaysiakini.* Accessed 30 June 2018 from https://www.malaysiakini.com/news/431931

Shamsul Amri Baharuddin. (1996). The construction and transformation of a social identity: Malayness and bumiputraness re-examined. *Journal of Asian and African Studies, 52,* 15–33.

Shamsul Amri Baharuddin. (1998). Bureaucratic management of identity in a modern state: Malayness in postwar Malaysia. In D. Gladney (Ed.), *Making majorities constituting the nation in Japan, Korea, China, Malaysia, Fiji, Turkey and the United States* (pp. 135–169). Stanford: Stanford University Press.

Shamsul Amri Baharuddin. (2006). A history of an identity, an identity of a history: the idea and practice of 'Malayness' in Malaysia reconsidered. *Journal of Southeast Asian Studies, 32,* 356–366.

Stevenson, R. (1975). *Cultivators and administrators: British educational policy towards the Malays, 1875–1906.* Kuala Lumpur: Oxford University Press.

Straits Government Gazette. (1859, November 04). Facsimile viewed at Malaysian National Museum, Kuala Lumpur, 2011.4.30.

Suulok Tawie. (2012, February 20). English an official language in Sarawak. *The Sun,* p. 2.

Tan, Poh-Ling. (1997). Malaysia. In P.-L. Tan (Ed.), *Asian legal systems* (pp. 263–313). Sydney: Butterworths.

Tate, Muzafar Desmond. (2008). *The Malaysian Indians. History, problems and future.* Petaling Jaya: Strategic Information and Research Development Centre.

The Economist. (2013, May 06). *Malaysia's election. A tawdry victory.* Accessed 08 May 2013 from http://www.economist.com/blogs/banyan/2013/05/malaysias-election-0?fsrc=nlw%7Cnewe%7C5-6-2013%7C5664297%7C36227794%7C

The Economist. (2018, March 10). *Malaysia's PM is about to steal an election.* Accessed 11 Mar 2018 from https://www.economist.com/news/leaders/21738363-american-officials-say-he-already-stole-millions-taxpayers-malaysias-pm-about-steal

The Malaysian Insider. (2013, October 06). *Perkasa chief warns of fresh race riot if Malays not helped economically.* Accessed 06 Oct 2013 from http://my.news.yahoo.com/perkasa-chief-warns-fresh-race-riot-malays-not-231639604.html

The Singapore Free Press and Mercantile Advertiser. (1849, March 29). p.2. [Advertisements].

The Star. (2013, September 20). *Income gap must be bridged,* p. 4.

The Star Online. (2009, December 11). *Court documents must be in English in Sabah and Sarawak.* Accessed 24 Jan 2012 from http://www.thestar.com.my/news/nation/2009/12/11/court-documents-must-be-in-english-in-sabah- and-sarawak/

The Star Online. (2012, January 21). *Umno VP: Govt gives money to help rakyat, not to garner votes*. Accessed 10 Jan 2013 from http://www.thestar.com.my/News/Nation/2012/01/21/Umno-VP-Govt-gives-money-to-help-rakyat-not-to-garner-votes.aspx

The Straits Times. (1896, June 20). *Untitled notice of court appointment*, p. 2.

The Straits Times (2018, April 16). *Malaysian opposition alliance hit by suspension of party*. Accessed 17 Apr 2018 from https://www.straitstimes.com/asia/se-asia/malaysia-opposition-alliance-hit-by-suspension-of-party

The Syonan Shimbun. (1942a, December 12). *Malai, Sumatra dialects to be standardised*, p. 1.

The Syonan Shimbun. (1942b, December 23). *46 pass written language test*, p. 2.

The Syonan Shimbun. (1943, January 11). *New order well established in Syonan*, p. 1.

The Syonan Times. (1942a, March 03). *Notification Non-British Lawyers*, p. 4.

The Syonan Times. (1942b, May 26). *Gunseibu notification*. Re-opening of the Courts in Syonan, p. 9.

The Syonan Times. (1942c, May 28). Police Courts Opened By Judge Nogi, p. 4.

The Syonan Times. (1942d, June 12). マナベニッポンゴ! [Learn Japanese!], p. 4.

The Syonan Times. (1942e, September 04). *Spanish language to be used in Philippines Law Courts*, p. 3.

Utusan Online. (2018, May 10). *BN tewas! Gabungan PKR umum menang* [BN loses! PKR coalition wins]. Accessed 10 May 2018 from http://www.utusan.com.my/berita/nasional/bn-tewas-gabungan-pkr-umum-menang-1.67013

Vaillancourt, François & Leblanc, Michel. (1993). *La propriété de l'économie du Québec en 1991 selon le groupe d'appartenance linguistique*. Montreal: Office de la langue française.

Varughese, George. [Malaysian Bar President] (2018, April 03). Press release.

Varughese, George. [Malaysian Bar President] (2019a, February 22). Press release.

Varughese, George. [Malaysian Bar President] (2019b, February 26). Press release.

Vengadesan, Martin. (2019, April 14). Orang Asli voices may go silent as languages face extinction. *Malaysiakini*. Accessed 15 Apr 2019 from https://www.malaysiakini.com/news/471967

Wade, Geoff. (2009). The origins and evolution of ethnocracy in Malaysia. *Asia-Pacific Journal* 47-4-09. Accessed 07 July 2011 from http://japanfocus.org/-Geoff-Wade/3259

Wain, Barry. (2009). *Malaysian Maverick. Mahathir Mohamad in turbulent times*. Basingstoke: Palgrave.

Whiting, Amanda. (2008). Desecularising Malaysian law? In P. Nicholson & S. Biddulph (Eds.), *Examining practice, interrogating theory: Comparative legal studies in Asia* (pp. 223–266). Martinus Nijhoff: Leiden.

Whiting, Amanda. (2012). The training and practice of Islamic lawyers in the Federal Territories of Malaysia. *Pacific Rim Law and Policy Journal vol., 21*(1).

Winstedt, Richard. (1961/1981). *Bidalan Melayu – Malay Proverbs* (Tan Chin Kwang Ed.). Singapore: Graham Brash.

Woon, Walter. (1997). Singapore. In P.-L. Tan (Ed.), *Asian legal systems* (pp. 314–355). Sydney: Butterworths.

World Bank. (2018). Data catalog. Accessed 12 Jan 2018 from https://data.worldbank.org/

Wu Min Aun. (1999). *The Malaysian legal system*. Petaling Jaya: Pearson Malaysia.

Yasuda Toshiaki. (1997). 帝国日本の言語編制 [The linguistic formation of the Japanese empire.] Yokohama: Seori Shōbō.

Yayasan Orang Asli Malaysia. (2012). *Malaysian Orang Asli Foundation*. Portal accessed 12 Dec 2012 from http://www.yos.org.my/index.php/pengenalan/orang-asli

Yuen Mei Keng & Martin Carvalho. (2014, April 01). Govt to look at 'one person, one vote' proposal. *The Star*, p. 17.

Chapter 3
Status Planning in Malaysian Law

The title of the Bill makes it clear to all that Malay is the official language, but measures are provided for smooth implementation (...) The courts will continue to use English and Malay, and other languages will be allowed, as at present, to be liberally used. At the same time I would warn the non-Malays that there is no excuse for them not to learn the Malay language if they profess undivided loyalty to this country.

Tunku Abdul Rahman (1967.3.03) (introducing National Language Act)

We are all aware that permission to use English could be refused. It depends on the case and the judge. So we need to be prepared.

Steven Thiru (Bar President) (2013.8.13)

3.1 Interrelation of Planning Activities

Status planning can be summarised as activity that aims to assign the use of certain languages to certain roles. Kloss's (1969) separation of status and corpus planning usefully distinguishes the external role and social orientation of those authorising domain-specific language use from the internal role and linguistic orientation of those facilitating authorised use. Cooper (1989:31–32) defined status planning as the allocation of language and language varieties to specific functions, and corpus planning as the creation of new forms and modification of old ones. Calvet (1987:282) employed a similar distinction between *actions sur les langues* and *actions sur la langue*. In practice, however, status planning intertwines with corpus, acquisition and discourse planning to a degree that can make it hard to isolate.

Linguists, who are more likely to be employed in corpus planning in activities such as lexicography, can scarcely avoid many of the prescriptive orientations of the legislators who bear primary responsibility for status planning. Legislators and judges, in turn, establish corpora as well as statuses when they produce authoritative texts in authorised languages. Status planning typically precedes corpus planning,

R. Powell, *Language Choice in Postcolonial Law*, Language Policy 22,
https://doi.org/10.1007/978-981-15-1173-8_3

with Sri Lanka's 26-volume Sinhala dictionary completed some 36 years after the 1956 Official Language Act that envisaged it (Coperahewa 2011:212). Cooper (1989:123–125) argues that action on form follows action on function because planners select and create certain language structures on the assumption that they can better serve projected functions, subsequent ideas about desirable forms being driven by non-communicative functions more than communicative needs. Internal language-specific reforms have external effects, however, and so status planning may be contingent upon, and even follow after, corpus planning. Haarmann (1990:106–7) lists the latter first in his taxonomy of planning. Malaysia's *Balai Pustaka* (later *Dewan Bahasa*), an institution focused on corpus reform, predated the key constitutional provisions (1957, 1963) that made Malay official (Kamarul et al. 2003:37). Tanzania's Law Dictionary Committee (1963) and BAKITA/ Institute of Kiswahili Research (1967) anteceded legal measures sanctioning courtroom Kiswahili (Rwezaura 1994:112–115).

The relationship between status and corpus planning is often collaborative. Thus Sri Lanka's 1946 Select Committee Report proposed needs analyses and terminological research to facilitate official use of Sinhala and Tamil as a prelude to reducing the status of English (Coperahewa 2011:196–199). But it may also take a less collaborative tack. There are perennial calls in Malaysia to enforce 'unadulterated' use of the national language (Mohamad Azim 2011.10.15) and periodic criticism of electoral candidates' deficiencies in it (Kuek 2010.10.29), and only recently the government and Dewan Bahasa discussed amending the 1963 National Language Act and 1996 Education Act so that those using 'broken' Malay could be fined (*Malaysiakini* 2017.11.14).

Status planning also interacts closely with acquisition planning, i.e. activity to ensure a language or variety is learnt by a target community, although the activities are distinct inasmuch as status measures do not necessarily lead to or even aim at language spread. In Singapore, for example, the politically motivated retention of Malay as the national language sits somewhat oddly with the effort that has gone into promoting English and Mandarin.

Running through all this is discourse planning, since governments inevitably seek to legitimise their reforms (Mead 1988:6). Status planning involves the production of constitutions, laws, authoritative reports and public texts in the service of elite-mediated national interests. Lo Bianco (2009:103) reminds us that discursive manipulation of social acceptance is more important to language planners than most public planners because of the mass social penetration of language.

Status planning is most evident in broad, symbolic constitutional measures (notably Art.152, which declares Malay the national language and Art. 160b, which allows the government to consider Malay translations of the constitution as authoritative), as well as in specific legislation (1963 National Language Act, 1976 Legal Profession Act, 1996 Education Act). But the enforcement of policy is often more closely related to judicial practice directions, circulars and rules. It will be seen that through all of these a role for English has been retained, although it is now a more limited role than 30 years ago. Language policy has also been elaborated on by a small body of case law, which among other things has ruled that judges' discretion

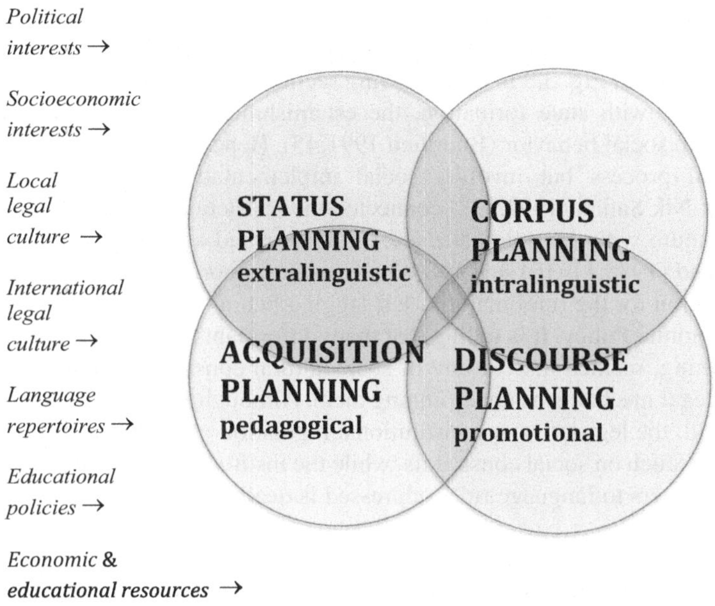

Fig. 3.1 Interrelation of language planning components and societal influences

to use English implies no corresponding right for lawyers to use it in proceedings unless the bench deems this to be in the interests of justice (*Dato' Seri Anwar Ibrahim* 2010). While not specifically addressing the legal domain, *Merdeka University* (1992) is also germane in controversially interpreting restriction of the use of other languages for 'official purposes' to include the medium of instruction of private bodies, which would appear to raise questions over the overwhelming use of English in law schools (Fig. 3.1).

The 1980s seems to have been the most active period of lower court Malayanisation, with a push to extend this to the higher courts coming in the 1990s, and renewed acceptance of English thereafter. Such a trajectory is largely supported in interview data from lawyers analysed in Chap. 8.

3.2 Status and the State

Linguists' conception of languages as equal seems quixotic when set against their lack of equivalence in the world of politics and economics, where language laws reflect power dynamics (Dovalil 2009). Revolving around legislation, the relationship between status planning and state politics is particularly close, though not always direct or transparent. While acknowledging that Malaysian law had little choice but to start off with the English it inherited, Mead (1988:6) speculates that the persistence of the language decades later suggests English serves the interests of the political classes. Political context is thus positioned at the forefront of this description and for reference, key language planning measures are set alongside political events in Fig. 3.3 in the following section.

Bound up with state formation, the establishment of official languages also reaches into social behavior (Bourdieu 1991:45). Hence status planning is not only a political process but involves social implementation (Kaplan and Baldauf 2008:41). Nik Safiah (1994:138) connected the restriction of English for debate in the legislature with the political rise of Mahathir and a new Malay middle class, while Mead (1988:11–16) saw 1980s policies in support of legal Malay as cultural compensation for the rural majority left lagging behind this middle class under the New Economic Policy. It is telling that many informants in this study, despite their legal training, seemed more aware of sociocultural constraints on language choice than the legal mechanisms underpinning them. Although this chapter is mainly concerned with the legislative and institutional regulation of language behaviour then, it will also touch on social constraints, while the institutional and individual orientations of lawyers to language rules addressed is dealt with in more detail in the following chapter.

In addition to the executive and legislative branches of the state, the judiciary itself plays an important role in implementing status planning. The courts are where language policy is most evidently and authoritatively on public view. The following summary excludes the *Syariah* system but includes East Malaysia's native courts and also the recently abolished Penghulu courts since these are referred to in common law enactments (Fig. 3.2).

The current financial jurisdictions of the Sessions and Magistrates Courts are the result of recent increases and were questioned within the Bar Council when first proposed because of the steep rise and the lack of prior investigation into the effect on the lower courts' capacity to deal with complex cases. The change is significant for this study as subordinate courts are more likely than the High Court to work in Malay.

The appointment of judges, magistrates, registrars, researchers and other judicial officers is administered by the Judicial and Legal Service. While this study did not extend to interviews with the judiciary, the significant role of justices in legal language policy was apparent from court observations and the comments of informants, including lawyers who have sat on the Bench. Many advocates consider the stance of individual judges to be the most important factor in courtroom language choice. Some senior informants mentioned the preferences of Chief Justices in explaining the ebb and flow of language policy (Chap. 9). It should be noted, however, that the Chief Justices at the helm in 1980–1984 and 1990–1994, when vernacularisation appears to have been accelerated, were all London-trained barristers.

Malay-dominated UiTM (Universiti Institut Teknologi MARA) and UIA (Universiti Islam Antarabangsa), the largest producers of law graduates, are increasingly important recruiting grounds for the judiciary[1] and as their alumni rise up the

[1] Multimedia University lecturer, p.c. 2013.2.

<table>
<tr><td colspan="3">Mahkamah Perseketuan / Federal Court (FC)</td><td></td></tr>
<tr><td colspan="3">Mahkamah Rayuan / Court of Appeal (CA)</td><td rowspan="6">Special Court[5]
1993 Constitutional Amendment Art 182(1)

Mahkamah Perusahaan/ Industrial Ct.
1948 Industrial Courts Ordinance: dismissals, trade disputes under 1967 Industrial Relations Act</td></tr>
<tr><td>Mahkamah Tinggi di Malaya/ High Court in Malaya
Civ, Crim, Commerce & Family Divs
Mahkamah Bagi Kanak-Kanak/ Court for Children
15 registries +circuit courts</td><td colspan="2">High Court in Sabah &Sarawak
Civ, Crim, Commerce & Family Divs
7 registries + circuit courts</td></tr>
<tr><td>Mahkamah Sesyen/Sessions Ct
Civil Div Crim Div
no capital offences; <u>RM1 million</u></td><td colspan="2">Sessions Court
Civil Div Crim Div
no capital offences; <u>RM1 million</u></td></tr>
<tr><td>Mahkamah Majistret/ Magistrates' Courts
5 yrs/<u>RM1 million</u></td><td colspan="2">Magistrates' Courts
5 yrs/<u>RM1 million</u></td></tr>
<tr><td colspan="3">Small Claims Tribunal
Tribunal for Consumer Claims</td></tr>
<tr><td>Mahkamah Penghulu/ Penghulu's Ct
Abolished 2013 by Subordinate Courts (Amendment) Act 2010</td><td>Native Ct. of Appeal of Sabah
no Penal Code offences

District Native Courts

Native Courts</td><td>Native Ct. of of Appeal Sarawak
no Penal Code offences
Resident's Ct.
Chief's Superior Ct
Chief's Ct
Headman's Ct</td><td></td></tr>
</table>

Fig. 3.2 Malaysian common law courts

hierarchy a corresponding rise in the legal and language culture of those institutions is to be expected. As will be shown in Chaps. 5 and 7, however, Malay-majority institutions do not necessarily favour Malay-medium teaching, with the picture further complicated by the greater likelihood of Malays gaining scholarships to study overseas. Entry into the Judicial and Legal Service (JLS) requires an SPM (*Sijil Pelajaran Malaysia*) school credit in Malay and a pass in English (AGC interviews 2014).

In the wake of a 2007 corruption and power-brokering scandal surrounding senior lawyer V.K. Lingam and Chief Justice Ahmad Fairuz (*Malaysiakini* 2008.5.10), a Commission was set up under the 2009 Judicial Appointments Commission Act, which requires the prime minister to uphold judicial independence (s.2). But justice and human rights news site *LoyarBurok* (Chen 2009.2.19) criticised the failure to appoint a member of the Bar Council among the Commissioners, who comprise the Chief Justice of Malaysia, Court of Appeal President, Chief Judges of Malaya and Sabah/Sarawak, and four others appointed for 2-year stints, all current incumbents being former senior judges (JAC 2015).

The Federal Court comprises the Chief Justice, Chief Judges of West and East Malaysia, President of the Court of Appeal and others appointed from the JLS or among High Court advocates of 10 years' standing (Wan Arfah and Bulan 2003:184–185). Five current judges were admitted to London Inns of Court; six, including one of these, have a UK LLB or LLM (Mahkamah Persekutuan 2014). All are Malay except for one Chinese and one Kadazan. Below them, the Court of Appeal comprises its President and ten others recruited from High Court judges (Wan Arfah and Bulan 2003:188), who number 47 in West Malaysia and 10 in Sabah and Sarawak (ibid:190). Sessions Court judges and 1st Class Magistrates are appointed from the Judicial and Legal Service where, according to an East Coast solicitor who had previously worked as a judge, training is largely in Malay. The Judicial and Legal Training Institute (ILKAP 2014) also runs courses in English in areas such as arbitration, construction law and legal opinion writing. Despite the generally Malay atmosphere of the JLS, many magistrates and prosecutors educated in English still prefer the language.[2] 2nd-class Magistrates, along with some 3000 Justices of the Peace (Aryeh Neier 2004.4.10), do not need legal qualifications (Wan Arfah and Bulan 2003:196). Law lecturers may also be recruited as judges.

Many of the senior judiciary have served with the Attorney General's Chambers (Mahkamah Persekutuan 2014). The AGC can be entered immediately after obtaining an LLB. The largest single employer of law graduates, its members include public prosecutors, Federal Counsel and Parliamentary Draftsmen. While one employee reported extensive use of English, both orally and in internal written communications, another recalled a preference for Malay, even in the International Affairs Division.[3] UM lecturers reported that academics are frequently involved in the drafting process and a KL-based corporate lawyer (p.c. 2013.7) revealed that bills are still generally prepared in English, even though the Malay translation is gazetted as authoritative. According to constitutional law lecturer Azmi Sharom[4] this undoubtedly contributes to the perception of the Malay text of statutes as unwieldy, something that was also mentioned by students at UM.

As for the bar, under the 1976 Legal Profession Act solicitor-advocates (*peguam bela-peguam cara*) must be 18, of good character, and Federal Citizens or permanent residents with a qualifying law degree (Majlis Peguam 2016). Direct admission can be obtained with an LLB or honours law degree from UIA, UiTM, UKM, UM, MMU or the National University of Singapore, the England and Wales solicitor's qualification, or a London or Dublin barrister's qualification (ibid, 2014). Universiti Utara Malaysia (UUM) graduates are also admitted provided they complete a training programme run by the Bar Council. More detailed discussion of the role of the bar in mediating language planning will be left until Chap. 5 as admission to the profession involves a number of measures bound up with language acquisition.

[2] Terengganu lawyer, p.c. 2014.2

[3] Interviews with AGC and former AGC employees, 2014.

[4] Interviewed at UM, 2013.8.

3.3 Main Status Planning Measures in Legal Domain

Status planning in Malaysia's legal domain reveals a legislative trajectory beginning with constitutional provisions and amendments, passing through statutes, then down to ordinances and court rules (subsidiary legislation that must conform to relevant enactments) and finally to practice directions issued by the Chief Judges of Malaya and East Malaysia after consultation with the Chief Justice (High Court Rule O.92r.3B). Constitutions are supremely authoritative yet often drafted widely, creating interpretative space for specific application. Directions, on the other hand, are narrowly drafted yet lack the full force of law, being created to regulate systematic and consistent procedure (Siti Norma Yaakob J in *Chua Choong Yin* 2002). The system thus leaves room for case law, which is rarely sealed off from the social and political imperatives of the day, to work out the practical implications of language status.

As argued in the previous chapter, political events either directly influenced or brought vital context to language events. For ease of reference key developments are laid out in Fig. 3.3.

The earliest general language provisions were in the 1948 Federation of Malaya Agreement (Government of Malaya 1948), which declared English and Malay as co-official and was published bilingually but made the English text authoritative. The judges in *Merdeka University* (1992) found Malay to have been used widely "in official circles…at the subordinate level" in the Federated States and indeed more than English in the Unfederated States, but they did not refer specifically to the courts. Allusions to the possibility of using Malay (e.g. in the 1948 Subordinate Courts Act) are rare and imply by default that law was administered in English.

While proclaiming Malay the national language (Art.152), the 1957 Constitution prohibited the suppression of other languages except for official purposes (Art. 152.1a), a provision cited unsuccessfully by proponents of a Chinese medium university in *Merdeka University*. English was to be used in the Federal and State legislatures (cl.2) and in the Supreme and High Court (cl.4) "for a period of ten years after Merdeka [Independence] Day and thereafter until Parliament otherwise approves". Thus as 1967 approached there were hopes, though no obligations, for a revision of the language policy. Also subject to 10-year review was a requirement that the authoritative texts of Federal enactments and subsidiary legislation be in English (cl.3a-3b), whereas a provision for subordinate court proceedings to be in English (cl.5) was reviewable at any time. Court testimony need not be translated into English if counsel on both sides agreed (cl.4), a measure presumably intended to cover the oral use of Malay.

In February, 1958 the Lord President issued a circular instructing all courts to reply in Malay to letters received in it, paralleling similar instructions to government departments, and discussed the possibility of introducing Malay in the lower courts with the Ministry of Justice (*The Straits Times* 1958.2.18). The chair of a seminar organised by UM's Socialist Club the following year concluded that Malay still lacked the necessary terminology for legal use, although one participant laid the

	POLITICAL	LANGUAGE PLANNING
1946	Malayan Union formed. UMNO founded under Onn Jaafar. MIC founded.	
1948	Federation of Malaya formed. Declaration of State of Emergency (till 1960).	Under Federation Agreement, Malay and English official.
1951	MCA political party formed. Tunku Abdul Rahman replaces Onn as UMNO leader. PM 1957-1970.	
1954	Alliance formed among UMNO, MCA and MIC.	
1957	Independent Malayan Federation established under Merdeka Constitution:	Malay the national language. English official for ten years. English for law.
1959	Election. Alliance:74 seats/52 votes%; Opp+ (PAS, MPSP,PPP):30 seats/29%	
1961		Education Act: Malay-medium National Schools, Chinese/Tamil National-type Schools;
1963	Malaysian Federation formed among Malaya, Sabah, Sarawak and Singapore.	
1964	Election. Alliance:89 seats/59%; Opp+ (PAS, MPSP, PAP, PPP):15 seats/14%.	
1965	Expulsion of Singapore from Federation. DAP founded by Malaysian members of PAP.	
1967		1963/1967 Language Act: New legislation bilingual. Courts Malay/English. English-medium schools, Chinese and Tamil secondary schools, to be phased out.
1969	Election. Alliance:95 seats/49.3%; Opp+ (PAS, DAP,Gerakan,PPP):49 seats/51%. Communalist rioting leads to State of Emergency, suspension of parliament.	
1970	Abdul Razak replaces the Tunku as UMNO leader. PM 1970-1976.	
1971	Parliament reconvened. New Economic Policy launched. Constitutional Amendment defines dissent over Malay language & privileges as sedition.	
1974	Alliance rebranded as Barisan Nasional. Election. BN:135 seats/61%; Opp+: 19 seats/39%.	
1976	Hussein Onn becomes UMNO leader and PM on Razak's death.	
1978	Election. BN:130 seats/57%; Opp+ (DAP,PAS): 24 seats/43%.	
1981	Mahathir replaces Onn as UMNO leader. PM 1981-2003	Directions require Malay for lower courts.

Fig. 3.3 Key Malaysian political and language planning events

1982	Election. BN:132 seats/60.5%; Opp+ (DAP,PAS): 2 seats/39.5%.	
1983		1976 Legal Profession Act amended to require BM proficiency for Bar admission.
1983		National Language (Amendment and Extension) Act
1988	Constitutional Crisis. Split between UMNO Baru and Semangat (Razaleigh).	
1990	Election. BN:127 seats/54%; Opp+ (DAP,Semangat,PAS):53seats/47%.	
1990		National Language (Amendment) Act: Proceedings in all courts to be in Malay; partial use of English permitted in interests of justice. Rules of High Court amended. English still required for documents submitted to Sabah and Sarawak courts.
1995	Election. BN:162 seats/65%; Opp+:30 seats/35%.	
1996		Education Act: Malay for National Primary & Secondary Schools; Chinese or Tamil for National-type Primary Schools; English a compulsory subject.
1997	Asian financial crisis. Arrest of DPM Anwar Ibrahim on corruption and sodomy charges.	
1999	Election. BN:148 seats/56.5%; Barisan Alternatif:45 seats/43.5%.	
2002		PPSMI (science and maths in English).
2003	Abdullah Badawi replaces Mahathir as UMNO leader. PM 2004-	
2004	Election. BN:198 seats/64%; Barisan Alternatif: 21 seats/36%.	
2008	Election. BN:140 seats/51%; Pakatan Rakyat:82 seats/48%.	
2009	Najib Razak becomes UMNO president. PM 2009~present.	2010: Dato' Seri Anwar ruling against court filing in English; 2012: phasing out of PPSMI begins.
2013	Election. BN:133 seats/47.4%; Pakatan Rakyat:89 seats/50.9%.	
2018	Election. Pakatan Harapan/Warisan :123 seats/ seats/51%; BN:79 seats/34%; PAS:18 seats/17%. Mahathir returns to premiership after 15 years.	

Fig. 3.3 (continued)

blame on lawyers' love of "difficult words" (*The Straits Times* 1959a.8.24). Recommendations were subsequently submitted to the government for a commission to coordinate efforts to introduce the national language in the courts (*The Straits Times* 1959b.8.25). In 1960, Minister of Justice Leong Yew Koh told parliament that Malay was being used in lower courts but was insufficiently developed and known for justice to be done were it made the judicial medium, a position that could be reviewed in 1967 (*The Straits Times* 1960.6.24). Several reports of courtroom Malay can be found in the press over the following decades, but they lack detail and are juxtaposed with calls for its introduction that imply use remained limited. For example, in 1960 DBP Director Zainal Abidin demanded a "start must be made" (*The Singapore Free Press* 1960.6.30); 5 years later his successor, Syed Nasir, called for Malay to be used in lower court proceedings and records (*The Straits Times* 1965.6.16). In 1962 Leong told the Senate notes of evidence in lower court civil proceedings were in Malay "wherever possible" (*The Straits Times* 1962.5.08).

Upon the entry of Singapore, Sabah and Sarawak into the Federation in 1963, constitutional amendments were passed allowing Mandarin and Tamil speech in the Singapore legislature, while confining legislation to English (Art.161F, repealed in 1966 after Singapore's expulsion). No restriction on English in the East Malaysian legislatures or courts could be introduced before 1967, and would require enactments in the respective state legislatures (Art.161(1–3)). Native languages were permitted in East Malaysian courts and also in the Sarawak legislature (Art.161(5)).

In an aside when commenting on proposals to draft legislation bilingually, the prime minister mentioned that courts in his home state of Kedah were already using Malay (*The Straits Times* 1964.12.04). In 1966 the Minister of Justice told the House Malay was "now being used in the lower courts" but could not be used in the Federal and High Courts because of Article 152 (*The Straits Times* 1966.8.24). The following year this constitutional restriction was lifted in the single most important piece of language legislation.

Announcing it as the peaceful implementation of national language policy in a multiracial society, the Tunku[5] introduced a constitutional amendment in March 1967, thereafter called the National Language Act, extending the use of Malay while preserving an important role for English (speech in *The Straits Times* 1967a.3.03). From September the national language was to be the "sole official language" in West Malaysia, but the bill would not apply to East Malaysia. While Federal and state bodies could use official documents in other languages in the public interest, the public had no right to demand translations (s.3).

Under the new Act, Federal and state legislation was to be bilingual (s.6). For new enactments Malay was authoritative unless otherwise prescribed (s.7(1)); for those passed before September, 1967 English remained authoritative unless a Malay translation was specifically given priority. Court proceedings could be in either language (s.8): the prime minister commented that "if cases can be argued in English it

[5]A royal title, sometimes spelt as *tengku*.

will be easier for our lawyers, whose command of Malay is not so good" as the "wheels of justice must go round, otherwise there will be no security for anybody living in this country". But he added that there was no excuse for non-Malays not to learn Malay "if they profess undivided loyalty to this country" (ibid).

The new Act ushered in discussion within the judiciary and legal profession over the balance between the two languages. In August, Lord President Azmi Mohamed announced that the bar had agreed to use the national language as much as possible in the lower courts, with Magistrates and Sessions Court judges having wide discretion to permit either or both languages (*The Straits Times* 1967b.8.06) and the views of counsel to be considered (*The Straits Times* 1967c.8.11). Statements of claim and defence could now be submitted to the lower courts in Malay (ibid).

By the early 1970s parliamentarians were excusing themselves (somewhat perfunctorily, with the phrase *dengan izin* – 'with permission') before using English in the House, the switch often triggered by the citation of legislation in that language, as in an exchange between V. Veerappan and Abdul Kadir Yusof over the wording of the constitution (Dewan Rakyat 1971.3.03). From 1975 English was disallowed for debate without express permission under Standing Order 8 (ibid, 1975.12.19). East Malaysian members were exempt but encouraged to try to use Malay (ibid, 1976.3.31). Nik Safiah (1994:138) claims permission is neither given nor requested lightly, yet use of English is not formally penalised and recently an extended exchange in it occurred between opposition and government parliamentarians, apparently for the benefit of visiting Australian MPs (*Malaysiakini* 2014.4.07). More recently a Sarawak-based opposition MP insisted on addressing the House in it, arguing that this was the constitutional right of East Malaysians (*Malaysiakini* 2015.11.17).

In 1979 Lord President Mohamed Suffian reported the national language being used "in most subordinate courts and some High Courts [and i]n time it might become nationwide" (*The Straits Times* 1979.10.30). Dato' Zamani Mohammad, head of a leading East Coast firm, recalls Terengganu public prosecutors using English in the High Court around 1980 but police officers already prosecuting lower court cases in Malay.[6] In that year the Attorney General proposed the establishment of a unit to promote legal Malay (*The Straits* Times 1980.6.09) and under his and Suffian's watch the recommendations of a committee on the implementation of the national language in the courts produced a flurry of reforms.

Despite a statement from the Prime Minister's office in April, 1981 that it was premature to use Malay in court (*Utusan Malaysia* 1981.4.17), under a September 9th judicial circular all justices of the Supreme, High, Sessions and Magistrates courts were instructed to use it wherever possible, the Department of Justice was to use it for correspondence, and the Bar Council to advise members to use it in court (Dewan Rakyat 1986.11.26). Speeches at official legal functions were to be in Malay and proposals were announced for a language test for lawyers (*New Straits Times* 1981d.10.21). A 1981 Chief Registrar circular emphasising Malay for the

[6] Interviewed at his offices, 2014.2.

subordinate courts was later referred to by a Deputy Minister from the Prime Minister's Office in acknowledging that it was more easily implemented at that level (*Utusan Malaysia* 1983.3.24). Bar Council President G.T.S. Siddhu reportedly regarded Malay as compulsory if justices, counsel and witnesses "have no trouble in speaking or understanding the language" (*New Straits Times* 1981c.10.14). In 1983 an amendment to the 1976 Legal Profession Act (s.11(2)) required all lawyers seeking admission after 1984 to certify proficiency in Malay. The following year a request from an Indian lawyer for admission without a Malay test was rejected in the High Court (*Utusan Malaysia* 1984.6.02).

Press interest in courtroom Malay in the 1980s suggests a period of more widespread implementation than anything that had gone before. "Smooth sailing" was reported for the first two Malay cases in Johor Bahru, despite lexical stumbling blocks (*New Straits Times* 1981a.10.01), but Kuantan lawyers fought over the correct way to address magistrates (*The Straits* Times 1981.10.08). A lower court official in KL, despite berating lawyers ignorant of, or willfully ignoring, the Chief Judge's direction, conceded there was no choice but to use "half Malay and half English" (*New Straits Times* 1981b.10.13). Mead (1988:103) cites examples of desperate Malay from *The Star*, including "*Saya akan* [I will] apply for costs" and "*Saya taruh sama engkau, engkau terbaring* [I put it with you, you are lying down]". Apart from their entertainment value these attest to the pressure some lawyers were under to perform outside their linguistic comfort zone. Fortunately for them, in 1986 a Deputy Minister reminded the House that the Language Act provided for flexibility in court (Dewan Rakyat 1986.11.26).

Continuous updating of procedural rules reflects the compromise between official Malay and discretionary, pragmatic English. The 1980 Rules of High Court were made available in Malay in 1990, although the English remained authoritative, with O.92.r.1, together with Court of Appeal Rule r.101, revised in line with the 1990 Amendment to the Language Act (below) to require documents for court to be in Malay unless submitted as exhibits. English "translations" could be attached and there was provision for urgent applications to be made in English subject to submission of a Malay translation within 2 weeks (Rashid Darham 1990.6.01). The 2012 Rules of Court, published bilingually, largely confirm this protocol. A recent innovation (O.41 r.13) permits depositions taken outside Malaysia to be submitted in English without translation. The Bar Council Task Force that produced the 2012 Rules in collaboration with the judiciary and AGC is now liaising with these two bodies with the aim of standardising the Malay and English versions by 2016 (Majlis Peguam 2016:362).

In 1988 Supreme Court judge Hashim Yeop advised that the discretion in the National Language Act to use English be reviewed in order to allow full implementation of Malay (*The Straits Times* 1988a.1.17). Soon after, hints were dropped by the government news agency about further reform (Rohana Mustaffa 1988.3.16) and in October an amendment opened the door wider for Malay in the higher courts without ruling out English (*The Straits Times* 1988b.9.18). Welcomed as "timely" by Lord President Abdul Hamid Omar (*The Straits Times* 1989a.6.03), described at a law seminar as a plan for "full court use of Bahasa" (*The Straits Times* 1989c.6.25), and claimed to imply Malay for all civil cases (*Utusan Malaysia* 1989.12.05, over-interpreting Hashim's announcement of the adoption of Malay translations of Civil Procedure rules), the 1990 National Language Amendment instituted Malay for all courts, but "of its own motion or on the application of any party…after considering the interests of justice" the court could order proceedings to be partly in English (s.8).

3.4 From Legislation to Political and Judicial Enforcement

We can see that the main legislative mechanisms to allow a fully Malay system were already in place 25 years ago. While polemically significant when interpreted in political contexts, such as the cultural nationalism of 1967 or the rising executive influence over the judiciary of the late '80s, these measures had neither an immediate impact on perceptions of language status nor a decisive effect on legal practice, however.

Soon after the passage of the 1990 Amendment Act, Justice Minister Sulaiman Daud questioned a judge's claim that he had been instructed to hear a case in Malay, denying the existence of any direction making Malay mandatory and insisting that discretionary English would continue (*The Straits Times* 1989b.9.27). On the other hand, on the day all courts were reported to have finally "switched to Bahasa Malaysia" following a 3-month postponement in implementing the policy (*The Straits Times* 1990a.6.02a), Abdul Hamid Omar reminded the press that the use of Malay was in accorded with relevant legislation (*The Straits Times* 1990b.6.02b). Six months later, new Justice Minister Syed Hamid advised courts to be strict when considering defence applications to use English (*The Straits Times* 1990c.12.15), the implication being that prosecutors from the Judicial and Legal Service were already using Malay. He also claimed that 70% of High Court cases were being heard in the national language (*The Straits Times* 1990d.12.18). Yet the following June he denied the government would do away with English "even when Bahasa Malaysia becomes the language of the courts" (*The Straits Times* 1991a.6.14). In December it was reported that English was still widely used in the higher courts because many lawyers and judges felt the use of Malay would "subvert the course of justice" (*The Straits Times* 1991b.12.05). Three years later Chief Justice Eusoff Chin called for more higher-court testimony and submissions to be in Malay (*The Straits Times* 1994.9.24). One East Coast lawyer recalled from his days as a magistrate in Kelantan in the early 1990s that although most cases proceeded in Malay lawyers were still permitted to use English. Looking back on her experiences as a young lawyer during that period, however, a KL-based corporate lawyer remembered a senior lawyer being ejected from the courtroom for refusing to speak Malay.

The gradual and partial effect of status planning measures leaves some room for arguing that they were largely political in origin and symbolic in intent, as seems to have been the case with earlier examples of language planning in common law such as the 1362 Statute of Pleading and 1731 Courts of Justice Act (see Chap. 10). But when put under judicial scrutiny they have emerged as rather more substantial.

Indeed case law, though not yet extensive, has contributed importantly to the construction of language status and rulings have always come down on the side of the National Language. In *Zainun Dahan* (1997), for example, justice Nik Hashim ruled that filing motions in English contravened not only High Court Rules but also the National Language Act. In *Dato' Seri Anwar Ibrahim* (2010), the court ruled Karpal Singh's use of English contravened the imperative to use Malay implied in the Language Act's use of "shall" (s.8). Academic and journalist Azmi Sharom[7] feels Karpal is unlikely to have been trying to score ideological points, even though his subsequent comment about the irony of justices using English to rule against its use by counsel was hardly apolitical, and may simply have been an underestimation of the propensity of the judiciary to dispense with its usual flexibility when adjudicating on high profile cases.

It should be noted that language policy is largely silent about the private sector. Despite periodic murmurs of government plans to require Malay for contracts in order to protect consumers (*The Straits Times* 2000a.1.22; 2000b.3.10) no restrictions apply. Mediation and arbitration, while framed by statute (e.g. 2005 Arbitration Act) and formally encouraged (High Court rule O.34), proceed out of the public eye in the language(s) preferred by parties, which in the case of the latter is invariably English (Powell and Azirah 2011a).

Cases Cited

Chua Choong Yin v Tan Boon Bak Trading Sdn Bhd & Anor [2002] 3CLJ 357 CA.
Dato' Seri Anwar Ibrahim v Tun Dr Mahathir Mohamad [2010] 3CLJ 444 CA.
Merdeka University v Government [1982] 2 MLJ 243 [Malaysia].
Zainun bte Hj Dahan lwn *Rakyat Merchant Bankers Bhd & Satu Lagi* [1997] 4 CLJ.

References

Aryeh Neier. (2004, April 10). Justices of the Peace. Sultan: JP is a trust, not an award. *Malaysiakini*. Accessed 27 Sept 2011 from http://www.malaysiakini.com/news/19500
Bourdieu, Pierre. (1991). *Language and symbolic power*. Cambridge, MA: Harvard University Press.
Calvet, Louis-Jean. (1987). *La guerre des langues et les politiques linguistiques* [Language war and language politics]. Paris: Payot.
Chen Mian Kuang. (2009, February 19). Judicial appointments commission: No representation from the bar. *LoyarBurok*.
Cooper, Robert L. (1989). *Language planning and social change*. Cambridge: CUP.
Coperahewa, Sandagomi. (2011). The language situation in Sri Lanka. In Kaplan & Baldauf (Eds.), *Language planning in the Asia Pacific: Hong Kong, Timor-Leste and Sri Lanka* (pp. 160–241). Abingdon: Routledge.
Dewan Rakyat. (1971, March 03). *Malaysian parliamentary proceedings*: DR-03031971.
Dewan Rakyat. (1975, December 19). *Malaysian parliamentary proceedings* (p. 9774).

[7] Interviewed at Universiti Malaya, 2013.8.

Dewan Rakyat. (1976, March 31). *Malaysian parliamentary proceedings* (pp. 28–29).
Dewan Rakyat. (1986, November 26). *Malaysian parliamentary proceedings: DR-26111986*. [Oo Gin Sun, Deputy Minister in Prime Minister's Office, in response to Mohd. Zain bin Abdullah].
Dovalil, Vítek. (2009, September). Ideological positioning in legal discourses on multilingualism: Equality of languages as an ideology and a challenge. Workshop on 'Ideological conceptualisations of languages in discourses of linguistic diversity', *Societas Linguistica Europaea*.
Government of Malaya. (1948). *Federation of Malaya agreement*. Kuala Lumpur: Government Printer.
Haarmann, Harald. (1990). Language planning in the light of a general theory of language: A methodological framework. *International Journal of Sociology of Language, 86*(1990), 103–126.
ILKAP. (2014). Official portal of *Institut Latihan Kehakiman dan Perundangan* [Legal and Judicial Training Centre] accessed 30 Apr 2014 from http://www.ilkap.gov.my/prime.php
JAC. (2015). *Official portal of the Judicial Appointments Commission* (Suruhanjaya Pelantikan Kehakiman). Accessed 12 Dec 2015 from http://www.jac.gov.my
Kamarul Zaman Shaharudin, Rossilawaty Sheriff, Sa'odah Abdullah, Mohamed Hamizi Ghazali & Ismail Karmun (Eds.). (2003). *Citra*. Kuala Lumpur: Dewan Bahasa dan Pustaka.
Kaplan, Robert, & Baldauf, Richard. (2008). An ecology perspective on language planning. In A. Creese, P. Martin, & N. H. Hornberger (Eds.), *Encyclopedia of language and education* (Vol. 9, 2nd ed., pp. 41–52).
Kloss, Heinz. (1969). *Research possibilities on group bilingualism: A report*. Québec: Université Laval, Centre International de recherches sur le bilinguisme.
Kuek Ser Kuang Keng. (2010, October 29). Tsen vows to improve on her Bahasa. *Malaysiakini*. Accessed 30 Mar 2011 from http://www.malaysiakini.com/news/146809
Lo Bianco, Joseph. (2009). Critical discourse analysis (CDA) and language planning (LP): Constraints and applications of the critical in language planning. In T. Lê, Q. Lê, & M. Short (Eds.), *Critical discourse analysis. An interdisciplinary perspective* (pp. 101–118). New York: Nova Science.
Mahkamah Persekutuan. (2014). *Pejabat Ketua Pendaftar Mahkamah Persekutuan Malaysia*/ Malaysian Federal Court portal accessed 2012.4; 2012.6; 2014.4 from http://www.kehakiman.gov.my/
Majlis Peguam. (2016). *Bar Council Annual Report 2015/16*.
Malaysiakini. (2008, May 10). *Correct, correct, correct, it's Fairuz*. Accessed 27 May 2011 from http://www.malaysiakini.com/news/82632
Malaysiakini. (2014, April 07). *MPs squabble in English to win over visiting Aussies*. Accessed 10 Apr 2014 from http://www.malaysiakini.com/news/259349
Malaysiakini. (2015, November 17). *'English' row in the house, Azizah told to make a stand*. Accessed 20 Nov 2015 from http://www.malaysiakini.com/news/319921
Malaysiakini. (2017, November 14). *'Broken' Bahasa Malaysia to cost you RM1k soon?* Accessed 20 Nov 2017 from http://malaysiakini.com/news/401903
Mead, Richard. (1988). *Malaysia's national language policy and the legal system*. New Haven: Yale.
Mohamad Azim Fitri Abd Aziz. (2011, October 15). *Gov't depts take steps on compulsory use of BM*. *Malaysiakini*. Accessed 30 Oct 2011 from http://www.malaysiakini.com/news/178737
New Straits Times. (1981a, October 01). *JB Sessions court goes Bahasa*. And legal jargon becomes case in point. p. 8.
New Straits Times. (1981b, October 13). *In the dark over bahasa in courts'* (p. 4).
New Straits Times. (1981c, October 14).
New Straits Times. (1981d, October 21). *Bahasa test for lawyers likely* (p. 3).
Nik Safiah Karim. (1994). The controlling domains of Bahasa Melayu: The story of language planning in Malaysia. In A. Hassan (Ed.), *Language planning in Southeast Asia* (pp. 133–150). Kuala Lumpur: Dewan Bahasa dan Pustaka.
Rashid Darham. (1990, June 1). *Penggunaan bahasa Malaysia di semua mahkamah mulai hari ini* [Use of Malay in all courts starts today] *Utusan Malaysia* (p. 13).

Rohana Mustaffa. (1988, March 16). Towards Bahasa as the language of the courts. *The Straits Times/Bernama* (p. 10).
Rwezaura, Barthazara. (1994). Constraining factors to the adoption of Kiswahili as a language of the law in Tanzania. *Afrikanistische Arbeitspapiere: Schriftenreihe des Kölner Instituts für Afrikanistik, 37*, 109–126.
The Singapore Free Press. (1960, June 30). *Start Malay in the courts now, says Dr Zainal* (p. 3).
The Straits Times. (1958, February 18). *Malay in the lower courts?* (p. 4).
The Straits Times. (1959a, August 24).
The Straits Times. (1959b, August 25). *Malay seminar group seeks action* (p. 2).
The Straits Times. (1960, June 24). *Malay is not accurate enough for all courts, says Leong* (p. 2).
The Straits Times. (1962, May 08). *Courts now record evidence in Malay* (p. 2).
The Straits Times. (1964, December 04). *Why bills must be in two languages: Tengku* (p. 1).
The Straits Times. (1965, June 16). *Use Malay in lower courts, call by Nasir* (p. 20).
The Straits Times. (1966, August 24). *The courts and the N-language, by Ismail* (p. 6).
The Straits Times. (1967a, March 03). *Language: I have chosen the peaceful way* (p. 8).
The Straits Times. (1967b, August 06). *Lawyers agree to National Language in court* (p. 1).
The Straits Times. (1967c, August 11). *Language in the courts* (p. 11).
The Straits Times. (1979, October 30). *Suffian: Why I don't agree with 3 demands* (p. 14).
The Straits Times. (1980, June 09). *A matter of making enough effort* (p. 12).
The Straits Times. (1981, October 08). *Lawyers at a loss over court terms* (p. 15).
The Straits Times. (1988a, January 17). *Use of Malay in court: Act 'must be amended'* (p. 9).
The Straits Times. (1988b, September 18). *Lawyers can apply to conduct High Court cases in English after Oct 1* (p. 14).
The Straits Times. (1989a, June 03). *Plan to use more Malay in courts wins support* (p. 16).
The Straits Times. (1989b, September 27). *Judges to be given option to hear cases in Bahasa or English* (p. 18).
The Straits Times. (1989c, June 25). *Law seminar participants accept plan for full court use of Bahasa* (p. 2).
The Straits Times. (1990a, June 02a). *Courts switch to use of Bahasa Malaysia* (p. 19).
The Straits Times. (1990b, June 6 02b). *Using Bahasa in court* (p. 2).
The Straits Times. (1990c, December 15). *'Be strict' in allowing English in courts* (p. 22).
The Straits Times. (1990d, December 18). *70% of High Court cases conducted in Bahasa: Minister* (p. 15).
The Straits Times. (1991a, June 14). *Govt won't scrap use of English in courts: Minister* (p. 22).
The Straits Times. (1991b, December 05). *English still widely used in higher courts* (p. 16).
The Straits Times. (1994, September 24). *Judges urged to use more Bahasa Malaysia* (p. 18).
The Straits Times. (2000a, January 22). *Sales contracts may soon have to be in Malay* (p. 32).
The Straits Times. (2000b, March 10). *KL govt will enforce the use of Bahasa* (p. 61).
Utusan Malaysia. (1981, April 17). *Masa belum sesuai tetapkan guna bahasa Malaysia di Mahkamah* [Time not yet suitable to use Malay in courts.] p. 18.
Utusan Malaysia. (1983, March 24). *Tarikh penggunaan Bahasa Malaysia dalam mahkamah belum ditetapkan* [Date for use of Malay in courts not yet fixed]. p. 6.
Utusan Malaysia. (1984, June 02). *Permohonan jadi peguam tanpa ujian bahasa Malaysia ditolak* [Application to become lawyer without Malay test rejected] p. 3.
Utusan Malaysia. (1989, December 05). *Semua kes sivil akan guna bahasa Malaysia tahun depan – Hashim* [Hashim – all civil cases will be in Malay from next year] p. 3.
Wan Arfah Hamzah & Ramy Bulan (2003). *An introduction to the Malaysian legal system*. Shah Alam: Penerbit Fajar Bakti.

Chapter 4
Corpus Planning

Laras perundangan khas, orang biasa tak faham [the legal register is special and not understood by ordinary people]. So it will take time to build up legal Malay.

Dewan Bahasa lexicographer (2013.12.17)

At the time of Maha Wangsa [the Great Dynasty] we were the power and Malay was used in law and everything else. But if we want to show our greatness again, have more dictionaries, more glossaries. Don't just dwell on the past.

Shah Alam advocate (2013.12.08)

4.1 Relationship with Status, Acquisition and Discourse Planning

Less overtly political than status planning, corpus reform is nonetheless generally undertaken by institutions related to centralised power structures. Bourdieu (1982:21) argues that language standardisation becomes indispensable with the emergence of nations as abstract, legal entities.

There are numerous examples from history of linkage between corpus planning and nationalism. While lacking a specific linguistic agenda, the Chancery played a key role in the standardisation of administrative English, as well as the centralisation of administrative procedures, in late medieval England. In Italy, when the Accademia della Crusca (1582) began winnowing out a national language two centuries after Dante had proposed the desirability of vernaculars as more 'natural' than Latin (Lo Bianco 2005:112), it chose to draw authority less from common usage than from a literary purism underwritten by the political power of Tuscany (Nencioni 1986:111). The Académie Française (1635) was central to Richelieu's campaign against disorder and power fragmentation (Cooper 1989:3–11). And Leibnitz's (1683/1917:19) proposals for making German a language of science called for nation and language to "bloom together". Moving on to postcolonial Asia, Academy Bangla (1955) emerged from political resistance to West Pakistani dominance and

R. Powell, *Language Choice in Postcolonial Law*, Language Policy 22,
https://doi.org/10.1007/978-981-15-1173-8_4

to this day relates its quest for literary excellence to national struggle (Bangla Academy 2014). Malaysia's Dewan Bahasa associates itself with the resolution of communal differences (Kamarul et al. 2003:viii) while promoting Malay as *jiwa bangsa*: "the soul of the nation" (Awang Sariyan 2013).

Inadequate terminology is frequently cited as a key impediment to vernacularisation. Sibayan (in Martin 2012:9) linked the capacity to develop lexical resources to the degree of intertranslatability among languages, which he deemed crucial to the adaptability of vernaculars to new domains. Kloss (1969:81) highlighted the importance of linguistic expertise for corpus planning, by default suggesting that linguists are less crucial for status planning. In the case of corpus planning for the legal domain legal expertise is required in addition to linguistic knowledge in order to factor in the professional ramifications of proposed innovations. With verdicts and reputations at stake, legal practitioners are understandably wary of the semantic and pragmatic implications of neologisms.

As for the connection between corpus reform and language acquisition, it goes without saying that innovations must be disseminated and inculcated to have any meaningful effect. Spolsky (2004:36) reminds us of the importance of social context when selecting or creating lexis and of the problems likely to arise when educated elites carry out reforms that overlook public feelings. In the case of professions such as law there must also be consideration of the differing needs of practitioners who live by legal language and lay participants who encounter it less often but may be affected by it more. The process is all the more complex if innovations need to be acceptable internationally as well as at home (Cooper 1989:125; Kaplan and Baldauf 1997:46). The international dimensions of science and technology are obvious enough, but they are also significant in law, and may be paramount in common law because of the cross-border authority of precedents.

Students interviewed for this study raised lexical issues early on when the question of language choice arose. Several students at UM's Faculty of Law, where nearly all tutorials (and most lectures) are in English, felt lexical deficiencies in Malay would make it burdensome to discuss legal cases in it, and when I suggested that bilingual tutorials might be the answer, one expressed fear that it could lead to confusion, "especially in terms". [1] Some students had witnessed court proceedings being interrupted by disputes over the equivalence of Malay and English terms during their professional attachments. While there is general awareness among students of the technical burden of legalese, it was notable that lexical deficiency was invariably associated with Malay rather than English, with some students explaining that this was because English law was the source for most Malaysian law. This attitude to Malay was not confined to terminology: many UM students commented that one of the main reasons they preferred to answer questions in English, even when Malay is an option, was because of a dearth of references in the latter.

Lawyers, too, frequently brought up Malay terminology as soon as they were probed about language difficulties at work. For some this was a minor barrier, over-

[1] University of Malaya law student, class of 2012.

come in their first few months of court appearances in the Malay-dominated lower courts and eased by the tolerance of many judges for English code-mixes. For Brendan Navin, former chair of the KL bar, it helped that many terms in English and Malay were "more or less the same".[2] However, according to a young practitioner interviewed in Ipoh, many law graduates rue leaving university still unable to write simple letters in Malay without considerable effort. Novices may be confused over the appropriate terms of address, with one UM attachment student reminding himself that it is *Tuan* [Sir] in the lower courts, not *Yang Arif* [Your Honour], and some even get into knots trying to Malayanise Latin terms that are usually untranslated (e.g. *prima facie*) and often abbreviated (*nemo dat…*). To add to the difficulties of the more studious, Law Latin is often quite different from general Latin. Kurzon (2013:136–7), for example, cites neologisms in Blackstone such as *feofsamentium* for ('deed of feoffment') that would baffle modern classicists, let alone the Romans.

Acronyms and abbreviations are a perennial feature of professional jargon and particularly common in the kind of routine applications that newcomers are likely to be involved in. One Melaka-based advocate, a native speaker of Malay but highly proficient in English, gave a poignant example of the difficulty bilingual abbreviations may pose even for those who know the full forms in both languages:

> I just needed an OIT – an Order In Terms. I introduced myself in Malay and explained my application and the judge goes PSD [*Perintah Seperti Dikehendaki*]? And I go Sorry? She gets mad at me and throws her pen down. (Melaka practitioner)

Corpus planning is also intertwined with the cultural social and political discourses behind code- and lexical choice. Public statements in support of the continued need for English made by Malaysian Justice Ministers and Chief Justices typically cite deficiencies in Malay terminology and jurisprudence, but what appear to be practical arguments often rest upon underlying sociostructural stances. Indeed L.A. Sheridan (*The Straits Times* 1963.2.01), founder of Malaya's first law faculty, recognised in the early days of language planning that applying Malay to complex discourses such as law would have political as well as technical implications. The indignation expressed 40 years later by national laureate Muhammad Salleh toward those yet to embrace Malay despite corpus reforms to expand its use as a vehicle of knowledge (Yusof Ghani 2002.8.12) encapsulates a widespread view that the marginalisation of the language among lawyers reflects cultural attitudes as much as lexical resources. The fact is that the adequacy of a lexicon is judged not merely by word counts but by perceptions about the associations surrounding words. Kaplan and Baldauf (1997:41) relate lexicogrammatical preferences to wider power relations, while Fairclough (2003) reminds us in his work on critical discourse analysis about how societal imbalances can be reconstituted in everyday and unconscious lexical choices. An indispensable component of corpus innovation is borrowing from other languages, but as Kurzon (2013:135) points out, loanwords frequently

[2] Interviewed in Kuala Lumur, 2013.12.

come with the powerful discourses with which they have been associated. For Bourdieu (1982:18), succinctly: "En fait il n'y a pas de mots neutres".

Ćapeta (2009:3) argues that, for all its claims to neutrality, legal language is no more receptive to single determinate meanings than non-legal language. Indeed Šarćevič (1997:70–71) equates the task of translating legal texts with that of translating entire legal systems, given that the translator must understand the legal effect of a text. Working with English and Turkish, Altay (2002) also sees a necessity for translators to understand wider legal and historical contexts if they are to approach pragmatic equivalence. Even within a broadly similar Roman law tradition, Alber and Palermo (2012:287) note the difficulty of describing Italian legal terms in German for bilingual districts of northern Italy because of differences between Italian and Germanic law.

Though blunter than some, one KL conveyancing lawyer typified the stance of many advocates and students with her comment: "Sufficient legal terms in Bahasa Malaysia? I don't think so!". A former magistrate with his own law practice in Terengganu recalled difficulties he had had in writing judgments in his native Malay because of a lack of terms. Constitutional law expert Azmi Sharom[3] pointed out the inadequacy of using *Negara Islam* to translate two critically different concepts: 'Muslim country' and 'Islamic state'. But whereas some practitioners find Malay terms vaguer than English, and others go so far as to doubt that bilingual terms can render equivalent meanings, many feel the existing Malay terms are adequate for the routine tasks they are most commonly used for.

4.2 Modernisation of Malay

Based on the diversity of Malayic languages found there, Borneo and southern Sumatra are the leading contenders for progenitor of Malay (Adelaar 2000:229). Stone inscriptions dated to the seventh century (Teeuw 1959:140) establish Malay in Brahmi script as the earliest written Austronesian language (Adelaar 2000:230), although little writing survives before the *Jawi* lawbooks and administrative rules of sixteenth-century Johor (ibid:231). The Portuguese and Dutch made some administrative use of the language, developing texts that served as models for Bible translations (ibid:232–234). The Royal Asiatic Society developed a *Rumi* script in the seventeenth century (Adelaar 1996:731) but there is no evidence of Malay (as opposed to Qur'anic) instruction until 1821 in Penang, 1867 in the FMS and 1897 in the Unfederated States. From 1916 Winstedt promoted it in Straits Settlements schools (Adelaar 1996:729) and established a Translation Bureau to produce and foster literature as well as oversee administrative translations (ibid:729).

Manuscripts have been discovered in a number of varieties of Malay (Teeuw 1959:140) and the nineteenth-century vernacular press drew on colloquialisms and

[3] Interviewed at UM, 2013.8.

loanwords (Adelaar 2000:235), but the Dutch and British alike scarcely looked beyond literary texts from Riau-Johor as models for a standard language (ibid:234). Indeed a tendency to conflate other forms with basilectal lingua francas has persisted, traditionalists expressing contempt for modernisers when tensions arise over the question of standardisation (Det 1949.4.24). Although a number of dictionaries were produced in the early twentieth century, including *Kitab Benih Bahasa*, (1917) and *Kamus Muhamudiah* (1925) (Kamarul et al. 2003:51), Adelaar (1996:729) finds little administrative use of the language before independence and suggests that its development in Malaya may have been slower than in Indonesia because competition from English was stronger than competition from Dutch. Mahathir (Det 1949.4.24) complained of lack of cooperation over language from Indonesia where, according to Adelaar (2000:238), Sanskrit and archaic Malay were prioritised as lexical resources rather than the Arabic and English that was favoured in Malaya.

Initially set up as an institute to tackle the shortage of Malay teachers, Dewan Bahasa dan Pustaka (DBP) started out as *Balai Pustaka* in 1956 before being made into a statutory body 3 years later under a chair appointed by the Ministry of Education. Asmah (2004:88) contrasts the centralised and systematised approach to Malay lexicography today with the piecemeal reforms that went on before the establishment of DBP. It now comprises five regional offices overseeing departments dedicated to corpus development, language research, lexicography, literature promotion, publications and terminological standardisation (Kamarul et al. 2003:1–9) and describes itself as the only authority to coordinate coining, formulation and standardisation (ibid:67). In the immediate postcolonial period the priority was lexical innovation in development-focused fields such as economics and science, guided by the principle of "seeking from within the Malay world" (Asmah 2004: 90). To "stabilize" terminology, spelling and grammar (Kamarul et al. 2003:39) it was therefore necessary to establish the bounds of that world. In principle, national and regional Malay dialects and Indonesian languages such as Javanese were preferred (Hawa 1992:4), with Arabic, and Sanskrit considered preferable to English (Asmah 2004:90).

For law too, UM's Nik Abdul Rashid (1989:9) advised coining new terms from Arabic or other Austronesian languages in preference to adapting English words. Heah (1989:3–5) claims that attempts to play down the role of the colonial language extended to substituting lexis from languages sharing etymologies with it, and as can be seen from examples in Fig. 4.1, a number of loans carrying the *–si* ending typical of Indonesian borrowings from *tie*-final Dutch have been favoured over *tion*-final English equivalents. English has nonetheless been the most productive resource (Hawa 1992:4–5). Collaboration with Indonesia stalled during the border conflicts of the '60s but in 1972 a joint Language Council (MBIM = *Majlis Bahasa Indonesia-Malaysia*, later MBBIM, when Brunei joined) oversaw a regional spelling agreement.

Extracted from DBP (1985) *Istilah Undang-undang*.

1. Unmodified loan from French/ German/Latin	*alibi, assumpsit, certiorari, en ventre sa mere, force majeure, pari pasu, ratio decidendi, res ipsa loquitur, stare decisis, thalweg, volonti non fit injuria*
2. Unmodified loan from English	abstain, *assizes*, award, *bare trust*, *Common Law*, fee, infer, informer, libel, moot, privity, relief, slander, tort, tribunal
3. Minor orthographic modification	anuiti, autoriti, beligeren, botomri, defendan, dividen, dures, endors, endowmen, eskrow, identiti, indentur, juvenil, koroner, mandatori, parol, royalti, testimoni, underait
4. Orthographic modification largely preserving phonology of loan	akuiesens [aquiescence], caj [charge], carter, catel [chattel], dekri nisi, inses, impaun, interplider, isemen [easement], kodisil, lokap [lock-up], majistret, prosiding, salvaj, sepena [subpoena], syer [share].
5. Orthographically & phonologically modified loan	akta, bankrap, devis dan bekues [devise and bequest], ejen [agent], indikmen, klien, usufruk [usufruct], waran.
6. Syntactically modified loan	entiti juridikal, kes litigasi, kes sivil, liabiliti vikarius, prinsip sektor, writ saman [writ of summons]
7. Morphologically modified loan	avulsi, aneksasi, keakruan [accrual], kerelevanan fakta [relevance of facts], ketaksolvenan [insolvency], memfraud, memprorog (prorogue), mendepos [depose], mengestop (estop), penggerenti (guarantor), rekuesisi
8. Syntactic & morphological modification	estet si bankrap [bankrupt estate], triti kapitulasi [capitulation treaty], yang digarnis [garnishee], writ terendors [endorsed writ]
9. Hybrid	afidavit jawapan [affidavit in reply], hak [right] *in rem*, jenayah inkoat [inchoate crime, liabiliti mutlak [absolute liability], kes ujian [test case], rizab kewangan [monetary reserve], alang [gift] intervivos, undang-undang antitrust [antitrust law], writ pelaksanaan [writ of execution]
10. Semantic extension of term transferred from other domains	amanah [trust], balasan [consideration], budi bicara [discretion], ganti rugi [damages], hakim [judge], jagaan ['watch'=custody kacau-ganggu [nuisance], perkongsian [partnership], wasiat [will], wasit [referee], zuriat [issue/offspring]
11. Loan translation/calque	akta induk [parent act], aset cair [liquid asset], pisah dan umpuk [sever and apportion], kontrak terkecewa [frustrated contract], saksi paksa [compellable witness], turun [stand down]

Fig. 4.1 Taxonomy of innovations in Malay legal lexicon

12. Translation involving conceptual transfer	badan berkanun ['codified~'= statutory body'], barang kes [exhibit], boleh dipatah [rebuttable], cek tak layan ['unserviced~'=dishonoured cheque], cuba membunuh [attempted murder], cukai tanah ['land tax'=quit rent], hutang lapuk ['obsolete~'=bad debt], izinlalu ['permission to pass'=wayleave], niat jahat terdahulu [malice aforethought], pekongsi lelap ['lapsed-' =sleeping partner], penggadai-janji ['charger of promise'=mortgagor], kos mengikut ['following cost'=cost in the cause], sewa tetap ['rent fixed'=dead rent]

Fig. 4.1 (continued)

A 28,000-word dictionary, *Kamus Dewan*, was published in 1970 (Kamarul et al. 2003:51), when DBP's focus shifted to support for phasing Malay into higher education (ibid:43), and is now in its fourth edition. In 1986 came a comprehensive grammar, *Tatabahasa Dewan*. Both commonly appear on the shelves of law firm libraries. Over 40 dictionaries have since been produced, mostly in scientific fields (ibid:69). The 1990s saw the development of digital corpora (ibid:55) and the establishment of a working committee to encourage use of Malay in the private sector (ibid:79). By way of comparison, Sri Lanka, which achieved independence a decade earlier, had indexed 43,000 Sinhala and 48,000 Tamil terms and phrases for public sector use by 1955 (Coperahewa 2011:219), an encyclopedia in 1963 that now runs to 11 volumes, and the 72-volume Sinhala dictionary in 1972 (ibid:220). Gill (2005:249) considers the 374 books translated between down to1994 a disappointing return on the RM38m allocated to DBP for enhancing the national language but concedes that even Japan has had difficulty keeping pace with the huge number of scientific articles published in English (ibid:249).

4.3 Development of Malay Legal Lexicon

Corpus planning was the main concern of early planners and continues to focus the attention of those doubting Malay's utility for complex law. It has been applied to the generation of legal lexis and enabled the generation of legal texts, even though the bulk of these appear to be translations from English.

Upon DBP's establishment the Attorney General sat on the Board of Control alongside the Director-General of Education (Kamarul et al. 2003:9), indicating early intentions to develop a Malay corpus for law. International jurist Tommy Koh, at that time part of an investigation into legal Malay at UM's new law faculty, recommended a combination of reviving disused terms, coining neologisms and translating or borrowing from other languages (*The Straits Times* 1959.8.24). The following year both the Minister of Justice (*The Straits Times* 1960.6.24) and the Director of DBP (*The Singapore Free Press* 1960.6.30) noted the prevalence of

Latin and French in English law; but whereas this led the former to express caution about the capacity of Malay to translate legal terms, the latter saw the ability of English legalese to absorb other languages as a reason to implement Malay in the courts immediately by adopting existing terms without waiting for them to be translated.

DBP established a committee for legal terms in 1963 (Dewan Bahasa 1986:xi) and brought out an English-Malay terminology, *Istilah Undang-undang*, in 1970. A second edition in 1986 "based largely on the first" incorporates the 1972 spelling reforms and adds a mirror Malay-English section for the 3404 entries, which suggests there was by then enough legal writing in Malay for practitioners to need this function. The 1986 preface stated that, except for international and maritime law, terms for specialised fields had yet to be worked out, and expressed the hope of 'completing' (*melengkapkan*) the terminology soon while conceding that the absorption of many existing terms was unavoidable, given the difficulty of matching the two languages in multiple legal contexts (ibid:xxii).

Lexical borrowing, which is almost inevitable in corpus planning, and code-mixing, its prevalent but less systematic cousin, can be controversial practices. Lo Bianco (2001:166) alludes to a key reason for the controversy: even though language 'modernisation' typically operates at technical and lexical levels, it is a loaded term that may also entail the reorientation of language communities toward external groups. A decade before independence, Mahathir (Det 1949.4.24) commented on journalists' departure from standard Malay through coinages like *diboykotkan* and the mimicry of English affixation and added that the language had become even more "slipshod" in the Unfederated States, where it was used in tandem with English, than in urbanised states where it was subordinate to English (ibid). In 1966 DBP's head of research defended the validity and value of absorbing English loanwords (*The Straits Times* 1966.7.18), but three decades later the Chief Justice announced (*Berita Harian* 1995.1.13) that Indonesia, which has a civil law system, was being trawled for terminology, presumably to lessen reliance on English. In 2002 Malaysian, Bruneian and Indonesian linguists met to discuss how to protect Malay from foreign words (*The Straits Times* 2002.3.09). Even today, the high proportion of English loans in Malay can make news articles about law partially accessible to non-Malay readers, as the example of "2 ahli DAP fail writ saman" (2 Democratic Action Party members file writ of summons) shows (Farabi Said 2013.9.30).

In legal Filipino, Sinhala and Tongan, orthographically modified borrowing is widespread. Spanish (e.g. *akusado*, *ebidensya*) is the main source for the first (Pasamba, p.c., in Powell 2012), while English (*apala*/appeal, *warenthuwa*/warrant) and Dutch (*ravukoopiya*/*rouwkoop*) are important influences on legal Sinhala (Fathima Marikkar),[4] and English (*Ateni Seniale*/Attorney-General, *peilifi*/bailiff, *lesisita*/registration) is vital for Tongan (Crown Law 2013). Substitution of indigenous semantic equivalents is also common, e.g. Tagalog/Cebuano *piyansa* for 'bail'

[4] Sri Lankan attorney, interviewed Tokyo, 2011.2.

and Tongan *hia* for 'offence'. A third and perhaps less common lexical strategy is coining new terms from indigenous elements, such as the Sinhala *ratshana stanaya* (haven place) for 'asylum'. All these methods are employed in *Istilah Undang-undang*.

In Fig. 4.1 the first eight sections exemplify different but overlapping adaptation strategies for loans. Most French, Latin and German terms, as exemplified in box (1), including some well-integrated loans such as 'alibi', are italicised but otherwise unmodified. Mashudi (1994:83) remarks that it would be difficult to translate Latin concepts that lack established English equivalents and further notes that since English common law employs a lot of Latin it follows that Malaysian common law should do the same.

Many English terms have been transferred without modification (2), although some are italicised to mark them as terms of art. Although it is difficult to predict their habitual pronunciation because of individual variation, as well as different institutional stances toward *bahasa baku*,[5] courtroom observations for this study found them generally to be pronounced as Malaysian English rather than following Malay orthography (hence /laibəl/ not /libəl/).

Other loans have minor orthographical modifications (3) that leave their derivation recognisable. While substitution of k for c and omission of final e seem intended to preserve donor phonology, in some cases visual continuity has been prioritised: -ow-, for example, never appears in indigenous Malay but it does in legal Malay. Many English loans and a few from Latin have undergone more extensive modification to preserve phonology (4), while a further group incorporate orthographic changes reflecting phonological nativisation (5).

Section (6) shows loan groups adapted syntactically as well as orthographically, notably to accord with post-modification of nouns. Section 7 shows borrowings subjected to affixation: *kesolvenan* combines a nominalising circumfix, *ke-an*, with a loan translation, *tak*, to negate *solven* (solvent). Another group (8) show both morphological and syntactic adaptation, Section 9 has examples of Malay-English and Malay-Latin hybrids.

The final three sections exemplify semantic strategies. Some Malay common law terms employ lexis transferred from other domains (10) including Islamic law (e.g. the Arabic loans *hakim*, *wasiat*), business (*perkongsian*, a rare instance of Chinese with Malay affixation in the *Istilah*), and everyday parlance (*balasan* means 'requital'). A small number of calques (11) are close translations from English. Finally, and perhaps most interestingly, are translations involving semantic analysis (12). *Boleh dipatah*, for instance, means 'able to be defeated'.

Zaiton and Ramlah (1994:116) evaluated innovations in the Malay legal lexicon from a translator's point of view and concluded that more time was needed to replicate the registers, style and authority of English legalese. After analysing *Istilah Undang-undang* Mashudi (1994:88) proposed looking to Indonesian rather than

[5] 'Standard language' commonly associated with initiatives by Anwar Ibrahim, as minister of Education in the 1980s, to promote pronunciation to the written form, a practice more common in Indonesia than Malaysia.

English for expansion, arguing that the language is more suitable not only because it is related to Malay but also because it is associated with anticolonialism.

The bulk of entries are nouns and the next largest category is verbs, although an attempt to transfer some of the deictic adverbs that litter legal English is witnessed by *hingga kini* (heretofor) and *kemudian dari ini* (hereinafter).

While some informants thought of Malay legalese as vague, few complained specifically of inaccuracies. Semantic accuracy appears to have been the first priority for lexicologists, with a combined strategy of preserving some terms, with or without orthographic or phonological modification, and unpacking others by translating components with semantic equivalents. Indeed a number of translations can be considered clarifications of the source terms. 'Authority', for example, can be *autoriti*, *kuasa* or *pihak berkuasa*, depending on whether it refers to case law, power, or an authorising body. 'Charge' yields *caj* (fee), *gadaian* (lien), *pertuduhan* (indictment) and *tanggungan* (liability). Documentary and material exhibits are distinguished (*eksibit* and *barang kes*).

A more common complaint among informants was that Malay neologisms were mere window-dressing. Some, including a KL advocate who had studied in England, thought cosmetically modified terms might just as well have been left in English. Others, including a Shah Alam lawyer frustrated with the lack of commitment made by language planners toward legal Malay, argued that equivalent terms should have been constructed from Malay components. The 1965 Companies Act (whose authorised version remains the English one) depends heavily on words barely changed from English, such as *artikel*, *aset*, *debentur*, *proksi*, *resolusi* and *transaksi*. *Injunksi* was a favourite object of scorn among informants. A student at Multimedia University wondered how *penghakiman ingkar* had been chosen for 'judgment in default' given that *ingkar* means 'disobedient' and presumably refers to the person the judgment is made against rather than the judgment itself.

Perhaps inevitably when comparing neologisms with long-established terms, Malay terms are often thought of as unstable and lacking authority. UMNO Supreme Council member Abdullah Ahmad (1991:14) felt they were revised too frequently. Two young lawyers from Johor Bahru pointed out that although they were aware of terms such as *kecuaian*, *kacau-ganggu* and *pehakiman ingkar*, they were largely confined to textbooks and 'negligence', 'nuisance' and 'judgment in default' invariably preferred when speaking Malay in court. Some informants also expressed uncertainty about whether they should use *Istilah* items when there were others with wider circulation. A UM lecturer who had worked in, as well as taught, insurance law gave the example of *pihak yang diinsurekan* (insured party) being preferred to *pengambil insurans* (taker of insurance) by practitioners.

The main criticisms voiced about *Istilah* did not concern inaccuracy, vagueness or lack of authority, but insufficiency. *Istilah* has no term for 'produce', a high-frequency term in courtroom discourse, with one corporate lawyer claiming that its rendition in some enactments as *keluarkan* could leave doubt about whether evidence had in fact been adduced (for which she preferred *hasilkan*) rather than merely shown. In conversations with a KL conveyancing lawyer it was also apparent that *Istilah* overlooks numerous terms of art that might not initially stand out as legalese. The phrase 'where is, as is', for example, is common in property sales contracts and crucially warns purchasers to check fitness for purpose, yet there is no standard Malay term and it must be translated ad hoc. Such complaints from within the profession are often reflected in commentary beyond. A speaker at the 4th Malay Language and Literary Congress (*Utusan Malaysia*, 1985.1.07) lamented the language's failure to emerge as a medium commanding the confidence of a modern country, specifically citing the poor development of legal Malay 28 years after independence. Mead (1988:71) contrasted the 3000 legal terms DBP devised in the 1980s with the 24,000 developed for medicine – a field former Chief Justice Zaki Azmi considers less dependent on language than law is (Koshy 2013.9.15) – and one Dewan Bahasa lexicographer acknowledged that there had been little terminological research since the 2003 edition, which itself added little to its 1986 predecessor. Another DBP lexicologist said he would welcome renewed collaboration with universities but does not expect it as they teach mostly in English and fail to prioritise legal Malay.

Many informants confessed to improvised code-mixing in court (see Ch. 9). There was generally greater acceptance of spontaneous English mixes when the Malay lexicon was deficient than of resorting to English where suitable Malay terms existed. A Shah Alam informant who directed most of the blame for Malay's lack of progress at the planning authorities also criticised individual practitioners for using 'maintain' when *senggara* was available and wondered whether those littering their speech with anglicisms such as *eksploitasi* actually knew what they meant. A legal translator[6] questioned persistent preference, including by the DBP itself, for *implementasi* over *melaksanakan*. Bar Council speeches, which tend to start out in Malay for politeness before shifting in to English, make use of coinages such as *implementasi, obligasi* and even *rekomendasi-rekomendasi*. Former bar president Hendon Mohamed[7] felt that code-mixing was better tolerated than it had been in her youth and concluded that, for all Malay's richness as a tool for interpersonal communication, the demands of courtroom language and dearth of legal texts in her mother tongue made mixing unavoidable.

Istilah may be the authorised Malay reference, but it is by no means the only one. The 3400 entries in Fajar Bakti's *Kamus Undang-undang* (1995), in English-Malay mode only, omit some items covered by *Istilah* but include some missing from the latter and add detailed explanations in Malay. Many practitioners also make use of online resources. Three lawyers interviewed in Melaka agreed on the utility of the Session Court's website.

The existence of terms does not guarantee their reception or circulation. Mead (1988:74) suggested that legal Malay may be less readily accepted than medical Malay because it needs to take account of the contextual determinants of language functions and lawyers' particular concern with hitting the appropriate style. One pro-Malay judge (Faiza 1993:105–6) pointed out that the legal loophole permitting

6 Interviewed at a corporate law firm in KL, 2013.12.

7 Interviewed in KL, 2013.12.

English in the interests of justice was designed to cover gaps in the Malay legal lexicon rather than in the Malay lexicon of individual advocates, let alone their reluctance to plug them. Yet it is not only the lawyers who have been slow to adopt new terms. At a seminar on legal language it was noted by Nik Abdul Rashid (1989) that despite the existence of the authorised term *kuasa*, the drafters of a legal amendment had decided to retain 'competency'.

Due weight should nevertheless be given to the view that legal language is unusually complex and resistant to change. Comprehensively describing and analysing legalese are forbidding tasks few linguists have been willing to take on. One feature of legalese that may help explain enervation in Malaysian corpus planning is the juxtaposition of specialised lexicogrammar opaque to outsiders with less specialised language that happens to be applied to legal contexts. This hybridity enables some to view legalese as too technical to be reworked and others to take the complications of corpus planning too lightly.

Goodrich (1984:188) typifies the majority of analysts of legalese in concentrating on archaic, specialised vocabulary and syntax reinforced by narrow definitions in the cause of context-independence. This is of a piece with Ng's (2009) view of English legal discourse as formalised and removed from the colourful uncertainties of Hong Kong society in a way that Cantonese is not. Goodrich, however, insists (1984:191) that legal language is related to "the everyday commitments and discourses of social and political practice and conflict". Durant (2013) reminds us that although technical terms have a tendency to form closed systems resilient to change, law itself is not closed: common law seeks professional legitimacy through precision, but also social legitimacy through claims to reasonableness and transparency. Lexically this duality is reflected in a broad range of terms, from expressions referring exclusively to legal matters (e.g. *mens rea*, act of *mandamus*), through ordinary words accorded special meanings (consideration, offer) or uses (find), to vocabulary employed across many domains that indexes legal contexts (usher, court) (ibid:2013). Some terms intimately associated with the legal register are not bound by legal definition at all. For an Australian judge to define 'reasonable doubt' to a jury, for example, would be construed as misdirection (Grey 2013). Orally, practitioners add prosodic variation to lexical range when shifting among styles in order to target different audiences or invoke different discourses, especially where juries are involved (Fuller 1993). Bilingualism adds another dimension to register choice, with bilingual lawyers negotiating their way through both semantic and pragmatic shifts.

Given that there is at least a four-way choice among acro- and mesolectal varieties of the two languages, the association of English with written and more formal discourse and of Malay with oral and more informal discourse is an oversimplification, and yet it is widespread at all levels of the profession. One Melaka practitioner felt standards for drafting in Malay were lower than for English because the former is typically used for more formulaic tasks such as drawing up statements of claim for which, as a KL corporate lawyer noted, templates and samples exist that can simply be amended for detail from case to case. Indeed if we consider how much legal work consists of the recycling of standard texts it makes sense that practitioners will prefer to use tried and trusted patterns, in either language, whenever innovation is unnecessary. By their nature, legal tasks in the higher courts are more likely to involve original circumstances and original arguments than those in lower courts, and as we shall see from accounts of office and court work, English tends to be preferred there.

In an interview in which he acknowledged the limitations of Malay legal vocabulary, former Chief Justice Zaki Azmi (Koshy 2013.9.15) contrasted the improved standard of documents drafted in Malay for the lower courts with those submitted to the higher courts, which were often mere translations from English "just to comply with procedural requirements". But he added that this caused few problems as most judges read the English versions. In the same interview he emphasised how in law, to a far greater extent than science, the ability of practitioners to express themselves is crucial. Yet in a poignant illustration of the range of opinion about the accessibility of legalese he also recalled his father, himself a Lord President[8], telling him that to enter the profession he just needed to master simple English.

4.4 Development of Malay Legal Corpora

A key problem facing the development of equivalent English and Malay legal terms is the ingrained inequality between the two languages in their legal lexicons. To support bilingual law in Italy's germanophone areas a Joint Commission for Terminology first looks for equivalents to Italian terms in Austrian and German law before considering translation (Alber and Palermo 2012:298), but its commissioners have an advantage over Malaysian language planners as there is a much larger corpus of modern law in German than in Malay. While most corpus planning studies focus on lexication (e.g. Heah 1989; Asmah 2004 on Malay and Mashudi 1994; Zaiton and Ramlah 1994; Powell 2004 on legal Malay), to promote literacy and discourse development in the target language there must also be generation of texts. Kaplan and Baldauf (1997:43) remind us that corpus planning is not just about lexicogrammar but requires the creation of texts in various registers in order to promote literacy. While investigating micro-level reforms that have been pursued to innovate the Malay legal lexicon, this study is also concerned with the generation of a Malay legal corpus in the form of statutes, cases and academic literature.

Writing perhaps plays a more crucial role in law than any other profession, and despite an ancient common law tenet about law being what is said by judges, in practice it is what is recorded in judgments and statutes. Legal texts contain performative acts regarding language use, evince the status and prestige of languages, and provide authoritative models of usage. Published texts constitute a sterner testing ground for new lexis than oral courtroom exchanges. Yet there is a dearth of academic literature on how legal corpora may be developed in new languages. Studies of legal translation, which is an essential part of the process, typically concentrate

[8] The term used for Chief Justice until 1994.

on technicalities such as lexical equivalence (e.g. Ćapeta 2009; Šarčević 1997) rather than educational and administrative support for drafters. Tiersma (1999) and Bhatia (1993) have highlighted law's interest in producing autonomous, authoritative texts, which gives legal writing something in common with scientific texts' "need to hold the world still" (Halliday 2001:187). Although Tiersma (1999:100) argues for a capacity to innovate, this study found the widely held conception (e.g. Lemmens 2011) of legal language as conservative to be largely shared by Malaysian language planners.

When UM's Socialist Club called in 1959 for pleadings to be done in Malay (*The Straits Times* 1959.8.24) they conceded the need for lawyers to cite statutes and law reports in English, arguing that the language could not be removed from the courtroom unless costly and time-consuming translation were undertaken, the entire legal system codified in Malay, or common law principles and procedures abandoned. In 1962 the leader of the People's Progressive Party advised keeping expatriates on at the legal department (*The Straits Times* 1962.12.02) as lack of books in Malay made it likely cases would continue in English. A translation bureau established within the AGC in 1964 was tasked with translating the constitution, Penal Code, Criminal Procedure Code and Evidence Ordinance (*The Straits Times* 1964a.1.27) and 3 years later the Chief Justice announced the completion of the Penal Code translation when advising prosecutors to prepare charge sheets bilingually (*The Straits Times* 1967.8.20). But citing shortages of stenographers as an obstacle to monolingual use of Malay, in 1964 the prime minister proposed bilingual publication of legislation, implying that the Malay would be translated from English drafts (*The Straits Times* 1964b.12.04). Section 6 of the 1967 Language Act establishes the principle of Malay as the authentic text for post-1967 legislation, while Section 7 gives authenticity to the English text for prior enactments, unless the head of state specifically prioritises a Malay translation. When introducing Section 7 the Tunku declared it would not be right to insist on Malay if its clarity were in doubt (*The Straits Times* 1967.3.03). In 2001 constitutional amendment 160b gave the head of state's discretion to declare the Malay text of the constitution itself authentic, despite it being translated from English.

Human rights lawyer Aston Paiva has argued that apparently superficial changes in a legal text may have far-reaching implications, citing the substitution of "Islamic law" and "syariah courts" for "Muslim law" and "Muslim courts" in the 1976 revision of the constitution as a referential shift from laws enacted by Malaysian Muslims to sacrosanct religious law (Koh Jun Lin 2015.9.23). When dual language texts are involved the complexity of retranslation is added to that of rewording, and former bar president Christopher Leong has voiced fears that Malay versions of some constitutional articles may be tantamount to amendment by stealth (Lavendran 2013.6.13). The implications of changing *ibubapa* (parents) to *ibu atau bapa* (mother or father) in 2002 in the Malay text of constitutional Article 12(4) has been discussed in several religious conversion cases, including *Shamala* (2003). The Article refers to parental rights over the religion of minor children, and while it could be argued that *ibu atau bapa* is a more literal translation of 'parent', the form used in the English text, thus implying the right of one parent to convert a child without the permission of the other, it is a less *legal* translation inasmuch as the Penal Code (s.9) applies the common law principle of the singular embracing the plural. This interpretation would appear to rule out unilateral conversions and was finally upheld in *Indira Gandhi* (2018).

In 1979 the government announced proposals to set up a special unit to oversee translation of pre-1967 laws (*The Straits Times* 1979.11.27). Mead (1988:43) notes that by 1982 only 60 had Malay versions. By 1991 the figure had risen to just 89, leading Zubaidah, (2002:159) to wonder how trials manage to proceed in Malay at all. Observations of law schools, offices and courtrooms suggest that lexical code-mixing and citation-triggered code-switching remain crucial (Chaps. 7, 8, and 9). In 1981 the Prime Minister's Department set up a committee under DBP to publish law books in Malay (*New Straits Times* 1981.10.21), but 2 years later Malaysia's first female High Court judge[9], Siti Norma Yaakob, averred it would be a long time before there were sufficient legal references (*Utusan Malaysia* 1983.4.26). Three years later *Utusan Malaysia* (1984.6.02) claimed lack of Malay versions of labour law was disadvantaging workers. Five years after that the Justice Minister declared his hope to DBP that legislative translations be completed as soon as possible, but he refused to give a time frame (*The Straits Times* 1989.11.06).

The legal field was a major source of frustration for delegates at the 4th Malay Language and Literature Congress, with some complaining that the bulk of Malay documents were mere translations (*Utusan Malaysia* 1985.1.07). While there was no detailed critique of the quality of translation, we should bear in mind Zaiton and Ramlah's view (1994:116–118) that translators tend to follow the structure of the original English rather than prioritise the natural structures of the target Malay – conceivably a time-saving strategy but also reflecting a fear of semantic shift. Abdullah Ahmad (1991:13) called for enactments to be prepared in BM from the start, but although the legislative process begins with discussions in parliament, which must be in Malay, followed by negotiation between ministries and the parliamentary draftsman, which *should* be in Malay, according to officers at the Attorney General's Chambers the initial drafting that commences in consultation with academics still seems to be done mostly in English. An administrator at the Legal Profession Qualifying Board suggested this made sense given the continued importance of Commonwealth legislative models, and in a letter to *Malaysiakini* in support of English, Selangor advocate P. Dev Anand Pillai (2015.11.23) argued that the country continued to benefit from the administrative system left by the British largely because of the continued practice of translating literally from English to Malay. Despite this, it is normally the Malay text of an enactment that is declared authentic, although there are exceptions, such as the Companies Act.

This study does not look at the quality of legislative translation but it does take note of some of the reservations about it that have been published in the press or expressed by informants. One UM student comfortable reading legal textbooks in

[9] Also the first female Chief Judge of Malaya; the current holder, Zaharah Ibrahim, is the second. In May, 2019, Tengku Maimun Tuan Mat was appointed the nation's first female Chief Justice.

Malay nevertheless preferred to refer to the English draft of the Evidence Act as he claimed the Malay was mere translationese. There was general agreement among both students and practitioners that Malay texts were longer than their English counterparts. A legal translator at a large KL corporate law firm put this down partly to the general problem of expansion when transferring any text drafted in one language into another, and partly to the more specific problem of Malay lexical deficiency, concluding that a number of English legal terms had to be unpacked as explanatory phrases in Malay. She added that a desire to avoid wordiness was one of the reasons for resorting to inelegant but readily understood anglicisms such as *deklarasi* (declaration).

Alongside enactments, judgments are the most authoritative legal texts and have traditionally been particularly important in common law systems. The need to read cases that are available only in English was the reason most frequently given by informants when justifying its continued use for jurisprudence and legal education. Zaki Azmi estimates that only 0.1% of the articles and judgments Malaysian lawyers need to know are in Malay (Koshy, 2013.9.15). Nor is this just a matter of cross-border jurisprudence as English is still widely used for Malaysian judgments as well. Almost three decades ago Abdullah Ahmad (1991:13) argued that as long as judgments are written in English the government has a duty to finance their translation into Malay, market demand not being strong enough for private publishers to shoulder the task. When interviewed in early 2014, however, former Terengganu bar chair Zamani Mohamad remarked on an increasing tendency among law journals to add Malay explanations to cases reported in English, thereby widening the platform for legal discussion in Malay and potentially ushering in the writing of more judgments in it.

Going beyond individual preference to evidence of national policy, former Chief Justice Abdul Hamid Mohamad has revealed (*The Star* 2013.8.07) that in the 1990s every High Court judge was required to write grounds of judgment in Malay at least once a month. One KL-based corporate lawyer recalled from her early days that many judges found the quota taxing and frequently tasked juniors with drafting opinions. In the same interview Hamid said that he chose Malay when producing decisions pertaining to jurisdictional conflict to ensure that they were accessible to *Syariah* judges. While Azmi Sharom thought the aim to reach a *Syariah* readership might similarly explain the choice of Malay for the majority opinions in *Lina Joy*, a high-profile religious conversion case that in 2006 prompted the first use of the language at apex level, former bar president Steven Thiru, who was involved in the case as an advocate, thought the choice also helped shield poor legal reasoning from wider audiences. When interviewed (as bar vice president in August, 2013), however, he cautioned against linking the increased use of Malay for judgments with the decreased quality of writing that many lawyers complain about, pointing out that sliding standards also coincided with rising pressure upon judges to churn out decisions more quickly in order to reduce backlogs.

Disclosing that he would use English if writing today in order to reach a wider readership, Hamid (ibid) elaborated that Malaysian law journals were still reluctant to report judgments in Malay. While perusal of *Malayan Law Journal* shows a gradual increase in the use of Malay, with web-based *CLJ.com* also carrying a number of Malay judgments from the lower courts, English remains the default medium for academic writing. When interviewed at UM, one law lecturer said that he would be happy to write more in Malay but the mounting pressure on dons to fulfill quotas for contributions to internationally recognised journals left little time for this.

In 2004 a lawyer publicly feigned shock that *MLJ* felt there had been only 13 Court of Appeal judgments in Malay worth publishing (Abdul Malik 2004.8.20). However, he also admitted that the pool from which legal journals could choose was still quite shallow, with no judgment above High Court level appearing at all until 1997. As for those Malay judgments that do get reported, a Kelantan lawyer interviewed in Kota Bharu in early 2014 thought *MLJ* was translating fewer of them into English than before but in any case found the Malay reports hard to read, mentioning that translation was not being outsourced to people without legal training. The language of reports is not necessarily an indication of the language in which decisions are written, but journals tend to preserve the authenticity of proceedings by reflecting the language used, often reporting primary decisions in Malay and then shifting to English for subsequent appellate decisions. Hence there is a growing body of bilingual texts in Malaysian law that reflects some of the bilingualism to be found in oral discourse:

***Harun Abdullah* (2006) Court of Appeal**
IN THE COURT OF APPEAL OF MALAYSIA HOLDEN IN FEDERAL TERRITORY OF PUTRAJAYA
CRIMINAL APPEAL NO. B-09-34-06 BETWEEN
HARUN BIN ABDULLAH ...APPELLANT
AND
PUBLIC PROSECUTOR ...RESPONDENT

[In the matters of Criminal Appeal No. 42(A)-17-2001 Before the High Court of Malaya in Shah Alam, Selangor Darul Ehsan

In this case the accused was indicted with the following charge:

"Bahawa kamu pada 9/1/90 di Lot 663, Jalan Kelinik di daerah Kuala Selangor dalam Negeri Selangor telah memalsukan cagaran bernilai iaitu satu lesen membeli senjatapi dan peluru siri no B113824 memberi kuasa pemindahan palsu hakmilik suatu senjatapi kepada Ng Yah Hai kp no 4103299 dan dengan curangnya menggunakan cagaran berharga palsu tersebut sebagai satu cagaran berharga yang sah yang kamu ada sebab mengetahui ia adalah palsu dan dengan itu kamu telah melakukan kesalahan yang boleh dihukum di bawah Seksyen 467 Kanun Keseksaan di baca bersama dengan Seksyen 471 Kanun Keseksaan [That you, on 1/09/90 at Lot 663, Jalan Clinic in Kuala Selangor, Selangor, falsified the collateral value of a licence to purchase firearms and ammunition, serial number B113824, to authorise falsely the transfer of ownership of a firearm to Ng Hai Yah (IC4103299) and dishonestly using forged security that you had a good reason to know was false and therefore you have committed an offense punishable under Section 467 of the Penal Code read together with Section 471 of the Penal Code]"

***Hashim bin Puteh* (2011) Industrial Tribunal**
INDUSTRIAL COURT MALAYSIA CASE NO : 24(17)/4-2726/04 BETWEEN
ENCIK HASHIM BIN PUTEH AND MOTOROLA MALAYSIA SDN. BHD.
AWARD NO : 1705 OF 2011 (...)
Y.A. PUAN YAMUNA MENON CHAIRMAN - (Sitting Alone)
Industrial Court, Kuala Lumpur (...)
Charge 1 It was reported that on **15 August 2000** between 12.50 pm to 1.00 pm, you have **swapped the new gold wire spool at the rework station Wire Bond m/c#2 with a used gold wire spool** at the CATV Back End (West Bond machine), Q-Building. The above allegation, if proven, is a major misconduct per Company Policy 1006 Clause D(1) – No. 16: "Any act contrary and prejudicial to Company Standard Operating Procedure".
Claimant's Reply:- "1. Tuduhan yang tidak berasas dan berniat jahat. Saya akui memang saya berada di mesin tersebut tetapi saya langsung tidak menyentuh bahagian gold wire [The allegations are baseless and malicious. I admit it I was at the machine in question, but I did not touch the gold wire]. "

Rules and regulations are now generally published bilingually and achieving equivalence is a perennial issue. The Bar Council is currently in discussion with the Judiciary and AGC over amendments to standardise and correct the two versions of the Rules of Court (Majlis Peguam 2016:362) and announced a delay in the gazetting of the Solicitors' Remuneration (Enforcement) Rules pending amendments in the BM text (ibid:354).[10] This suggests that regulations, like statutes, tend to be drafted in English first and then translated. The importance attached to accuracy in a profession conscious of the implications of subtle differences can be illustrated by the requirement that law firms seeking to go by a vernacular name seek Bar Council approval to ensure that "the translation conveys the same meaning as in English" (ibid:312).

A lack of teaching material is a further barrier to the development of a legal Malay corpus. A DBP lexicographer recalled complaints about lack of Malay teaching materials from more than 20 years, a problem that Abdullah Ahmad (1991:10) blamed largely on academics. An East Coast practitioner who was asked to teach business law in Malay at a private law college found the few textbooks available in the language to be basic and dated. The preference for writing materials in English continues today and, according to several UM law lecturers, demands on Malaysian academics to publish more in overseas journals (hence in English) in order to raise their employers' international rankings further reduces their incentive to publish textbooks in Malay. Those teaching increasingly popular subjects such as medical

[10] *Bertikaian*, for example, is to be substituted for *berhujah* for ('contentious').

and environmental law are especially likely to produce materials in English. One exception to the trend is family law, which has produced a range of materials in Malay. This reflects the local nature of much family law, which is particularly rich and complex in Malaysia' multicultural context.

Cases Cited

Indira Gandhi A/P Mutho v Pengarah Jabatan Agama Islam Perak [2018] 1LNS 86

Lina Joy v Majlis Agama Islam Wilayah Persekutuan, Kerejaan Malaysia Rayuan Sivil no. 01-2-2006(W)

Shamala Sathiyaseelan v Dr. Jeyaganesh C Mogarajah (2003) S8-24-1727 2003

References

Abdullah bin Ahmad. (1991). *Strategi dan persediaan ke arah perlaksanaan bahasa Malaysia sebagai bahasa undang-undang* [Strategy and preparation for implementing Malay as a legal language]. Paper presented at *Seminar Bahasa dan Undang- undang* [*Seminar on Language and Law*], *Dewan Bahasa*, 1991.12.3–4. [Viewed Arkib Negara, Kuala Lumpur].

Abdul Malik Abdul Hakim. (2004, August 20). *Mahkamah abai bahasa Melayu?* [Court neglecting Malay?] *Utusan Online*. Accessed 21 Feb 2012, from http://www.utusan.com.my/utusan/info.asp?y=2004&dt=0820&pub=utusan_malaysia&sec=Rencana&pg=re_07.htm

Adelaar, Alexander K. (1996). Malay: Its role and spread. In S. A. Wurm, P. Mühlhäusler, & D. T. Tyron (Eds.), *Atlas of languages of intercultural communication in the Pacific, Asia, and the Americas* (pp. 673–693). Berlin/New York: Mouton de Gruyter

Adelaar, Alexander K. (2000, 2). Malay: A short history. *Oriente Moderno, XIX* (LXXX), 225–242.

Altay, Ayfer. (2002). Difficulties encountered in the translation of legal texts: The Case of Turkey. *The Translation Journal 6*(4). Accessed 10 Sept 2004, from http://accurapid.com/journal/22legal.htm

Alber, Elisabeth., & Palermo, Francesco. (2012). Creating, studying and experimenting with bilingual law in South Tyrol: Lost in interpretation. In Xabier Arzoz (Ed.), *Bilingual higher education in the legal context. Group rights, state policies and globalisation*. Martinus Nijhoff: Leiden.

Asmah Haji Omar. (2004). *Muafakat Bahasa: Sejarah MBIM/MABBIM sebagai Pembina Bahasa* [*Language agreement: a history of MBIM/MABBIM as language-builders*]. Kuala Lumpur: Dewan Bahasa dan Pustaka.

Awang bin Sariyan. [Direct-General, Dewan Bahasa] (2013, November 30) .*Memperkasa Sistem Perundangan Negara melalui Bahasa Melayu* [Empowering the legal system through Malay]. Keynote paper presented at *Ceramah Memperkasa Sistem Perundangan Negara melalui Bahasa Melayu* [Forum on empowering the legal system through Malay]. Malaysian Bar Council, Kuala Lumpur.

Bangla Academy. (2014). Official website accessed 30 Jan 2014, from http://www.banglaacademy.org.bd [Bangla pages translated by Dr Mahmud Hasan, University of Liberal Arts, Dhaka].

Berita Harian (1995, January, 13). *Perundangan: Malaysia kaji istilah Indonesia* [Law: Malaysia studying Indonesian terminology], p. 12.

Bhatia, Vijay. (1993). *Analysing genre. Language use in professional settings*. London/New York: Longman.

Bourdieu, Pierre. (1982). *Ce que parler veut dire. L'économie des échanges linguistiques* [*What speech means. The economics of linguistic exchange*]. Paris: Arthème Fayard.

Ćapeta, Tamara. (2009). Multilingual law and judicial interpretation in the EU. In L. Sočanac (Ed.), *Curriculum, multilingualism and the law*. Zagreb: Nakladni zavod Globus.

Cooper, Robert. L. (1989). *Language planning and social change*. Cambridge: Cambridge University Press. *Planning across the curriculum*. Clevedon: Multilingual Matters.

Coperahewa, Sandagomi (2011). The language situation in Sri Lanka. In Kaplan & Baldauf (Eds.), *Language planning in the Asia Pacific:Hong Kong, Timor-Leste and Sri Lanka* (pp. 160–241). Abingdon: Routledge.

Crown Law Tonga. (2013). Official portal of Tongan Justice Department. Accessed 12 Sept 2013, from www.crownlaw.gov.to/

Det, C. H. E. (1949, April 24). Malay – "modern" and standard. *The Straits Times*, p. 6.

Dewan Bahasa dan Pustaka. (1986). *Istilah undang-undang* [Legal terminology]. Kuala Lumpur: Dewan Bahasa dan Pustaka.

Durant, Alan. (2013). *The interaction between ordinary and technical language in the functioning of law*. Paper presented at 11th Biennial Conference on Forensic Linguistics (IAFL), Mexico City, June 2013.

Fairclough, Norman. (2003). *Analysing discourse. Textual analysis for social research*. London: Routledge.

Faiza Tamby Chik. (1993). Language and the law: The role of Malay and English in legal education and the practice of law. In K. L. Tee (Ed.), *Legal education in Malaysia quo Vadis?* (pp. 103–107). Kuala Lumpur: University of Malaya.

Farabi Said. (2013, September 30). Guan Eng:2 ahli DAP fail writ saman [Guan Eng:2 DAP members file writ of summons]. *Mingguan Malaysia*, p. 14.

Fuller, Janet. (1993). Hearing between the lines: style switching in a courtroom setting. *Pragmatics, 3*(1), 29–43.

Gill, Saran Kaur. (2005). Language policy in Malaysia: Reversing direction. *Language Policy, 4*, 241–260.

Goodrich, Peter. (1984). Law and language: An historical and critical introduction. *Journal of Law and Society, 11*(2), 173–195.

Grey, Peter. (2013). *Is advocacy an art?* Paper presented at 11th Biennial Conference on Forensic Linguistics (IAFL), Mexico City, June 2013.

Halliday, M. A. K. (2001). Literacy and linguistics: relationships between spoken and written language. In Burns & Coffin (Eds.), *Analysing English in a global context* (pp. 181–193). London: Routledge.

Hawa Abdullah. (1992). *General guidelines for the formation of terms in Malay*. Kuala Lumpur: Dewan Bahasa dan Pustaka.

Heah Lee Hsia, Carmen. (1989). *The influence of English on the lexical expansion of Bahasa Malaysia*. Kuala Lumpur: Dewan Bahasa dan Pustaka/Malaysian Ministry of Education.

Kamarul Zaman Shaharudin, Rossilawaty Sheriff, Sa'odah Abdullah, Mohamed Hamizi Ghazali, & Ismail Karmun. (2003). *Citra*. Kuala Lumpur: Dewan Bahasa dan Pustaka.

Kaplan, Robert, & Baldauf, Richard. (1997). *Language planning from practice to theory*. Clevedon: Multilingual Matters.

Kloss, Heinz. (1969). *Research possibilities on group bilingualism: A report*. Québec: Université Laval, Centre International de recherches sur le bilinguisme.

Koh Jun Lin. (2015, September 23). *Small change in constitution confused nation on Islam*. Accessed 30 Sept 2015, from http://www.malaysiakini.com/news/313218

Koshy, Shaila. (2013, September 15). Language makes the law. *The Star* (Online edition). Accessed 15 Sept 2013, from http://www.thestar.com.my/News/Nation/2013/09/15/Education-Tun-Zaki-English-Medium-Schools.aspx

Kurzon, Dennis. (2013). Foreign and archaic phrases in legal texts. *The International Journal of Speech, Language and the Law, 20*(1), 117–142.

Lavendran, G. (2013, June 13). Bar Council: Translating Constitution causing confusion. *Free Malaysia Today*. Accessed 14 June 2013, from http://www.freemalaysiatoday.com/category/nation/2013/06/18/bar-council-translating-constitution-causing-confusion/

Leibniz, Gottfried Wilhelm von. (1683/1917). *Ermahnung an die Deutschen. Von deutscher Sprachpflege* [Admonition to the Germans: On German language cultivation]. Darmstadt: Wissenschaftliche Buchgesellschaft.

Lemmens, Koen. (2011). The slow dynamics of legal language. Festina lente? *Terminology, 17*(1), 74–93.

Lo Bianco, Joseph. (2001). Viet Nam: Quoc Ngu, colonialism and language policy. In N. Gottlieb & P. Chen (Eds.), *Language planning and language policy: East Asian perspectives* (pp. 159–206). Richmond, Surrey: Curzon Press.

Lo Bianco, Joseph. (2005). Globalisation and national communities of communication. *Language Problems and Language Planning, 29*(2), 109–133.

Majlis Peguam. (2016). *Bar Council Annual Report 2015/16.*

Martin, Isabel Pefianco. (2012). Expanding the role of Philippine languages in the legal system: The dim prospects. *Asian Perspectives in the Arts and Humanities, 2*(1), 1–14.

Mashudi Kader. (1994). Peristilahan Undang-Undang [Legal Terminology]. In Nik Safiah Karim & Faiza Tamby Chik (Eds.), *Bahasa dan Undang-Undang* (pp. 81–91). Kuala Lumpur: Dewan Bahasa dan Pustaka.

Mead, Richard. (1988). *Malaysia's National language policy and the legal system.* New Haven: Yale.

Nencioni, Giovanni. (1986). L'Accademia della Crusca e la lingua italiana. In P. Ramat, H.-J. Niederehe, & K. Koerner (Eds.), *The history of linguistics in Italy* (pp. 107–120). Amsterdam: Benjamins.

New Straits Times. (1981, October 21). Bahasa test for lawyers likely, p. 3.

Ng Kwai. Hang. (2009). *The common law in two voices. Language, law and the postcolonial dilemma in Hong Kong.* Stanford: Stanford University Press.

Nik Abdul Rashid Majid. (1989). *Keupayaan Bahasa Melayu sebagai Bahasa Undang-undang* [The capability of Malay as a legal language]. *Seminar Kebangsaan Undang-undang: Isu Bahasa dan Common law* [*Seminar on national law: the issue of language and common law*]. Kuala Lumpur: Dewan Bahasa dan Pustaka.

P. Dev Anand Pillai. (2015, November 23). We can't do without English. *Malaysiakini.* Accessed 24 Nov 2015, from http://www.malaysiakini.com/letters/320664

Powell, Richard. (2004). Terminological creation and language shift in Malaysia's legal system. *Current Issues in Language Planning, 5*(3), 109–130.

Powell, Richard. (2012, July 4–7). *Legal vernacularisation and access to justice.* Paper presented at the Asian regional conference of the International Association of Forensic Linguists, Kuala Lumpur.

Šarćevič, Susan. (1997). *New approach to legal translation.* The Hague: Kluwer Law International.

Spolsky, Bernard. (2004). *Language policy.* Cambridge: Cambridge University Press.

Teeuw, Andries. (1959). The history of the Malay language. A preliminary survey. *Bijdragen tot de taal-, land- en volkenkunde, 115*(2), 138–156. Accessed 10 Nov 2011, from http://www.kitv-journals.nl

The Singapore Free Press. (1960, June 30). Start Malay in the courts now, says Dr Zainal, p. 3.

The Star Online. (2013, August 7). Abdul Hamid: Proficiency in English vital to legal sector. Accessed 10 Aug 2013, from http://www.thestar.com.my/News/Nation/2013/08/07/Abdul-Hamid-Proficiency-in-English-vital-to-excel-in-legal-sector.aspx

The Straits Times. (1959, August 24). Malay for courts? 'Not now', p. 7.

The Straits Times. (1960, June 24). Malay is not accurate enough for all courts, says Leong, p. 2.

The Straits Times. (1962, December 2). Keep expats in law dept – plea by the PPP, p. 14.

The Straits Times. (1963, February 1). Malay can be used in lower courts- Sheridan, p. 4.

The Straits Times. (1964a, January 27). Bureau to put law papers in national language, p. 5.

The Straits Times. (1964b, December 4). Why bills must be in two languages: Tengku, p. 1.

The Straits Times. (1966, July 18). New words won't corrupt language: Expert, p. 11.

The Straits Times. (1967, March 3). Language: I have chosen the peaceful way, p. 8.

The Straits Times. (1979, November 27). Speeding up the move to translate laws into Bahasa, p. 12.
The Straits Times. (1989, November 6). Translation of laws into Bahasa Malaysia being speeded up, p. 11.
The Straits Times. (2002, March 9). Experts aim to protect Bahasa from foreign terms, p. 22.
Tiersma, Peter. (1999). *Legal language*. Chicago: University of Chicago Press.
Utusan Malaysia. (1983, April 26). *Penggunaan Bahasa Malaysia di mahkamah tak perlu dilaksana segera* [Use of Malay in courts need not be implemented immediately], p. 5.
Utusan Malaysia. (1984, June 2). Permohonan jadi peguam tanpa ujian bahasa Malaysia ditolak [Application to become lawyer without Malay test rejected], p. 3.
Utusan Malaysia. (1985, January 7). *Penggunaan Bahasa Malaysia di bidang kehakiman gambaran krisis intelektual* [Use of Malay in field of law depicts intellectual crisis], p. 7.
Yusof Ghani. (2002, August 2). Opponents of English policy invited to roadshow. *Malaysiakini*. Accessed 30 Mar 2011, from http://malaysiakini.com/news/12595
Zaiton Ab. Rahman, & Ramlah Muhamad. (1994). *Penterjemahan karya undang-undang* [Translating the law]. In Nik Safiah Karim & Faiza Tamby Chik (Eds.), *Bahasa dan Undang-Undang* (pp. 113–121). Kuala Lumpur: Dewan Bahasa dan Pustaka.
Zubaidah Ibrahim. (2002). *Court interpreting in Malaysia in relation to language planning and policy*. Unpublished doctoral thesis, Universiti Malaya. [Viewed Universiti Malaya].

Chapter 5
Acquisition Planning

You have a system of law that came from England, but then you have the local education system, and one year everything will be in English and the next everything will be in Malay, so there's no stability, and you change one thing in one place and something will change somewhere else.

Shah Alam law student (2014.3.10)

We emphasise English here because it is where the market demand is. They'll have a chance to practise their legal Malay during pupillage. And it's not that difficult since it's mostly for the lower courts.

East Coast law lecturer (2014.2.20)

5.1 Bilingualism and Language-in-Education Policies

In positioning bilingual lawyers at the heart of the Malaysian legal model, this investigation is particularly interested in how English-Malay professional competence is planned and supported. While law schools and legal offices are key sites for the acquisition of legal lexis and discourses, the capacity of young lawyers to work in two languages is heavily dependent on the *general* language education they receive. In this chapter it will be shown that the ability to use Malay for legal tasks is widely presumed to have been covered by general schooling, thereby making English the main medium and concern of legal education and professional training. It is a presumption based partly on the roles of the two languages in the education system and partly on how they are employed in the legal domain.

The LPP (language planning) paradigm is rarely applied to use-based language varieties such as legalese. The preponderance of research targets acquisition or maintenance of user-based varieties for national education or minority speech communities. Inasmuch as the majority of Malaysian lawyers come to the profession with a general academic bilingualism inculcated at primary and secondary school, before looking at law faculty and professional language policies we need to review

R. Powell, *Language Choice in Postcolonial Law*, Language Policy 22,
https://doi.org/10.1007/978-981-15-1173-8_5

Malaysia's intricate language-in-education policies in order to bring exegetic context to the bilingual experiences of lawyers, students and lecturers.

Malaysian LPP researchers perennially characterise acquisition planning there as a compromise between integrative and instrumental factors (e.g. Asmah 1979; Gill 2005). However, in view of Bourdieusian accounts of how social environments reproduce unequal distributions of linguistic capital in ways that are neither entirely forced nor entirely free, studies elsewhere have moved beyond dichotomising the integrative and instrumental components of language acquisition to focusing on the psychological, social and material investments that learners make. Norton (2001:159), for example, draws on Benedict Anderson's concept of imagined communities in arguing that investment in a target language is also investment in one's own identity and status (ibid:166). The extent to which people feel accepted in the community they envisage joining can be critical to their language proficiency (ibid:169). This study is interested in how law students, in employing two languages to attain academic knowledge and vocational skills, are motivated in their language preferences by perceptions of the professional culture they are orientating themselves toward.

Malaysia has a complex state education system reflecting three well-established yet fluctuating policy orientations that continue to cohabit uneasily: partial recognition of multiculturalism through 'vernacular' primary schools; the goal of universal competence in both the national language and English; and affirmative action on behalf of the majority Malay community, which is constructed as economically disadvantaged and educationally underperforming.

5.1.1 Vernacular Schooling

From the perspective of global common law this study uses 'vernacular' to refer to Malay. But within Malaysia itself the term is reserved for languages other than the national language, with vernacular schooling usually meaning Mandarin or Tamil. It never refers to English, even though that is the first language of many urbanites (Pillai 2006) as well as an additional medium in state schools and the main medium of private schools. 'Vernacular' is often conflated with 'mother tongue', yet many pupils in vernacular schools have a different home language from the one they study in.

MOI (medium of instruction) was a key issue in national identity debates during the pre-independence decade. The 1951 Barnes Committee recommended single stream education in Malay or English (Tate 2008:165), declaring these the natural choices of those "who regard Malaya as their permanent home" (cited by Wade 2009), whereas the Fenn-Wu Committee of the same year found Chinese-medium schooling consistent with Malayan national consciousness (Kua 1999:6). The Central Advisory Committee (Federation of Malaya 1951) hedged, proposing instruction in English, Malay or both with some provision for spoken and later for written Mandarin and Tamil. It was more forthright in declaring that the "last racially segregated Vernacular primary school in Malaya will close when the parents of the children attending it believe that a local national school would provide a more acceptable education" (ibid:6). To this day this argument is heard from parents who decide against sending their children to Malay-medium state schools.

The system adopted at independence reflected the 1956 Razak Report's proposals for Malay 'national' primary and secondary schools, English, Chinese and Tamil 'national-type' primary schools and English and Chinese 'national-type' secondary schools, both Malay and English to be compulsory subjects throughout (Tate 2008:165–166). Unity was to be achieved through a common syllabus (Andaya and Andaya 1982:239) as much as a common language. The 1996 Education Act (s.17(1)) also reaffirmed the principle of making Chinese or Tamil available as a subject at national schools where parents of at least 15 pupils requested it, with the same provision for "indigenous languages" if "reasonable and practicable" allowing the teaching of East Malaysian languages such as Iban.

There has never been provision for Tamil secondary education. Although proposals to instate it continue to be raised (Aw 2013b.12.01), Tamil language nationalists come up against others who question the language's instrumental value for an ethnic community that is disproportionately affected by social deprivation (Appudurai and Dass 2008:47–49). Some call for the abandonment of Tamil after Standard 3 in order to facilitate integration into Malay secondary schools (Tate 2008:174–175), others for outright abolition (Tong 2003.4.07). Another divisive factor is the largely anglophone outlook of the Indian elite. While the Tamil-speaking grass roots have become increasingly important for the MIC (Tate 2008:175), the phasing out of English education in the 1970s brought stronger reactions than any policies to restrict Tamil, the middle class seeing this, alongside pro-Malay economic measures, as eroding their influence in professions such as law (ibid:168). The picture Tate (ibid:177) paints of Indian lawyers enjoying gracious living in the 1960s is to some extent borne out by their high profile in the pages of *Insaf* from that period, a Malaysian bar journal replete with advertisements for expensive cars and imported alcohol. But nowadays "the rat race ha[s] become a reality for lawyers, doctors, accountants and business executives" (ibid:177). UM lecturers admit the traditional 10% allotment for Indian students has not been filled for many years. Meanwhile high drop-out rates and painful transitions to secondary education plague Indian vernacular schools (Appudurai and Dass 2008:25–26). Currently, only 152 of the remaining 524 Tamil schools receive full government funding (*Malaysiakini* 2014a.2.12). Seven of the Indian lawyers interviewed for this study had Tamil ancestry but none, including a Tamil court interpreter's son (KVL4), had attended a vernacular school.

In contrast, Chinese schools thrive, perpetually enflaming discussion of what Kua (1999:5) dubs the "inseparable issues of language and citizenship". Official policy appears to have assumed they would gradually fade away. As Barisan Nasional learned to expect less support from Chinese voters, calls from some UMNO ranks to abolish the schools (Aw 2013a.5.12) or withdraw state funding from them (*Malaysiakini* 2013a.6.11) grew. Incorporating the Taib Committee's recommendations to phase out funding for national-type secondary schools, the

1961 Education Act led to half the Chinese secondary schools converting to Malay and the rest going independent, with a further blow coming from derecognition of Chinese-medium exam qualifications (Kua 1999:9). When the ninth Malaysia Plan proposed nationalising all remaining partially-funded schools, vernacular educationalists scoffed that 'national-type secondary schools' no longer existed anyway (Puah 2004.8.17). Yet partial funding continues, evincing government interest in maintaining administrative control and gaining some votes. Torn between abandoning Chinese voters and wooing them back, after the last election the government promised at least to continue paying teachers' salaries (Koh 2013.10.30). Leading up to the 2018 general election BN also promised to recognise the Unified Examinations Certificate for university entrance for students who had obtained a credit in Malay language (*Malaysiakini* 2018.4.08), although it remained vague as to whether an exam set by independent Chinese schools since 1975 and recognised by some institutions overseas would be admitted by national universities.

Despite the mixed messages from the government, Chinese-medium schools have not only maintained their importance for the Chinese but, according to a report by Dong Jiao Zong (the Federation of Chinese School Boards, published by the Centre for Public Policy Studies 2017) are increasingly popular with non-Chinese pupils, whose participation schools rose from 12% in 2010 to 15% in 2014. In urban areas as many as 33% are Malay (Zainul Arifin 2012.9.19), which suggests they attract parents unable to afford the English-dominated private sector but seeking better education than the Malay-medium national schools provide.

In some locations Chinese culture and language also pervade national schools. Several Chinese students at UM's law faculty described the Malay-medium schools they had attended as having a 'strong Chinese culture', with Mandarin used extensively outside the classroom. One Malaysian Indian lecturer at the faculty recounted how she had had to withdraw her daughter from a national school in a Chinese catchment area because so much Mandarin was being used both inside and outside class.

Transition from national-type primary school to national secondary school may be difficult, especially if Chinese students have to shift social communication, as well as learning, into Malay. But two law students said they had not needed to fall back on the additional Malay language classes provided for them as they had picked up enough Malay from daily life. Reports of Chinese pupils scoring higher than Malays in BM exams go back decades (Mead 1988:38), and Kua (1999:x) writes of the pragmatism of Chinese in learning Malay "naturally and legitimately as a second language". Whereas a KL-based Chinese lawyer interviewed in December, 2013 remembered working hard at school to get good marks in Malay but thereafter finding little use for it in professional life, a newly qualified advocate from Johor Bahru called it his "second mother tongue".[1]

With many Chinese informants confident in their Malay, and several Malay informants confessing to difficulties when using it formally, this study bears out

[1] Interviewed 2013.12.

others (David 2003; Powell 2008) in finding linkage between ethnicity and language proficiency in the legal profession to be weak (see Chap. 6). Discursive links between medium of instruction and nationalist politics remain strong, however.

In 1965 the Minister of Information accused proponents of multilingual education of ignoring the "interests of the people in general" (*The Straits Times* 1965.7.27). In *Merdeka University* (1982) the Federal Court sided with the government by interpreting constitutional Article 152(1)'s prohibition on *official* use of other languages as ruling out the establishment of a predominantly Chinese-medium private university. The 1987 Ops Lalang incarceration of educationalists, NGO activists and (mostly opposition) politicians followed Chinese protests and Malay backlashes surrounding proposals to appoint non-Mandarin-speaking Malay administrators for Chinese schools (Kua 1999:12). When curricular reforms to strengthen Malay, or English, entail reduced hours for Mandarin in school they are routinely interpreted as moves to curtail vernacular education. Indeed some UMNO voices call for just that (*Utusan Malaysia* 2001.3.19; *Malaysiakini* 2011.10.12), even though the government denies any agenda to phase out Chinese instruction (Tan 2004.12.20). The majority of *Kempen Satu Sekolah untuk Semua* ('one school for all campaign') petitioners are Malay and support unity through instruction in the national language (Kempen Satu Sekolah 2013). Several ethnic Chinese practitioners, including a partner interviewed in a small firm in Ipoh and a young lawyer from a medium-sized Penang practice, commented that since Malay and English are now taken for granted in the legal profession, proficiency in Mandarin was becoming an important asset for prospective employees. The latter also mentioned that many Chinese colleagues who had been educated in English or Malay were sending their own children to Mandarin schools.

5.1.2 The National Language and the 'Second Language'

While Mandarin's heightened international instrumentality is a relatively recent challenge to the hegemony of the national language, English has always been regarded as competitor in a range of domains. In the early years following independence, Malay primary education had low status and its best pupils went on to English secondary schools (Abdul Rahman 2007:162). Some educated only in Malay did succeed in going on to lecturing posts in technical colleges but former prime ministerial secretary Ahmad Mustapha Hassan (2007:13–14) recalls even ethnic Malay teachers punishing children for speaking Malay as they thought it would never achieve true national status (ibid:117). The 1958 National Language Seminar to promote Malay was actually conducted in English (ibid:135).

Asmah (1979:19) concludes that the new nation couldn't afford the potential divisiveness of bilingualism and on a level playing field Malay couldn't have competed against English (ibid:55). Hence restrictions on the use of the latter were phased in from the 1960s and 1970s. Malaya's English primary and secondary schools were converted to Malay medium by 1976 and 1985 respectively, with a similar conversion process in Borneo after a 4 - year time lag (ibid:23). This delayed phasing in of Malay, along with a distinct political and ethnic identity, means that the possibility of reviving English-medium state schooling is even now raised more often in East Malaysia than Malaya (*Malaysiakini* 2016.2.26).

One ethnic Chinese law lecturer at UM felt that entering the school system in the period when everything was switching over to Malay had left him lacking confidence in English, even though it was his preferred medium for legal writing. An ethnic Malay KL lawyer in her forties recalled starting at an English-medium school when Malay was being introduced for the humanities in Malaya, relocating to Sarawak because of her father's work, where everything was still in English, then returning to her old school in KL a few years later to find all subjects in Malay.

Following the 1969 communal riots, a pass in Malay was made compulsory for the Certificate of Education and for government employment (Ting 2010:400). While this pushed some Chinese toward private (Mead 1988:34) or overseas (Ting 2010:401) employment, a former UM lecturer involved in human rights law felt it may have boosted Mandarin rather than English proficiency among the Chinese as more of them began to be attracted to Taiwan and elsewhere. Older informants recalled private education as out of reach, except for the elite, but today 'international' schools are booming. According to a report by the International School Consultancy Malaysia has the highest proportion of children attending such schools in Southeast Asia (*Malaysiakini* 2017.3.17). Undoubtedly this is partly because of their use of English, but it also reflects disillusionment with the quality national schools which, according to PKR Youth Leader Nik Nazmi,[2] are widely perceived as decreasingly academic and decreasingly secular. Nevertheless the private sector remains too costly for many urban and most rural parents (Toh 2012.5.14). In addition to financial burdens, leaving state education has long-term consequences as their different exam structures, in addition to different media of instruction, channel pupils away from national universities toward education abroad or in local/overseas twinning programmes.

Although 50% of the lawyers in this investigation had studied law in private institutions or overseas (compared with 60% for the bar as a whole),[3] most had attended state primary and high schools, with two thirds undergoing Malay-medium primary education. One officer from the Legal and Professional Qualification Board suspected that BM test scores exaggerated proficiency levels because of the memory-based format of exams, given the problems reported in formal written communication, very few lawyer informants apart from a handful of the more senior practitioners rated their Malay as poor. For almost all of them, English standards were of much greater concern. For former bar president Steven Thiru,[4] the competitive relationship between Malay and English meant that with higher standards imposed for the former, including a requirement to pass the Malay test on the SPM

[2] Interviewed in Shah Alam, 2013.10, when he was Deputy Speaker of the Selangor Assembly.

[3] Majlis Peguam (2013).

[4] Interviewed when vice president, 2013.8.

exam in order to get a school-leaving certificate, it was inevitable that students had less time to focus on the latter. Given the importance of language in general for lawyers and of English in particular for common law, Thiru's remarks might be thought to reflect the special position of law, but they are often voiced in other professions. In 2015, for example, it was reported that 1000 medical students had dropped out primarily because of their lack of English (*Malaysiakini* 2015.11.09).

Despite the perennial alarm calls, individual accounts from informants for this study add up to a picture of English resilience – even in state education. For a *bumiputera* minority Junior Science Colleges offer the Cambridge International General Certificate of Secondary Education in addition to the SPM. While vaunting the educational opportunities they give to bright children from rural areas, they cover only 2% of the secondary school population and according to DAP MP Ko Chung Sen (in Aidila 2013.11.07), many of these are from wealthy backgrounds.

The anglophone and anglophile outlook of many national schools in middle-class catchment areas is another sector helping to maintain English. One Melaka advocate recalled it being the main language spoken outside the classroom at her Malay-medium school and found she was further encouraged to maintain high standards at the former Catholic school she went on to, while her colleague from the same city recounted enthusiasm for the language being reinforced by the stance of the PTA.[5] Several other informants, including a UM lecturer and a Johor Bahru lawyer, described English being used outside and even inside the classroom in Malay-medium schools, with the stock of novels in the library mainly in English even if textbooks were in Malay.

In addition to Junior Science Colleges and the middle-class urban national schools encouraging gifted or wealthier children to excel in English, it should not be forgotten that the language has long been a compulsory subject in both national and national-type schools (a stance reaffirmed by the 1996 Education Act, s.17). Measures to stem the decline of English go back as far as the nationalistic 1970s (Mead 1988:30), when it was promoted as a "strong second language" (third Malaysia Plan, in Mukherjee and David 2011:17) even as Malay was being prioritised, and support for English can be found among some considering themselves Malay nationalists (*The Straits Times* 1990.6.30).

The most comprehensive and controversial instrument promoting English was PPSMI (*Pengajaran dan Pembelajaran Sains dan Matematik dalam Bahasa Inggeris*), which required it for science and maths classes from 2002 until the policy was phased out a decade later. Introduced at the end of Mahathir's premiership and consistent with his tendency to prioritise economic over cultural development, the PPSMI opened up fault lines in public opinion that did not neatly follow political or communal divisions. In general the diverse opposition were more united against the policy than the government was united behind it. Malay-majority PKR and PAS backed Chinese teachers association Dong Jiao Zong's stand on mother tongue education (Yusof Ghani 2002.8.15), as did a number of Tamil NGOs (Kuek 2005.12.09)

[5] Both interviewed at the Melaka bar offices, 2014.4.

despite MIC's official support for the policy (Yusof Ghani 2002.8.02). Samuel et al. (2012.2–3) note that *The Star*, an MCA mouthpiece, focused on PPSMI's threat to Mandarin when PPSMI was first introduced (eventually Chinese schools were allowed to teach the subjects in Chinese as well as English), but shifted to calls to retain English when it seemed that Malay was to be reintroduced.

While many lawyers disliked maths at school (Chap. 7), routine drafting of higher performing pupils into the science stream means that under PPSMI most recent law graduates spent more time studying in English than in Malay at high school. Some UM law students seemed weary of the politicised fluctuations of medium of instruction policies, but many took a pragmatic stance. Several Chinese students thought they were more burdened that other groups as they had had Mandarin, as well as Malay and English, to cope with, but acknowledged the support of teachers who code-switched in class to make sure they understood English materials. One student said his teachers had anticipated the policy by introducing more English even before PPSMI was official. Similarly, several Malay students recalled their teachers orally explaining English content in Malay.

Most of the 1st- and 2nd-year student informants had been at school during the phasing out of PPSMI, when pupils who had started in English were given the choice of continuing with it. The fact that most take up the option has been touted in some quarters of the press as a sign of the language's instrumentality in employment (*The Star* 2009.2.30). However, students generally took a shorter-term view, saying that in order to get through their school exams it made more sense to stick to the language in which more materials were available. In practice English-medium instruction lingers on in different guises, such as the recent Dual Language and Higher Immersive programmes (Wan Saiful 2016.2.11). A number of political leaders, including former International Trade and Industry Minister Rafidah Aziz (Koh Jun Lin 2015.11.18), have come out in favour of bilingual education, with science and "anything that has got to do with international exposure" in English.

5.1.3 Affirmative Action

Justified in principle by constitutional Article 153's assertion of the Malays' "special position", but controversial in detail (Kua 2014.5.26), educational affirmative action has enabled more Malays than ever before to enter universities and hence professions such as law, but at the same time it has encouraged them to use more English. One lecturer interviewed in Melaka suggested provisions to help Malays were specifically targeted at helping them overcome the disadvantage in English they have traditionally perceived themselves as suffering from. Among the measures in place, Kua (2002:21) highlights *bumiputera* monopoly of state loans for domestic and foreign degrees, while Wade (2009) emphasises the role of the quotas introduced in 1998 for public university admissions. UiTM overtly reserves 100% of places for *bumiputera* (*Malaysiakini* 2008.8.13). Rumours of the survival of covert quotas elsewhere draw complaints from Chinese (Lee 2013.7.22) and Indian

(Palanasamy 2013.7.15) politicians even within BN. The Legal Profession Qualifying Board insists vehemently that the CLP (Certificate of Legal Practice) results reflect exam scores and nothing else (LPQB 2013, MYP3), with one administrator who had worked there complaining that dealing with allegations of ethnically-skewed adjustments was a consequence of such practices being followed elsewhere.

Subtler forms of affirmative action are also influential. According to Wade (2009), 90% of scholarships for overseas study are earmarked for *bumi*, and several lecturers at both UM and MMU acknowledged the greater difficulty non-Malays experience in getting funding for undergraduate and postgraduate study. Differential university entrance procedures also play their part. Those entering by the STPM (*Sijil Tinggi Persekolahan Malaysia*) exam normally taken at the age of 19 after 2 years of study are more likely to be Chinese since alternative routes, viewed as easier by many Chinese (and some Malay) students, are generally unavailable to them, including *matrikulasi* (matriculation) and *asasi* (foundation) courses run at residential colleges reserved for Malays. *Sekolah Kluster*, *Teknik* and *Agama* (cluster, technical and religious schools) complete a network of pre-tertiary boarding schools catering to Malays selected from mainstream schools. To prevent a surge in non-*bumi* intake when direct ethnic quotas were dropped in 2002, UM was required to allocate a proportion of places to *asasi* students, and many of its law students come from UiTM's law foundation. UIA (International Islamic University) does admit non-Muslims into its LLB programme and is attractive because of its low fees, but according to one Chinese lawyer who chose UIA primarily for financial reasons, the bulk of places are for Malays.[6]

The *asasi* and *matrikulasi* system has undoubtedly helped reduce traditional Malay weaknesses in English. With the exception of religious schools, residential colleges use it as their main medium. A Johor Bahru lawyer who did pre-law at UiTM before going on to UM's law faculty, and a Terengganu lawyer who got her law degree from UiTM, both attested that English was almost exclusively used for the law *asasi* at that university, which is open only to *bumiputera*. Two other Terengganu lawyers confirmed that English was the medium of UIA's law *matrikulasi*.

With the help of scholarships, residential colleges channel a growing percentage of Malays toward foreign universities. In some local public universities this has had the effect of reducing the number of high-performing Malays, inadvertently reinforcing the stereotype of Chinese success. But it is in private schools that non-*bumi* presence is most obvious. An ethnic Chinese lawyer who had done her pre-law and LLB programmes at ATC (Advanced Tertiary College) and a Malay lawyer who had attended HELP University both recalled most of their fellow students being Chinese or Indian and felt that this, along with the medium of instruction, helped to push social interactions into English – something that Malay-dominated public sector schools such as UiTM also encourage through informal rules, according to a recently

[6] Interviewed in Ipoh, 2013.1.

qualified advocate from Johor. However, another HELP graduate, now working in corporate law, remembered half the Chinese students preferring to use Mandarin among themselves.

5.2 Language Proficiency and Bar Admission

As shown in Fig. 5.1 below, bar entry can be gained directly through an approved law degree from four local public universities (UIA, UiTM, UKM, UM), one local private university (MMU), from NUS in Singapore, or via English and Irish solicitor's and bar examinations. Provided a bar-approved training course is completed, graduates of UUM may also be admitted. Entry can be achieved with a degree from UniSZA, London University's external programme or 49 approved institutions in Australia, Britain and New Zealand if the CLP (Certificate of Legal Practice) is then passed (LPQB 2013).

According to a UM law lecturer who had graduated from the same department she was teaching in, the CLP was inaugurated in 1984 primarily to give Malaysians studying overseas another way of entering the Malaysian bar after Britain made an upper second-class degree or above a requirement to enter the barrister's or solicitor's course there. Nowadays, however, many CLP candidates study partly or entirely in Malaysia at private colleges such as HELP that offer London University's external LLB. Originally available only in English, the CLP can now be taken in Malay. There is no Chinese version of the exam, but in 2018 the Legal Professional Qualifying Board agreed to allow candidates holding the largely Chinese-medium Unified Examinations Certificate to sit the exam provided they also had three credits at SPM or O Level. In 2019 the requirement was raised to five credits (*Malaysiakini* 2019.3.30).

At least three regulatory systems ensure those entering the profession have a certain level of bilingualism. First, the government makes Malay proficiency a condition for entry to most tertiary institutions. Second, law-teaching institutions themselves, including those overseas, require proof of adequate English. Third, the legal profession imposes a Malay requirement on anyone who, typically by studying overseas, has failed to gain a formal qualification in Malay. Whether the level of Malay thereby imposed is sufficient for legal practice is keenly debated.

5.3 Language Checkpoints at Colleges and Universities

Apart from exemptions for international students, there is a Malay language requirement to enter public universities. In most cases it is fulfilled by the SPM exams, sat around age 17, as the Malay paper, alongside history (which is taught in Malay) must be passed to earn full SPM certification and this in turn is normally required for the various routes (STPM, *matrikulasi* or *asasi*) into university. A July Paper

(Sources: LPQB, 2013; university websites as in references)

Qualification	Institution	Location	Notes
APPROVED LLB FROM MALAYSIAN PUBLIC UNIVERSITY	**UM** Universiti Malaya	KL	Law programme since 1972 CLP exemption.
	UKM Universiti Kebangsaan Malaysia	Selangor	Law programme since 1984. CLP exemption.
	UiTM Universiti Teknologi MARA	Selangor	Law programme since 1968 (for London degree); 3-yr ordinary LLB + final year to attain LLB (hons.) for Bar admission. CLP exemption.
	UIA Universiti Islam Antarabangsa/IIU	Selangor	Law programme since1981. CLP exemption.
	UUM Universiti Utara Malaysia	Kedah	Law programme since 2003. CLP exemption if take BC training course
	UniSZA University Sultan Zainal Abiddin	Terengganu	Law programme since 2009. CLP exemption.
APPROVED LLB FROM MALAYSIAN PRIVATE UNIVERSITY	**MMU** Multimedia University	Melaka	Law programme since 2004 CLP exemption.
APPROVED LLB FROM SINGAPORE	**National University of Singapore**	Singapore	(Formerly part of UM.) Malaya's first law dept.1957. CLP exemption.
APPROVED EXTERNAL LLB FROM MALAYSIAN PRIVATE UNIVERSITY/ COLLEGE	**Brickfields Asia** **HELP** **ATC**	KL Selangor Selangor Selangor	University of London the only external LLB that can be taken entirely in Malaysia (as well as partly overseas). LLB holders approved for, but not exempt from, the CLP exam. Several colleges (including ATC, Brickfields, HELP) have CLP preparation programmes. A number of Malaysian institutes (e.g. Taylor's University) currently in negotiation with LPQB for approval for graduates to sit CLP.
BARRISTER-AT-LAW	**Inner Temple** **Middle Temple** **Grey's Inn** **Lincoln's Inn** **King's Inn**	London (4) Dublin (1)	CLP exemption.
SOLICITOR	**Law Society of England and Wales**	England	CLP exemption.
APPROVED AUSTRALIA, NEW ZEALAND & UK LLB	**Currently 49 universities**		At least Second Class Lower Honours. LLB holders not exempt from CLP.

Fig. 5.1 Malaysian bar admission

gives those who failed school Malay a second chance. UM, UKM, UiTM and UIA require at least a credit (grade C) on the SPM Malay paper (Universiti Malaya 2013; Universiti Kebangsaan Malaysia 2013; Universiti Teknologi MARA 2013; Universiti Islam Antarabangsa 2013). Law faculties may impose higher conditions than those set by the university. UM currently asks for a grade B. MMU, the only private law faculty whose graduates can be admitted directly to the bar, also requires a credit in Malay (Multimedia University 2013), as does HELP, whose website (HELP University 2014) reminds students that this is a condition for bar admission. ATC requires a pass/grade D (Advanced Tertiary College 2014) and according to a Penang lawyer who attended it, students who scored lower than a C are encouraged to take the July Paper.

As for English, although it is one of the required papers at SPM level, a passing grade is not obligatory to gain the school-leaving certificate. There have been government proposals to make it so (*Malaysiakini* 2013b.9.06), but some argue that this would disadvantage rural pupils (Anand 2013.9.07). A UM lecturer interviewed in 2013 said that he and many of his colleagues did not expect a pass in English to become compulsory any time soon, despite all the rhetoric, yet 1 year later the Education Minister announced plans to make it a compulsory subject at university (*Malaysiakini* 2014b.9.02).

According to Asmah (2003:107), even students with an SPM credit can have difficulty with English. And law faculties impose higher standards than most faculties. UM and UiTM require MUET (Malaysian University English Test) band 4. For comparison, UiTM's engineering school requires MUET Band 3. UKM (University Kebangsaan, the national university set up to promote higher education in Malay) will consider candidates with MUET band 3 if they have at least grade 2A on the English SPM paper, but according to a lecturer there in practice it is difficult to get onto the LLB with less than band 5. All UIA faculties require IELTS 6.0, TOEFL PBT 550 or an equivalent on a placement test. MMU requires a B on the SPM English paper for its law foundation and band 4 MUET for its LLB. From 2013 UM also started interviewing all candidates, and according to lecturers who had been involved, with most law applicants are questioned in English. UniSZA imposes higher English standards for its LLB than for its other programmes (except for its BA in Teaching English as a Second Language), including a distinction at SPM and band 4 MUET. Yet one lecturer there admitted that only 10% of those progressing from the university's law diploma to the LLB programme have fulfilled these requirements and are required to make efforts to catch up after they start.

Most law programmes include compulsory language classes. At UKM English for Law is taught in the first semester and Arabic in the second (UKM Law 2015). In 1983 UM instituted language classes for law students in either Malay or English, whichever was assessed as weaker (Nik Ramlah 1993:136), but now the emphasis is so much on English that when I asked students there what was taught during "language class" there was surprise I could have thought it might referred to Malay or anything else. Students wanting more English classes seem to be outnumbered by those feeling the English classes they are sufficient or superfluous. Several said that rather than general English they would prefer instruction in legal argument or writing. But in discussions with law lecturers and the linguists brought in to teach English at the law faculty, differences emerged within each group over whether to introduce legal content or focus on general English.

It is not only the type of classes, but also their role in academic assessment, that is under debate. During my research at UM moves were afoot to make grades on the English course count towards total marks, but in the event the course itself was dropped in the wake of proposals to institute a new course on Law Through Literature.

UniSZA law students take two credits in English per semester in general English and also have an English for Specific Purposes class, which was formerly taught as a legal English class a court interpreter. MMU teaches all subjects in English, including Islamic law, but lecturers informed me that English language classes are no longer obligatory for law students. A recent graduate from UIA, however, said there were annual English tests that must be passed to progress to the next year.

As for Malay, although it is a medium for some law courses at UM (see Chap. 7), it is not taught as a subject at the faculty. A lecturer who had previously been a student there explained that Malay was generally regarded as in need of less support than English, to which her senior colleague commented that this was a volte face from the faculty's early days when the introduction of instruction in Malay caused problems for students and lecturers alike. UM student informants were fairly evenly split about BM classes, some questioning the assumption that all the younger generation, including Malays, were proficient in the language or seeing a need to prepare graduates for court work in it, and others maintaining that it was enough to learn Malay legal terms as they expected to be working with documents drafted in English, even if they had to be translated for court. Several UM students felt that they already had more Malay-medium classes than their counterparts in other universities.

Lawyers who had graduated from UIA and UiTM confirmed that their first 3 years of study were entirely in English, but they also noted that courses in legal Malay form part of the final year, in preparation for legal practice. A UIA graduate from Terengganu, however, remembered theses courses as primarily focused on memorising word lists and felt that his UKM-graduated colleagues had gained a better grasp of terminology because students there actually work with Malay documents. A UiTM graduate practising in KL remembered legal Malay classes consisting mainly of translating English documents. From interviews about work practice (Chap. 8) this emerged as one of the main tasks given to junior lawyers. Indeed emphasis on learning lists of Malay words would be consistent with a preference in the profession for translating texts from English to Malay rather than the other way round, or with using the latter in formulaic documents rather than to create original texts. MMU students, however, are required to prepare and deliver a moot, which many lecturers and lawyers alike see as the best way to simulate the various stages of legal practice, and there is a ballot to ensure 50% do so in Malay. A senior lecturer there recalled that when there had been a free choice, everyone had opted for English.

The 1996 Education Act states that the government "may require" Malay and Malaysian studies to be taught in private post-secondary schools not using Malay as the MOI, and the Private Higher Educational Institutions Act of the same year permits "a course of study" to be taught in English provided Malay (s.41), Malaysian studies and Islamic or moral studies (depending on students' religion) are also taught (s.43). ATC now combines these criteria by making law students pass Malaysian and moral studies in Malay, whereas according to a recent graduate they had previously been offered in English. An ethnic Indian graduate from HELP University just starting out in practice reported that most students see these compulsory Malay courses as inconvenient, but unchallenging in terms of language.

5.4 Professional Requirements

Although the CLP exam is now offered in Malay after being set only in English for its first 15 years (when, according to a Malay advocate, even Malaysian legislation was cited in its English version in the questions), according to LPQB officials fewer than 20 a year choose to answer in the national language. This presumably reflects the fact that it targets those who studied law in private colleges, as well as those from Australian, British and New Zealand schools that are approved by the LPQB but not recognised for direct admission to the bar. The pass rate for first-time examinees is around 30%, with a further 30% passing after retaking one of the papers; those who fail more than one have to resit all five (LPQB 2013).

Examiners' reports of declining English have contributed to a push by the bar for new common bar entry procedures, something former president Steven Thiru discussed at length when interviewed (as vice president) in 2013. Five years on a scheme has yet to be implemented. In the Annual Report for 2017 Thiru argues that the bar, judiciary and Attorney-General's Chambers are in agreement about the need for a Common Bar Course but the law faculties oppose what they see as an attempt to remove their capacity to qualify students directly (Majlis Peguam 2017:114).

The view that poor English is keeping down the CLP pass rate is questionable, however. According to a former administrator of the LPQ, assessors are instructed to ignore lexicogrammatical errors provided answers are understandable and correct. In its advice to candidates, LPQB (2013) focuses more on the problem of examinees who regurgitate facts without answering questions.

While three SPM or O level credits are among the requirements for sitting the CLP, there is nothing specific about Malay language (LPQB 2013). However, since 1984 no one may be admitted to the profession without passing (or gaining exemption from) the Malay Qualifying Examination (1976 Legal Profession Act, s.11(2)). Exemption is usually obtained by having an SPM credit in the national language, but alternatives include a UK or Singapore GCE in Malay language or literature (LPQB 2013). A legal translator who coaches would-be lawyers in Malay[7] found some people preferring the GCE to the bar's language exam as it requires written

[7] Interviewed at corporate practice in KL, 201312.

rather than oral answers. On the other hand a recently qualified ethnic Indian lawyer who had studied in the UK said she had opted for the bar's exam as it is offered frequently and results are announced immediately. She noted that many fellow candidates were Chinese, but former bar president Hendon Mohamed,[8] who has sat on the examining panel since its inception, found that "quite a few of them" were Malays who had scraped through their SPM Malay with only a passing grade and not a credit.

The exam consists of general conversation followed by questions in Malay on an English legal passage that examinees must translate (LPQB 2013), hence reinforcing the position of English as the source of law and the default written language. Candidates are advised to prepare by reading judgments, legal articles and Rules of Court in both languages, together with *Istilah Undang-undang* (ibid). An LPQB officer revealed that the test, which lasts about 15 min, is taken by about 50 people every year and about half pass each time. A small amount of English code-mixing seems to be tolerated and the Indian lawyer mentioned in the previous paragraph said examiners helped her with prompts. According to a legal translator-cum-coach who enjoys a reputation for getting candidates through the test first time, about 3 months' preparation should suffice. She advised focusing on legal lexis but also stressed the importance of keeping up with current affairs for the general conversation section. Most of her pupils were headed for legal sectors that function predominantly in English, and the young Indian lawyer confessed to dropping her Malay studies as soon as she passed the test.

From 1200 members in 1980 the profession grew tenfold by 2005 (Majlis Peguam 2013) and now numbers some 17,000 (Majlis Peguam 2017). A decade ago, 75% were 'young lawyers' of under 7 years' standing (Beh Lih Yi 2005.2.25) and today, 53% are below the age of 40 (Majlis Peguam 2017). Chooi Mun Sou's reminiscences of the old days, when everyone knew each other from studying in London, must seem increasingly distant to a younger generation, over half of them female, working in a more dynamic bar (Fahri et al. 2004.4.07). Malays, comprising 41%, compared with 39% Chinese and 19% Indian (Majlis Peguam 2017) remain underrepresented in comparison with 2010 national census figures of around 60% Malays,[9] 25% Chinese and 7% Indians (Jabatan Perangkaan 2013). While half work in the Klang Valley (Majlis Peguam 2013), where English is widely used, nearly 90% of firms have fewer than six lawyers. A UM lecturer with decades of legal practice pointed out that some firms do very little litigation or criminal work and may spend as much time liaising with clients in Chinese or other languages as drafting documents in English or Malay.

What was an overwhelmingly a foreign-trained profession a few decades ago is now mostly domestically educated. According to Bar Council figures (Tan

[8] Interviewed in KL, 2013.12.

[9] The Department of Statistics gives only a combined figure of 67% *bumiputera* but since 61% report their religion as Islam (http://www.statistics.gov.my/), all Malays are officially Muslim, and large minorities of non-Malays also profess Islam, the percentage of Malays can be assumed to be no more than 60%.

2011.2.06), only 21% of practitioners were admitted through overseas qualifications, the largest cohort being English-trained barristers, followed by graduates of Commonwealth universities before the CLP was required. Twice this number (42%) are local university graduates: 2607 from UIA, 885 from UiTM, 1336 from UM, 695 from UKM, 59 from MMU and 54 from UUM. UIA is currently the largest source of lawyers, providing 215 in 2010, compared with 195 from UiTM, 95 from UM and 89 from London Inns of Court. Those admitted directly from local universities in 2010 outnumbered barristers and CLP-holders 624:284 (ibid). However, 36% of lawyers currently in practice came through the CLP and as we know that most of them come from private colleges, taken with the overseas graduates we can conclude that over half the bar did their law degrees entirely in English.

The final hurdle to admission is 9 months' pupillage (chambering) at a law firm, a term which, according to a recent entrant to the Malaysian bar with years as an English solicitor behind him, is occasionally reduced by the LPQB for those with relevant experience. It seems to be common for pupils to chamber at firms where they completed work attachments as undergraduates. After 6 months pupils receive a 'short call' allowing them to plead cases before registrars. For the full call, which allows pleading in open court, proof of Malay proficiency is required.

5.5 Medium of Instruction Policies in Law Schools

The relationship between Malay and English in law faculties in many ways follows the ebb and flow of tertiary education in general, with promotion of the former in the 1970s being tempered in the 1980s and 1990s by concerns about the decline of English that continue to this day. As Malay was being phased into primary and secondary education and affirmative action for *bumiputera* stepped up, tertiary education was expanded through the raising of technical colleges to public university status, including USM in Penang in 1969, UiTM in 1969 and UPM in 1971), and in 1970 the National University, UKM (Universiti Kebangsaan Malaysia) was opened. Mead (1988:34) notes that whereas Malays comprised 20.6% of UM students in 1963, by 1975 they made up 65% of this expanded university population. UKM prioritised instruction in the national language from its inception (ibid:34), translating 106 scientific books in its first three decades (Gill 2005:249). In 1983 all five public universities announced a switch to BM as the sole medium for first years (*The Straits Times* 1983.6.30), whereupon USM claimed to be using it for all arts subjects and 80% of science classes (Mead 1988:25). Yet by the late '70s there was already renewed interest in English because of university entrants' decreased proficiency in it (Asmah 1994:72). This led to an easing back on Malay for science in 1993 (Asmah 2003:107). The reversion to English for science and maths in school 10 years later came in the wake of reports of employer preference for private sector graduates because of the poor English of public university graduates, 40,000 of whom were unemployed in 2002 (Gill 2005:256). In that year UKM announced proposals to teach half its courses in English (*The Straits Times* 2002.3.29). As for the private sector, according to DBP (*Malaysiakini,* 2002.12.20), there were already 750 English-medium colleges 10 years ago.

After Singapore's exit from Malaysia in 1965 there was no local legal education other than London external courses until law began in English at UM in 1972. A Malay-medium stream was added 3 years later (Nik Ramlah 1993:136). Zamani Mohammad recalls this being for those entering via the STPM school exam, with those entering with the Higher School Certificate continuing to taught in English, and often by expatriates. By 1979 all lectures were supposed to be in Malay unless taught by foreigners (Nik Ramlah 1993:136). However, in 1980 a UM survey concluded not only that English was necessary for law students but that many had insufficient proficiency in it (Asmah 1994:75) and in 1983 a bilingual system was adopted (Zubaidah 2002:161), with lectures in Malay and tutorials in English (Ahmad et al. 1993:161). An advocate from Kelantan and another from Melaka who had been UM students in the 1990s remembered strict adherence to the bilingual policy, with the latter adding that bilingualism was far less of a burden than the legal content he had to master. The faculty's official policy remains bilingual. During my visits, the curriculum, notices about tutorials and test results were posted in Malay, while semester exams were announced in English. In theory students may answer exams in either.

UKM started teaching law in Malay in 1984; the policy is now bilingual, and a graduate practising in Kelantan described a pattern similar to UM of lectures in Malay and tutorials in English. There is a choice of medium for assignments and semester tests but for exams each language must be used for at least one question on every paper, with a recent graduate reporting that marks are deducted if only one is used. This differs from UM where, according to students, the same language must be used throughout an exam.

Like the private universities and colleges, UIA, UiTM and UniSZA officially teach law in English. UIA has taught all lectures, tutorials and exams in it since 1983 except for the *Bahasa Melayu Perundangan* (Legal Malay) course for final year students. Terengganu lawyer Mukhtar Abdullah recalled other language requirements, such as basic Arabic, and Malay for international students, that did not affect legal studies. The foundation courses for students aiming to study law at UIA and UiTM are also in English. According to advocates from Johor Bahru and KL who had taken the UiTM foundation, students are assigned to an intensive English class after a placement test. UniSZA's syllabus states English to be the MOI and explains all law courses except for *Bahasa Malaysia Undang-undang* (legal Malay) in it (UniSZA 2013). As for exams, a lecturer there commented: "No matter how terrible their English is they have to try to use it". MMU and HELP teach all courses in English, with a student at HELP saying this included Malaysian Legal System and an MMU lecturer confirming that Islamic Law was no exception.

Aware of the dominance of English in most law-teaching institutions, a number of lecturers at UM felt that attempts there to retain an important role for Malay were unrealistic. One lecturer, despite being very supportive of bilingual education, wondered if it was necessary to draft exam questions in both languages for subjects that no student had chosen to answer in Malay for years, and noted that the external BA in Jurisprudence, which had started out entirely in Malay as it targets those with practical experience from the public sector, also now gave students the option of answering in English. Several of her colleagues agreed that there was encouragement from the university's higher echelons to emphasise English in lecturers but cautioned that this remained unofficial.

Although limited by what is available, the legal materials law faculties provide is another indication of language policy. Ahmad et al. (1993:168) reported on students' inability to make use of library resources because they were overwhelmingly in English. A UM graduate from Terengganu and a UKM graduate working in KL commented independently that the theoretical choice of medium that their respective institutions offered for answering exams was constrained by the paucity of materials in Malay for most subjects.

Asked to explain the law schools' de-emphasis of Malay, one UniSZA lecturer highlighted the job market: even if many lawyers ended up working mainly in Malay, the ability to place graduates with prestigious firms prioritising English is a selling point for law faculties. Perceived proficiency is another factor. A young UM lecturer voiced the common view that Malay was less of a burden for most students, partly because of their pre-university schooling and partly because the professional tasks they are likely to use it for are less complex and generally confined to the lower courts where, as a UniSZA lecturer pointed out, they will have sufficient opportunity to reinforce their skills in the early years of practice. An MMU lecturer also argued that since the legal system originated in English, moving from English into Malay was more natural than the other way round.

5.6 Professional Support for Bilingualism

In 1981 the bar president estimated that only 10% of members knew Malay (Hickling 2001:36). When the state bar committees announced plans to hold Malay classes in response to the Lord President's direction to use BM in the lower courts, these were described as 'crash courses' focusing on technical terms (*New Straits Times* 1981.10.14). A series of seminars in the late '80s and early '90s to examine the slow progress of legal Malay were heavier on polemic than practical solutions. In 1989 the Institute of Policy Studies, in collaboration with DBP, held a one-day seminar on language issues in common law at which UM law faculty's Nik Abdul Rashid (1989) proposed a timetable for phasing in Malay that involved updating legal terminology by 1989 and using Malay for all Magistrates and Sessions courts pleadings by 1991, but participants failed to elaborate on how to disseminate terms or prepare advocates. A seminar held for the judiciary a year later seems to have viewed the difficulty of conducting trials in Malay largely as one of terminology and proposed the establishment of regional committees to remedy this (in Wan Adnan 1991:12). A symposium on language at UM's law faculty in 1992, when low proficiency in Malay was concern for the whole university according to a former lecturer there, was more comprehensive in connecting courtroom skills and strategies with legal education. It covered a range of positions and included a judge who saw the continuance of English as evidence of lawyers' poor progress in Malay (Faiza 1993), as well as a linguist who interpreted courtroom code-switching as a sign of language proficiency rather than deficiency (David 1993). The disappointment expressed then with the professionals' level of Malay (Mhd. Ariff Yusof 1993) was still being echoed a decade later (Zubaidah 2002:161; Rodziah 2004:287).

Abdullah Ahmad (1991) was more specific in putting teachers at the centre of Malay implementation strategies, arguing for sabbaticals for legal scholars, translators and lexicographers and for close collaboration among academics, legal practitioners, judges and legislative draftsmen.

DBP occasionally organises language courses for the AGC, most recently at the Department of Law Revision and Reform in April 2013 when legal drafters, law journal editors and a linguist who has written on Islamic law were invited to discuss legal translation and editing (Jabatan Peguam Negara 2014). A DBP representative described her main role there as giving a briefing on the use of dictionaries.

The Bar Council has a committee for Malay that meets about twice a year and holds annual promotional events. Mukhtar Abdullah, a former head of the Terengganu bar, explained that the chair of the committee is typically given to representatives from Malay-majority states and so he and a colleague found themselves running it for 2 years (he was also put on a committee in charge of *Syariah* liaison). Asked to organise an event to promote legal Malay he concluded that the Bar Council had insufficient expertise or resources and so invited the director general of the DBP to give a speech "because they have all the facilities, budget and whatever". In late 2013 I attended this speech, entitled 'Strengthening the national legal system through Malay' (Awang Sariyan 2013.11.30). Delivered in Malay with intermittent asides in English, most of it focused on the administrative role of the language under the Melaka Sultanate 500 years ago. Despite calling for newer models of legal Malay through case reports and theses, it offered no practical advice on how to do so. Specific questions from the floor about the scarcity of Malay legal resources went unanswered, and the speech ended after two hours with poetry recitations.

The Bar Council's Malay committee also organises annual events, such as visits to DBP and language workshops (Jawatankuasa Bahasa Melayu 2013a). Several of these have been run by a UM language lecturer with a degree in law, but the one I participated in (Jawatankuasa Bahasa Melayu 2013b) had little legal content beyond an explanation of some orthographic reforms (DBP has recently declared *peguam bela*, and not *peguambela*, the correct form for 'solicitor') and a list of correct forms of address for various government officers. About half the participants seemed to be Malay legal clerks, some of whom were gently admonished for answering questions in English. The workshop leader took great care not to impinge on the authority of language planners (especially the DBP) or legal planners (the judiciary and AGC) in a way redolent of discussions witnessed between lawyers and linguists at UM where wariness and modesty conspired to impede concrete planning.

The fact is that the Bar Council remains far more concerned about English than Malay standards. Former president Steven Thiru emphasised the need to upgrade communication skills in the language when discussing the proposed Common Bar Course (Thiru 2011) and when legal practitioners for this study were asked to comment on the course, all assumed the priority would be to improve English standards. It should nonetheless be noted that an outline of the course published in the Bar Council's 2016/2017 Annual Report (Majlis Peguam 2017) states that both languages will be used and the Introduction to the Malaysian Legal System is to include a section on "Bahasa Malaysia for Lawyers".

Nowhere is the obsession with English standards stronger than in corporate law. Chooi Mun Sou, who had organised Malay classes as head of the Selangor Bar Association in the 1960s and even hired Malay tutors for employees when he set up his own firm, finds nowadays that he is more concerned about standards in English than Malay. A legal translator reported declining attendance for the in-house Malay classes that a corporate law firm hired her to offer its lawyers and staff – even though she felt Malay standards had barely improved over the years. A partner at another large firm said some of its younger lawyers were being sent to the British Council for graded English courses, and an advocate with the AGC said her own department was doing the same.

5.7 Bilingual Law without Bilingual Legal Education

Acquisition planning has been explained above in some detail because it consists of a complex web of mechanisms that contribute to bilingual law rather than a systematic plan for bilingual legal education. With Malay, Mandarin or Tamil used as a medium at primary schools and Malay and English compulsory subjects there, general bilingual proficiency is then pursued at secondary level by requiring Malay as a medium (1996 Education Act) and English as a compulsory second language. English has been further reinforced by the PPSMI policy, still lingering on in some schools, of teaching the key subjects of maths and science in it. The legal education that follows this at tertiary level throughout the public and private sectors is based upon support for English. The law schools embrace this stance as English is perceived as the weaker language for most students, recognised as the medium of most academic materials and legal sources, and assumed to constitute a higher professional hurdle in legal practice. Law faculties and law schools generally have English language requirements, and these are often higher than for other courses, but the Bar has not set a specific requirement because it is clear that there is currently no way of gaining admission without studying law predominantly in English.

Legal education does include some instruction in Malay at some public institutions, but this tends to target specific areas such as Islamic law and to concentrate on the acquisition of legal lexis in students' final year. To insure against lawyers entering the profession without a certain standard of Malay, bar admission is contingent upon proof of competence via school certification or a dedicated exam. But interviews and personal observations suggest that there is little support in the teaching institutions, the bar, or even from the DBP, for more vocational Malay, the assumption being that general BM proficiency and on-the-spot practice will be enough for new lawyers to learn how to perform the tasks it is most often used for.

Cases Cited

Merdeka University v Government [1982] 2 MLJ 243.

References

Abdul Rahman Arshad. (2007). *Unity and education in Malaysia*. Kuala Lumpur: Dewan Bahasa dan Pustaka.

Abdullah bin Ahmad. (1991, December 3–4). *Strategi dan persediaan ke arah perlaksanaan bahasa Malaysia sebagai bahasa undang-undang* [Strategy and preparation for implementing Malay as a legal language]. Paper presented at Seminar Bahasa dan Undang- undang [Seminar on Language and Law], Dewan Bahasa.

Advanced Tertiary College. (2014). Admissions brochure for ATC College Law Department. Accessed 10 April 2014, from http://www.atc2u.com/download/courses/undergraduate/llb/LLB-brochure.pdf

Ahmad Mhd Yusof, Mansor Jusoh, Juneidah Ibrahim, & Abd. Kahar Yaakob. (1993). *Laporan Kaji Selidik Penggunaan Bahasa Melayu dalam Bidang Kehakiman dan Undang-undang* [Investigative report on the use of Malay in judicial and legal sectors]. Kuala Lumpur: Dewan Bahasa dan Pustaka. Accessed 31 July 2005, from http://www.geocities.com/CapitolHill/Congress/5544/law1207.htm

Ahmad Mustapha Hassan. (2007). *The unmaking of Malaysia. Insider's reminiscences of UMNO, Razak and Mahathir*. Petaling Jaya, Selangor: SIRD.

Aidila Razak. (2013, November 7). Don't limit English education to elite. *Malaysiakini*. Accessed 10 Jan 2014, from http://www.malaysiakini.com/news/245988

Anand, Ram. (2013, September 7). Anwar: M'sia not ready to make English a 'must pass'. *Malaysiakini*. Accessed 8 Sept 2013, from http://www.malaysiakini.com/news/240511

Andaya Watson, Barbara., & Andaya, Leonard. (1982). *A history of Malaysia*. London: Macmillan.

Appudurai, Jayanath, & Dass, David G. A. (2008). *Malaysian Indians: Looking forward*. Petaling Jaya: Strategic Information and Research Centre.

Asmah Haji Omar. (1979). *Language planning for unity efficiency: A study of the language status and corpus planning of Malaysia*. Singapore: RELC.

Asmah Haji Omar. (1994). Nationism and exoglossia: The case of English in Malaysia. In Abdullah Hassan (Ed.), *Language planning in Southeast Asia* (pp. 66–85). Kuala Lumpur: Dewan Bahasa dan Pustaka.

Asmah Haji Omar. (2003). *Language and the language situation in South East Asia with a focus on Malaysia*. Kuala Lumpur: Akademi Pengajian Malaysia, Universiti Malaya.

Aw, Nigel. (2013a, May 12) Don – Abolish vernacular schools for unity's sake. *Malaysiakini*. Accessed 16 May 2013, from http://www.malaysiakini.com/news/229913

Aw, Nigel. (2013b, December 1). *Tamil secondary school? DPM put on the spot*. Accessed 2 Dec 2013, from http://www.malaysiakini.com/news/248129

Awang bin Sariyan [Direct-General, Dewan Bahasa]. (2013, November 30). *Memperkasa Sistem Perundangan Negara melalui Bahasa Melayu* [Empowering the legal system through Malay]. Keynote paper presented at *Ceramah Memperkasa Sistem Perundangan Negara melalui Bahasa Melayu* [Forum on empowering the legal system through Malay]. Malaysian Bar Council, Kuala Lumpur.

Beh Lih Yi. (2005, February 25). *Bar Council reforms: Young lawyers meet put off*. Accessed 20 Feb 2012, from http://www.malaysiakini.com/news/33872

Centre for Public Policy Studies. (2017). Portal accessed 12 Dec 2017, from http://cpps.org.my/wp-content/uploads/2017/10/Vernacular-Education-in-Malaysia-Factsheet.pdf

David, Maya Khemlani. (1993). Language and law: Communicative strategies in a court of law a Malaysian experience. In Khaw Lake Tee (Ed.), *Legal education in Malaysia Quo Vadis?* Kuala Lumpur: University of Malaya.
David, Maya Khemlani. (2003). Role and functions of code-switching in Malaysian courtrooms. *Multilingua 22*. Accessed 1 Nov 2003, from http://www.degruyter.de/journals/multilin/2003/pdf/22_5.pdf
Fahri Azzat, Edmund Bon, Amer Hamzah, & Shanmuga Kanesalingam. (2004, April 7). Lawyers a close second to prostitutes? *Malaysiakini*. Accessed 27 Sept 2011, from http://malaysiakini.com/letters/27483
Faiza Tamby Chik. (1993). Language and the law: The role of Malay and English in legal education and the practice of law. In Khaw Lake Tee (Ed.), *Legal education in Malaysia Quo Vadis?* (pp. 103–107). Kuala Lumpur: University of Malaya.
Federation of Malaya. (1951). *Report on the Barnes report on Malay Education and the Fenn-Wu report on Chinese education*. Central Advisory Committee on Education.
Gill, Saran Kaur. (2005). Language policy in Malaysia: Reversing direction. *Language Policy, 4*, 241–260.
HELP University. (2014). Official portal accessed 10 April 2014, from: http://www.help.edu.my
Hickling, Reginald Hugh. (2001). *Malaysian Law*. Kuala Lumpur: Pelanduk.
Jabatan Peguam Negara. (2014). *Official portal of Attorney General's Chambers of Malaysia*. Accessed 2011~2014, from http://www.agc.gov.my
Jabatan Perangkaan. (2013). *Portal of Malaysian Department of Statistics*. Accessed 8 Aug 2013, from www.statistics.gov.my/
Jawatankuasa Bahasa Melayu. (2013a). *Malaysian Bar Council Malay Committee annual reports*. Accessed 2 Nov 2013, from http://www.malaysianbar.org.my
Jawatankuasa Bahasa Melayu. (2013b, December 19). *Malaysian Bar Council Malay Committee workshop*, Kuala Lumpur.
Kempen Satu Sekolah untuk Semua. (2013). *Website of 'One School for All' petition*. Portal accessed 10 Aug 2013, from http://www.thepetitionsite.com/1/kempen-satu-sekolah-untuk-semua/
Koh Jun Lin. (2013, October 30). *Doors still open to national-type Chinese schools*. Accessed 30 Oct 2013, from http://www.malaysiakini.com/news/245398
Koh Jun Lin. (2015, November 18). Rafidah ayes bilingual education system. *Malaysiakini*. Accessed 18 Nov 2015, from http://www.malaysiakini.com/news/320056
Kua Kia Soong. (1999). *A Protean Saga. The Chinese Schools of Malaysia*. Kajang, Selangor: Dong Jiao Zong Higher Learning Centre.
Kua Kia Soong. (2002). *Malaysian critical issues*. Kajang, Selangor/Selangor: Petaling Jaya/SIRD.
Kua Kia Soong. (2014, May 26). Article 153 doesn't condone UiTM bumi policy. *Malaysiakini*. Accessed 26 May 2014, from http://www.malaysiakini.com/news/263904
Kuek Ser Kuang Keng. (2005, December 09). Language switch – Tamils back DJZ. *Malaysiakini*. Accessed 2012.11.27 from http://www.malaysiakini.com/news/44289
Lee Way Loon. (2013, July 22). Wee: Varsity intake system 'more quota than quota'. *Malaysiakini*. Accessed 26 July 2013, from http://www.malaysiakini.com/news/236426
LPQB. (2013). Portal of the Legal Profession Qualifying Board, Malaysia. Accessed 1 Sept 2013, from http://www.lpqb.org.my/
Majlis Peguam. (2013). *Bar Council Annual Report 2012/13*. Accessed 30 Nov 2013, from http://www.malaysianbar.org.my/general_notices/bc_general_statistics_2013.html
Majlis Peguam. (2017). *Bar Council Annual Report 2016/17*.
Malaysiakini. (2002, December 20). *DBP magazine slams English language policy*. Accessed 1 Nov 2011, from http://www.malaysiakini.com/news/14015
Malaysiakini. (2008, August 13). *PM vetoes call to open UiTM to non-Malays*. Accessed 20 Sept 2011, from http://www.malaysiakini.com/news/87721
Malaysiakini. (2011, October 12). *Govt urged to abolish vernacular schools*. Accessed 15 Oct 2011, from http://www.malaysiakini.com/news/178488

Malaysiakini. (2013a, June 11). *NGOs want PM to rescind promises on Chinese schools*. Accessed 11 June 2013, from http://www.malaysiakini.com/news/232633

Malaysiakini. (2013b, September 6). *Highlights of Educational Blueprint 2013-2025*. Accessed 7 Sept 2013, from http://www.malaysiakini.com/news/240426

Malaysiakini. (2014a, February 12). *Convention to gather final input on Tamil schools plan*. Accessed 13 Feb 2014, from http://www.malaysiakini.com/news/254173

Malaysiakini. (2014b, September 2). *English to be a must-pass at public universities*. Accessed 2 Sept 2014, from http://www.malaysiakini.com/news/273468

Malaysiakini. (2015, November 9). *1,000 would-be doctors quit due to poor English*. Accessed 10 Nov 2015, from http://www.malaysiakini.com/news/318859

Malaysiakini. (2016, February 26). *S'wak MP: Revive English schools as autonomy show of faith*. Accessed 27 Feb 2016, from https://www.malaysiakini.com/news/329616

Malaysiakini. (2017, March 10). *In SEA, M'sia has most kids in English language international schools*. Accessed 10 April 2017, from https://www.malaysiakini.com/news/375265

Malaysiakini (2018, April 8). *Najib makes vague election pledge on UEC*. Accessed 10 April 2018, from https://www.malaysiakini.com/news/418853

Malaysiakini (2019, March 30). *CLP exam: Requirements for UEC holders changed*. Accessed 30 Mar 2019, from https://www.malaysiakini.com/news/470117

Mead, Richard. (1988). *Malaysia's National language policy and the legal system*. New Haven: Yale.

Mhd. Ariff Yusof. (1993). Language and the law: The role of Bahasa Malaysia and English in legal education and the practice of law. In Khaw Lake Tee (Ed.), *Legal Education in Malaysia Quo Vadis?* (pp. 117–125). Kuala Lumpur: University of Malaya.

Mukherjee, Dipika & David, Maya Khemlani (Eds.). (2011). *National language planning and language shift in Malaysian minority communities – Speaking in many tongues*. Amsterdam: Amsterdam University Press.

Multimedia University. (2013). Official website of MMU, Melaka. Accessed 2013.11.21 from https.www.mmu.edu.my

New Straits Times. (1981, October 14). *Crash courses in court Bahasa*, p. 6.

Nik Abdul Rashid Majid. (1989). *Keupayaan Bahasa Melayu sebagai Bahasa Undang-undang* [The capability of Malay as a legal language]. Seminar Kebangsaan Undang-undang: Isu Bahasa dan Common law [Seminar on national law: The issue of language and common law]. Kuala Lumpur: Dewan Bahasa dan Pustaka.

Nik Ramlah Mahmood. (1993). Language and legal education in Malaysia – Past and emerging trends. In Khaw Lake Tee (Ed.), *Legal education in Malaysia Quo Vadis?* (pp. 134–146). Kuala Lumpur: Universiti Malaya.

Norton, Bonny. (2001). Non-participation, imagined communities and the language classroom. In M. Breen (Ed.), *Learner contributions to language learning: New directions in research* (pp. 159–171). London: Longman.

Palansamy, Yiswaree. (2013, July 15). Kamalamathan working to fix university, matriculation situation. *The Malaysian Insider*. Accessed 10 Sept 2013, from http://www.themalaysianinsider.com/malaysia/article/kalamanathan-says-working-to-fix-university-matirculation-situation

Pillai, Stefanie. (2006). Malaysian English as a first language. In David Maya Khemlani (Ed.), *Language choices and discourse of Malaysian families: Case studies of families in Kuala Lumpur, Malaysia* (pp. 22–42). Petaling Jaya: SIRD.

Powell, Richard. (2008). *Motivations for language choice in Malaysian courtrooms and implications for language planning*. Kuala Lumpur: Universiti Malaya.

Puah, Pauline. (2004, August 17). Vernacular educationists unmoved by funding proposal. *Malaysiakini*. Accessed 27 Mar 2011, from http://www.malaysiakini.com/news/29254

Rodziah Matled. (2004). Rape and constitutional law on trial. In Zubaidah, Alnian, Fauziah, Lohanayadu, & Rajesway (Eds.), *Language, linguistics and the real world, vol II: Language practice in the workplace. Selected papers from the First International Conference on language, linguistics and the real world, Kuala Lumpur, 2002*. Kuala Lumpur: University of Malaya.

Samuel, Moses, Mahmud Hasan Khan, Lee Luan Ng & Kin Wai. (2012). Articulation of medium of instruction politics in the Malaysian Chinese press. *Discourse: Studies in the Cultural Politics of Education.* Accessed 10 Aug 2013, from https://doi.org/10.1080/01596306.2012.745731

Tan Chee Kwan. (2004, September 20). *Sesi kelas Bahasa Cina tidak dikurangkan dengan sengaja* [Chinese classes not being reduced intentionally]. Accessed 31 Mar 2011, from http://www.malaysiakini.com/news/32306

Tan, Roger. (2011, February 06). High time for a new Bar. *The Star Online.* Accessed 2014.5.26 from http://www.thestar.com.my/story.aspx/?file=%2f2011%2f2%2f6%2ffocus%2f8011437&sec=focus

Tate, Muzafar Desmond. (2008). *The Malaysian Indians. History, problems and future.* Petaling Jaya: Strategic Information and research Development Centre.

Thiru, Steven. (2011, July–September). A first class legal profession. A common bar course to transform the training of new entrants to the Malaysian legal profession. *Praxis*, 7–10.

The Star. (2009, February 30). *Majority want Science, Maths taught in English,* p. N13.

The Straits Times. (1965, July 27). *Multi-lingualism supporters thinking only of own interests*, p. 8.

The Straits Times. (1983, June 30). *Varsities to switch to Bahasa soon*, p. 18.

The Straits Times. (1990, June 30). *Pass in English may soon be compulsory, says ministry*, p. 16.

The Straits Times. (2002, March 29). *M'sian U to teach science, humanities in English*, p. 2.

Ting, Su-Hie. (2010). Impact of language planning on language choice in friendship and transaction domains in Sarawak, Malaysia. *Current Issues in Language Planning, 11*(4), 397–412.

Toh Boo Huat. (2012, May 14). English medium schools available - but not to all. *Malaysiakini.* Accessed 16 May 2012, from http://www.malaysiakini.com/letters/197845

Tong, Y. S. (2003, April 7). PPP chief calls for closure of Tamil schools. *Malaysiakini.* Accessed 26 Mar 2011, from http://www.malaysiakini.com/news/15024

UKM Law. (2015). *Portal of Universiti Kebangsaan Malaysia Law Faculty.* Accessed 11 Nov 2015, from: http://www.ukm.my

UniSZA. (2013). *Panduan Prasiswazah Fakulti Undang-undang dan Hubungan Antarabangsa* [Undergraduate guide for Faculty of Law and International Relations].

Universiti Islam Antarabangsa. (2013). Official portal of International Islamic University Malaysia (UIA/IIUM). Accessed 20 Nov 2013, from http://www.iium.edu.my/

Universiti Kebangsaan Malaysia. (2013). Official portal of UKM. Accessed 20 Nov 2013, from http://www.ukm.my

Universiti Malaya. (2013). Official portal of UM. Accessed 20 Nov 2013, from http://www.um.edu.my/

Universiti Teknologi MARA. (2013). Official portal of UiTM. Accessed 20 Nov 2013, from http://www.uitm.edu.my/index.php/en

Utusan Malaysia. (2001, Mar 19).

Wade, Geoff. (2009). The origins and evolution of ethnocracy in Malaysia. *Asia-Pacific Journal* 47-4-09. Accessed 7 July 2011, from http://japanfocus.org/-Geoff-Wade/3259

Wan Adnan bin Muhamad. (1991, December 3–4). *Peranan Bahagian Penyelidikan dan Sekretariat Bahasa Mahkamah Agung dalam Usaha Meningkatkan Penggunaan Bahasa Malaysia dalam Bidang Kehakiman* [Role of the Research Department and Secretariat for legal language in efforts to increase use of Malay in field of justice]. Paper presented at Seminar Bahasa dan Undang-undang [Seminar on Language and Law], Dewan Bahasa.

Wan Saiful Wan Jan. (2016, February 11). Critics should stop acting like they are smarter than parents. *Malaysiakini.* Accessed 20 Feb 2016, from https://www.malaysiakini.com/letters/330023

Yusof Ghani. (2002, August 15). Opponents of English policy invited to roadshow. *Malaysiakini.* Accessed 21 Aug 2011, from http://www.malaysiakini.com/news/12595

Zainul Arifin Md Isa. (2012, September 19). More Malays going to SJK(C)s. *New Straits Times* (Online). Accessed 10 Oct 2013, from http://www.nst.com.my/opinion/columnist/more-malays-going-to-sjk-c-s-1.145419

Zubaidah Ibrahim. (2002). *Court interpreting in Malaysia in relation to language planning and policy.* Unpublished, doctoral thesis, Universiti Malaya [Viewed Universiti Malaya].

Chapter 6
Discourse Planning

In countries like France, Germany, Thailand and China it's the respective national languages that are used in the courts, although they also consider English an important language as far as international and commercial matters are concerned. (My translation)

Ahmad Fairuz (former Chief Justice) (*Utusan Online* 2008c.12.17)

If you don't understand English you will be left behind in the law (…) If you want to limit your practice to the lower courts, fine. But if you want to expand, you have no choice.

Zaki Azmi (former Chief Justice) (in Koshy 2013.9.15)

6.1 Discourse as a Component of Language Planning

Although discourse has always played a crucial role in the formation and implementation of language policy, scholastic recognition of its importance was not apparent until the 1990s. Haarmann (1990:105–105) saw psychological preparation for the application of policy to practice as sufficiently independent of corpus and status planning to warrant a distinct analytical category, which he labeled 'prestige planning'. Neustupný (1994:50) characterised planning as a process that begins with the discursive construction of language problem and ends with their discursive resolution. More recently, Tollefson (2002:5) has called on researchers to pay more attention to how policies mobilise public opinion, and Lo Bianco (2009:103) has highlighted how public texts, as constituents of performative action, shape social alignments behind policies.

Whether we can isolate discourse as a discrete instrument of planning is debatable, however. For one thing, it is intimately entangled with every stage of status-, corpus- and acquisition planning, often sitting crucially at the juncture between policy and practice. For another, even if we accept unanticipated outcomes as an important aspect of language planning, status, corpus and acquisition measures

R. Powell, *Language Choice in Postcolonial Law*, Language Policy 22,
https://doi.org/10.1007/978-981-15-1173-8_6

have a deliberateness about them that may be lacking in the discourses leading to and emerging from them. Indeed one motivation driving Critical Discourse Analysis has been to reveal interests and agendas that may be hidden even to policymakers themselves. Discourse can certainly be manipulated in the service of political, cultural or professional agendas, but it cannot be approached as a manipulable resource in quite the same way as status rules, lexis innovation or educational reforms, being less amenable to central control or objectification.

The documents and speeches that expound Malaysian language policy are rarely comprehensive or unambiguous. Both the policies and the ways they are interpreted reflect compromises among different positions and between idealism and pragmatism, but as Ball (2006:49) has argued, these compromises are situated within discursive frames, albeit dynamic ones. As there are relatively few documents laying out Malaysian language-in-law policy (constitutional Article 150, some legislative provisions according with it, a handful of judgments and some procedural rules), this chapter focuses less on analysing the discourse that appears to underlie texts than on identifying the range of leading discourse through which policies and practices are filtered in public and professional life. In keeping with the primarily political framework within which Malaysian language-in-law planning has been approached here, the main focus is on publicly influential discourses, especially those that see policymaking in terms of resolving conflicts between competing interests, national conceptions or legal interpretations. Drawing on Gramsci's concept of hegemony, which views discourse as a vital support, and even a replacement, for material control, Lo Bianco (2009:110) emphasises the instrumentality of powerful policy statements, while nonetheless acknowledging the influence of resistant discourses on outcomes. The centralised nature of legal systems constrains counter-discourses, especially when there has been decades-long management of public debate as in the case of Malaysia, but within these constraints we can find a range of positions on language-in-law policy that feed not only on the heterogeneity of opinion among politicians, justices and legal practitioners but also on flexibility and ambiguity in official policy itself.

The chapter begins (Sect. 6.2) with a review of the relationship between discourse and the language in the Malaysian legal domain, an area of vital sociopolitical importance yet much less the subject of public debate than the educational domain. We will then (Sect. 6.3) look at the constraints on policy formation and dissemination in Malaysia, a democracy that holds regular elections yet didn't have a change of regime for 60 years and experienced an increasing level of control over dissent as prospects for political change grew. In Sect. 6.4 we then focus on discussions about language within the legal profession itself, before going on (Sect. 6.5) to the main discursive frames within which discussions are typically organised. The chapter concludes with a discussion of the discourses of justice as this concept is invariably the endpoint of arguments in support or defiance of policies and practice. Schiffman (1996: 13) characterises language policy as a juxtaposition of *de jure* or overt statements and informal, covert behaviour, and we can similarly see discourse as working both in official planning and in the habitual yet often unconscious decisions made by practitioners. Hence this chapter pivots between the political and societal measures described in the chapters that preceded it and the accounts of the motivations behind grounded practice that follow.

6.2 Discourse and Language-in-Law Policy

Like acquisition planning, discourse planning is seldom linked to the legal domain. It should be. While language planning in general is reliant on persuasive discourses because of its deep social impact (Lo Bianco 2009:103), its application to the legal domain is heavily dependent on the deployment of legitimising discourses because of the powerful symbolic dimensions of the law. For most citizens, however, there is much less contact with the legal domain than the educational domain. Galanter's (1974) contention that "repeat players" enjoy advantages over "one-shotters" in civil litigation is largely true of the law in general. The government offices and well-resourced law firms that regularly engage with the judicial system have considerably more influence and hence higher awareness than citizens involved once or twice in a lifetime. In a Malaysian poll about threats to democracy (Merdeka Center 2010), only 7% ranked the independence of the courts in their top two concerns. Similarly, Malaysian debates on language-in-education policy tend to be more pervasive than those about language-in-law. This does not, however, prevent political and legal figures from invoking the rights or will of the people in support of language preferences.

Although many aspects of the law are highly technical, when it comes to language planning technical considerations, such as the clarity of legislation or effectiveness of interrogations, compete with non-technical and highly politicised motivations. Fishman's (1994:97) assertion that "... very little language planning practice has actually been informed by language planning theory" still holds good today, and in Malaysian law language planning is driven by political and cultural agendas as much as linguistic or legal analysis.

In light of evidence that language planning is forced by circumstance (Corson 1989:141) or shaped by compromise (Ricento 2000:7) as much as crafted through ideological alignment (ibid:3), the extent to which discourse is planned at all can be questioned. While issues about agency and conscious reflection impinge upon the analysis of all aspects of planning, at least with status, corpus and acquisition planning we have relatively accessible legislative, terminological and curricular processes to explore, and we can also consider individual and institutional orientation to the products of planning in the form of laws, lexical innovations and medium of instruction policies. The genesis and evolution of discourses on legal language can be more challenging to track.

The highest expressions of language-in-law policies are legal texts themselves. In common law traditions these texts are reinforced by a nexus of interdiscursive reasoning, and also by a hierarchy of privileged interpretation. Enactments on legal language constitute performative action as well as models of performance, their messages borne not only by what they say but also by the language in which they say it. The 1967 National Language Act, for example, performs the illocutionary act of prescribing the national language for official uses (s.2) while permitting government-authorised translations in the public interest (s.3) and the use of English if deemed fit (s.4). It further declares English to be the authentic version of laws enacted before September 1st, 1967, thereby including itself. Rather than define 'national language' the Act refers to constitutional Article 152, where this is stated to be Malay. The register in which the enactment is written is clearly legalistic, yet short on accessible or nationalistic rhetoric, and it combines surface flexibility with underlying authoritarianism by emphasising the government's discretion to interpret provisions in the public interest.

Compared with laws, other texts and speech may be more obscure or subtle in their orientation because of the complex and collective nature of policymaking. Among LPP theorists themselves, some sociopolitical positioning is more overt (e.g. Nekvapil's (2006:2) descriptions of planning as an objective process) and some more subtle (e.g. Rubdy's (2008:212) construction of language as a plannable resource – a position that may sound apolitical enough until we consider the cultural and identity-linked implications of treating languages as mere commodities). Similarly, the ideological dimensions of Malaysian academics' labelling of Malay as "the most natural" choice for national language (Asmah 1987:65), or announcements on government-controlled TV3 extolling *Satu bangsa, satu bahasa* (One people, one language), are transparent enough, whereas Malay subtitling of Indonesian soap operas is more ambiguous, being motivated at least in part by communicative concerns.

A number of analytical approaches propose ways of clarifying the sociopolitical impact of discourse, including critical discourse analysis (CDA, e.g. Fairclough 1989), genre theory (Bhatia 1993) and Systemic Functional Grammar (SFG, Halliday 2001). But identifying the effects and functions of texts is not the same as revealing the motivations of those who produce them. For Giddens (1979:42), texts are autonomous products whose functions can nevertheless be traced to the historical and material situations of the humans producing them (ibid:7), with discourse a continuous flow of such texts (ibid:55) linking the old and new (ibid:70). More recently Wagenaar (2011) has striven for a theory of discourse that problematises the idea that texts are self-consciously constructed by individuals at the centre and unilaterally imposed on the periphery, while falling short of a structuralist conception of texts as intention-free. He turns to Foucault's *gouvernementalité* (1991, in Wagenaar 2011:112) in construing discourse as a loop system that filters individual interests through interplay between a centre that disperses power and a periphery that receives, but also recharges, this power. Foucault (e.g. 1980) himself made frequent reference to legal (especially penal) systems in emphasising the role of discourses and microlevel practices in subtly conditioning citizens to conflate their individual aspirations with those of the state. Hence modern states have come to rely less on coercion and more on knowledge-based control. Nevertheless we should not forget that legal domains stand apart to the extent that coercive power always lurks in the shadows of epistemological manipulation.

While not in itself a critical discourse analysis, the chapter draws on CDA's self-representation as an approach to studying text and talk that focuses on the wider power relations underlying policy statements and criticisms (van Dijk 1995:17).

6.3 Formation and Dissemination of Discourses on Malaysian Law

Writing from a CDA standpoint, van Dijk (1995:20) highlights the control of politicians, journalists, academics, corporate managers and judges over formal and informal discourses. In Malaysia the degree to which most civil domains were politicised during six decades of BN rule tended to restrain counter-discourses to an unusual extent for a polity that holds regular elections. The state arsenal of discursive control includes the Sedition Act (1948), the Defamation Act (1957), the Copyright Act (1987), the Computer Crimes Act (1997) and the Communications and Multimedia Act (1994). Under Najib Razak's premiership (2009–2018) restrictions accelerated, culminating in an Anti-Fake News Bill rushed through prior to the 2018 elections with a provision in s.8(3) to remove publications "likely to be prejudicial to public order". The Pakatan Harapan government succeeding Najib repealed the law 3 months after taking power (*Malaysiakini* 2018g.8.16).

Despite Najib's promises to abolish the colonial-era Sedition Act (*Malaysiakini* 2012a.7.11) he chose instead to update it (Koh 2016.3.05). The Act contains broadly-drafted sanctions against exciting disaffection against the government (s.3(1)a) or justice system (s.3(1)c). In the latter part of BN's reign it was used among other things to convict Karpal Singh after he questioned a sultan's constitutional powers; charge N. Surendran (Karpal's successor as Anwar's lawyer) for alleging political interference in trial proceedings (*Utusan Online* 2014b.8.18); prosecute constitutional lawyer Azmi Sharom for expressing an opinion on constitutional law (*Utusan Online* 2014c.9.02); and investigate human rights lawyer Edmund Bon after he argued, as most lawyers would, that non-Muslims are not subject to *Syariah* (*The Malaysian Insider* 2014.9.12). Crucially, for our purposes, the Sedition Act was extended (s.3(1)f) after the 1969 race riots to bring criticism of constitutional provisions about the national language (e.g. Art. 152) within the purview of seditious tendency', and it has been used to incarcerate critics of the pro-Malay language policy (Mead 1988:27–29). In January, 2019 a lawyer who had helped draft amendments to the Sedition Act in the wake of the 1969 racial riots claimed that even calling for the abolition of the Act was seditious unless the sultans gave their consent (Koh 2019.1.20).

The political neutrality of the judiciary that administers the Act has long been debated in public, from the days when Mahathir accused the Bench of being unfavourable to his government (*Time* 1986.11.24, in *The Straits Times* 1986.11.29) to more recent claims in media forums that judges may not be reliable arbiters of fake news (*Malaysiakini* 2018b.3.27). It should be noted that sedition cases initially go to the Sessions courts where they are likely to be dealt with by junior judges relatively fresh from civil service training. Selective prosecution and a compliant judiciary were widely considered to be part of the government's political armory. Bon, Malaysia's current representative to ASEAN's Intergovernment Commission on Human Rights, goes as far as to argue (2013:372) that the judiciary has never recovered from the constitutional crisis of 1988, when Lord President Salleh Abas and other leading judges were removed from office to prevent the courts finding Mahathir's reelection as UMNO leader illegal (Wain 2009:72–73).

A key question at the time of writing is whether the Mahathir of 2019 will be able to resist the controlling stance he adopted toward the judiciary 30 years ago. But there has always been a degree of unpredictability in the deployment of centralised control informed by the unwritten rules of power games. Hence the clamping down on Anwar Ibrahim's use of English in court, which another litigant might have got away with it. Hence the widespread debate about the special position of the Malays and their language, even though this is supposed to be beyond question according to the constitution and the Sedition Act.

Similarly, media controls do not so much deny space to counter-discourses as threaten them with suppression should they be voiced by the wrong people at the wrong time. Under BN, few print newspapers departed from a broadly pro-government line, although it is clear that Chinese dailies tended to be bolder than papers in other languages in their response to the high-level corruption scandals that gradually drowned BN (*Malaysiakini* 2016b.4.01). The absence of opposition opinion on television (Loone 2013.3.25) and frequent exclusion of unfavourable journalists from press conferences (*Malaysiakini* 2013.12.12, 2014a.1.27) allowed political criticism to be demonised as unpatriotic and un-Islamic (Al Hafar 2014.2.14). Online news portals enjoyed more freedom under BN[1] but were periodically threatened with censorship (*Malaysiakini* 2011.1.25), lawsuits (*Malay Mail Online* 2014.6.03) or prosecution for fake news (*Malaysiakini* 2018a.3.05). BN's last Communications and Multimedia Minister admitted that 399 websites had been blocked (*Malaysiakini* 2016a.3.22) and according to *Malay Mail* (Zurairi 2018.5.19) *Malaysiakini*'s reporting of election results was censored during the last general election. In 2018 Malaysia was ranked 145 out of 180 countries on the World Press Freedom Index (*Malaysiakini* 2018c.4.25).

The new government has promised a more tolerant policy, but one veteran journalist warns that even if the practice of issuing *wahyu* ('instructions') from on high ceases, the press may continue to suffer intimidation from civil servants as keen to defend their new masters as they were to protect their old ones (A. Kadir Jasin 2018.10. 28). We should nevertheless question the extent to which the media shapes

[1] While this study mined a wide range of media in both English and Malay, for relative objectivity it relied heavily on online portals under less government control, especially *Malaysiakini*, whose independence has been recognised by international press monitors; its reader comments have been largely critical of BN yet it regularly carried articles from the government press agency *Bernama* under the BN regime, including an attack on Pakatan's election manifesto by the UMNO Youth deputy chief within hours of its announcement on 2018.3.09.

opinion in a society where 61% (around twice as many as in Hong Kong or Singapore) believe the news to be tainted by undue political influence (*Malaysiakini* 2016e.11.12).

Other potential instruments of discursive control under BN included the manipulation of school curricula (*The Sun* 2002.3.09) and censorship of books (Wade 2009). With an average of 37 books banned each year between 1971 and 2017 (41% of them in Malay, 30% in English and 27% in Chinese) this might seem an overtly political tool, but it should be noted that two thirds of banned Malay books relate to religion, with both religion and sex outweighing political criticism as grounds for censorship across all languages (Ooi 2017). But one publication confiscated in 2010 was a handbook on legal rights (Paulsen 2010.10.21). Recently a book in Malay deemed sympathetic to the formerly Chinese-dominated Communist Party was banned (*Malaysiakini* 2018h.12.07).

Despite the barrage of controls, Malaysia has not lacked vigorous debate on language policy, or on economics, politics and law. To some extent this discursive heterogeneity reflects materially implicated polarisation between those who are more dependent on government largesse (rural communities, *bumiputera* needing educational and employment support) and those who either do not need it or do not expect it (e.g. most of private commerce). The BN government had a habit of ramping up cultural policies, such as reviving the idea of Malaysia as an Islamic state (Shazwan 2014.5.29), whenever doubts over its economic capacity to support rural areas arose (*Malaysiakini* 2014b.6.17), but the economy's steady growth (arguably exaggerated by massive overseas borrowing) slowed down its slide into ideological dictatorship.

Also muddying the picture is diversity within influential institutions. Whilst the bar has typically been represented as resistant to the Home Ministry, the judiciary and the AGC, particularly in the final years of BN monopolisation of power, all such historically constituted bodies should be seen as incrementally evolving. Giddens (1979:119) reminds us that institutional practices are routinised gradually through sedimentation processes that create tensions between the needs of actors and the roles associated with institutional identity. Hence there is always space for circumscribed dissent and compromise in policymaking. In the case of Malaysian law the flexibility and ambiguity built into language policy itself may also push back the boundaries of that space. Legal practitioners' agency in language choice has benefitted from BN's struggle to balance sociopolitical and economic agendas, with the largely anglophone minority on whom the private sector depends enjoying a degree of autonomy as long as it embraces the principle of Malay hegemony and the pragmatism of bilingualism.

Indeed there is ample evidence of a diversity of opinion from prominent actors in the legal domain. The British-born Colonial Legal Service officer who was parliamentary draftsman when Malaya's constitution was devised went on, decades later, to call for "a confrontation between English and Malaysian common law" in order to remove vestigial cultural domination by English-trained barristers (Hickling 2001:37). One Chief Justice extolled the virtues of common law through the international medium of English (Koshy 2013.9.15) just a few years after another had accused English-based law of sophistry (Faridah 2004.10.13) and recommended its replacement by *Syariah* (Bell 2007.9.01).

The capacity of counter-discourses to resist hegemonic discourses is, however, severely inhibited when the latter are backed by political power and economic resources. In acknowledgment of Butler's (1993:187–188) development of Foucauldian discourse into a model of unstable and immanent power whereby actors establish their own boundaries of identity, Bourdieu (2000:160–161) conceded that habituses (institutionally inculcated predispositions) may be destabilised by contradictions and internal divisions; but his insistence that they don't merely dissolve at the behest of those who resist them is especially pertinent for institutions like law that are supported by authoritative discourses and potentially coercive forces. Lo Bianco (2004:748) indexes the Bakhtinian concept of dialogic processes to explain how the discourses that have most influence on policy are those that are fused with political power in "authoritative" contexts and recursively reinforced by practice in institutional settings. Thus in Malaysian law we find there is more room for a range of positions on the desirable balance between Malay and English than for outright rejection of the use of either language, let alone for proposing other languages for legal use.

The key vehicles of policy discourse are the constitution, other enactments, judicial decisions, and statements by authoritative government and judicial figures disseminated mostly through the media. Given the degree of media control, newspaper editorials and articles themselves may also serve as instruments of government policy. More diffuse, but of high symbolic value, are government-sponsored seminars and cultural campaigns. Civil society sites for disseminating responses to policy include Bar Council statements, other professional forums and academic surveys.

Referring to state-authored public texts as conduits of discourse, Lo Bianco (2010:12–13) highlights laws as vital links in the chain between planning and practice, constituting potent instruments of performative action (Lo Bianco 2009:103). The National Language Act stands out as the source for language policy in general and law in particular. In introducing it the Tunku explained the partial retention of English as the "peaceful way" of prioritising justice and pragmatism over nationalism: "The wheels of justice must go round, otherwise there will be no security for anyone…" (*The Straits Times* 1967a, b, c). Yet he also warned non-Malays against shunning the national language "if they profess undivided loyalty to this country" (ibid). Incorporated into the constitution (Art.152), the Act is invoked in most discourses on policy. While the official role of English has been reduced by subsequent amendments, the Act is also cited to justify its continued use. Soon after its adoption it was reported that the secretary of the Bar Committee inferred from it that moves toward Malay should proceed with caution and consultation (*The Straits Times* 1967b.8.09). On the other hand Karpal Singh cited it when sarcastically calling for the voiding of all judgments written in English (Hafiz 2010.9.27).

Judicial decisions not only constitute the most authoritative performative statements after enactments but their grounds of judgment often include discourses about the social functions of legislation and moral duties of litigants. The majority opinion in *Merdeka University* (1982) does not address legal language itself but is an important example of how an apparently technical matter may index sociocultural discourses. In arguing that a discretion under the Universities and University Colleges Act to authorise new universities in the national interest implied the right to reject those not teaching in Malay it delves into decades of legislative and administrative practices before finding the national language to be a unifying instrument that universities, deemed to be statutory bodies, have a duty to use. The Lord President further referred to the Indian case of *Pathumma* (1978) to emphasise that social settings, national needs and popular aspirations must be considered in constitutional interpretation. In *Zainun Dahan* (1997) a motion filed in English was judged to be not merely a procedural error but a "willful violation" that could render proceedings "chaotic". In *Dato' Seri Anwar* (2010), the technical grounds on which an English memorandum was rejected were embellished with personal attacks describing its submission as a flagrant act that was the "hallmark" of the appellant. Subsequent strategic attempts by Anwar's counsel to overturn other judgments in English, including one involving a death-row client (Hafiz 2011.2.10), failed in their immediate purpose but succeeded in forcing the Bench to clarify their own right to use the language, thereby calling into question their denying the same right to advocates.

Judges' courtroom comments, which may constitute legally persuasive *obiter dicta,* often reveal the stance of individual justices and also their institutional culture, thus showing how trial proceedings constantly weave between language policy and practice. David (1993:115) describes a judge fearful of the impression he would leave if he allowed English in his courtroom. Powell (2008:51–52) heard defendants being asked why, as young Malaysians, they needed a Chinese interpreter, and while it is possible that the defendants themselves were adopting an ideological position in insisting on their right to an interpreter, *LoyarBurok*, a blog focused on justice issues, has drawn attention to continued deficiencies in either Malay or English among many Chinese, including the young (Ng 2011).

During investigations for this study a Melaka Sessions judge was observed preventing an expert witness from speaking English on the grounds that he was Malaysian, even though he had come unprepared to give medical testimony in Malay and struggled to do so (Chap. 9). Insufficient evidence has been gathered to claim that the broad principle of proceedings being in Malay is now being extended to witness testimony, but a Johor Bahru lawyer and a UM lecturer independently reported an increase in the practice of translating English evidence into Malay rather than hearing it directly. While many advocates claim they can predict the expectations of individual judges from their reputations or from the nature of the case, most feel they have to come prepared to use either language.

The public statements of Chief Justices, other judges, and justice ministers, along with legal administrators and politicians, constitute influential discourses that give weight, context and clarification to planning measures. In the early days of Malayanisation, for example, the provision in the National Language Act (s.2) implementing Malay for "official purposes" was interpreted by Perak's Legal Adviser to mean that letters to government departments in languages other than Malay could be responded to as long as the reply including a reminder to use the national language (*The Straits Times* 1967c.9.02). In 1990 the Justice Minister urged judges to be strict when considering whether to allow English (*The Straits Times* 1990.12.15) but 6 months later he saw fit to assure the profession that even when BM became the language of the courts (thereby admitting that this was not yet the case in practice) English would continue and lawyers would need to be bilingual (*The Straits Times* 1990.12.15). In 1994 the Chief Justice urged judges to use more Malay (*The Straits Times* 1994.9.24) and in 2002 the *de facto* law minister declared he would set a personal example to lawyers by using it exclusively for official speeches (*The Straits Times* 2002.3.09).

Discourse on legal language policy also emerges from parliamentary debate. UMNO backbenchers periodically question ministers about the language's lack of progress in law despite its extensive adoption in administration (Dewan Rakyat 1983.8.05) after decades of independence (ibid, 1986.11.26). On a different tack, Malay's official position in law has been invoked to demand more extensive use in higher education (ibid, 1995.11.28). Karpal Singh used parliament as a platform to warn against politicised enforcement of Malay without regard for legal needs (ibid, 1984.3.20), as well as to lampoon government ministers' fondness for code-mixes and anglicisms despite their purist rhetoric (Beh Lih Yi 2006.9.07).

Where we find a range of editorial emphasis within what has generally been a tightly controlled press we may infer a range of opinion within government itself. In the 15 years following the Language Act, *Utusan Malaysia* (e.g. 1981b.4.17, 1983.4.26) focused mostly on practical impediments to the progress of legal Malay, whereas in 1990 it gave prominent coverage to the Chief Justice's announcement of measures to promote the language in law and his description of the legal and judicial field as the 'strongest bulwark' (*benteng terkuat*) of English in the country (Rashid Darham 1990.6.01). Railing at the higher courts 18 years later, the paper called on judges to "fulfill the pledge" embedded in the amended Act (*Utusan Online* 2008a.12.09). English-language *The Star*, which has emphasised the importance of a multiethnic judiciary (2008.5.01) and generally supported English for science and maths instruction (2009.2.03), once placed former Chief Justice Zaki Azmi's pro-English comments in its educational section (Koshy 2013.9.15).

Other instruments of discourse planning are perhaps more symbolic than substantive, such as Dewan Bahasa's cultural campaigning through public seminars (*Berita Harian* 1990.11.20) or its nomination of Chief Justice Abdul Hamid Omar as Man of the Year for upholding Malay in the courts (*Berita Harian* 1992.4.03).

6.4 Lawyer Perspectives

The rapid growth and diversification of the bar make it increasingly difficult to construct a common legal culture or gauge its role in the formation of discourse on language policy, especially given lawyers' limited scope to initiate and empower new discourses. However the orientations of the Bar Council, the body that regulates the profession and coordinates State bar committees, can be construed from perusal of *Insaf* and *Praxis* (the former and current bar journals), from the bar website, and from press releases where language choice is a perennial if relatively infrequent topic. Periodically criticised for its lukewarm embrace of Malay (*The Straits Times* 1981.3.10; *Utusan Online* 2013.4.18), the Council is generally cautious about issuing statements directly in favour of English, preferring to focus on the linguistic needs of professionals and litigants (*The Straits Times* 1989a.6.21), the continuity of common law traditions (*Malaysiakini* 2004.10.14), and the problem of inaccurate BM translations of texts (Lavendran 2013.6.13), all of which imply support for English.

Praxis, like *Insaf* before it, carries few articles in Malay. A suspicion that the Council's leading lights lack confidence in BM is sometimes the subject of discussion on its web forum (*Majlis Peguam* 2014), where reported judgments, notices and comments are 95% in English. One 2005 posting[2] congratulated a high-profile lawyer for responding to a challenge to give his comments in Malay, but tempered this by wry speculation about who had translated his response from 'Mat Salleh' (white man's) language. Official speeches published on the website often begin ceremonially in Malay before proceeding to English, and personal observations of Bar Council events suggest some leading members rarely use the national language, despite acknowledging its status. Larger firms and anglophone lawyers appear to play a disproportionate role in local bar committee activities. According to an advocate from Melaka, meetings and events there are mostly in English. However, lawyers in Kota Bharu report that Kelantan bar meetings have been shifting steadily toward Malay.

The Bar Council has a long track record of criticising perceived interference in judicial independence (Donoghue 2013:46). When it condemned police brutality against participants in the Bersih 3.0 rally against electoral corruption, Mahathir accused it of acting as a political party (*Malaysiakini* 2012c.5.16). The Prime Minister's Department has revived the idea of setting up an alternative organisation to represent lawyers (*Malaysiakini* 2012b.5.14). In 2016 the bar president rejected accusations of being a 'busybody' in calling for the resignation of Attorney General Apandi, arguing it was within the Council's legal obligations to criticise an official who appeared to have failed to carry out his obligations to investigate a PM-linked financial scandal (Tong 2016.3.19). Later that year he issued a press release ridiculing suggestions by the deputy prime minister that the Council was in league with bodies aimed at toppling the government (Thiru 2016.12.10).

Although a weak marker of individual language preferences, ethnicity continues to feature prominently in perceptions about political and cultural orientations in the profession. It may be relevant, for example, that middle-class Indians have traditionally not only been overrepresented among lawyers but also associated with prowess in English, although there has been a gradual shift in the leadership of the Council, from domination by Indians to a more even ethnic balance (*Insaf*

[2] http://www.malaysianbar.org.my/component/option,com_joomlaboard/Itemid,/catid,36/func,view/id,509/#509

1968~2013).[3] In 2013 *LoyarBurok* carried an article accusing the Council of hypocrisy for constantly reminding the government of the need to respect the constitution while continuing to refer to the national language as Bahasa Malaysia in its reports and speeches when the constitution has always called it Bahasa Melayu (Aidli Khalid 2013.7.02), the former indexing the cultural diversity of Malaysia rather than the primacy of Malay culture.

The appointment of Tommy Thomas, an ethnic Indian and non-Muslim, as Attorney General in June, 2018, apparently aroused concerns from some sultans on the Council of Rulers despite being a unanimous decision by the new government (Goh 2018.6.2). It has resurrected politicised divisions over the cultural position of a profession periodically accused of marginalising Malay, especially in its elite divisions. (*Utusan Online* 2014a.8.17), with the new appointee's lack of proficiency a prime target for critics of the new government. While denying that race and religion were material to their objections, Concerned Lawyers for Justice and Young Professionals attacked the AG's inexperience in constitutional matters and concomitant unfamiliarity with Islamic laws and the Malay-weighted national social contract, and specifically condemned his inadequate grasp of the national language (*Malaysiakini* 2018d.6.04). PAS has gone so far as to claim that Thomas, together with new Finance Minister Lim Guan Eng, are "sidelining the use of Bahasa" (*Malaysiakini* 2018e.7.05). Such rhetoric partly reflects a cultural reaction from some circles to the fact that the country now has not only an Indian AG but also a Chinese *de facto* law minister (Liew Vui Keong) and a Sabahan Chief Justice (Richard Malanjum, a Sabahan). PAS's information chief labelled Malanjum as not on the side of Islam (*Malaysiakini* 2018f.7.12). In *Lina Joy* (2006), his was the only opinion in support of freedom to change religion, and the only one written in English. But caution should be adopted before casting the bar in a single light since nationwide ideological divisions are found within the profession as well. In July, 2018, for example, a Muslim law pupil claimed that her master refused to authorise her admission to the bar because he felt her participation in a civil action against a radical Muslim preacher made her a potential threat to Islam (Hafiz 2018.7.21).

6.5 Dominant Discourses

Language-in-law policy figures less prominently in public discourse than educational policy, presumably because citizens participate less regularly in the legal system and take a back seat to professionals employing legalese that can baffle non-lawyers, whatever language it is encoded in. Leading discourses line up along a range of positions about the desired balance between Malay and English, with other languages scarcely considered. No one openly calls for a return to English (which could be construed as seditious), but proposals for BM to take over all legal

[3] The current Malay President follows two Indians and a Chinese.

functions remain in the minority and are rarely framed specifically. The Constitution and Language Act are the most important authorities cited to legitimise views. Since these are broadly drafted, rhetorically favouring Malay while pragmatically allowing English, discourses tend to be richer in principle than in specific proposals.

Certain persistent discourses in official statements, press coverage and civil society forums continue to frame public discussions on legal language and also recur in the private comments of lawyers and law students. These can generally be placed along two axes, one charting preferences for Malay or English, and a second charting orientation toward symbolic or pragmatic values. The latter spectrum evokes Haviland's (2003:764) polarisation of theoretical and practical arguments whereby he distinguishes interest in linguistic rights and in language as a sociopolitical tool from concern about courtroom translation and literacy. Similarly, De Schutter and Robichaud (2016) separate identity and non-identity issues in discourses on linguistic justice. Identity-based discourses are not merely symbolic as they draw on the view that equal access to the opportunities offered by a polity depends on ability to access them in one's first language, but they tend to focus on non-communicative matters such as the rights, self-worth and dignity of communities. Non-identity issues, on the other hand, target more communicative matters such as efficiency and transparency.

In the Malaysian context both orientations are often found within the same statements, as in a recent speech by the Sultan of Perak, currently Chancellor of UM, in which he associated the dignity and glory of Malay with the spirit of the independence agreement but also stressed its knowledge, administrative and commercial value in a globalised era (*Malaysiakini* 2016c.10.05).

6.5.1 Replacing Common Law

The idea of replacing common law altogether is not in itself a linguistic one, but it generally implies cutting out the need for English. Counterviews in support of common law are linked, though less imperatively, to presumptions that English should remain along with the legal tradition that was developed in it.

Shortly after independence, rejection of common law was discussed by young lawyers as a way of avoiding the colossal task of translating precedents (*The Straits Times* 1959.8.24). Three years later in an exchange of letters in the press (Malayan Malay 1962.11.02; Wong 1962.11.06) readers debated whether English law was an un-Malayan anachronism and an impediment to unification. Echoing the State Advocate-General's view of English law as "universally accepted as the characteristic of a free society", Malaysia's first Lord President declared "a common law… just as essential a unifying force as a common language" (*The Straits Times* 1963.10.15). Conversely Ahmad Fairoz, who according to UM's Azmi Sharom is the Chief Justice with the strongest record on promoting Malay, more than once proposed moving to some inquisitorial, socialist (Faridah 2004.10.13) or Islamic (Bell 2007.9.01) system and was lauded by a minister for contributing to justice

(*The Star Online* 2007.8.24) but criticised by the Bar Council for undervaluing the current system's proven flexibility (*Malaysiakini* 2004.10.14). Outright calls to make *Syariah* the basis of Malaysian law (Zurairi 2013.10.19) provoke more controversy than evolutionary stances such as Farid's (2011) suggestion that judicial decisions refer to Islam and indigenous custom rather than foreign precedent. Proposals for strengthening *Syariah* frequently characterise English law as an interloper that has overextended its legitimacy (Mohamed Azam 2013.12.10). One UIA law lecturer has argued that the constitution, while supreme, wasn't necessarily intended to be secular (Shazwan 2014.5.29).

Without going so far as to call for an end to common law, the country's first parliamentary draftsman came to the opinion that it should unshackle itself from its foreign past:

> To adopt words of Mr Justice Holmes, the "morally-tinted words" used by
> common law lawyers "have caused a great deal of confused thinking".
> Malaysia belongs not to Europe but to Asia.
> (Reginald Hickling 1994:12)

There is a counterpart to polemic in favour of replacing English, alongside English law, in the arguments of those who fear the expansion of legal Malay will inevitably entail the erosion of common law culture. L.A. Sheridan's sense that the use of Malay in law had political implications (Sect. 4.1) appeared to anticipate Karpal Singh's warnings (in Mead 1988:45) about alien concepts hitching a ride on the back of a new legal language, and parallels with the fears expressed by Hong Kong lawyers about the cultural impact of Cantonese were mentioned in Chap. 1.

6.5.2 Legal Malay in the Service of National Unity and Dignity

Most discourse is framed by the assumption that English-based law will to some extent continue and therefore turns on the degree to which English should continue to be the medium of this law. Malay is seen as embodying the spirit, unity and dignity of the nation so failure to use it in an important national institution such as law constitutes betrayal of the postcolonial agenda. The preponderance of nationalistic and symbolic language, rather than appeals to legal transparency and intelligibility, adds weight to a default position among language planning theorists that reforms are primarily shaped by extralinguistic problems. Even legal arguments tend to take a back seat: in what could have been framed as a constitutional debate over the right of an East Malaysian politician to use English in parliament, cabinet minister Ismail Sabri Yaakob chose to denounce the practice as *demeaning* the official language that is "even used in the courts" (Anne Muhammed 2015.11.24). A decade before, one lawyer described those same courts' neglect of Malay as the *persecution* of the national language (Abdul Malik 2004.8.20).

A lot of rhetoric in this vein draws on the history of Malay as a pre-colonial medium of law (Nik Abdul Rashid 1989:2) and diplomacy (Awang Sariyan 2013), but the most common starting point is based on the premise that any denial of its constitutional supremacy is improper (Norlizah Abas 2009.12.09) and by extension impugns the nation's aspirations (Mohd Yusmadi 2006.4.05). Words like *biadap* (insolent) litter the rhetoric of those who take this stance against English (e.g. Ismail Sabri Yaaokob, cited by Anne Muhammad 2015.11.24). Furthermore no excuse for lack of proficiency is entertained since studying the official language is obligatory (Tay et al. 1981.3.17), so the recalcitrance exemplified by the legal profession is characterised as an attitudinal or cultural problem rather than a pedagogical one (Abdullah Ahmad 1991:17). The judiciary's fondness for anglicisms has been dubbed tantamount to forcing citizens to study English in order to understand Malay (Nik Abdul Rashid 1989:13). Association between English and *kolonialisme mental* (Abdullah Ahmad 1991:9) reaches down into civil society. One lawyer informant heading a human rights body felt the police and other government servants responded better to enquiries and complaints expressed in Malay, even if they understood English, while a UM law student said she refrained from using English in her provincial home town in case people thought her arrogant. At the same time, poor English is regularly cited, even in the Malay-targeted press, to throw doubt on public figures' education or intelligence (*Harakah Daily* 2013.1.15).

While lawyers are regularly singled out for resisting national policy (Dewan Rakyat 1995.11.28), with *Utusan* even calling for those not fluent in Malay to be suspended (*Utusan Online* 2008b.12.10), the strongest criticism is reserved for ethnic Malay academics and politicians who don't take their own language seriously. National laureate Muhammad Salleh (Yusof Ghani 2002.8.12) has spoken of Malay being marginalised by the very people who should be promoting it. Comments about politicians who send their children to study in England (Tan Peek Guat 2013.6.15, in *Majlis Peguam* 2014) or use English in Cabinet meetings (Praba Ganesan 2011.11.03) align with Beaugrande's (1999:108) characterisation of elites as indifferent or even hostile to the language planning that they oversee.

In general discussions about the medium of law as an instrument of unity constitute a subset of the ongoing debate about whether English is alien, divisive and elitist rather than a part of national identity. When Sarawak Chief Minister Adenan Satem called for his state to declare English co-official with Malay in reflection of its historical importance there, former Information and Communications Minister Rais Yatim responded: "Isn't this a disintegration and will it not cause a split in the society?" (*Malaysiakini* 2015.11.24).

The discourse of dignity is sometimes attached to Malay in international contexts too. Rais Yatim (*Malaysiakini* 2017.11.25) has added his views to a decades-long polemic about the language being denied its rightful place as an official medium of ASEAN (now generally implying a co-official role, when the body was first formed it was often touted as preferable to English). There is a pragmatic basis to such claims since Malay and Indonesian between them have more L1 and proficient L2 speakers than any other language in the region, but they are attenuated by the two nations' perennial orientation toward cultural demarcation from, rather than association with, each other. Any possibility of extending international legitimacy to legal Malay is further undermined by the disparate origins of jurisprudence in each nation, notwithstanding the occasional foray by Malaysian jurists into the Indonesian legal lexicon (*Berita Harian* 1995a.1.13).

6.5.3 Potential of Malay as a Medium of Law

Some polemic gives more weight to pragmatic and technical considerations than cultural resistance, negotiating a discursive space identified by Zubaidah (2002:142) when pointing out the difference between accepting Malay as a national symbol and embracing it as a means to economic and academic attainment.

Riding a crest of language planning initiatives in the 1980s, one parliamentarian voiced support for amending the 1976 Legal Profession Act to require lawyers to know Malay by describing it as a practical, as well as 'decent' (*layak*), language that should be good enough for the courts if it was good enough for the legislature (Dewan Rakyat 1983.8.05). In ridiculing the notion that there had been no justice in Malaya until English was introduced, law academic Nik Abdul Rashid (1989:2) suggested the judiciary was ignoring Malay's intellectual capabilities by treating it as a Proton (the somewhat maligned national car) and English as a Mercedes.

In 1990 the Justice Minister (*Utusan Malaysia* 1990.6.30) urged lawyers to stop harping on inadequacies in Malay texts and instead become part of the solution to the problem. Alongside rhetoric about Malay as "the medium from which the nation itself draws life", Hickling (2001:37) argued that its use would advance Malaysian jurisprudence. More recently, a head of DBP (Awang Sariyan 2013) attempted to link the expansion of Malay to the strengthening of the legal system, although he offered few concrete proposals for how to do so.

6.5.4 Access to Justice

Although arguments based on the delivery of justice in specific cases figure more prominently in the discourse of practitioners than policymakers, support for Malay in the service of more transparent and accessible legal processes goes back 50 years or longer. A *Straits Times* reader (1962.11.02) argued that even if political expediency was the main reason for doing away with English, judicial expediency was not a sufficient reason to retain it, and accused those who felt law could not operate properly in another language of giving no thought to capital defendants at the mercy of inadequate interpreters because of their lack of English. *Utusan Malaysia* (1984.6.02) claimed the voice of most workers went unheard because labour laws had not been translated into Malay. Somewhat defensively, deputy prime minister Ghafar Baba once assured the House that BM would "not affect the process of ensuring justice is accorded to everyone" (*The Straits Times* 1989b.10.20). A few years later the Chief Judge of Malaya tried similarly to assuage the concerns of foreign residents about the expansion of Malay (*Berita Harian* 1995b.7.22). More recently, Karpal Singh unsuccessfully sought review of a judgment (Kow 2012.8.02) on the grounds that the poor Malay of one of the judges – from East Malaysia – constituted coram failure.

In an article in *Insaf* prominent for its length and its choice of Malay medium, an Indian-Malaysian lawyer (Balakrishnan 1990) put forward several reasons for using the national language, including its potential for reducing the backlog of cases, the right of litigants to understand procedures and arguments, and, citing a case of professional misconduct, the need to restrain lawyers who mislead their clients. Another practitioner writing in *Utusan* (Salleh Buang 2003.4.29) dubbed Malay a 'client-friendly language' and wondered why sale and purchase agreements and complex civil cases were still mostly in English. Without addressing legal differences between common law and *Syariah* he went on to recommend the latter as an example of how a legal system can be administered in the national language:

> In short, the question I want us to ponder this week is why Malay is marginalised or neglected by the legal profession and civil judicial institutions of our country. If you want to see court proceedings entirely in Malay, take a day or two off to attend a Syariah court somewhere.
>
> 'Salleh Buang', *Utusan Malaysia* (2003.4.29) [4]

Judicial transparency has long been marshalled in support of English, as well as Malay. Insisting that the wishes of the many who were happier using the national language in court were already substantially complied with, Lord President Mohamed Suffian (*The Straits Times* 1979.10.30) declared those demanding complete use of Malay to be as emotional as those wanting complete use of Islamic law and insisted that the independence and fairness of the existing English-based system was appreciated by most Muslims. Thirty years later one of his successors, Zaki Azmi, argued that English was still needed for complex legal agreements (Koshy 2013.9.15). Former bar president Steven Thiru[5] has expressed concern that Malay may sometimes be used to mask poor legal reasoning.

Some discourse avoids preference for either language in favouring whichever is more capable of delivering justice in the circumstances. Zaki (Koshy 2013.9.15) suggested that although judges tend to prefer English texts they find it useful to have the Malay version alongside them when there is doubt about legislative intentions. But such pragmatism seems to be voiced more in opposition to Malay nationalism than in support, as on a bar website forum (2011.12.13, in Majlis Peguam 2014) that cited cases of witnesses feeling reluctant to admit to their deficiencies in the national language. In a posting in June 2013 (ibid), one commenter begins in neutral enough terms but clearly comes down on the side of English:

> I am of the opinion that so long as the justice has been served, language shall not be a bearer to a justice system in Malaysia as many legal terms have not been defined and provided for in Bahasa Malaysia.
>
> (Tong Kuan Ling 2013.6.13)

---

[4] My translation.

[5] Interviewed in Kuala Lumpur, 2013.8.

6.5.5 Malay for Domestic Law, English for International Law

With common law widely recognised as an international system with local applicability, a labour division between English for international law and Malay for domestic law seems acceptable to many. One Multimedia University lecturer suggested this was a logical dichotomy in legal practice that mirrored academic approaches to the two languages. Karpal Singh, while taking care to dub Malay the language that unites the country, called English the language "which unites nations" (*New Straits Times* 2009b.12.11). The chair of a pro-PPSMI (English for maths and science) pressure group argues that BM alone is not enough for Malays as it is not an international language (*New Straits Times* 2009a.3.21) and the Chief Minister of Sarawak cited the need to have international trade contracts in English when justifying its promotion in education (*Malaysiakini* 2016d.10.17). In a recent address to Certificate of Legal Practice graduates the Sultan of Perak combined internationalism and nationalism when reminding his audience that English proficiency was necessary to prevent Malaysians from being left behind in the global race and that its use did not imply waning patriotism (MLTC 2016.4.28), adding:

> The people must equip themselves with instruments to compete with the world's citizens. We have to boldly step forward because the war is not won by just building a fortress…

The statements by two former Chief Justices heading this chapter reveal subtly contrasting perceptions of the international dimension of Malaysian law, each broadly within the middle ground that encompasses the majority of opinions while allowing for differential rhetorical positioning. Both recognise a role for English, but Fairuz builds a case for more Malay (*Utusan Online* 2008c:12.17) by applauding the use of national languages in the courts of civil law jurisdictions and seeing English as important primarily for international affairs and trade. Zaki (Koshy 2013.9.15), on the other hand, addresses the cross-border interdiscursivity of common law and stresses the value of Commonwealth and American jurisprudence for criminal and commercial jurisprudence. By adding that Malay is fine for the lower courts but not "if you want to expand", Zaki's stance recalls Mahathir's emphasis on English for the acquisition of knowledge in a competitive world (Nik Ramlah 1993:134) and implies that private practitioners have to engage with forces beyond Malaysia even when not working specifically on international cases.

It is evident that constructions of 'domestic' and 'international' go beyond geography in pitting concerns for government control and social stability against orientations toward economic expansion and market forces. Just as international schools evoke the private sector and detachment from government control more than they evoke foreign students, international law firms evoke something more than contracts with overseas companies.

The private sector is often cast as unresponsive to national language policy (*Utusan Malaysia* 1981a.4.01), with ethnicity routinely invoked to reinforce this characterisation given non-Malays' apparent inability or reluctance (*Malaysiakini* 2006.3.25) to join the public sector and Malays' complaints of discriminative hiring practices in private firms (Koon 2012.11.10). Discourses linking private law to English typically refer to competiveness, responsiveness to market forces and globalisation. Even when commending the rise in Malay standards and focusing on the working of the domestic courts and the Attorney-General's Chambers, former Chief Justice Abdul Hamad Mohamed (*The Star Online* 2013.8.07) drew associations between English and employability, competitiveness, and reaching out to wider audiences.

6.6 Discourses of Justice

It is only to be expected that justice is frequently invoked in discussions about language policy in the legal domain, whether on behalf of Malay, English or bilingualism. But justice is a loaded term that indexes wider concerns than the workings of the judicial system itself, and discourses need to be unpacked in order to determine what kind of justice speakers have in mind and whose justice they are referring to. At one end of the scale is justice for participants in individual legal cases and at the other, justice for the entire nation. Neither construction is independent of ideological underpinnings.

Discourse focused on individual cases and proceedings, whether voiced by practitioners supporting Malay to help litigants understand proceedings (Balakrishnan 1990) and consumers understand sales contracts (Salleh Buang 2003.4.29), or by a bar president attributing injustice to non-Muslim parents to mistranslations of English legal texts (Lavendran 2013.6.13), rests not only on pragmatic assessments but on underlying ideas about what different languages are capable of, and such ideas are seldom linked to linguistic analysis. Senior Malaysian lawyers frequently voice suspicions about the quality of Malay legal texts despite their own lack of facility in the language, and the idea that common law is inevitably more effective and transparent in English is a default position for many. While hardly addressed by linguists or lawyers in Malaysia as yet, the influence of language ideologies in justice systems is of increasing interest to analysts elsewhere, having been studied in officially monolingual contexts (Nakane 2013, in Japan), unofficially bilingual contexts (Angermeyer 2015, in the United States) and officially bilingual contexts (Ng 2009, in Hong Kong).

The ideological framing of other types of justice is more transparent. In arguments in support of Malay, appeals to justice for the Malays as long-term custodians of the land, or for the nation emerging from colonial domination, shape much of the discourse of dignity and may be more persuasive than arguments about the rights of individual defendants or litigants. Frequent criticism of the courts' neglect or demeaning of Malay implies a positioning of law as a servant of the national language rather than of the national language as serving the law. Such discourses are linked to the idea that the Malay language itself is an object deserving of justice. The concept of justice for languages, a relatively recent development in political philosophy as it grapples with the management of multilingualism from postmodernist perspectives (e.g. De Schutter and Robichaud 2016), has historical echoes in the ideas of nationalists such as Leibnitz in Germany and Richelieu in France, and there may be parallels between the discourse of liberation from Latin in early modern Europe and discourses against English in present-day Asia.

Haviland (2003:765) argues that multilingual contexts tend to produce a different set of ideologies from monolingual settings, which may help explain why Malaysian lawyers and language planners generally find the existence of bilingual law itself unremarkable, even if they argue about the roles and values of the languages supporting it. Hence we rarely find polemic about the ambiguity of bilingual law, only criticism of discrepancies in particular texts. The pervasiveness of ethnic and cultural discourse in Malaysia feeds an intuitive sense of the diachronic and interdiscursive dimensions of day-to-day language choices among legal practitioners that echoes the theoretical perspectives of Bakhtin or Bourdieu. Linkage between professional language practices and societal perspectives will be explored in the following three chapters, on law schools, law offices and courtrooms respectively.

Cases Cited

Dato' Seri Anwar Ibrahim v Tun Dr Mahathir Mohamad [2010] 3CLJ 444 CA
Lina Joy v Majlis Agama Islam Wilayah Persekutuan, Kerejaan Malaysia Rayuan Sivil no. 01-2-2006(W)
Merdeka University v Government [1982] 2 MLJ 243
Zainun bte Hj Dahan lwn *Rakyat Merchant Bankers Bhd & Satu Lagi* [1997] 4 CLJ

References

Abdul Malik Abdul Hakim. (2004, August 20). *Mahkamah abai bahasa Melayu?* [Court neglecting Malay?] *Utusan Online*. Accessed 21 Feb 2012, from http://www.utusan.com.my/utusan/info.asp?y=2004&dt=0820&pub=utusan_malaysia&sec=Rencana&pg=re_07.htm

Abdullah bin Ahmad. (1991) *Strategi dan persediaan ke arah perlaksanaan bahasa Malaysia sebagai bahasa undang-undang* [Strategy and preparation for implementing Malay as a legal language]. Paper presented at Seminar Bahasa dan Undang- undang [Seminar on Language and Law], Dewan Bahasa, 1991.12.3–4.

Aidil Khalid. (2013, Jully 2). *Language, The law and the elephant in the room. What has happened to the language of the Malaysian courts?* Accessed Oct 2014, from http://www.loyarburok.com/2013/07/02/language-law-elephant-room/

A. Kadir Jasin. (2018, October 28). Returning the press to journalists. *Malaysiakini*. Accessed 29 Feb 2018, from http://www.malaysiakini.com/letter/449307

Al Hafar. (2014, February 14). Why Teresa Kok's video is 'insulting to Islam'. *Malaysiakini*. Accessed 14 Feb 2014, from http://www.malaysiakini.com/letter/254373

Angermeyer, Philipp Sebastian. (2015). *Speak English or what? Codeswitching and interpreter use in New York City courts*. New York: Oxford University Press.

Anne Muhammad. (2015, November 24). *Minister: DAP MP 'biadap' [rude] for wanting to debate in English*. Accessed 25 Nov 2015, from http://www.malaysiakini.com/news/320802

Asmah Haji Omar. (1987). *Malay in its sociocultural context*. Kuala Lumpur: Dewan Bahasa dan Pustaka.

Awang bin Sariyan [Direct-General, Dewan Bahasa]. (2013, November 30). *Memperkasa Sistem Perundangan Negara melalui Bahasa Melayu* [Empowering the legal system through Malay]. Keynote paper presented at *Ceramah Memperkasa Sistem Perundangan Negara melalui Bahasa Melayu* [Forum on empowering the legal system through Malay]. Malaysian Bar Council, Kuala Lumpur.

Balakrishnan, R. (1990, 12). Kewibawaan BM menjamin keadilan dalam undang-undang sivil [BM integrity guarantees justice in civil law]. *Insaf, XXI*(3), 1, 47–60.

Ball, Stephen. (2006). *Education policy and social class: The selected works of Stephen J. Ball*. London: Routledge.

Beaugrande, Robert de. (1999). Theory and practice in the discourse of language planning. *World Englishes, 18*(2), 107–121.

Beh Lih Yi. (2006, September 7). Karpal: Why nobody dare to touch Khairy? *Malaysiakini*. Accessed 20 Mar 2011, from http://www.malaysiakini.com/news/56484

Bell, Thomas. (2007, September 1). Malaysia considers switch to Islamic law. *The Telegraph*. Accessed 12 Dec 2013, from http://www.telegraph.co.uk/news/worldnews/1561896/Malaysia-considers-switch-to-Islamic-law.html

Berita Harian. (1990, November 20). Bahasa di mahkamah [Language in court], p. 4

Berita Harian. (1992, April 3). *Ketua Hakim dipilih Tokoh Dewan Masyarakat* [Chief Justice chosen as man of the year by *Dewan Masyarakat*], p. 3.

Berita Harian. (1995a, January 13). *Perundangan: Malaysia kaji istilah Indonesia* [Law: Malaysia studying Indonesian terminology], p. 12.

Berita Harian. (1995b, July 22). *Hakim: guna bahasa Melayu tidak jejas keadilan* [Judge: Using Malay doesn't impair justice], p. 2.

Bhatia, Vijay. (1993). *Analysing genre. Language use in professional settings*. London/New York: Longman.

Bon, Edmund. (2013). An accidental footnote. In B. Welsh & J. U. H. Chin (Eds.), *Awakenings: The Adbullah Badawi Years in Malaysia* (pp. 371–388). Petaling Jaya: SIRD.

Bourdieu, Pierre. (2000). *Pascalian meditations*. Cambridge: Polity Press.

Butler, Judith. (1993). *Bodies that matter. On the discursive limits of "sex"*. New York: Routledge.

Corson, David. (1989). *Language planning across the curriculum*. Clevedon: Multilingual Matters.

David, Maya Khemlani. (1993). Language and Law: Communicative strategies in a court of law a Malaysian experience. In K. L. Tee (Ed.), *Legal education in Malaysia Quo Vadis?* Kuala Lumpur: University of Malaya.

De Schutter, Helder, & Robichaud, David. (2016). Van Parijsen linguistic justice – Context, analysis and critiques. In H. De Schutter & D. Robichaud (Eds.), *Linguistic Justice. Van Parijs and his critics* (pp. 1–26). London/New York: Routledge.

Dewan Rakyat. (1983, August 5). Malaysian parliamentary proceedings: DR-05081983 [Tan Mamat Ghazalee bin Abdul Rahman, Ulu Nerus].

Dewan Rakyat. (1984, March 20). Malaysian parliamentary proceedings: DR-20031984. [Karpal Singh].

Dewan Rakyat. (1986, November 26). Malaysian parliamentary proceedings: DR-26111986 [Oo Gin Sun, Deputy Minister in Prime Minister's Office, in response to Mohd. Zain bin Abdullah].

Dewan Rakyat. (1995, November 28). Malaysian parliamentary proceedings: DR-2111995 [Tuan Haji Mohamed bin Haji Abdullah, Pasir Puteh].

Donoghue, Tim. (2013). *Tiger of Jelutong*. Singapore: Marshall Cavendish.

Fairclough, Norman. (1989). *Language and power*. Harlow: Pearson Education.

Farid Sufian Shuaib. (2011). Towards Malaysian common law: convergence between indigenous norms and common law methods. *CLJ Legal Network* [2011] 1 LNS(A)ix. Accessed 30 Aug 2012, from www.cljlaw.com/

Faridah Begum. (2004, October 13). CJ plans to review justice system. *The Star Online*. Accessed 14 Oct 2004, from https://www.thestar.com.my/news/nation/2004/10/13/cj-plans-to-review%2D%2Djustice-system/

Fishman, Joshua A. (1994). Critiques of language planning. *Journal of Multilingual and Multicultural Development, 15*(2/3), 91–99.

Foucault, Michel. (1980). *Power/Knowledge: Selected interviews and other writings 1972–1977*, Ed. Gordon and trans. Gordon, Marshall, Mepham and Soper. New York: Vintage.

Galanter, Marc. (1974). Why the "haves" come out ahead: Speculations on the limits of legal change. *Law and Society Review, 9*(1), 165–230.

Giddens, Anthony. (1979). *Central problems in social theory. Action, structure and contradiction in social analysis*. London: Macmillan.

Goh, Norman. (2018, June 2). Source: Thomas is sole AG nominee, give time for rulers to deliberate. *Malaysiakini*. Accessed 3 June 2018, from https://www.malaysiakini.com/news/428014

Haarmann, Harald (1990). Language planning in the light of a general theory of language: A methodological framework. *International Journal of Sociology of Language, 86*, 103–126.

Hafiz Yatim. (2010, September 27). Karpal: Written judgments must be in BM. *Malaysiakini*. Accessed 29 Sept 2010, from http://www.malaysiakini.com/news/143709

Hafiz Yatim. (2011, February 10). Ex-cop on death row loses final appeal. *Malaysiakini*. Accessed 9 Dec 2011, from http://www.malaysiakini.com/news/155702

Hafiz Yatim. (2018, July 21). Law grad claims call to Bar denied due to Zakir Naik lawsuit. *Malaysiakini*. Accessed 23 July 2018, from http://www.malaysiakini.com/news/435292

Halliday, M. A. K. (2001). Literacy and linguistics: Relationships between spoken and written language. In Burns & Coffin (Eds.), *Analysing English in a global context* (pp. 181–193). London: Routledge.

Harakah Daily. (2013, January 15). Zoh1ra's SW1M fights back, only to expose grasp of English language. Accessed 17 Jan 2013, from http://en.harakahdaily.net/index.php/berita-utama/6562-zohras-sw1m-fights-back-only-to-expose-grasp-of-english-language.html

Haviland, John B. (2003). Ideologies of language: Some reflections on language and U.S. law. *American Anthropologist, 105*(4), 764–774.

Hickling, Reginald Hugh. (1994). 'The Progress of Malaysian Law'. Annual Lecture delivered on December 6, 1994. *Journal of the Malaysian Branch of the Royal Asiatic Society, LXVII*(pt. 2), 1–16.

Hickling, Reginald Hugh. (2001). *Malaysian Law*. Kuala Lumpur: Pelanduk.

Koh Jun Lin. (2016, March 5). Worse to come when Sedition Act amendments come into force. *Malaysiakini*. Accessed 5 Mar 2016, from http://www.malaysiakini.com/news/332817

Koh Jun Lin. (2019, January 20). Move to abolish Sedition Act is seditious, lawyers claims. *Malaysiakini*. Accessed 21 Jan 2019, from http://www.malaysiakini.com/news/461026

Koon Yew Yin. (2012, November, 10). Hiring discrimination study a half-finished product. *Malaysiakini*. Accessed 11 Nov 2012, from http://www.malaysiakini.com/news/213938

Koshy, Shaila. (2013, September 15). Language makes the law. *The Star* (Online edition). Accessed 15 Sept 2013, from http://www.thestar.com.my/News/Nation/2013/09/15/Education-Tun-Zaki-English-Medium-Schools.aspx

Kow Gah Chie. (2012, August 2). Karpal's review application in sedition case dismissed. *Malaysiakini*. Accessed 5 Aug 2012, from http://www.malaysiakini.com/news/205334

Lavendran, G. (2013, June 13). Bar Council: Translating Constitution causing confusion. *Free Malaysia Today*. Accessed 14 June 2013, from http://www.freemalaysiatoday.com/category/nation/2013/06/18/bar-council-translating-constitution-causing-confusion/

Lo Bianco, Joseph. (2004). Language planning as applied linguistics. In A. Davies & C. Elder (Eds.), *The handbook of applied linguistics* (pp. 738–763). London: Blackwell.

Lo Bianco, Joseph. (2009). Critical Discourse Analysis (CDA) and Language Planning (LP): Constraints and applications of the critical in language planning. In T. Lê, Q. Lê, & M. Short (Eds.), *Critical discourse analysis. An interdisciplinary perspective* (pp. 101–118). New York: Nova Science.

Lo Bianco, Joseph. (2010). Language policy and planning. In N. H. Hornberger & S. L. McKay (Eds.), *Sociolinguistics and language education* (pp. 143–173). Clevedon: Multilingual Matters.

Loone, Susan. (2013, March 25). DAP rejects 10-minute airtime for election manifesto. *Malaysiakini*. Accessed 27 Mar 2013, from http://www.malaysiakini.com/news/224845

Majlis Peguam. (2014). Malaysian Bar Council website. Accessed Dec 2012, Mar 2013, May 2014, from http://www.malaysianbar.org.my

Malayan Malay. (1962, November 2). Replacing English with Malay in our courts. *The Straits Times* (Letters to the editor), p. 16.

Malaysiakini. (2004, October 14). Bar Council rejects changes to current legal system. Accessed 27 Sept 2011, from http://www.malaysiakini.com/news/30780

Malaysiakini. (2006, March 25). TI way to attract more non-Malay civil servants. Accessed 10 Apr 2011, from http://www.malaysiakini.com/news/48891

Malaysiakini. (2011, January 25). Online news sites to be included under PPPA. Accessed 31 Jan 2011, from http://www.malaysiakini.com/news/154483

Malaysiakini. (2012a, July 11). National Harmony Act to replace Sedition Act. Accessed 19 June 2014, from http://www.malaysiakini.com/news/203363

Malaysiakini. (2012b, May 14). Nazri: Cabinet to discuss plan to set up legal academy. Accessed 15 May 2014, from http://www.malaysiakini.com/news/197888

Malaysiakini. (2012c, May 16). Mahathir: Bar Council has become political party. Accessed 16 May 2012, from http://www.malaysiakini.com/news/198108

Malaysiakini. (2013, December 12). Ministry bars M'kini from press conference on Shiites. Accessed 12 Dec 2013, from http://www.malaysiakini.com/news/249215

Malaysiakini. (2014a, January 27). Malaysiakini barred from Muhyiddin function. Accessed 28 Jan 2014, from http://www.malaysiakini.com/news/252913

Malaysiakini. (2014b, June 17). 70pct Malaysians feel the pinch in 2014. Accessed 19 June 2014, from http://www.malaysiakini.com/news/265886

Malaysiakini. (2015, November 24). S'wak asked to reconsider English official language decision. Accessed 25 Nov 2016, from http://www.malaysiakini.com/news/320741

Malaysiakini. (2016a, March 22). MCMC blocked 399 websites till Feb 2016. Accessed 23 Mar 2016, from http://www.malaysiakini.com.news/334886

Malaysiakini. (2016b, April 1). Local dailies snub WSJ's exposé. Accessed 2 Apr 2016, from https://www.malaysiakini.com/news/336107

Malaysiakini. (2016c, October 5). Perak sultan expresses concern over Malay language. Accessed 10 Oct 2016, from http://www.malaysiakini.com/news/357965

Malaysiakini. (2016d, October 17). Stupid! S'wak CM censures past education policy. Accessed 18 Oct 2016, from http://www.malaysiakini.com/news/359331

Malaysiakini. (2016e, November 12). Do M'sians trust the news they read? Accessed 10 Jan 2017, from http://www.malaysiakini.com/news/362604

Malaysiakini. (2017, November 25). Make Malay official language of Asean, Rais says. Accessed 26 Nov 2017, from https://www.malaysiakini.com/news/403334

Malaysiakini. (2018a, March 5). Anti-fake news law to be tabled to cabinet in 'weeks'. Accessed 5 Mar 2018, from https://www.malaysiakini.com/news/414483

Malaysiakini. (2018b, March 27). NUJ: Anti-fake news bill will likely end up stifling the media. Accessed 28 Mar 2018, from https://www.malaysiakini.com/news/417178

Malaysiakini. (2018c, April 25). Press Freedom Index: M'sia drops a rank, affected by China media control model. Accessed 30 Mar 2018, from https://www.malaysiakini.com/news/421513

Malaysiakini. (2018d, June 4). Naming Thomas makes Harapan no different from BN, say lawyer groups. Accessed 5 June 2018, from https://www.malaysiakini.com/news/428228

Malaysiakini. (2018e, July 5). PAS: Guan Eng, Thomas sidelining use of Bahasa. Accessed 5 July 2018, from https://www.malaysiakini.com/news/432879

Malaysiakini. (2018f, July 12). Muslims restless as non-Muslims now 'control' legal system, PAS claims. Accessed 12 July 2018, from https://www.malaysiakini.com/news/433838

Malaysiakini. (2018g, August 16). Anti-Fake News Act repealed. Accessed 12 July 2018, from https://www.malaysiakini.com/news/439219
Malaysiakini. (2018h, December 7). Home ministry bans book on Malayan Communist Party. Accessed 18 Dec 2018, from https://www.malaysiakini.com/news/455221
Malay Mail Online. (2014, June 3). Umno, Najib, officially sue Malaysiakini for defamation. Accessed 4 June 2014, from http://www.themalaymailonline.com/malaysia/article/umno-najib-officially-sue-malaysiakini-for-defamation
Malaysian Insider. (2014, September 12). Lawyer Edmund Bon investigated over alleged seditious comment. Accessed 12 Sept 2014, from http://www.themalaysianinsider.com/malaysia/article/lawyer-edmund-bon-investigated-over-alleged-seditious-comment#sthash.bzSy9htC.dpuf
Mead, Richard. (1988). *Malaysia's National language policy and the legal system.* New Haven: Yale.
Merdeka Center. (2010). *Political Values Survey* 2010.
MLTC. (2016). Portal of the Malaysian Legal and Tax Information Centre. Accessed 28 Apr 2016, from http://malaysianlaw.my/general/news/sultan-nazrin-wants-legal-practitioners-to-master-english-Y15795.html
Mohamed Azam Mohamed Adil. (2013, December 10). *Transformasi mahkamah Syariah di Malaysia: kemajuan dan pencapaian melalui tanda arus global* [Transformation of Malaysia's Syariah courts: progress and achievement in global terms]. Paper presented at *Seminar on Islamic law in practice with global perspective*, Akademi Pengajian Islam, Universiti Malaya.
Mohd Yusmadi M. Yusoff (2006, April 5). Bahasa kebangsaan sebagai bahasa keadilan [National language as a language of justice]. *Utusan Online.* Accessed 30 April 2012, from http://www.utusan.com.my/utusan/info.asp?y=2006&dt=0405&pub=utusan_malaysia&sec=Rencana&pg=re_02.htm
Nakane Ikuko. (2013). Language Rights in Japanese Criminal Courts: Bridging the gap between legal professionals and language professionals. *Asian Studies Review, 37*(3), 302–318. https://doi.org/10.1080/10357823.2013.771134.
New Straits Times. (2009a, March 21). English must be in the equation, pp. 12–13.
New Straits Times. (2009b, December 11). Karpal: Make English the second official language, p. 6.
Norlizah Abas. (2009, December 9). Mendaulatkan bahasa kebangsaan [Uphold the national language]. *Utusan Online.* Accessed 30 Apr 2011, from http://www.utusan.com.my/utusan/info.asp?y=2009&dt=1210&pub=utusan_malaysia&sec=Dalam_Negeri&pg=dn_22.htm
Nekvapil, Jiří. (2006). From language planning to language management. *Sociolinguistica, 20*, 92–104. Accessed 4 Apr 2012, from http://uk-online.uni-koeln.de/remarks/d5134/rm2169329.pdf
Neustupný, Jiří (1994, May). Problems of English contact discourse and language planning. In Thiru Kandiah, John Kwan-Terry (eds.) *English and Language planning.* Singapore: Academic Press, 50–69.
Ng Kwai Hang. (2009). *The common law in two voices. Language, law and the postcolonial dilemma in Hong Kong*. Stanford: Stanford University Press.
Ng, Lisa. (2011). *Malaysian. Chinese. Totally Foreign.* Accessed 10 Apr 2014, from: http://www.loyarburok.com/2011/05/13/malaysian-chinese-totally-foreign/
Nik Abdul Rashid Majid. (1989) *Keupayaan Bahasa Melayu sebagai Bahasa Undang-undang* [The capability of Malay as a legal language]. Seminar Kebangsaan Undang-undang: Isu Bahasa dan Common law [Seminar on national law: the issue of language and common law]. Kuala Lumpur: Dewan Bahasa dan Pustaka.
Nik Ramlah Mahmood. (1993). Language and legal education in Malaysia –past and emerging trends. In K. L. Tee (Ed.), *Legal education in Malaysia Quo Vadis?* (pp. 134–146). Kuala Lumpur: Universiti Malaya.
Ooi Kok Hin. (2017, October). The policing and politics of the Malay language. *Penang Institute Issues.*
Paulsen, Eric. (2010, October 21). Red Book: Are lawyers just not bothered? *Malaysiakini.* Accessed 2 July 2011, from http://www.malaysiakini.com/letters/146002

Praba Ganesan. (2011, November 3). Lying in two languages: English in our schools. *The Malaysian Insider.* Accessed 30 Mar 2011, from http://www.themalaysianinsider.com/opinion/article/lying-in-two-languages-english-in-our-schools/

Powell, Richard. (2008). *Motivations for language choice in Malaysian courtrooms and implications for language planning*. Kuala Lumpur: Universiti Malaya.

Rashid Darham. (1990, June 1). *Penggunaan bahasa Malaysia di semua mahkamah mulai hari ini* [Use of Malay in all courts starts today] *Utusan Malaysia*, p. 13.

Ricento, Thomas. (2000). Introduction. In T. Ricento (Ed.), *Ideology, politics and language polices* (pp. 1–8). Amsterdam/Philadelphia: Benjamins.

Rubdy, Rani. (2008). Language planning ideologies, communicative practices and their consequences. In M. Martin-Jones, A. M. de Mejia, & N. H. Hornberger (Eds.), *Encyclopedia of language and education* (Volume 3: Discourse and Education) (2nd ed., pp. 211–223).

Salleh Buang. (2003, April 29). Guna bahasa mesra anak guam [Use client-friendly language]. *Utusan Online.* Accessed 30 Apr 2013, from http://utusan.com.my/utusan/info.asp?y=2003&dt=0429&pub=utusan_malaysia&sec=Rencana&pg=re_03.htm

Schiffman, Harold. (1996). *Linguistic culture and language policy*. London: Routledge.

Shazwan Mustafa Kamal. (2014, May 29). 'Secular Malaysia' claims based on wrong court precedent, ex-top judge argues. *The Malay Mail* (Online). Accessed 29 May 2014, from http://www.themalaymailonline.com/malaysia/article/secular-malaysia-claims-based-on-wrong-court-precedent-ex-top-judge-argues

Tay, Douglas, Razak Rashid & Kamal Zailani. (1981, March 17). Akta Bahasa:Pembankang dikecam [Language Act: Opposition parties criticised]. *Utusan Malaysia,* p. 2.

The Star. (2008, May 1). Multi-ethnic judiciary needed, p. N8.

The Star. (2009, February 03). *Majority want Science, Maths taught in English*. p. N13.

The Star Online. (2007, August 24). Minister: Study proposal on switch to Syariah Law thoroughly. Accessed 11 Nov 2011, from http://www.thestar.com.my/story.aspx/?file=%2f2007%2f8%2f24%2fnation%2f18681665&sec=nation

The Star Online. (2013, August 7). GE13: 13th Malaysian General Election. Accessed 10 Aug 2013, from http://elections.thestar.com.my

The Straits Times. (1959, August 24). Malay for courts? 'Not now', p. 7.

The Straits Times. (1962, November, 2) Justice in English. (Letters to the editor), p. 8.

The Straits Times. (1963, October 15). Common law a 'must' to unite Malaysia: Thomson, p. 20.

The Straits Times. (1967a, March 3). Language: I have chosen the peaceful way, p. 8.

The Straits Times. (1967b, August 9). N-language in courts: Bar Committee to meet, p. 6.

The Straits Times. (1967c, September 2). A 'berjaya' start. N-Language in courts, p. 1.

The Straits Times. (1979, October 30). Suffian: Why I don't agree with 3 demands, p. 14.

The Straits Times. (1981, March 10). Muslim lawyers hit out at Bar Council, p. 14.

The Straits Times. (1986, November 29). Mahathir 'did not ridicule judiciary', p. 11.

The Straits Times. (1989a, June 21). Bar Council wants all to give views, p. 17.

The Straits Times. (1989b, October 20). At the Dewan Rakyat. [Reprinted from *New Straits Times*], p. 21.

The Straits Times. (1990, September 15). 'Be strict' in allowing English in courts, p. 22.

The Straits Times. (1994, September 24). Judges urged to use more Bahasa Malaysia, p. 18.

The Straits Times. (2002, March 9). Minister to use only Malay in his speeches, p. 22.

The Sun. (2002, March 9). History move will not burden students, p. 2.

Thiru, Steven. (2016, December 10). Bar Council Press Release: Allegation that the Bar Council is involved in a movement to topple the government is absurd.

Tollefson, James. (2002). Introduction: Critical issues in educational language policy. In J. Tollefson (Ed.), *Language policy in education, critical issues* (pp. 3–16). Mahwah, NJ: Lawrence Erlbaum.

Tong, Geraldine. (2016, March 19). Bar not busybody or political, just upholding rule of law. *Malaysiakini*. Accessed 20 March 2016, from https://www.malaysiakini.com/news/334455

Utusan Malaysia. (1981a, April 1). *Soal pekasaan bahasa bergema lagi* [Language policy implementation question continues to reverberate], p. 13.

Utusan Malaysia. (1981b, April 17). *Masa belum sesuai tetapkan guna bahasa Malaysia di Mahkamah* [Time not yet suitable to use Malay in courts], p. 18.

Utusan Malaysia. (1983, April 26). *'Penggunaan Bahasa Malaysia di mahkamah tak perlu dilaksana segera'* ['Use of Malay in courts need not be implemented immediately'], p. 5.

Utusan Malaysia. (1984, June 2). *Undang-undang buruh patut diterjemah dalam Bahasa Malaysia* [Labour laws should be translated in Malay], p. 8.

Utusan Malaysia. (1990, June 30). *Peguam dan pengamal undang2 digesa jadi pengamal bahasa Melayu* [Lawyers and legal practitioners urged to become practitioners of Malay], p. 3.

Utusan Online. (2008a, December 9). *Kotakan janji bahasa Melayu di Mahkamah* [Fulfill the pledge for Malay in court]. Accessed 30 May 2013, from: http://www.utusan.com.my/utusan/info.asp?y=2008&dt=1209&pub=utusan_malaysia&sec=Rencana&pg=re_03.htm

Utusan Online. (2008b, December 10). *Lucut keistimewaan peguam tidak fasih bahasa Melayu* [Forfeit privileges of lawyers not fluent in Malay]. Accessed 30 May 2013, from http://www.utusan.com.my/utusan/info.asp?y=2008&dt=1210&pub=utusan_malaysia&sec=Dalam_Negeri&pg=dn_15.htm

Utusan Online. (2008c, December 17). *Bahasa Melayu dalam mahkamah* [Malay in the courts]. Accessed 30 Apr 2013, from http://www.utusan.com.my/utusan/info.asp?y=2008&dt=1207&pub=utusan_malaysia&sec=Rencana&pg=re_01.htm

Utusan Online. (2013, April 18). Keputusan batal saman peguam 8 Mei [Decision on striking out summons May 8]. Accessed 10 April 2013, from http://www.utusan.com.my/utusan/Mahkamah/20130418/ma_02/Keputusan-batal-saman-peguam-8-Mei

Utusan Online. (2014a, August 17). *Pulih integriti Majlis Peguam* [Recover the Bar Council's integrity]. Accessed 22 Aug 2014, from http://www.utusan.com.my/utusan/Rencana/20140817/re_03/Pulih-integriti-Majlis-Peguan

Utusan Online. (2014b, August 18). *Surendran ditahan di bawa Akta Hasutan* [Surendran arrested under Sedition Act]. Accessed 19 Aug 2014, from http://www.utusan.com.my/utusan/Jenayah/20140818/je_07/Surendran-ditahan-di-bawah-Akta-Hasutan

Utusan Online. (2014c, September 2). *Pensyarah UM mengaku tak bersalah sebut perkataan menghasut* [UM lecturer pleads not guilty to uttering seditious words]. Accessed 2 Sept 2014, from http://utusan.com.my/utusan/Dalam_Negeri/20140902/dn_38/Pensyarah-UM-mengaku-takbersalah-sebut-perkataan-menghasut

van Dijk, Teun. (1995). Aims of critical discourse analysis. *Japanese Discourse, 1*, 17–27.

Wade, Geoff. (2009). The origins and evolution of ethnocracy in Malaysia. *Asia-Pacific Journal*, 47-4-09. Accessed 7 July 2011, from http://japanfocus.org/-Geoff-Wade/3259

Wagenaar, Hendrik. (2011). *Meaning in action: Interpretation and dialogue in policy analysis.* New York: Armonk.

Wain, Barry. (2009). *Malaysian Maverick. Mahathir Mohamad in turbulent times.* Basingstoke: Palgrave.

Wong, L. C. (1962, November 06). A language goal. *The Straits Times* (Letters to the editor), p. 12.

Yusof Ghani. (2002, August 12). *Bahasa Melayu dipinggirkan bangsa sendiri, kata sasterawan Negara* [Malay marginalised by the people themselves, says laureate]. *Malaysiakini.* Accessed 12 Dec 2012, from http://www.malaysiakini.com/news/12542

Zubaidah Ibrahim. (2002). *Court interpreting in Malaysia in relation to language planning and policy.* Unpublished, doctoral thesis, University of Malaya. [Viewed University of Malaya]

Zurairi Ar. (2013, October 19). Make syariah Malaysia's only law, urges ISMA. *The Malay Mail Online.* Accessed 19 Oct 2013, from http://www.themalaymailonline.com/malaysia/article/make-syariah-malaysias-only-law-urges-isma

Zurairi Ar. (2018, August 19). MCMC says censored sites providing GE14 'live' results to preserve 'public order'. *Malay Mail Online.* Accessed 20 August 2018, from https://www.malaymail.com/s/1632665/mcmc-says-censored-ge14-live-results-to-preserve-public-order

Chapter 7
Language Practices in Legal Education

It's like an irony that I'm Malay and my mum actually teaches lawyers Bahasa and here I am struggling with it. I find English much easier after five years of learning law in it.

KL corporate lawyer (2014.3.06)

The competency level of those who are going to be hearing the matter is also an issue for me, I mean, if you don't understand English well how are you able to read the cases and understand the cases? To me it's that simple. Every Commonwealth authority is in English. How are you studying the law, how are you comprehending the law if you are not comfortable in English?

Melaka litigation lawyer (2014.4.29)

7.1 Language Policy, Professional Practice and Individual Choice

In the last three chapters we explored how Malay has been phased into the legal domain in a way that leaves an option, and sometimes a necessity, for English in professional practice. The investigation now turns from policy to practice, beginning here with legal education and going on in the following two chapters to law offices and courtrooms. Most of the data for this chapter comes from a bricolage of questionnaires, interviews and observations. Questionnaires on language preferences for study and expectations about language use in the workplace were collected from some 500 law students at UM, MMU and UniSZA, which attract students from all over the country (including East Malaysia, where there are no law schools). This was supplemented by focus group discussions with about 100 students and interviews with some of them, together with interviews with 20 students from other institutions. Law lecturers and language teachers at law faculties were also interviewed, and most of the 60 legal practitioners interviewed about professional practice were also asked about their experiences as law students. In addition

R. Powell, *Language Choice in Postcolonial Law*, Language Policy 22,
https://doi.org/10.1007/978-981-15-1173-8_7

to questionnaires and interviews, observations of law lecturers were carried out at UM, MMU and UniSZA.

In classrooms, offices and courtrooms Malaysian legal practice encompasses daily compromises between institutionalised recognition of the authority of the national language and pragmatic acknowledgment of the value of English on the part of judicial and administrative authorities. The communicative needs of students, clients and courtroom participants play an important role in these compromises, and bilingual proficiency, reinforced by pragmatic awareness, increases the agency of practitioners.

Bilingualism is inevitably an ambiguous construct. Kaplan and Baldauf (1997:137) propose a taxonomy ranging from monolingualism to balanced bilingualism. Baker (2001:31) distinguishes competence from dominance, while Mackey (2000:27–37) distinguishes frequency and duration from function and then goes on to separate the latter into external (e.g. home, school) and internal (task-based skills) competencies. While the patterns of bilingualism and orientations to language-in-law policy described here have no claim to be representative of young lawyers, many common concerns, stances and strategies emerged.

In Chap. 5 we saw how bilingual legal practice depends less on integrated acquisition planning than on a complex of checks and balances that generate varying levels of general proficiency in Malay and English at school and prioritise legal English at law school. The rationale for this is that Malay is now seen as less of a burden for students than English and general proficiency in it is assumed to be readily transferable to most of the legal tasks it will be used for. In this chapter we will see how an inchoate policy is bolstered by pragmatism and societal multilingualism, with UM and UKM bending official bilingual policies toward English while UniSZA has an official English MOI, supported by unofficial Malay-English code-switching.

7.2 Language Repertoires of Malaysians Entering the Profession

While it is beyond the scope of this study to assess communicative competence at individual or cohort level, the topic of language proficiency arose frequently in questionnaire and interview data and is relevant when evaluating reported language preferences for legal sites and tasks. The language proficiency of individuals should be viewed as another structural constraint upon language choice in addition to language rules and the lexicogrammatical capacities of the Malay and English languages as it involves societal as well as individual factors. It is important to contextualise individual Malay-English legal bilingualism within the complex societal multilingualism that emerges from the data. There are perhaps few countries where language issues are so controversial and yet where people are so unconsciously multilingual.

Given the high rate of school attendance (96% at primary level[1]) and the high degree of political intervention (Abdullah Hassan 1994:143; Gill 2005:242) in schools, Malaysian language-in-education policy can be assumed to have considerable influence over language repertoires. However, although the national census still collects data about ethnicity, using similar categories to those introduced by the British in the 1870s (Shamsul 1996:19), language data is no longer collected. Two university researchers who had been involved in compiling census questions recounted both conceptual difficulties, such as how to distinguish languages from dialects or L1 from L2 competence, and logistical complexities, such as soliciting sufficiently detailed responses without overburdening the public.[2] 'Mother tongue' and 'first language'/'L1' are problematic constructs in general and in Malaysia approximate at best. Ricento (2002:2) ties definitions to strategic ends, and notes that allegiance to a mother tongue tends to be more important for minorities than majorities as it may serve as a defensive in-group marker (ibid:7). Wee (2010:431) suggests that the way the term 'mother tongue' is employed in Singapore rides roughshod over local sociolinguistic complexities. Pennycook (2004:8) finds the very concept of a native language questionable.

While Malay is the home language of most Malays, varieties in Sarawak (Ting 2010), Kelantan (Azirah and David 2011) and elsewhere may be phonologically and lexicogrammatically distinct enough to compromise intelligibility for Malays from elsewhere. According to the former head of a law department,[3] in most homes a variety other than the standard taught in schools is spoken, and some studies (e.g. Abdullah Hassan 1994:121) have reported cases of children experiencing difficulty with standard BM. One Melaka-based lawyer recalled being scolded at school for spelling a word as she and most of her Kedah classmates pronounced it: "In a Standard 1 test I spelt *perempuan* [woman] as *pompuan* and had to stand on a chair. When I went home I got so mad I stood on a chair and wrote *pompuan* on the wall". As for other languages, Mandarin is consistently referred to as a 'mother tongue' (e.g. in Kua 1999, 2005, 2011) even though Hokkien and Cantonese have traditionally been used more in Malaysian homes, and a large minority of Malaysian 'Tamils' speak Malayalam rather than Tamil at home (Knowles 2004:38). Previous studies have shown a significant number of urban Malays, Chinese and Indians using English at home (Pillai 2006; Sankar 2007) and this was often borne out in the accounts of students and lawyers during this investigation, as well as by invitations to homes where the only people speaking Malay were the Indonesian cooks.

Asked about their main home language (or languages where there was balanced multilingualism), 46% of student informants at UM, 44% at MMU and 18% at UniSZA stated Chinese, with 39% at UM, 18% at MMU and 66% at UniSZA stating Malay and 10% at UM, 24% at MMU and just 4% at UniSZA stating English.

---

[1] World Bank (2015) World Development Indicators. Accessed 2015.12.12 from: http://wdi.worldbank.org/table/2.9

[2] Interviewed at UM's Asia Europe Institute, 2016.10.04.

[3] Interviewed in KL, 2013.8.05.

Language(s) (rounded %)	UM (n=349)	MMU (n=55)	UniSZA (n=74)
Mainly Mandarin	**20%**	**16%**	
Mand + other Ch	**9%**	**3.6%**	**3%**
Cantonese	**3.5%**		**1.4%**
Hokkien	**1%**	**1.8%**	
Other Ch	**2%**		**1.4%**
Ch + E	**10%**	**13%**	**7%**
Ch +E+BM		**9%**	**5%**
CHINESE+	***46%***	***44%***	***18%***
Mainly BM	**26%**	**9%**	**55%**
BM+E	**13%**	**7%**	**9%**
BM+Ch	**0.5%**	**1.8%**	**1.4%**
BM+	***39%***	***18%***	***66%***
Mainly English	**10%**	**24%**	**4%**
ENGLISH	***10%***	***24%***	***4%***
Tam+E	**2.6%**	**3.6%**	**1.4%**
Tamil	**1.7%**	**1.8%**	**8%**
Tam&BM	**0.3%**	**1.8%**	**1.3%**
Tam&E&BM		**5.5%**	
TAMIL+	***>5%***	***13%***	***11%***
Kadazandusun	**0.3%**		
Other Indian	**0.3%**	**1.8%**	**1.4%**
Semai	**0.3%**		
Suluk	**0.3%**		
OTHER	***1.2%***	***2%***	***1.4%***

Fig. 7.1 Main home language(s) of law student informants

Tamil was the main home language of under 5% at UM but 13% at MMU and 11% at UniSZA (Fig. 7.1). Within these categories lay considerable complexity, with those using a Chinese language other than or in combination with Mandarin outnumbering those mainly using Mandarin, and most Tamil speakers using that language in balance with English and/or BM.

Accounts from UM focus groups shed some light on this multilingualism. Declaring Malay and English as balanced home languages could mean the whole family code-switches, but it was also used to describe replying in Malay to parents who favoured English, or using Malay with parents and English with siblings. 'Mainly Malay' could mean mainly Kelantan dialect rather than standard BM. 'Chinese' could mean Mandarin, Cantonese, Hakka, Teochew or, for one UM student, "Foochow with parents and Mandarin with friends". An example of the less commonly reported pattern of 'Malay and Chinese' included a Malay student whose parents sent him to Chinese primary school to "mingle with others". Indian

Language(s)	UM (347)	MMU (56)	UniSZA (74)
BM	22%	37%	35%
BM+English	28%	14%	20%
Mandarin	31%	29%	3%
Mandarin+BM	3.6%	3.5%	32%
BM+English+Mand	5%	3.5%	
Mandarin+English	4%	3.5%	4%
Tamil	1.7%	1.8%	4%
English	4.8%	7%	1.5%
Other	1.4%		

Fig. 7.2 Law students' main medium of primary education

languages tended to be spoken together with English and indigenous East Malaysian languages together with Malay and/or English.

Interviews with lawyers also revealed rich multilingualism. Former bar president and long-term Bar Council member Hendon Mohamed had spoken English as much as Malay as a child because her father worked for the royal family in Johor. Another Bar Council member, Brendan Navin, had a Tamil father and Chinese mother who communicated with each other in Malay while speaking to him in English. A former chair of the association of Kelantan, a heavily Malay state, remarked "if [most Malays] hear someone reading English, everything we can understand; only speaking is difficult". The Melaka lawyer who had rebelled against being told how to spell *perempuan* considered Kedah Malay rather than BM as her mother tongue and recalled being encouraged to use English at home. Most ethnic Chinese lawyer informants were at least trilingual: an advocate from Penang was brought up with Hokkien, English, Cantonese and Teochew and "everything is mixed", while another Melaka lawyer, originally from Perak, considered Cantonese her home language as it was what her Hakka mother and Cantonese father used with each other, but she had spoken Hokkien in the neighbourhood, Mandarin in the family business, Malay at primary school and English in her convent secondary school:

> I just took it that if I have to communicate with this person I have to know this language, if I want to get through that class I have to use that language.

As for education, all of Malaysia's main MOIs featured in accounts of primary schooling (Fig. 7.2), although few students (>5%) reported being educated *mainly* in Tamil. Nearly a third at UM and MMU on the west coast had attended Mandarin primary schools, but only 3% at UniSZA on the East Coast.

Most students had experienced PPSMI (maths and science in English), with 37%, 32% and 30% at each site respectively describing their secondary schooling (Fig. 7.3) as Malay/English, although 23% at all three institutions remembered it as mainly Malay. 26% at UM and 15% at MUU reported Mandarin as a major component of their secondary education, but only 6% at UniSZA, where 41% said their secondary schooling was mainly in English. As this was double the number who had reported English+Malay primary schooling it suggests that many UniSZA students

Language(s)	UM (347)	MMU (56)	UniSZA (74)
BM	23%	23%	23%
BM+English	37%	32%	30%
BM+English+Mand	5%	5%	
Mandarin	10%	7%	
Mandarin+BM	5%	1.8%	3%
Mandarin+English	6%	1.8%	3%
Tamil	-	-	-
English	14%	29%	41%
Other	0.2%		1%

Fig. 7.3 Law students' main medium of secondary education

attend residential secondary schools, which are attended mostly by Malays but usually teach classes in English.

The problem of switching languages when switching schools was mentioned more often by Chinese lawyers than others, perhaps because most need three languages, as with an Ipoh practitioner who went from Chinese primary to Malay secondary school, "and then at UIA it was all English".

There is thus some support in the data for the idea, discussed in Chap. 5, that language planning has loosened traditional associations between language and ethnicity. Indeed many informants specifically warned against essentialism. For one ethnic Indian lecturer at UM, English was "no divider of race, religion or gender". A UM Malay student from a province with a large Malay majority insisted she had no advantage when it came to legal arguments in BM, while a Malay student from MMU boasted of coming second in the school's BM-medium moot before adding, almost as a matter of course, that it was won by a Chinese classmate. After declared that Malay was "in my blood" a student at UiTM, an institution reserved for Malays and other *bumiputera*, related how his father, a carpenter, had insisted he study English seriously and voiced trepidation about coming before lower court judges since he felt he argued better in English than in Malay. A number of Chinese practitioners, including a partner in a small Ipoh practice, thought Malays had better English than the Chinese because of the *asasi* residential school system, while a KL-based corporate lawyer saw many Chinese as handicapped in English because, apart from those able to afford private education, they had to study in Mandarin and Malay before they got to English-medium classes.

Socioeconomic divisions certainly complicate, and sometimes cut through, ethnic divisions. A Malay student privately educated in Malaysia and then at a British law school described his BM as "rubbish", whereas a publicly educated Chinese from Johor favoured Malay for court submissions. According to a KL corporate lawyer the handicap in English that is often attached to Malays did not hold for the middle classes. Another KL advocate felt that PPSMI had divided the economic haves and have-nots through English regardless of ethnicity. While being interviewed in an upmarket café he pointed out a multiethnic group of executives on a neighbouring table: "Look at these guys. All Malaysian and all speaking English.

Why can't we do what the Indons have achieved where Indonesian is used even in the boardroom?"

Linkage between language and ethnicity is not irrelevant, however. The 2012 cohort of professional attachment students at UM were given no instructions about which language to write their reports in: half the Malays, but only a third of the Indians and just 5% of the Chinese, chose BM. Furthermore, ethnic-based calculations about the language choices of others persist. There was consensus among focus group informants at UM about Malay schoolteachers being more likely than others to use BM in class, and it may be that institutional and cultural pressures override individual preferences and proficiencies. But it is not necessarily the case that Malays feel under more pressure than others to use the national language: on one of my first visits to a Malaysian law firm a senior partner arranged, perhaps not randomly, for me to interview an ethnic Malay, Chinese and Indian practitioner and I noted the surprise expressed by the latter two at how freely their Malay colleague discussed using English in court without asking permission.

7.3 Motivations for Studying and Practising Law

Most interviewees and focus group participants were asked about their interest in law, although this was not put into quantifiable form in the questionnaires. Informants' comments revealed a wide range of motivations, many of them connected with language.

The most commonly cited attraction of law among students was that it was a prestigious option for those who disliked maths and science and doubted they would do well in medicine or scientific, the career sectors most in favour by parents. One UM student thought law had "a wow factor, accountancy does not". A number of lawyers from several locations also saw their dislike for maths and science as significant in their career choice. An aptitude for arguing was mentioned by many student and lawyer informants, with love of reading also referred to frequently. While an ethnic Chinese Penang practitioner was the only one to specify *English* reading, from the context it was clear that most of those expressing their interest in reading and debating had that language in mind. In acknowledging comments by former Information, Communications and Culture Minister Rais Yatim about the consistent appeal of books in English in contrast to falling demand for Malay texts, DBP director Awang Sariyan conceded that interest in English was enduring but claimed it remained confined to "elite families" (*Malaysiakini* 2016.5.04). However, this study failed to connect English literacy more closely to socioeconomic status than to diverse cultural and individual factors. A smaller number of students and lawyers, in several locations, specifically associated their career choice with personal aptitude for English.

After a propensity for literature, debate or the English language, and lack of enthusiasm for science, the next most commonly cited attraction of law was concern for social justice. Two UM students stressed the importance of knowing one's rights while another hoped to make money in corporate law so that she could do pro bono work for NGOs. A blind lawyer from Kota Bahru felt law was the best means for advocating on behalf of those with disabilities. A KL-based conveyancing lawyer (not a field commonly associated with rights or social justice) described justice, fairness and equality as more important than material motivations. A practitioner at a large corporate firm related her desire to join the profession and "protect my family" after seeing her mother being "cheated by lawyers" in her childhood. Hendon Mohamed connected an interest in justice with a love of literature in confessing to childhood idolisation of Portia in *The Merchant of Venice*.

As in many countries, law in Malaysia is often attractive to those intending to pursue politics, whether motivated by social justice or material gain. A Chinese lawyer from Ipoh found his profession an asset when entering local politics, but found Malay more useful than English. Only two informants, from Kota Bahru and Kuala Terengganu respectively, volunteered the financial opportunities of the profession as a motivation. It may be significant that both were from the East Coast, where according to another Terengganu practitioner law was traditionally considered an ambitious goal. Yet another East Coast lawyer, Mukhtar Abdullah, recalled how out-of-reach law had seemed in his youth because "you must be well-versed in English and it's all controlled by West Coast people".

The role of chance also plays its part, not least because the educational system often directs young people to careers that were not their first choice. Two UM students reported having to accept offers to study law after failing to get places in accountancy. A Melaka practitioner who rejected the place for ophthalmology she received instead of her first choice of medicine unexpectedly received a scholarship for law. Despite being the top student at her school, one ethnic Chinese law lecturer recalled watching many of her Malay friends get scholarships to study overseas and halfheartedly applying for various courses at Malaysian institutions before ending up doing law as a third choice. Another Melaka practitioner claimed her boyfriend had financed her through law school to distract her from interfering in his family business, never dreaming she might actually pass her exams and enter the profession.

In sum, Malaysian lawyers bring a rich and complex range of linguistic and cultural experiences and diverse instrumental motivations to the profession, but facility with language and interest in reading and debating seem common to many of them.

7.4 Law School Policy and Practice

Following up the findings about medium-of-instruction policy at Malaysian law schools laid out in Chap. 4, this section explores policy implementation and the ways students and lecturers orientate to it. MOI on the ground emerges less as a fixed protocol than as a compromise between policy and pedagogical needs. At UniSZA, for example, a lecturer who had stated that he was obliged to teach entirely in English was later observed using Malay for at least a third of his class. Students similarly walk a path between conformist and pragmatic responses to official rules.

During a lecture at MMU I heard only English from the lecturer and students alike, but immediately the class ended students started code-switching with other languages and several told me that many lecturers did so too. On first approaching UM about my proposal to observe lectures I was handed the law curriculum and warned that it was only in Malay, but after being invited to sit down over coffee I was regaled with concerns about falling standards in English and informed that the vice chancellor had recently, though unofficially, called for more emphasis on the language.

7.4.1 Policy and Practice at Universiti Malaya

Since the student questionnaires focused on study preferences without asking directly about MOI, the bulk of the data on language of instruction comes from interviews with UM students and lecturers, but interviews and observations at MMU and UniSZA and interviews with legal practitioners and students who attended other public or private law schools suggest that flexible interpretation of MOI policy is not confined to UM.

Among UM focus groups there was general agreement that the subjects of Law and Society, Legal Methods, Advocacy and Drafting were taught entirely in English, whereas Islamic Law was taught entirely in Malay. Family Law and Crime involved lectures in Malay and tutorials and texts in both languages. For Contracts, first years said the course was entirely in English but second years remembered their lecturer speaking both languages while using an English textbook. The first years' tort lecturer taught in English but second years had had one teacher using English and a second using Malay. No one seemed aware of the official lectures-in-Malay/tutorials-in-English policy, but a number of student comments evinced a strong expectation that tutorials would be in English, with Malay more likely to be used alongside it, or even instead of it, in lectures.

All UM students felt English was prioritised over Malay. As one focus group participant put it, "We know English is the main medium in this faculty…it's not a policy but we all feel that because most profs are using it". Another reported that some lecturers refused to use BM. When I asked a third what she meant by few teachers being bilingual enough to produce "really bilingual students" she described their reluctance, and hinted at their inability, to use BM. Notwithstanding the complications of university entrance, whereby applicants may get assigned to schools and courses low on their preference lists, one student felt "UM tends to attract people happier with English". Most elective courses are in it. Priority for the language is reinforced by its use in nearly all tutorials, where more active participation is expected than in lectures. Indeed one student commented: "We've never tried to argue in BM". Another said that if a lecture were in BM and the corresponding tutorial in English she would take notes in the latter because tutorials counted for more.

This emphasis upon English seems common across all law schools. But whereas lawyers graduating from UiTM and UIA described how their schools had introduced more Malay in the fourth, vocationally-oriented year, UM brings in legal practitioners at this stage who lecture entirely in English.

No lecturer at UM was described as a stickler for Malay. One informant brought up a lecturer who was thought to be "much tougher on use of correct Malay", adding that this motivated him to write in English instead. Other students recalled a foreign teacher being denied departmental permission to lecture in English, and while other lecturers were surprised to hear this, given that foreign lecturers have traditionally been exempt from using BM, several of them commented independently that it was one thing to implement the language policy flexibly and quite another to seek official leave to depart from it.

Although few students felt they had a genuine language choice, several mentioned lecturers (e.g. on the Tort and Family Law courses) asking them which medium they preferred. Malay had recently become an option for mooting in the faculty – though not because of local demand so much as because of the National University of Singapore's desire to hold debates with Malaysian counterparts in it. When asked what factors influenced MOI, individual lecturer preference was most often cited, followed by the medium of the textbook and other study and research materials.

Of nine UM lecturers asked which language they 'mainly' taught in, six said English, two Malay, and one reported balanced bilingualism. Within these generalisations a number of strategies emerged. One lecturer had "followed the trend" in moving away from a bilingual lecture-tutorial divide toward more English. Another confessed to code-switching, especially in order to reinforce understanding when wrapping up lectures, while his colleague, who had studied law bilingually when balance between the two languages was promoted, gave little thought to medium as long as students understood content. UM's Baseline Study (2014), carried out to explore language concerns at the time I was conducting interviews and observations there, found some flexibility among lecturers, with the exception of one teacher who confessed to poor Malay, and another who told students while he had locus standi to switch languages they had to answer in English. Three lecturers teaching mainly in English commented that they used BM for explanations and examples. Two others said they adhered to the policy of Malay for lectures and English for tutorials, although one of these gave students the option of presenting in English during lectures.

Lecture halls and tutorial rooms are not the only place where law learning goes on. Interviews yielded some insights into language choice outside class, including a buddy system whereby seniors pass on lecture notes to juniors — a practice one KL advocate had resisted as a student for fear the notes were out of date. Echoing reports from Sri Lanka Law College (see Chap.10), the language of the notes students make and circulate appears to influence the medium of self-study. Some study groups use Facebook, which a first-year UM student described as a medium that encouraged English, but there are also informal debate groups that use BM. Another dimension of legal education is the outreach programmes students take part in, such as giving legal advice at shelters and in prisons. Most students identified Malay as the most useful language for such work, with one second-year student saying it could be challenging if legal details had to be explained as he was more used to discussing law in English.

7.4.2 Policy and Practice at MMU and UniSZA

At MMU where, according to one senior lecturer, BM is considered "less of an educational burden" than English, even though Malay students are in a minority, there seems to be widespread adherence to the school's all-English policy. The three lectures I observed were entirely in English, although it should be noted that two of them were taught by non-Malaysians, and some students reported code-switching in other classes. When there had been a choice most students had opted to moot in English, and so a ballot system was introduced whereby 50% have to moot in Malay, while the foreign language option on the curriculum is much more popular than an alternative Malay option. Even outside the classroom one student felt that conversation among his classmates tended to drift to English because of the multiracial and Malay-minority intake.

At UniSZA, although lecturers reported a preference for Malay in faculty meetings and for internal correspondence, in the last 3 years instruction has moved from bilingualism to an all-English policy. In practice, however, several lecturers also use BM in class to reinforce understanding. One lecturer with a senior administrative position and another with a local legal practice reported teaching in English but following up with explanations in Malay during after-class discussions. Another lecture noted that student participation was keener when he started adding examples in Malay to his English-medium talks: "The first thing I taught them is if they don't understand, if they want to ask questions, then don't worry about the language. The main intention is for them to understand the concept".

7.4.3 Policy and Practice at other Institutions

Judging by the recollections of UKM graduates interviewed as lawyers and to the reports of a lecturer employed there, most lectures are now in English despite an official Malay-English split for lectures and tutorials policy, a practice formerly tolerated only for expatriate lecturers. A policy of requiring at least one exam question per paper to be answered in a different language from the others continues, but a recent graduate now working in corporate law recalled BM being accepted for all the questions on the Islamic law paper because of a shortage of English terms. Another UKM graduate from the same firm said that the lack of BM materials and the tendency to conduct lectures in English had made it more challenging for her to write answers in Malay, even though she had attended a Malay-medium secondary school, and she had consequently kept to her Malay answers to one question per exam and tended to answer more briefly than when writing in English.

Those informants who had studied law in private sector institutions such as Brickfields and ATC remembered all LLB courses being in English. Some university lecturers who had also taught pre-law diploma courses, however, mentioned the need to code-switch with Malay.

7.5 Classroom Code-Switching

Given the accounts of many law students and lawyers about schoolteachers code-switching to reinforce content, it was anticipated that the practice would play an important role in law schools too and bilingual teaching was discussed in interviews and focus groups as well as witnessed directly in many classes. After generously giving up part of their classes for me to distribute questionnaires many UM lecturers allowed me to stay to observe the rest of the class, and I was also able to sit in on lectures at MMU and UniSZA.

A common practice at UM seems to be to use Powerpoint slides in English, often based on textbook extracts, and add oral explanations in a mixture of English and Malay. One lecturer used Malay to encourage students to answer questions while another code-switched almost to the point of teaching everything twice. Another, however, adhered strictly to English. None of the observed lectures was entirely in Malay, but the practice cannot be ruled out as there was no time to observe lectures in family law or Islamic law, two subjects reported to favour the language. According to one student, if the textbook was in Malay that was also the medium of the lecturer's slides, with teachers who used BM materials less likely to stray into English than the other way round. Although this might indicate a stance on language policy it could also reflect an assumption that BM is better understood by students.

A final year MMU student who had reported a propensity on the part of some lecturers to code-switch showed some evidence for this in his notes, which appeared to contain verbatim extracts containing numerous examples of lexical code-mixing. His professional practice teacher, for example, used Malay when referring to documents such as *borang gadaian* (mortgage form) and *borang pindahmilik* (transfer form), as well as for professionals involved in conveyancing such as *pesuruhjaya sumpah* (commissioners of oaths). His criminal procedure instructor switched between languages for everyday terms (*waran tangkap* = arrest warrant; *orang kena tuduh* = suspect; *orang kena tangkap* = arrestee) and also when explaining 'arrest and seizure':

> *Bila I pegang dia baru* constitute arrest. *Kalau tak pegang tak* arrest. Arrest *pun boleh jadi kalau I sebut "Jangan bergerak!"*. Arrest *pun boleh jadi kalau I cakap: Jangan bergerak! Kalau tak kena tembak!*
> [It constitutes arrest if I just hold him. There's no arrest if I don't. It can also be an arrest if I say: Don't move! or Don't move or you'll get shot!]

At UniSZA I also observed more extensive code-switching, notably in two classes on trust law and one on contracts. While the latter revolved around Malaysian cases, the former applied seminal English cases to Malaysian contexts. Much of the code-switching arose from lexical code-mixing, especially the insertion of English phrases into Malay explanations. Some mixes were clearly coherence strategies drawing directly on cases

> *Binatang dekat zoo* – yes you can *sebab ada* educational value, *kalau tapi* for group of animals *mesti* prove *ada* benefit lah.
> [Animals in the zoo – yes you can because they have educational value, but for a group of animals you must prove there's a benefit.]

> *Dalam kes* [In the case of] Pettingall vs Pettingall, I bequeath £50 a year for my favourite black mare.

and some lexical insertions might be seen as legalese

> *Kalau* you *tak boleh* transfer *sebagai* charitable, can just put under NCPT
> [If you can't transfer as charitable you can just put under NCPT (non-charitable purpose trust)]

> *Boleh* presume *tak* transfer *kalau tak jelas.*
> [You can assume no transfer made if it's not clear.]

where both 'charitable' and 'presume' have Malay equivalents (*khairat* and *menganggap*) yet are commonly heard untranslated in lawyer talk. Legalese such as 'beneficiary' (which is almost the same in Malay) and 'non-ascertainable' (which would probably be unpacked into a clause if translated) was frequently used alongside habitual lexis that might be found in non-legal domains, as in the following, where 'transfer', 'problem', 'you' and 'IC' can be considered integrated loans:

> *Boleh* transfer *kalau punya IC,* but *nanti ada* problem – *jadi* non-ascertainable beneficiaries. What if children *masuk Islam?*
> [There can be a transfer if there is an identity card, but later there will be a problem – they'll be non-ascertainable beneficiaries. What if the children become Muslims?]

To a lesser extent Malay was embedded in English, for example for local cultural terms

> If dispute arise regarding *wakaf* [a Muslim benefaction] it will not go to civil courts.

and for reiterations:

> It is illegal since it is illegal to hunt foxes for sports – *untuk sukan* – [for sport] so it is most unlikely this category would be relevant.

In these and many other instances of intrasentential code-mixing and intersentential code-switching we see something more than the translation of language thought by lecturers to be burdensome for students: after all, it is unlikely students who are expected to know technical terms like 'NCPT' (above) will need words like 'cat' and 'eat' translated. Rather, code-switching constitutes a comprehensive pedagogical strategy whereby teachers constantly weave two languages in order to create rapport between themselves and the students and cohesion between English-language texts, often embedded in historical English contexts, and contemporary Malaysian society. By code-switching and inserting a local example a trusts lecturer brought the law alive when explaining the potentially dry topic of trusts for tombs and monuments:

> *Contohnya Nirwana kat Nilai. Yang kaya kaya*, those who are wealthy, build a plot. *Ada lif dan lain lain* and some plot there *ada makam iaitu mausoleum, ada* air con. The upkeep of that mausoleum is based on the trust set up for the beneficiaries. For trusts for monuments, if it is limited to 21 years then prima facie it is a valid purpose trust. The trust cannot be made under perpetuity. *Untuk monumen 21 tahun.* [Take Nirwana in Nilai (a Chinese cemetery near KL). Those rich people, those who are wealthy, build a plot. They got lifts and everything, and some plots there have graves, you know, mausoleums, with air-conditioning. The upkeep of that mausoleum is based on the trust set up for the beneficiaries. For trusts for monuments, if it is limited to 21 years then prima facie it is a valid purpose trust. The trust cannot be made under perpetuity. For monuments, 21 years.]

Similarly, in the contracts class the teacher shifted from language taken from a case that seemed to have been reported in English to his own view, thereby triggering some Malay, and then on to his personal experiences:

> In Parimala the court gave damages to the passengers despite the fact that they are not party to the contract. And then *dia kata* [it was said] there is no contract but the parties can sue under negligence. *Kalau I telah* [if I had been the] lawyer I argue they share the toll ticket. They share the contract. But my time in court, sometime I *tak* [don't] focus *majistret* [magistrate] *lah. Sebab* [because] I look for words to translate in my head.

The paradigm of Systemic Functional Grammar may shed some light on this bilingualism with its concept of communication having multiple metafunctions: an ideational one conveying ideas and experiences; an interpersonal one expressing relationships; and a textual one organising discourse according to mode and structure. Thus code-switches to repeat or rephrase, for example, might be interpreted as elaborating on propositional context, and also refocusing students' attention on the speaker, while at the same time punctuating speech in the way that italics or parentheses do for written texts. This last 'textualising' function, emphasised by Chan (2004) to show how speakers code-switch to frame and structure discourse, and suggested by Powell (2008) as a reason many advocates switch languages when breaking off to refer to exhibits, recurred throughout the lectures. There was already modal separation between the English text and Malay oral explanation, and the teacher constantly referred students to his slides and to parts of the textbook by switching from English to *Tengkok* [look at] page 161, or *I bagi tahu u kes...* [let me tell about you the case of...].

Despite departmental MOI policies, then, classrooms emerged as pragmatic and even collaborative sites of bilingual communication. While such a degree of flexibility is unlikely to be repeated in courtrooms, examples given in Chap. 9 will show that language alternation does go on there and involves coherence- and rapport-building strategies that similarly go beyond strategies to compensate for language deficiency.

7.6 Student Preferences for Study

The student questionnaire for UM, MMU and UniSZA included items about language preference for study activities and revealed a clear preference for English at all three schools for all activities (Fig. 7.4). When UM's 2013 cohort was given the same questionnaire the English bias was even stronger, perhaps reflecting the fact that most had been interviewed in English as part of admissions procedure. The high percentages for writing exams in English at MMU (100%) and UniSZA (99%) presumably reflect university requirements. However, 90% of UM students also chose English for most of their tasks, even though BM remains part of official policy. The only task where MMU preference for English fell below 90% was mooting, for which 50% are required to use BM. The fact that the preference at UniSZA for reading online in English was as strong as at UM is probably indicative of the medium of relevant websites as much as of literacy skills. Research conducted by David Chong in 2015 found 60% of Malaysians reading Wikipedia in English rather than Malay or Chinese, leading Chong to suggest more could be done to improve the Malay version of the site (Foong 2018.7.09).

In light of the comments reported in the previous chapter about PPSMI (science and maths in English) that revealed how the availability of materials limits language choice, overall preference for English in law school may indicate institutional constraints – including the perceived preferences of departments – rather than academic proficiency. But even for practices less likely to be under institutional constraints, such as online discussions, 80–90% at UM and MMU, and two thirds at UniSZA, favoured English. The somewhat lower percentage at UniSZA (64%) nonetheless supports comments from several of their lecturers about students' lack of confidence in spoken English, with a similar number (67%) favouring English when talking in lectures.

	UM 2009~2012 n=246				**MMU** n=56				**UniSZA** n=74			
Malay - both equal -English	M	b/e	E		M	b/e	E		M	b/e	E	
% favouring English				E %				E %				E %
Read textbooks		24	222	87%			56	100%		5	69	93%
Read course material	2	33	211	86%			55	98%		4	70	95%
Read books& journals		21	225	91%		1	54	96%	1	11	62	84%
Read online	2	37	206	84%		5	51	91%		11	63	85%
Listen to lectures	1	63	178	74%		1	54	96%		18	56	76%
Listen to tutorials		34	212	86%			55	98%		12	62	84%
Speak in lectures	1	63	178	84%			54	96%		26	48	67%
Speak in tutorials	1	30	214	87%			55	98%		20	54	76%
Online discussions	1	42	200	82%		4	52	93%		27	47	64%
Moots & debates		19	227	92%		10	46	82%		4	70	95%
Write essays & reports		22	224	91%			56	100%		1	73	99%
Take tests & exams		22	223	92%			56	100%		1	73	99%

Fig. 7.4 Language preferences for study tasks

Although several students at UM and MMU claimed higher general proficiency in English, with some attributing this to PPSMI, they were outnumbered by those for whom language strength depended on the activity or topic in question. Many among UM's 2013 intake, for instance, preferred Malay for discussing daily life, politics and administration, and also for reading judgments and case summaries because of the complexity of the language. But some of their classmates and seniors said they avoided Malay legal texts because they were more familiar with the English terms. One fourth-year student commented that using English textbooks not only brought familiarity with English terminology but also with thinking and arguing in the language. In a focus group discussion with second-years several students, many of them Malay, went as far as to suggest that BM was too vague, informal, mixed, or unstable for academic study.

Many indicated that the medium of legal materials is crucial for language preference. One UM first-year preferred Malay to discuss cases if they were reported in Malay, while several UniSZA students preferred it for Islamic law as most of the sources are in it. A point often heard among the majority of English-favouring students at all three schools was the preponderance of cases in the language, as well as its position as the source of common law. Two MMU students also mentioned the greater exposure and international opportunities English offered. A small number in UM's 2013 cohort thought Malay should be confined to a few subjects such as Islamic law, and one or two even suggested it be scrapped from the curriculum altogether.

One item on the questionnaire asked for suggestions for improving legal study in both languages. The question thus ran the risk of steering students toward a favourable stance on bilingual study, yet three MMU students used the prompt to describe studying law in BM as "troublesome" or even "impossible". Four others from MMU, and two from UM, responded to this question by stating that using two languages would be confusing.

In general, those going to the trouble of offering advantages for bilingual study were in a minority. Around 10% of UM's 2013 intake emphasised the importance of being able to explain law in both languages and called for a balance of English and Malay lectures, but only one volunteered the idea that bilingual study would enhance understanding of law. Lack of opportunities to practise arguing in BM was noted by a fourth-year UM student, presumably mindful of his impending need for the language in court, and there was a suggestion from a UM first-year that it be used for mooting. Perceived weakness in English seemed to be behind many UniSZA calls for more BM at school, including Malay explanations in class, bilingual reading materials and bilingual teaching. Three specifically proposed specialised legal Malay courses and three others suggested they be given a choice of medium for classes and exams. Some at UniSZA also pointed out the disjoint between English being used heavily at law school and the likelihood of Malay being needed more at work. At MMU, which appears to use less BM than the other two institutions, only ten students (from a relatively small sample of 56) went as far as to propose BM courses or bilingual teaching, but 20 recommended partial use of BM in lectures or greater availability of Malay materials and lecture notes. One had noticed that his non-Malay friends had started to talk to him more in BM as they approached graduation and chambering.

Even if student preferences were paramount, it would be difficult to distill this diversity of opinion into proposals for policy reform. The general preference for English largely aligns with teaching practice yet also reflects a wide range of positions, with enthusiasm for the language as the best tool for legal practice less apparent than acceptance of it as the medium of most materials, the preference of law schools, and the priority for those who feel they lack proficiency in it. One UM second-year felt "it would be great to master both languages…in the legal field, but the core problem is, do we have the time and do we have the motive to change what is currently available to us?" It should also be noted that a large number of students didn't express a clear preference, or felt they could adapt to whatever was required, which might be an indication of their proficient bilingualism or of their years of experience of adapting to fluctuating language policies in general education.

7.7 Perceptions of Law Students' Language Skills

The language proficiency of law graduates, especially in English, is of growing concern in the profession and law schools. Yet little has been done to assess language proficiency in the profession or even formulate criteria for assessment. When the Sultan of Perak enjoined CLP graduates to master the language (MLTC 2016.4.28) his audience consisted largely of those who had chosen – successfully – to answer the exam in it, so passing English-medium law exams is apparently not enough. The key issues that emerged from discussions with law lecturers and lawyers were whether English proficiency was declining; if so, whether this was due to emphasis upon Malay in general education; the degree to which poorer English is thought to influence legal study; and the possibility that any fall in English has been compensated for by improved levels of Malay. This section concentrates on language at law school, with legal practitioners' expectations of lawyers in the workplace dealt with in the next chapter.

As early as 1980 a UM survey found the English of young lawyers to be declining (Asmah 1994:75). A former head of department there felt that reduced confidence in students' English skills was one of the main changes in the 20 years since she had organised a symposium on language and law, but added that the problem was not confined to law; moreover a fall in proficiency among non-Malays had to some extent been balanced by rising proficiency among Malays. One of the current law lecturers at UM sensed a decline in English upon her return to the faculty after a five-year break but refused to attribute this to any shift to BM in general education since her own generation had also been educated largely in Malay. Another UM lecturer estimated that only 5% of his graduates were linguistically equipped for high-level legal work, by which he appeared to mean English. Azmi Sharom, however, thought mounting criticism of students' English was too harsh: "Do they want Lord Denning after four years?"

No clear view of students' weakest areas emerged from interviews with lecturers, although writing was the skill most frequently mentioned, possibly because it is the main means of assessment. While one UM lecturer focused on sentence-level errors such as syntax, two others noted text-level problems such as resorting to bullet point answers and failure to link arguments. Some comments linked language difficulties and plagiarism, with a Terengganu practitioner who also lectured at UniSZA describing hiatuses between flawless cut-and-pasted sections and less coherent original prose and a UM lecturer remarking that the new intake, who were generally regarded as being better at English than their seniors, were scoring worse in writing because they had been scared off copying.

Poor reading skills were discussed by several lecturers, two UM teachers attributing the problem to the displacement of traditional research methods by web searches, but in general reading was more of a concern for practitioners than lecturers. One from KL and another from Johor Bahru, both in their 40s, regretted that the younger generation read less, the first remembering how novels had helped him absorb grammatical patterns painlessly. A lexicographer liaising between Dewan Bahasa and the Attorney-General's Chambers presumably had Malay in mind when averring "*Orang muda kurang membaca buku*" [young people rarely read books], but in general reading was more often associated with English than Malay. An ethnic Chinese corporate lawyer from KL thus stood out in recalling that she grew up enjoying Malay novels, despite speaking English and Hokkien at home and attending English-medium schools.

Before drawing conclusions about a generational shift away from literature it should be pointed out that several lawyers relating their confidence in English to childhood reading were only in their 20s or 30s.

Speaking skills were more often discussed in terms of confidence or soft skills than grammatical or phonological features. One UM lecturer advised weaker speakers to slow down since it was more important for lawyers to be accurate than to be fast. Feedback from supervisors in the reports of UM professional attachment students tended to focus on communicative features such as clarity and relevance. Lexicogrammatical accuracy seemed more of a concern with regard to writing. One supervisor wrote in his intern's log: "We need to improve in his meticulosity as he has made some careless mistake".

For all the negative comments about English from lecturers, a pilot study at UM (UM Baseline Study 2014) found 85% of the 2013 intake to be good or competent in English, based on IELTS banding, but recommended remedial classes for the bottom 15%. Writing emerged as the weakest skill and speaking and listening the strongest. The study noted that this cohort had been the first for many years to be interviewed as a part of admissions procedure, and largely in English, so they may have had higher proficiency than their predecessors.

Lecturers and especially attachment supervisors were far less critical of students' Malay than their English. One supervisor commented on his UM intern: "The student is at ease when dealing with others and communicating in BM". While the obvious conclusion is that proficiency in it is higher, the possibility that standards are less exacting should also be considered, given lawyers' awareness that Malay is likely to be used mostly for oral discussion in the lower courts or to translate documents drafted in English. Azmi Sharom felt that lecturers were stricter about Malay than lawyers. Two of his UM colleagues recalled that as recently as the 1990s law schools were more worried about Malay standards than English, and for one of them the main task remained to transform the everyday Malay spoken "in short bursts, mixed up with other languages, and readily understood from context" into something more academic. Another UM teacher and an administrator at the Legal Profession Qualifying Board concurred that while emphasis on BM during general schooling had raised standards, it had also brought overreliance on memorisation and test techniques that did not necessarily provide a foundation for proficient legal discourse. UM's own pilot investigation into the language skills of law students (UM Baseline Study 2014) nevertheless found general satisfaction with Malay proficiency and noted that only a small minority of students wanted BM language classes to be reintroduced.

7.8 The Role of Language in Evaluating Law Students

Evaluating the importance of language in legal education is problematic, even in common law jurisdictions where English is considered a first language. Stone (1983:314) described language acuity as "the basic tool" of the legal profession when addressing the dilemma US law schools face about whether to divert limited curricular resources from substantive law to reading and writing skills (ibid:316), and the difficulties may be particularly challenging for those instructing students who lack regular contact with acrolectic English in intensely multilingual and multicultural societies like Malaysia.

UM's law faculty offers all exams bilingually, and while few students choose to answer in Malay nowadays, the observations of some lecturers there and recollection of former students show that many refer to both versions of test papers in order to reinforce their understanding of questions. As for assignments, whereas Azmi Sharom enforced use of English in anticipation of students' need to use it for exams, one of his colleagues tolerated the marked preference his students had for Malay. One lecturer reported to the UM Baseline Study (2014) that students would rather answer in Bahasa "when they are given the option", which raises the question of how much choice they feel they really have. Most reported choosing mainly according to the medium of instruction and resources. One stated "I prefer BM for family law because the lecture and textbooks are in it, but contracts, torts, I use English". Another said that while he would prefer to write in Malay it was difficult to do so because of lack of references. The language of seniors' notes emerged as a key factor for some students. Two UM lecturers commented that an increasing tendency to regurgitate memorised examples rather than analyse test questions (a problem also noted by a Legal Profession Qualifying Board administrator with regard to the CLP) had reinforced the connection between the language of texts, notes and exams. One sophomore at UM said he tended to "learn cases and memorise key points so

I'll come up with them more easily in the same language". However, a few students reported taking notes in a different language from the medium of lectures. A UM lecturer and a KL lawyer, both in their 40s, recalled doing the same students, and the latter also mentioned friends who had taken notes in Chinese in HELP's all-English law classes.

Some students considered whether language choice influenced grades, although none said this would override factors such as the medium or lecturers, textbooks and notes. A fourth-year UM student assumed that a lecturer who taught in BM would be "more comfortable" marking tests in it. A second-year at the same institution wondered whether the standards were the same for both languages. A Melaka practitioner who had graduated from UM recalled speculating about which language would get him better marks, but ended up using English simply because he found it easier. A lecturer there commented that students, including ethnic Chinese, used to feel they would score better by answering in BM but largely concurred with her colleague, Azmi Sharom, that if anything Malay was now marked more strictly than English. Whichever language they chose, all the students said they had made their decision long before entering the exam room.

UM gives no instruction about what language law students are to write their reports on their professional attachments in. (The logbook supplied for attendance notes has a cover in Malay, but this may simply reflect the widespread practice of making the language *visible*). For the 2012 programme, 75 reports were written in English and 27 in Malay. Of the 39 logbooks submitted, 22 were filled in predominantly in English, 14 in Malay, and three in a balance of the two.

Lecturers at UM, MMU and UniSZA alike, as well as lawyers and administrators involved with the CLP, wrestled with the question of whether examinees could be assessed on legal knowledge independently of linguistic proficiency. The dilemma was most often discussed with reference to English. A senior lecturer at MMU reported focusing on failures of content rather than language, and former bar president Steven Thiru recalled CLP examiners being instructed to overlook grammatical errors. One UniSZA lecturer reasoned that "even though they have broken grammar, so long as they understand the concept it's ok". Leniency with language may go beyond Malaysia, given that an Ipoh lawyer who had studied at HELP remembered friends with questionable English proficiency sailing through exams marked by British assessors for the university's twinning programme. A KL lawyer who had studied partly in Wales remarked: "Even in the UK we could get by mostly on memorisation".

On the other hand one East Coast-based practitioner and lecturer argued that poor English got in the way of legal knowledge and saw this as the main reason UniSZA graduates had not yet been exempted from taking the CLP in order to qualify for the bar. A UM lecturer confessed to difficulty in ignoring persistent petty errors like "This is means…" even when they did not impede understanding. One of his colleagues noted a division between younger lecturers wanting to concentrate on legal content and older ones who felt language was paramount because it affected legal understanding. For another UM lecturer, now heading a human rights organisation, it was not merely a question of whether examiners understood what students wrote: declining English had affected basic study skills. While her attempts to raise MUET requirements at UM had been labeled elitist by some colleagues, she insisted that her concern was not for English per se but for academic standards.

Some lecturers endorsed the views I put to them of Australian barrister and academic Rowena Cantley-Smith (2006), who has proposed oral assessment as better preparation for legal practice than written tests. The UM lecturer who had noted a generation gap among her colleagues over attitudes to language accuracy reported that she tried to discourage memorisation by replacing written tests with oral presentations based on problems to be solved using whatever legal knowledge and resources students could muster. They were free to use English or BM and apparently responded well after the initial shock of being asked to be inventive. However, one of her former students, interviewed as a recently qualified lawyer, felt that it was pointless to introduce students to creativity in their final 12 months after years of factory education.

The extent to which law courses should include vocational as well as academic education fuels further debate. Differential entry requirements for graduates from different institutions reflect the Malaysian bar's concerns about the level of communicative as well as legal skills and help explain its intention to play a larger role in legal education. The latest proposal is for a Common Bar Course (CBC) comprising two 5-month semesters for graduates of 3-year degree programmes (the final year of 4-year programmes is normally dubbed the 'professional year'), with the first semester to include courses on communication skills and opinion writing (*Majlis Peguam* 2016: 231). For all pupils regardless of their law degree an Advanced Professional programme is also planned, with training in advanced communication to begin in the first semester (ibid). Both English and Malay are proposed as media of instruction for the CBC, with a 160-h Introduction to Malaysian Legal System course for overseas degree holders to include classes in Bahasa Malaysia for Lawyers.

Soft skills were frequently described by informants, without specific mention of English or BM. Two UM lecturers emphasised the importance of imparting the practical components of legal culture, such as producing documents and greeting court personnel in ways likely to win favour. In their reports, most UM attachment students mentioned at least one thing they had learnt about dealing with people, such as putting clients as ease, being persuasive and projecting confidence, adopting appropriate body language, employing productive questioning techniques or expressing empathy, all the while learning how to turn the fractured stories that clients commonly told into legal facts.

7.9 Relating Curricular Policy to Classroom Practice

While the legal education component of this study has been skewed toward UM because of the greater number of interviews there than at other schools, it seems clear that pedagogical pragmatism is central to legal instruction in Malaysia. This often produces more bilingualism in classroom practice than in curricula. English is prioritised across the board, whether because it is identified as the weaker language of most students or regarded as more useful for legal study or legal practice. No school translates the status of Malay as the official legal medium into predominantly BM-medium teaching. Lecturer and student preferences also confirm the inadequacy of corpus planning for Malay.

Two complimentary patterns of managing the importance of English emerge from the data. Where the official MOI is English, as in the private sector (e.g. HELP, MMU) and in *bumiputera*-majority public schools (UIA, UiTM, UniSZA), different degrees of supportive code-switching are employed, based on assessment of students' needs, and ranging from something close to monolingual instruction at institutions teaching London University external programmes, through a degree of code-switching at MMU, to extensively bilingual discourse at UniSZA. There are elements of compulsion in language policies, such as an insistence at many institutions that exams be answered in English, but this seems to reflect a pedagogical rather than an ideological stance. Where the MOI is officially bilingual, however, teaching practice has moved more toward English. UM and UKM now teach more in it than in Malay, although the latter still requires some exam questions to be answered in BM. No data on classroom code-switching was collected from UKM, but it certainly goes on at UM. UM strengthens English content in the final, professional year, even though many students are likely to need BM more in their early years of practice. Speculatively this is because, as the traditional apex university (despite this status officially being reserved for Universiti Sains Malaysia in Penang), it envisages high-level private sector work for its graduates – a goal that UniSZA also strives for while accepting that it is somewhat more remote. The fact that UiTM and UIA bring in more Malay before graduation is undoubtedly a counterweight to the all-English instruction conducted there in the first 3 years, but it may also reflect the fact that their graduates enter public service in much larger numbers than those from UM, where they will need Malay as much if not more than English.

Even when offered a choice, students' language preference is constrained by educational materials and legal resources, as well as by the policies of individual lectures, and all this adds up to a strong preference for English. Recognition of the need for more bilingual instruction and materials seems to outweigh lingering disdain for the utility of BM or fears that use of two languages may be confusing. However, for most students the reality is that comprehensive legal education is being implemented in English but not in Malay.

References

Abdullah Hassan. (1994). Problems of language assimilation in West Malaysia. In H. Abdullah (Ed.), *Language planning in Southeast Asia* (pp. 103–132). Kuala Lumpur: Dewan Bahasa dan Pustaka.

Asmah Haji Omar. (1994). Nationism and exoglossia: The case of English in Malaysia. In H. Abdullah (Ed.), *Language planning in Southeast Asia* (pp. 66–85). Kuala Lumpur: Dewan Bahasa dan Pustaka.

Azirah Hashim, & David, Maya Khemlani. (2011, June 2–5). Comparing language policy and practice in the East and West Malaysian courts. Paper presented at *The Law and Society Association 2011 Annual Meeting*, San Francisco.

Baker, Colin. (2001). *Foundations of Bilingual Education and Bilingualism*. Clevedon: Multilingual Matters.

Cantley-Smith, Rowena. (2006). The role of oral assessment in undergraduate law studies. *13 James Cook U.L. Rev 30 2006*, 30–63.

Chan, Brian Hok-shing. (2004). Beyond "contextualization": code-switching as a "textualization cue". *Journal of Language and Social Psychology, 23*(1), 7–27. http://jls.sagepub.com/cgi/reprint/23/1/7. Accessed 20 Feb 2005.

Foong, Jasmine. (2018, July 09). More M'sians reading Wikipedia in English than in BM, Chinese. *Malaysiakini*. http://www.malaysiakini.com/news/433316. Accessed 10 July 2018.

Gill, Saran Kaur. (2005). Language policy in Malaysia: Reversing direction. *Language Policy, 4*, 241–260.

Kaplan, Robert, & Baldauf, Richard. (1997). *Language planning from practice to theory*. Clevedon: Multilingual Matters.

Knowles, Gerry. (2004). English 2020: The future of English in Malaysia. In Knowles, Jamaliah, Jariah, Su'ad and Zuraidah (Eds.), *Language, linguistics and the real world, vol 1. Making Linguistics Relevant. Selected papers from the First International Conference on Language, Linguistics and the Real World.* Kuala Lumpur, 2002, pp. 23–49. Kuala Lumpur: University of Malaya Press.

Kua Kia Soong. (1999). *A protean Saga. The Chinese schools of Malaysia*. Kajang, Selangor: Dong Jiao Zong Higher Learning Centre.

Kua Kia Soong. (2005). *The Malaysian civil rights movement*. Petaling Jaya, Selangor: SIRD.

Kua Kia Soong (2011). *Patriots and pretenders. The Malayan people's independence struggle*. Petaling Jaya, Selangor: SUARAM.

Mackey, William. (2000). The description of bilingualism. In L. Wei (Ed.), *The Bilingualism Reader* (pp. 26–54). Abingdon: Routledge.

Majlis Peguam. (2016). Bar Council Annual Report 2015/2016.

Malaysiakini (2016, May 04). Affirmative approach needed in raising Malay language proficiency. http://www.malaysiakini.com/news/340249. Accessed 4 May 2016.

MLTC. (2016). Portal of the Malaysian Legal and Tax Information Centre. http://malaysianlaw.my/general/news/sultan-nazrin-wants-legal-practitioners-to-master-english-MY15795.html. Accessed 28 Apr 2016.

Pennycook, Alastair. (2004). Performativity and language studies. *Critical Inquiry in Language Studies, 1*(1), 1–26.

Pillai, Stefanie. (2006). Malaysian English as a first language. In D. M. Khemlani (Ed.), *Language choices and discourse of Malaysian families: Case studies of families in Kuala Lumpur, Malaysia* (pp. 22–42). Petaling Jaya: SIRD.

Powell, Richard. (2008). *Motivations for language choice in Malaysian courtrooms and implications for language planning*. Kuala Lumpur: Universiti Malaya.

Ricento, Thomas. (2002). Introduction. In T. Ricento and T. Wiley (Eds.), Revisiting the mother tongue question in language policy, planning, and politics. *The International Journal of the Sociology of Language*, 1–9.

Sankar, Lokasundari Vijaya. (2007, November 23). Ramifications of TESL for Malaysian L1 English speakers. Paper presented at Colloquium on Language Education and Policy, *2nd Language, Education and Diversity International Conference, Waikato University.*

Shamsul Amri Baharuddin. (1996). The construction and transformation of a social identity: Malayness and bumiputraness re-examined. *Journal of Asian and African Studies, 52*, 15–33.

Stone, Elizabeth Walker. (1983). A plan for the special preparation of attorneys in effective writing skills. *The Journal of Negro Education, 52*(3), 314–331.

Ting, Su-Hie. (2010). Impact of language planning on language choice in friendship and transaction domains in Sarawak, Malaysia. *Current Issues in Language Planning, 11*(4), 397–412.

UM Baseline Study. (2014). *Baseline study on the communication skills of law students*. Universiti Malaya, 2013.6.11~2014.6.10.

Wee, Lionel. (2010). Neutrality in language policy. *Journal of Multilingual and Multicultural Development, 31*(4), 421–434.

Chapter 8
Bilingualism in Law Offices

> *I have Malay staff so you'll hear some yelling from my cubicle asking for terms.*
>
> Melaka lawyer (2014.4.29)

> *The national will is to have things in Malay but at the same time there is another will, from the private sector, especially commerce, wanting English. There will be conflicts.*
>
> Dato' Zamani Mohammad, Terengganu lawyer (2014.2.14)

8.1 Investigating Language in the Law Office

For most lawyer informants in this study, legal and linguistic skills were intimately connected. One Johor practitioner was emphatic: "I would put language first (...) The legal points you want to make depend on your language". A young corporate lawyer said she hadn't thought much about language as a student but had come to understand its importance since starting to practise. Whereas some lecturers thought it possible to concentrate on legal skills while overlooking their students' language problems, former bar president Steven Thiru[1] was typical of practitioners in seeing the two as inseparable.

The keenest concerns were voiced about English rather than Malay. One corporate lawyer argued that problems communicating in English were affecting legal practice and another pointed out that errors in documents, even when not altering meaning, put his firm in a bad light. That Malay was generally considered less problematic may indicate perceptions that proficiency in it is higher but it may also reflect the fact that it is assigned to tasks that are less demanding – if not necessarily less in demand.

There are a few academic commentaries on the early effects of vernacularisation on professional practice. Mhd Ariff Yusof (1993) and Faiza (1993) referred to defi-

[1] Interviewed in KL, 2013.8.

R. Powell, *Language Choice in Postcolonial Law*, Language Policy 22,
https://doi.org/10.1007/978-981-15-1173-8_8

ciencies in practitioners' Malay, while Ahmad et al.'s (1993) survey of language practice in 1123 firms and Nik Safiah and Faiza's (1994) collation of language-related reports implied that the advance of Malay was slower than had been anticipated. On the other hand Nik Ramlah (1993) expressed fears that shift toward Malay had led to declining standards in legal training.

In this chapter, which explores how language choice influences work in Malaysian law offices, I have been cautious about characterising any task, let alone any work environment, as 'English' or 'Malay', taking heed of Bhatia's (2011a, b) view of legal practice as genre-bending, hybrid and interdiscursive and of lawyers as professionals who mix identities in daily practices that pull them between different jurisdictional (e.g. common vs civil law) as well as different professional (legal, corporate) and cultural (national, ethnic) loyalties. Nevertheless distinct associations between a particular language and particular kinds of work did emerge, and some professionals gave hints about which language they felt was better suited to which kind of work.

Questionnaires and reports based on UM students' professional attachment programmes helped frame interviews with lawyers. The 102 reports from 2012, with a further 20 obtained from the 2013 programme,[2] were mostly appended with handwritten *Rekod Kehadiran* (attendance notes) containing numerous direct and indirect references to language by the students themselves and by their supervisors. Most attachment students were involved in three or more legal areas. Conveyancing was perhaps the most common activity. Family cases (both civil and *Syariah*) and litigation were also frequently reported, followed by financial law (bankruptcy, corporate agreements, Islamic banking) and crime (from traffic violations, metre-tampering and immigration infringements to capital offences). Other areas included employment disputes; defamation; negligence; native land cases; and intellectual property (patent registration, trademark infringement, raiding a software firm). Courtroom and police station visits featured in many of the 2013 reports, with a small number also recording visits to penal and immigration detention centres. In addition to basic administrative tasks such as filing and delivering documents, most students drafted court forms, did land and bankruptcy searches and answered client letters. Many participated in client interviews or liaised with government departments and other law firms. As it is a matter of course for most professional Malaysians to work bilingually, many of the 2012 reports made few specific references to the languages used, so a short questionnaire including items about language choice was sent out to the 2013 students. But even when language was not mentioned it was often apparent from reports that more than one was needed, and often in the same task.

Given logistical and confidentiality considerations, focused law office observations were not conducted, but the orientations that many informants gave when I visited their workplaces, and the practices that surrounded and sometimes interrupted office-based interviews, helped to contextualize the data.

[2] The remainder had yet to submit their reports during my UM visits in 2014.

The analysis begins by assessing language preference for various communicative tasks (Sect. 8.2) and continues by exploring situational factors such as office location (Sect. 8.3) and work sector (Sect. 8.4). Attitudes to workplace bilingualism will then be addressed (Sect. 8.5), followed by professional evaluation of the evolution of communicative skills (Sect. 8.6). The section concludes with discussion of how language influences career choices (Sect. 8.7).

8.2 Language Preferences for Office-Based Tasks

8.2.1 Overview

Figure 8.1 summarises questionnaire data collected from UM students about the "main language(s)" for office tasks according to mode (speaking or reading/writing) and interlocutor/correspondent. While based on a sample of only 72 (some 72% of the attachment batch for 2012), a wide variety of worksites was covered and some patterns that emerged were borne out in student reports and interview data, with Malay having a more important role in oral communication and government dealings and English carrying more weight in documents (except for those submitted to court) and in the private sector.

Eng, Malay, Chinese (Rounded %; n=72)	E	M	C	E /M	E/C	M/C	E/M/C
SPEAKING:							
Conversation among office colleagues	**28**	**45**	**1.5**	**14**	7		**4**
Office meetings	**51**	36		**11**	**1.5**		
Meetings with/ calls to clients	**38**	**25**		**17**	**4**	**1.5**	**15**
READING & WRITING:							
Instructions from clients	**44**	**25**	**1.5**	**18**		**1.5**	**10**
Emails/letters to clients	**54**	**26**		**18**	**1.5**		
Emails/letters to govt depts	**17**	**72**		**11**			
Documents for court	**25**	**46**		**28**			
Private agreements	**72**	**11**		**14**			
Legal research	**91**	**6**		**3**			

Fig. 8.1 General language preferences in law offices

Almost half the attachment students reported conversation with office colleagues to be mainly in Malay, with 28% finding it mainly in English and 14% in a blend of both. In the more formal setting of office meetings, however, English (51%) was the main language more often than Malay (36%). English also scored higher in conversations with clients (38%:25%), considerably higher in written communication from (44%:25%) and to (54%:26%) clients, and much higher for private agreements such as contracts (72%:11%) and for legal research (91%:6%). On the other hand BM was more widespread for documents prepared for court (46%:25%) and much more so for correspondence with government departments (72%:17%). It should also be noted that nearly a third reported a mixture of English and Malay for court documents and nearly a fifth for client correspondence. Chinese came a poor third as a main language but was reported by 11% in use alongside English, or English and Malay, for conversation with colleagues and by 20% for conversation with clients. One attachment student found English, Malay, Hokkien and Mandarin all being used with clients while another mentioned "some use of Chinese and Tamil".

8.2.2 Communicating with Staff and Colleagues

In order not to overload attachment students, the questionnaire did not differentiate between interlocutors. However, in comments, reports and interviews, many students and lawyers distinguished conversations with staff from those with lawyers. A student completing his studies in the UK recalled the use of English "even with runners and clerical staff" at his KL corporate practice, and some lawyers reported speaking to employees in it to encourage them to, as a Melaka lawyer put it, "reach out to a certain type of clientele". But in most offices, even in KL firms where lawyers interacted in English, there was a tendency to use Malay or to code-switch with clerks. Two practitioners from Ipoh and another two from Penang said Malay was more common with Malay employees and Chinese or English with non-Malays. One attachment student found Chinese used with clerks and Malay with dispatch riders.

For conversation among lawyers, English emerged from student reports as the main preference. A Penang practitioner described this as a matter "of course" and a Melaka advocate went as far as to say "among lawyers it is 100% English". Two more at large KL practices agreed it was "very unusual for us to be using Malay". One Malay practitioner had just gone into partnership with another Malay but reported that both conversed in English. There were regional differences, however. Several East Coast informants, in both Kota Bharu and Kuala Terengganu, spoke to staff and lawyers alike in Malay.

8.2.3 Communicating with Clients

As might be expected, language accommodation toward clients is common. For a Melaka practitioner, "With clients it depends on them". Client ethnicity was often mentioned, with a Chinese lawyer from Kota Bharu mostly using BM, as 90% of his clientele were Malay, while speaking Mandarin to Chinese clients, a Malay from the same city using BM for the Malays and Siamese but English for the Chinese, and Mukhtar Abdullah, down the coast in Kuala Terengganu, reserving English for Chinese and Indians and otherwise sticking to Malay. While a KL practitioner put the balance at 70% English, 20% Mandarin and 10% Malay in his firm, a Penang practitioner described her workplace as "an English environment" but found Malay clients assuming they could use BM as soon as they entered the office. A Melakan noted that at least 50% of her non-Malay clients were more comfortable in BM than English.

As well as ethnicity, the professional and social background of clients was a frequently cited factor in language choice. A Chinese in partnership with Malay practitioners in Melaka conversed with state government clients entirely in BM but with corporate clients mostly in English. A KL lawyer involved in construction litigation observed that many of his wealthiest clients were self-made Chinese businessmen who had never achieved proficiency in Malay or English. In the case of legal aid clients, former bar president Hendon Mohamed found that a wide variety of languages and communicative styles might be needed, with English and legal jargon not very high on the list.

Code-switching was commonplace. An attachment student from the 2013 batch observed that "the language used to communicate with clients will always be more than one"; his classmate noted how mixed language might "attract the client's attention more". An Ipoh practitioner described clients coming in speaking English, "but when we see from the facial expression they don't understand our reply we switch to Chinese".

It was rather clear that English carries greater weight in written than spoken communication. One 2013 attachment student found client phone calls to be mostly in Malay but emails often in English, while a Melaka lawyer said Chinese was common when speaking to clients but English preferred when writing to them. For a Kota Bharu lawyer, correspondence was in BM for individual clients and government bodies but English for corporate clients, including property developers.

8.2.4 Reading, Research and Writing

Enquiries about the language of legal research invariably brought comments such as "all in English" and "definitely in English" (both from the Malay-dominant East Coast) across the board. The main reason given was that most reading materials are in it, including law reports, books and judgments. A practitioner from Kota Bharu and another from the Klang Valley pointed out that even case reports posted by the Attorney-General's Chambers are mostly in English. Assigned to mooting in Malay, an MMU student found difficulty in conducting his preparatory research in it. It was sometimes also suggested that English resources were "easier to comprehend" (KL practitioner) and a Melakan stated he would opt for the English version of a statute even where Malay was available. While there may be some circularity in finding texts easier to understand in the language that a practitioner is more accustomed to reading them in, another Melakan described English texts as "more natural" and a Kota Bharu advocate advanced the idea that the English background of the law made texts more readable in that language. A KL litigator cited the important role of legal research as one of the main reasons English was more of an impediment than Malay to professional success, with those lacking English proficiency confined to less innovative work.

Written aptitude tended to be evaluated in relation to specific tasks rather than as a general skill. A KL-based graduate from a UK law school and a UM graduate working in Melaka agreed that opinion-writing, normally the end product of research, called for English. Client correspondence varied with client preference but tended to be in English even for clients who were spoken to in other languages, with clients themselves favouring it for written instructions. On the other hand documentary drafting was likely to be in BM if it was for the court, although the frequency with which translation was mentioned in connection with the drafting process suggests there is a continuing propensity to think of English as the base language of law.

8.2.5 Translating and Interpreting

15% of UM's 2012 attachment students mentioned translating documents or interpreting for clients in their reports, but many of their observations implied that translation was also involved in activities where it was not specifically mentioned, which suggests that it is often taken for granted. An item about translation and interpreting was therefore included on a questionnaire given to 2013 attachment students, and just under half reported being tasked with one or the other.

In both the 2012 and 2013 data, Malay and English were the main languages discussed in relation to translation. The numerous examples of translation in both directions confirmed its pivotal position in legal practice. Malay translations were done for both government departments and individual clients. One student had been asked to translate sales and purchase agreements, deeds of assignment, statements of claim, affidavits and originating summons and logged the translation of a statement of claim for a government office. Among the lawyers, a Terengganu practitioner discussed translating "various documents for government departments" while another from Kelantan described the need to translate tenancy agreements into Malay for clients. As for translation from Malay into English, several examples were given of foreign clients presented with official documents, including applications for judicial review, High Court submissions, State Authority Consents and other forms for which BM is mandatory. However, a Penang litigation lawyer said that many of the clients who requested English versions of documents were Malaysian.

Older lawyers routinely task juniors with translation and many appear to regard law students as language resources, assuming most of them to have been educated bilingually. Several students reported helping their seniors with Malay as if it were only natural that the older generation of lawyers lacked proficiency in it:

> In the afternoon I translated a few affidavits from Bahasa Malaysia to English as my boss is having difficulties in understanding BM. (UM student attached to Kuching firm, 2012)

Few students seemed to set much store by translation as details were scant, although a Chinese student who chose to write most of his attachment log in Malay received a special allowance from his Penang firm after proving adept at translating affidavits. A newly qualified lawyer who had been attached to a KL corporate firm before transferring to a smaller practice in Ipoh described translation simply as "an unwritten part of the job" for juniors.

One of the most frequent office tasks is translating documents prepared in English so that they can be submitted to court. In Steven Thiru's firm everything was written in English and then translated, rather than drafted directly in Malay; another KL practitioner described translation as the final stage instead of being incorporated into the drafting process. While many practitioners, on both the East and West coasts and even in larger firms in KL, did their own translations, some firms practise labour division. "One person is very good at translating into BM", reported a Melaka lawyer, while a KL counterpart noted "We have one lawyer who is a very good translator and in fact that's all she does". It was not necessarily the Malays who were best at translating into Malay: "Sometimes I have to do English-BM translation but many non-Malays here are better than me", commented an informant in a small KL partnership. Translation may also be outsourced, as in the case of one of the larger KL firms where interviews were conducted.

A KL litigator was typical of both lawyers and students in commenting that translation was "an important skill for a lawyer" without going into details about how it is done. According to a Terengganu advocate, no particular training was needed to change the main points of cases into BM when drafting submissions as "we follow previous patterns". A Malay student, educated mostly overseas and confessing to poor Malay, was told by his firm: "Just use google translate".

However, a young Kota Bharu practitioner admitted to difficulty translating documents into BM despite it being her mother tongue:

> I had to google some words but (...) it's a direct translation, we cannot match it to the word but thanks to Whatsapp and Facebook we can ask around our colleagues.

A KL lawyer advised against directly translating into BM as "it looks funny". A Terengganu lawyer said his firm preferred to stick to English as "the meaning might change" while his senior declared: "We have to follow what has been written before, we don't have the skill to translate into Malay". Although Steven Thiru found colleagues rarely referring to the BM translations of documents submitted to court, another KL-based practitioner warned of the importance of checking them thoroughly as judges had the right to rely solely on the Malay: "If you ask for something [that is] in the English document but not in the BM they can refuse you".

Translation is a function not only of the bilingual policy but also societal multilingualism, and here other languages, especially Chinese, may be important. Attachment students reported translating oaths into Chinese or Chinese texts into English. One Melaka lawyer translated sale and purchase agreements into Mandarin; her colleague translated client instructions from Mandarin into English and the firm's replies into Mandarin. Chinese literacy brings the added advantage of enhancing communication with foreign clients. Both Melaka and Penang are popular with overseas investors and retirees. One practitioner from the former had several clients from Taiwan; a conveyancing lawyer in KL served property purchasers from China – although she said many were happy to sign English agreements once they had been explained orally in Chinese and a few signed even without an explanation. Secondment to a Singapore firm made one ethnic Chinese UM graduate regret her poor Mandarin.

Examples of oral interpreting recorded in the student data included: "minor interpreting"; translating between Chinese and English for a Thai client in a police station; Malay into English for a foreign lawyer; Malay or English into Mandarin for clients; and "translating Malay into English during trial for defence counsel who cannot understand Malay well". One of the 2013 attachment students mentioned helping a chamberee who lacked fluency in Malay. Another student took pride in helping her senior, whose communicative skill overshadowed her lack of BM: "The ways she handles the distress client who has been cheated by her husband is phenomenal. She couldn't understand Malay so I translated for her in English and the flow of the advising process is smooth as ever". Some students were surprised to come across Malaysians seeking advice at government legal aid departments who knew neither Malay nor English, with one of the 2012 batch noting this "bitter truth" as a particular problem with legal aid clients.

Chinese also featured among the languages that students were asked to interpret, including English into Malay, Mandarin and Cantonese for the benefit of clients. A conveyancer emphasised the duty of practitioners to attest in a jurat (clause attached to an affidavit) that loan agreements, which banks generally prefer to be in English, had been explained to borrowers; hence it was paramount to gain client trust by striving for equivalent Chinese terms. Mandarin was used by many students in dealings with foreign clients, with Hokkien and Cantonese also mentioned.

In comparison with Chinese, Tamil seldom appeared in the data. I often heard the language spoken among lawyers in pre-session conversations at court, especially in KL, with several lawyers reported is as a home language and one 2013 attachment student logging interpreting for Tamil-speaking clients, but few students or lawyers mentioned using the language at work, even though it is the most important Indian language in Malaysia and spoken by some 1.3 million (Ethnologue 2018). This may in part reflect a shortcoming in the sampling, since fewer than 2% of the UM and MMU students gave Tamil as the main home language, although this rose to 8% at UniSZA (Fig. 7.1). Several UM law lecturers remarked on the fall in the numbers of Indian students and assumed that they had shifted to private colleges, but data from these was collected only through interviews with a dozen students and from comments about education from lawyer informants. It is also likely that Tamil takes a back seat to English and Malay for most Indians entering law. 12 of the 60 lawyer informants described their ethnicity as Indian, but only four had been educated even partly in Tamil and none predominantly in it. One from Johor Bahru, another based in Ipoh and a third working in KL mentioned social use of Tamil, alongside English and Malay, but none referred to it in discussions about the office. Malaysians speaking northern Indian languages are numerous enough to constitute a separate category from other Indians in Bar Council data on the profession, and few speak South Indian languages. One Melakan practitioner said that she needed an interpreter for the many Tamil clients coming to her office as the only Indian language she spoke was Gujerati.

Two 2012 attachment students logged office discussions about Arabic terms for Islamic banking contracts, and some 20% of the batch mentioned involvement in *Syariah* cases, including visits to the family courts, but none reported a need to write or speak Arabic.

8.3 Influence of Office Location

While language choice is framed primarily by bilingual policy (BM for official functions, English where judges find it convenient and in much of the private sector), and is further influenced by societal multilingualism and international liaison, regional culture and work-sector practices are also significant.

Former bar president Ambiga Sreenevasan (2013) acknowledged that legal and political reforms are unlikely to go beyond preaching to the converted in urban areas unless people in the provinces are engaged in their own languages. Conducting interviews with legal practitioners across seven sites brought opportunities to explore regional differences. Student questionnaires and reports covered locations nationwide, and although students were not asked specifically to comment on local conditions, many did so in passing.

Students and lawyer informants themselves came from a variety of regions (Figs. 8.2, 8.3 and 8.4) and often made regional comparisons. Although 42% of the lawyer informants worked in the Klang Valley (where 50% of the nations lawyers are based), only 30% had been raised there. 8% were from East Malaysia (Sabah or Sarawak), 6% from Penang in the north, and the rest from other West Malaysian states, including Kelantan, Terengganu and Pahang on the East Coast, Perak, adjacent to the Klang Valley, and Johor and Melaka in the south. Many had been employed or done professional attachments in multiple locations.

Comments from East Malaysians suggest that most return to their home states after completing LLBs – which are only offered in West Malaysia. One UM student intending to take up criminal law back in Sarawak declared "English will be enough" since it is the official medium of law there. A UM lecturer generally found East Malaysians, especially Sabahans, to be above average in English, although one Sabahan lawyer mentioned a greater need for Malay in smaller towns there.

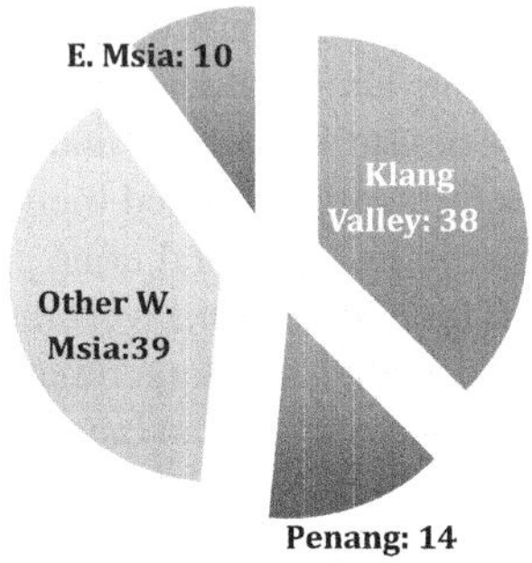

Fig. 8.2 Hometown of UM2013 students (%) (n = 80)

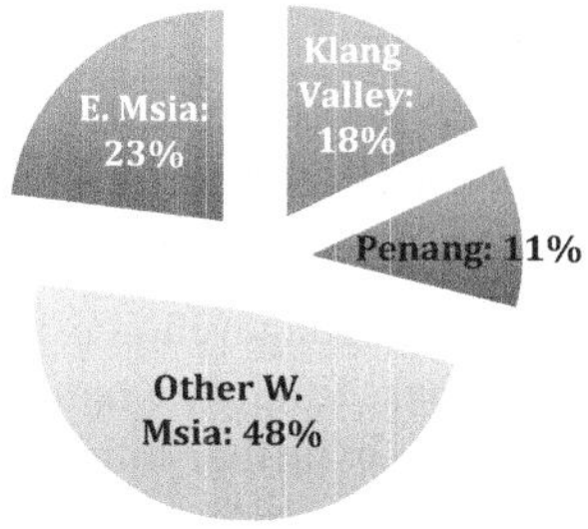

Fig. 8.3 Hometown of UniSZA students (%) (n = 74)

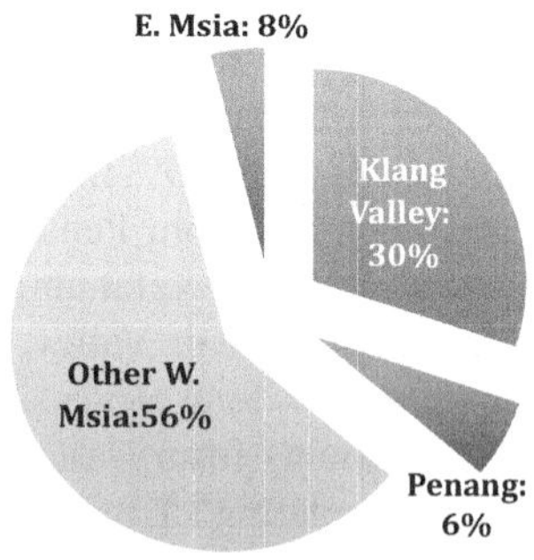

Fig. 8.4 Hometown of lawyer informants (%) (n = 60)

While there is some truth in stereotypes about different parts of Malaysia having distinct language ecologies, the only clear patterns emerging from the data were that the Klang Valley tends to favour English and the East Coast strongly favours Malay. Penang in the north, and Johor, next to Melaka, perhaps also tend to lean toward English, but both have large Chinese populations and offices tend to include speakers proficiency in Mandarin or other Chinese languages.

Many practitioners emphasised the contrast between the competitive Klang Valley and the more collaborative provinces. For a Melaka lawyer it was "KL on the one hand and everywhere else on the other". Former bar president Hendon Mohamed recalled a sense of anonymity upon moving from Johor to KL 40 years ago, even though that was a time where there were still only 200 lawyers in the whole city. A practitioner from Ipoh and another from Melaka commented independently on the difficulty of specialising in the provinces, where economic survival may depend on serving a variety of clients. A Terengganu lawyer educated in KL complained of having to fly back just to buy or borrow specialised law books, while a lawyer up the coast in Kota Bharu described the difficulty of getting Kelantanese firms to take on corporate work: "We have to call in big firms from KL". In terms of language there was a general consensus that more English is used in and around the capital than elsewhere.

Malay was felt to be indispensable on the East Coast, with a Terengganu-based lawyer concluding "As long as they stay in KT it shouldn't be a problem if [lawyers] don't speak English but if they went to KL then there is a problem". Another Kuala Terengganu lawyer found civil litigation involved much more Malay there than in KL. English is now used less than Malay at the Kelantan bar association because, according to a Kota Bharu practitioner, "the younger ones can't understand it. This shift is also taking written form, with the annual report for the local bar in BM, even though the accountant's report remains in English.

Localisation is attenuated by the mobility of lawyers and judges. A disproportionate number have been educated in the Klang Valley and many have worked there before moving to other states. The language preferences of courtroom judges was thought to be difficult to predict because of regional transfers, as well as individual experience, and a young lawyer who had moved from KL to Ipoh thought that differences among law firms in any one town could be more important than differences among towns. According to a Melaka practitioner, many clients choose firms where they expect to be able to converse in their mother tongue, so most towns have practices that tend to attract certain ethnic groups.

Informants nevertheless highlighted some local characteristics. Hokkien was reported to be widely used among lawyers as well as their clients in Penang, while Cantonese was important in KL and Ipoh. East Coast Malaysians, including non-Malays, often favour their distinct dialects over standard Malay: one MMU student from the West Coast described difficulties in understanding clients during his chambering in Terengganu. According to a local practitioner, anglophones still hold sway at Melaka bar association meetings because Chinese and Indian members tend to be the most active, even though the number of Malay lawyers has grown. Something similar might be said of the national Bar Council.

8.4 Influence of Work Sector

The main sector-related division emerging from the data was between the Malay-dominant government sector and English-favouring private sector, but there were also language-based differences related to particular areas of work.

8.4.1 Government Sector

According to a Johor Bahru lawyer, "For those going into government service of course BM is fine". While a UM 2013 attachment student reported use of several languages, including English, at a Bar Council Legal Aid Centre in the capital, another attached to a government Legal Aid Bureau (LAB) in Kelantan found "Malay used for everything, including legal research". A 2012 attachment student assigned to an LAB in Johor was the only one able to speak Chinese to clients, suggesting that most of her colleagues were Malay. Her classmate, attached to a private firm functioning in English with some Mandarin, found BM the sole language used for contacting government departments. While one Sabah lawyer reported wide use of English with government officials another, whose office operated overwhelmingly in English, said Malay was used for official correspondence with government departments, including the courts, even though trials there proceeded mostly in English. A student attached to a Sabah LAB described legal officers conversing and preparing court documents in English but correspondence for government offices and conversation with clerical staff being mostly in BM.

Hendon Mohamed recalled private law firms using BM with government departments as early as the '70s and most lawyers now adhere to this strictly. A Kelantan practitioner remarked: "Correspondence to government departments? All in BM, no exception". A KL conveyancer said BM was used for "all letters to the Land Office" and it was the same for a Penang lawyer when checking insolvency status with the Identity Card Department. A KL-based conveyancing lawyer noted that documents for the Finance Ministry and State Government were among the few in the housing loan process that were not completed in English. According to a Terengganu practitioner also involved in conveyancing, government departments would not reject English documents if everything were in order, but replies would come back in Malay.

8.4.2 Corporate and Non-contentious Work

If the government sector pulls legal communication toward Malay, business tugs back in the direction of English, the preference not only of large top tier firms but also boutique ones that "follow the money".[3] The English version of the Companies

[3] Amanda Whiting, Asian Law Centre, Melbourne University, 2013.3.16.

Act remains the authentic one and all documentation for setting up a company can be drafted in English apart from the Certificate of Incorporation. (One KL corporate practitioner pointed out that the government has been reissuing older English-medium certificates in BM). A Klang Valley lawyer specialising in corporate and arbitral work and rarely attending court said that he seldom took affidavits in anything other than English. Another Klang Valley practitioner specialising in construction arbitrations confessed to "getting a bit lazy" about Malay as he rarely needed it. Another corporate lawyer confirmed Azirah and Powell's (2011) findings that arbitration, which is promoted by the government in order to reduce litigation backlogs, is dominated by English even when all parties are Malaysian. Like Ng (2009) in Hong Kong, this study refrained from directly soliciting information about salaries yet similarly concludes that the level of remuneration is a factor in language attitudes, with those serving well-funded commercial clients likely to favour English.

8.4.3 Banking and Insurance

Three Kuala Terengganu lawyers and one KL lawyer who had served in the legal department of banks agreed that English was the working language of banking, as did lawyers and attachment students corresponding and conversing with banking sector clients. For most banking lawyers court appearances were the only area that called for Malay, with one Penang practitioner using the language in litigation and a Terengganu practitioner using it for prosecuting financial crimes. But one UM student was asked to translate affidavits into English for a banking litigation. At a Penang firm English copies were kept for any matter involving international law or foreign clients, but I was also told that some clients preferred private documents in Malay and correspondence in Malay or Chinese. A Terengganu lawyer confirmed that Islamic banking is also mainly done in English, this expanding sector being embedded in common law and statute rather than *Syariah* (Abdul Hamid Mohamad 2012).

The banking sector's preference for English affects related work sectors such as insurance. A lawyer based in Kota Bharu, which leans strongly toward Malay, claimed his work for a local insurance panel was 100% in English. A newly qualified Malay lawyer in Johor Bahru found Malay terms in the field to be scarce and unfamiliar and one lecturer recalled having to create her own terminology when asked to teach insurance law in Malay at UM. A recent study of insurance communication (Wan Irham Ishak et al. 2013) found Malay documents contained extensive English lexis, with *Takaful* (Islamic insurance) agreements commonly in English despite containing numerous Arabic concepts. Many insurance clients are not comfortable with documents in English, however, and the UM lecturer who had taught insurance warned of possible legal implications if clients sign agreements they later claim not to have understood. Bank Negara (the Central Bank) now provides documents in Malay and brokers take pains to recruit agents from a range of language backgrounds (Wan Irham Ishak et al. 2013). Sales pitches typically involve code-switched oral explanations of documents written partly or wholly in English: "Waiver of control *ni kita tak dapat* [We did not receive this waiver of control]" (ibid).

8.4.4 Conveyancing

The language preference of the banks also affects practices in the field of conveyancing since property purchases usually entail loans. Unsurprisingly, lawyers involved in commercial property on both the West and East Coasts described English as dominant, but from Penang and Ipoh all the way down to Johor, residential conveyancing, the bread and butter of many smaller firms, also seems to be mostly in English. As a Terengganu practitioner put it, "the banks prefer it". It seems that few firms even issue Malay versions of loan agreements. A Penang conveyancer said she had never seen a sale and purchase agreement in Malay, although she was sometimes asked for Chinese translations.

The various documents required for property transfers are invariably complex and it might be thought that the use of English presents a risk for clients. Given what is at stake, however, it could also be argued that the legal system prefers to keep things in English as it has stood the test of time. During his professional attachment a UiTM student observed how lengthy documents were generated from the stock of existing agreements simply by substituting names and property details. A Terengganu lawyer who mostly served Malay clients, and a KL lawyer mostly serving Chinese, found it was generally enough explain crucial passages orally in the preferred language of the purchaser or vendor. However, three other East Coast practitioners said that an increasing number of purchases there were being processed in BM, unless corporations or foreigners were involved: foreign buyers are still thin on the ground on the East Coast, but an important clientele for lawyers in Penang, Melaka and Johor Bahru. If more agreements are now being drawn up in Malay it will be interesting to see if more equivalents are coined for English terms of art that few non-lawyers understand, or whether drafters shift toward more lay-friendly language. One Melaka lawyer felt that there were limitations to recycling tried and tested formulaic language because of local variations in property practices.

8.4.5 Family Law

Being defined as Muslim under the constitution, Malays bring family matters to *Syariah* courts, except where non-Muslim parties are also involved. Family proceedings in the civil courts are therefore brought by non-Malays, which may bring a preference for English even though documents are supposed to be submitted in the national language. One lawyer with a practice in an upmarket part of KL found clients preferring to speak English and even asking for court documents to be translated into it, and even in Terengganu practitioner a young practitioner found many family cases among Chinese and Indian parties conducted in English. A Melaka lawyer said many judges there allowed English documentation in probate and divorce matters. Another Melaka practitioner noted that the lack of a specialised family court there means that cases are heard before judges usually involved in civil litigation who tend to be "fairly flexible" about language. She estimated that half of her clients spoke to her in Malay, with many of the others requesting Chinese or Tamil interpreters. Observations of a number of family cases (see next chapter) suggest that the socioeconomic level of parties may be a significant indicator of language preference.

One Johor lawyer considered linguistic flexibility part of the communicative skills that are vital in family practice, along with empathy and the ability to draw on experience, and both before and after being interviewed at her office she was heard code-switching between Malay and English with clients.

8.4.6 Civil and Criminal Litigation

Court appearances entail drafting and submitting a range of documents. While official policy requires Malay, in practice the anticipated language of proceedings and the particular stage of proceedings influence the language of documents. Most litigation lawyers agreed on the importance of drafting cause papers or pleadings in the national language as they contain specific claims for relief and defences against the claims of the other party; but for submissions (arguments) many thought a skeleton in Malay would suffice. Several litigators – most based in the Klang Valley but one working in Melaka – didn't even bother with the Malay skeleton if they expected oral proceedings to be in English. Brendan Navin, a national Bar Committee member, echoed the view of many in suggesting that the English 'translation' that many firms submit along with Malay papers may be the one that is given more attention by judges. Lawyers in both Johor Bahru and Melaka confirmed that witness statements and supporting documents in English need not be translated into Malay.

As will be seen with proceedings themselves, court hierarchy influences the language of documentary drafting. A young practitioner based in Kelantan submitted papers for the Court of Appeal in English, even though for all courts below she stuck to BM. Steven Thiru followed a practice common in KL of submitting bilingual sets of papers to the High Court in the expectation that judges would concentrate on the English. Brendan Navin did the same, but for the lower courts he did not bother with English, even though the Malay documents he submitted were usually translated from English. While he did most translations himself, two partners in large KL corporate firms, and a senior lawyer with a small firm in Johor Bahru, drafted papers in English and then had juniors translate them.

Age, in addition to area of law, seems to have an impact on language preference for drafting. This is only to be expected given that most senior lawyers qualified before Malay became a requirement for qualification in the 1980s, with many moving up to High Court litigation as Malay started taking over the lower courts. Ng

(2009: 210) too found seniority to have a significant bearing on attitudes towards language among Hong Kong lawyers, where Cantonese started to be used 15 years ago. Malaysian attachment students are normally assigned to senior practitioners. 72% of those supervising UM's 2012 cohort wrote their comments in English (with most of the 28% who chose BM employed in legal aid offices). Younger Malaysian lawyers today have more opportunities to use Malay because of rites of passage through the lower courts, where it is the main medium, and they are also more likely to have been educated in the national language prior to their legal studies. One practitioner from Penang and another from Ipoh, both in their 30s, drafted directly in BM. The former recalled feeling comfortable doing this within a few months of starting out in practice, despite having studied law entirely in English. The latter mentioned being helped by the use of templates.

Some informants reported differential language preferences for civil and criminal matters. A UM attachment student noted the "use of dwilanguage [bilingualism] for civil cases and BM for criminal cases". Many attachment students attend police stations, and several reported that discussion there was entirely in Malay unless foreigners were involved. An advocate from Ipoh and another from Kuala Terengganu drafted most of their papers in BM but the latter said it was not necessary to translate authorities that were reported in English. Despite finding English widely spoken in the High Court, a KL advocate described criminal lawyers there as more fluent in Malay because of the preferences of defendants and witnesses. While Malay generally seems to be favoured for criminal matters, English comes more into play as cases proceed up the court hierarchy.

For documentary submissions in both criminal and civil matters, the preferences of justices, as well as the anticipated medium of oral proceedings, seem to influence the language of drafting, and one Johor advocate emphasised the importance of checking which language individual judges were more comfortable with, something that may be easier to do in provincial cities with a smaller Bench.

8.5 Attitudes to Workplace Bilingualism

With the exception of practitioners specialising in non-contentious matters and the diminishing generation of senior lawyers dependent on bilingual juniors, English-Malay bilingualism emerges from the data as part and parcel of the Malaysian law office. Given that lawyers could get by with English alone a generation or so ago, this bilingualism is undeniably a result of vernacularisation policies, but the comments of students and practitioners about their own preferences and those of clients suggest that these policies are seen less as an imposition than as in line with societal changes and market forces.

Undoubtedly there are still some practitioners with poor Malay who resent becoming marginalised. A Johor litigator who felt he had been pushed out of advocacy commented: "It's tough lah. This dual language thing makes it very difficult". Chooi Mun Sou was not alone among the older informants in suggesting that the promotion of Malay had accompanied a decline not only in English but also in legal standards. Conversely some informants who would welcome greater use of Malay expressed frustration with the lack of effort put into developing its legal register Malay. After commenting "Do we think justice – I'm sorry – is only in English?", an advocate based in Shah Alam, in the Klang Valley, saw little choice but to continue with English until legal Malay evolved further.

Possibly some informants had reasons to be cautious about criticising the official language policy, even in anonymous interviews, but the overall impression from interviews and questionnaires was that bilingual law is accepted as pragmatic, given societal multilingualism, or as expedient, given the Malayanisation of education and other domains. While continuing to feel more confident in English than Malay, an Indian lawyer from Johor said she had long stopped translating from English drafts as it was now easier for her to write directly in Malay. Despite working predominantly in BM, a Malay lawyer based in Shah Alam had seen his English flourish once he started to use it for legal research.

For many, bilingual practice is automatic and unremarkable. A partner in a large KL firm stated: "For High Court and above we will normally submit in both languages"; a junior lawyer in a medium-sized Melaka firm noted: "In the Melaka High Court we file in BM but in KL we file in English as well". One attachment student from UM's 2013 batch had been tasked with drafting a bilingual report for a VIP's visit to a Legal Aid Bureau. Nowhere was the normalisation of bilingualism more apparent than in student recollections of their workplace experiences, which often skated over language choice in activities that were clearly bilingual. Many reports themselves contained code-switching that appeared to reflect the languages used in practice. The majority of the attachment reports written in BM were submitted by students who had been posted to legal aid offices, but nearly all of these contained English legal lexis, such as "setting aside default judgment", "grounds of defence" "dock brief" and "mitigate". Some 20% of the UM2012 reports written in English were accompanied by logbooks filled out predominantly in BM, and although there was no opportunity to follow the idea up, it seems plausible this indicates some preference for Malay for routine and spontaneous tasks, and for English for more reflective or formal writing. On-site language also seemed to influence the medium of note-taking, with 2013 students using BM to log police station activities much more than office-based tasks.

Most logbook entries in BM included extensive English legal terminology. One 2012 student embedded "pleading", "bill of costs" and "material change to vary maintenance" in a single entry in Malay. Another switched to English for "personal injury" and "Deed of Mutual Covenant". English appeared quite frequently for terms that have widely-known Malay equivalents, such as "case management" and "hire-purchase". Some students added English terms after their Malay notes:

> *Belajar bagaimana untuk membuat pemfailan kes* [Learnt how to file cases] *(case filing)* (2012 attachment student).

Others flagged untranslated English terms with inverted commas: "'mention' *di mahkamah majistret untuk kes dadah*" [a mention in the magistrate's court for a drugs case], "*mengemaskini dan mencatit* 'list of hearing/mention'" [update and record list of hearings/mentions] (2012 student). But terms in different languages were more commonly left unmarked and unexplained: "*Membuat draf pendaftaran* [draft registration of] power of attorney"; "*Kes buruh* [industrial case] – malicious prosecution".

The comparative lack of Malay terms, or lower familiarity with them, might be behind the fact that Malay terms appeared in English sentences less often than the reverse. In some instances a switch to Malay appeared to indicate the language in which a task was conducted: "Learn how to amend *afidavit jawapan* [affidavit in reply]", and if the language which activities were reported in is anything to go by, research in English often accompanied tasks performed in BM: "Research setting aside judgment in default – *deraf petisyen penceraian berasingan* [draft petition on matrimonial separation]"; "*Pengurusan kaunter* [manage counter]. Research on 'distress'".

8.6 Professional Evaluation of Lawyers' Communicative and Legal Skills

Concerns about the communication skills of those entering the profession arose frequently in in lawyer and lecturer interviews. Many practitioners became noticeably more engaged when the topic of communication standards was raised. Gaining access to students at the three main research sites was also facilitated in part by institutional expectations that my investigations would shed light on language proficiency, and indeed during my initial approaches there was an assumption that this was my primary aim. In fact my main objective was to explore bilingual legal education and gain insight into the concerns of legal practitioners and lecturers about communicative standards, rather than to evaluate language proficiency. My involvement nevertheless led to a set of general proficiency tests being incorporated into UM's Baseline Study (2014), as well as to discussions among lecturers and administrators at all three law schools about how to support and measure English (and to a lesser extent Malay) standards and legal communication skills.

8.6.1 English Standards

English was invariably uppermost in the minds of informants when communication skills were mentioned In 2008 the Bar Council set up an ad hoc committee to explore common entry procedures (Thiru 2011: 7) after "abysmal language skills" contributed to a 60% failure rate in its ethics courses for chambering pupils (ibid: 8). In 2011 the head of the bar's Qualifications Evaluation Team proposed requiring new entrants pass an English test (Tan 2011). At the end of the year the bar conducted an employability survey of 393 firms of all sizes throughout West Malaysia and found respondents (10% replying to online surveys and 90% interviewed by phone) primarily interested in three factors when hiring young lawyers: written English proficiency; oral English proficiency; and commitment to the firm (Thiru and Ang 2012: 17). Only 13% of local graduates were rated as having high English writing skills, with 20% deemed to have high oral skills, compared to 65% of those educated overseas and approximately 50% of those who had taken an external LLM (ibid: 17). Declaring language and communication skills essential to legal practice (ibid: 19), the report, which according to Steven Thiru (2013 interview, see footnote 1) was only partially released to the press for fear of embarrassing local universities, showed "without doubt the main concern voiced by employers was new entrants not sufficiently capable in spoken or written English".

As might be expected, senior practitioners were the least equivocal about the idea that lawyers' English had declined. Chooi Mun Sou, who back in the 1960s had hired Malay language tutors for his juniors, recalled decades later how a prospective pupil asked his interviewers to switch from English to Malay as he couldn't follow them. Another KL lawyer confessed to bringing English tutors into his firm. A Terengganu advocate in his 30s remarked on a proficiency gap between his own and the older generation and regretted his firm's decision to start conducting recruitment interviews in BM. A Penang advocate of around the same age, however, felt her peers' English was "not bad", and UM lecturer Azmi Sharom believed that many of his seniors were unnecessarily pessimistic.

In addition to views about English standards, opinions also varied about the extent to which any decline in them might be affecting legal performance. The KL lawyer who was hiring English tutors felt the main need was to avoid creating a bad impression with clients, but a senior practitioner in Kelantan cited examples of advocates misunderstanding important points in court and attributed this to the younger generation being unable to read law journals properly. As an examiner for the CLP, Steven Thiru felt many candidates with adequate legal knowledge were being betrayed by their English.

8.6.2 Malay Standards

Many of the senior lawyers who were concerned about English were conversely impressed by the rise in Malay standards, and few practitioners who believed themselves to be proficient in the language complained about the Malay of others. One Melakan declared: "I've never encountered any lawyer with really bad Bahasa but many with really bad English", while another from the same city, despite reservations about the legal content of his juniors' writing in Malay, was satisfied with the quality of the language itself. A KL advocate still in his 40s admired the ability of those younger than him to draft directly in BM rather than translate from English. But one Penang practitioner noted problems with juniors' formal Malay, even though their conversational Malay was fluent, especially when they translated documents from English, and a teacher hired to translate and teach Malay at a large KL firm felt lawyers could be very inaccurate in BM documents – "they even mix up the parties" – and were too ready simply to draft in English pass and get others to translate.

The spread of BM across ethnic groups was often mentioned. A Shah Alam-based Malay practitioner in his 60s acknowledged that "Even many of the non-Malays are very good" while an Indian lawyer in his 40s remarked "Some of the people who come through are brilliant – you close your eyes and you won't realise they're not Malays". An Indian lawyer from Johor Bahru who considered English her first language felt she had had a better grounding in Malay grammar than many younger native speakers. The Malay teacher mentioned in the previous paragraph thought the poor grammar and lack of formality of many Malays was precisely because they took their own language for granted, adding that lawyers needed time to acquire Malay legal terminology whatever their ethnic background. A Shah Alam advocate recalled with embarrassment having to ask permission to use English to express himself in court, whereas "now it's an automatic thing because BM is my mother tongue". While claiming to think in Malay himself, however, a young Chinese lawyer from Johor Bahru was critical of some of his Chinese colleagues: "The way she speak it's like Bahasa Pasar [marketplace Malay]. *Saya tak tahu lah*! [I dunno!]. The judge got annoyed".

In the bar's employability survey over 50% of local graduates scored much higher than overseas and extension students on spoken and written BM (Thiru and Ang 2012: 17) and several informants, including three from prestigious KL firms, also thought that local graduates' legal skills were as good as those returning from abroad. The latter nevertheless seem to be more employable, and are especially sought after by firms with corporate and international clients. Steven Thiru attributed his firm's preference for overseas graduates to their English rather than their law, as proficiency in Malay was less prized. It also seems that proficiency expectations for Malay may be lower than for English. Two UM graduates practising in Johor Bahru felt their alma mater underestimated legal Malay. One of them saw the lack of advocacy and drafting classes in the language there as indicative of the low regard in which Malay was held, while her colleague was at pains to point out distinct discursive norms of the language. He advised against direct translation: "If you use Malay to submit it is different, English is more straight to the point". His former lecturer, an advocate for more bilingualism, commented: "In Malay you have to build your case, you cannot take short-cuts".

8.6.3 Opinions on Bilingualism

Just as in legal education, where medium of instruction policy tends to respond to an English bias among prospective employers instead of supporting the two languages in tandem, many legal practitioners had a habit of evaluating Malay and English as separate skills with distinct functions rather than seeing bilingualism as a composite dynamic skill that can maximise the capacity to perform legal tasks. It was nevertheless apparent that many advocates who reported being at ease in either language preferred to focus on legal and communicative skills during their interview rather than on linguistic skills.

A UKM graduate felt equally adept at drafting in BM or English and put this down to her lecturers' emphasis on both languages. A Melakan practitioner who had graduated from UM when the policy was more bilingual there believed excellence in both languages had become a matter of course for the profession, to the extent that recruiters were now focusing on Mandarin and additional languages and on legal skills rather than on English or Malay proficiency. Another Melakan saw legalese as a distinct language, rather than a variety of either English or Malay, and believed proficiency in it came mainly through legal practice itself.

8.6.4 The Importance of Soft Skills

Many practitioners emphasised communicative skills that were not directly linked to English or Malay, with "soft skills" a recurrent buzzword in interviews. On Melakan argued that persuasiveness did not depend on grammar. An Ipoh lawyer felt confidence was more important than specific language skills, coupled with the ability to read unfamiliar situations and know where to go for help. A KL practitioner suggested that it was greater confidence, rather than superior legal skills, that made overseas graduates stand out; in comparison, local graduates tended to be less assertive, but they could also be inappropriately direct. A Johor practitioner believed that using the correct forms of address and other courtesies could achieve a great deal in both the office and at court. Hendon Mohamed advised those entering the profession to learn how to get on with people, including their clerical staff.

The Ipoh lawyer emphasising the role of confidence felt young lawyers should worry less about language and more about underlying analytical skills. An advocate from KL noted that while technology had greatly speeded up legal research, it had not replaced the need to analyse data and construct arguments, and these were the skills on which confidence and creativity were founded.

8.7 Influence of Language Policy on Office Work and Career Choice

This survey of office practice revealed a complex picture in which bilingualism plays an important role for most practitioners. The influence of status planning is evident in the likelihood of work involving government departments or court appearances involving Malay. There is a corresponding tendency for private sector work to involve less Malay, although this is less clear-cut because of diversity in client preferences. Acquisition planning in general education continues to accommodate multilingualism and is reflected in the legal profession with various patterns of English-Malay bilingualism coupled with a significant role for Chinese in many work sectors and geographical locations.

Professional specialisation influences language choice, with criminal litigation pulling toward Malay and financial work toward English. The register and mode in which legal tasks are conducted are other factors. Research, written communications and formal meetings are more likely to involve English, which constitutes evidence of the limitations of corpus planning for legal Malay, while spoken communication and informal conversation are likely to lean more toward Malay, depending on the interlocutor.

With some exceptions – perhaps corporate work in KL, which may be entirely in English, or criminal work on the East Coast, which may be entirely in Malay – bilingualism is essential for most lawyers. The overall impression from interviews and questionnaires is that language policy is pragmatic enough to encompass official Malay, societal multilingualism, and the English bias of business and legal tradition. This does not mean that most lawyers are balanced bilinguals, however, and it is likely that language proficiency and preference influence individual career choices. Although the study did not look into this directly, it did ask future lawyers how they connected career planning and language.

While not included for the first class polled at UM, an item was subsequently added to the general questionnaire about the language students expected to use most at work, with a choice of BM, English, or a balance of the two. Those expecting a bilingual balance outnumbered those mostly expecting to use English by 5:4 overall at UM and by 5:3 at UniSZA, although MMU students anticipated the use of English somewhat more than balanced use of English and BM (Fig. 8.5). Overall only 6% expected mostly to use BM, but this rose to 12% at UniSZA.

With a third of students not aiming to practise law at all, or unsure about their future (Fig. 8.6), no attempt has been made to quantify explanations about expected language use given in the comments section of the questionnaire or in focus group discussions, but it is worth looking at the comments that arose to see what associations students make between language and career.

Among the slight majority who anticipated an equal need for Malay and English, the most frequent explanations related to client needs: "Different kinds of clients", noted one student from UniSZA, with one of his colleagues mentioning the need to "Create conducive environment for the parties" and another remarking "Malaysia is multiracial". A first year UM student commented: "Our clients can be coming from

UM2009~12 (253)			**MMU** (55)			**UniSZA** (74)			**TOT** (382)		
BM	**Equal**	**Eng**	**BM**	**Equal**	**Eng**	**BM**	**Equal**	**Eng**	**BM**	**Equal**	**Eng**
10	134	109	2	24	29	9	41	24	21	199	162
4%	**53%**	**43%**	**4%**	**44%**	**53%**	**12%**	**55%**	**32%**	**6%**	**52%**	**42%**

Fig. 8.5 Language students expect to use most in legal career

	UM(2009~13) (278)	MMU (55)	UniSZA (74)
Public sector law	16%	18%	34%
Private sector law	55%	56%	36%
Non-lawyer but law-related	12%	4%	17%
Non-legal	4%	9%	5%
Overseas employment	2%	9%	3%
N/K	10%	4%	4%

Fig. 8.6 Students' anticipated work sector

any range of economic status". There were many allusions to diversity of office location, summed up succinctly by a UM student as "English for big city like KL but Malay for small city". The bilingual nature of some work sectors was also mentioned. "In conveyancing I'll need both", concluded a UM first year, while her classmate anticipated that "as a prosecutor I'll need both". A UniSZA student wrote: "Office may require English but in court they will use the national language". The few references to language policy acknowledged its bilingual aspects, with a UM fourth-year acknowledging "We have to use different languages in different courts" and his classmate writing "Malay more for documents but English for arguments".

Among those expecting mainly to use English at work, the most commonly given reasons were the language's wide use in the private sector and commercial law, its international and global dimensions, and the large amount of legal materials in it, with one MMU student citing statutes and cases and another pointing out the language's domination of law journal articles. Two UniSZA students commented that Malay was easier for them but most sources were in English. Comments emphasising English as the main medium of legal study and also research were prevalent, but several students also referred to the language's association with legal culture: "I don't want to look inferior", commented one UniSZA informant, while a UM second-year contended "In most firms English is the professional language and Malay is not". Among these students, then, official requirements for Malay did not appear to be constraining, although one student at HELP University said that although she expected English to be more useful "it also depends on the judges". An East Malaysian commented: "I come from Sarawak where it's not compulsory to use Malay" and an MMU student confessed to a personal preference for English but added: "I would expect to use more Malay at work due to the 'requirements' of the country".

The minority of informants expecting to use more BM than English were generally more likely than the others to refer to the language policy. A UM student wrote: "More Malay because in court there is a sign which say 'Gunakan Bahasa Kebangsaan'" while another commented: "We can only apply to use English in higher court" and a third cited "…rules of court" (UMS2010C.3). However, there was also pragmatic justification for Malay, with one ethnic Chinese commenting "More Malay people around and it is better to speak in Malay to foster better relationship" and another declaring in discussions that "society have more understanding in this language".

A student at a private college intending to complete her legal education overseas hoped to work in English but anticipated problems upon returning as she had never studied law in BM, and for one Chinese student at UM, language worries (presumably about Malay) were decisive:

> I won't stay in legal field mainly because of language problems. At first I thought I had lost interest in law because of subject matter but when I met Taiwanese law students I felt the main barrier was language.

A UiTM student expected to leave legal practice after a few years and go into business because "English is more in my comfort zone". He added that where students were headed in 5 years could be matched to their current language skills, the ones really good at English picturing themselves in big firms and the ones who struggled, or who lacked ambition, aiming for the public sector.

Among practitioners there were no accounts of lawyers leaving the profession because of the language policy, but several had curtailed their courtroom appearances when Malay was phased in and some mentioned a preference for corporate work because it need not entail BM. A Melaka lawyer working in both languages felt poor BM should not be a major barrier for ambitious advocates as long as they could get through their early years in the lower courts and read – or get others to translate – notes of proceedings. Chooi Mun Sou saw language policy as affecting the judiciary more than the bar since judges were not only more in the public spotlight than lawyers but were now predominantly Malays because of affirmative action in recruitment.

Exemplifying the diverse ways in which language policy can influence individual careers, a KL corporate lawyer mused that the downgrading of English on the school curriculum may have actually steered her into law: "I did law instead of something directly related to language because they stopped English literature at school". At the same time she felt shut out from practising in Singapore, where she had once lived, as the republic stopped admitting Malaysian lawyers in the 1990s when compulsory English was dropped from the Malaysian school-leaving STPM test.

References

Abdul Hamid Mohamad. (2012). Harmonisation of Shari'ah and common law in Malaysia:the way forward. *2nd International Seminar on Shari'ah and Common Law 2012*, Universiti Sains Islam Malaysia, 2012.3.06. Accessed 2013.3.30 from http://www.tunabdulhamid.my/index.php/speech-papers-lectures/items/317-harmonisation-of-shariah-and-common-law-in-malaysia-the-way-forward

Ahmad Mhd Yusof, Mansor Jusoh, Juneidah Ibrahim, & Abd. Kahar Yaakob. (1993). *Laporan Kaji Selidik Penggunaan Bahasa Melayu dalam Bidang Kehakiman dan Undang-Undang* [Investigative report on the use of Malay in judicial and legal sectors]. Kuala Lumpur: Dewan Bahasa dan Pustaka. Accessed 31 July 2005, from: http://www.geocities.com/CapitolHill/Congress/5544/law1207.htm

Ambiga Sreenevasan. (2013, December 7). 9th Kuala Lumpur Young Lawyers Association Meeting, Kuala Lumpur.

Azirah Hashim, & Powell, Richard. (2011). Exploring language choice in Malaysian trials and arbitrations: Common aims, complementary methods. In M. Petersen & J. Engberg (Eds.), *Current trends in LSP research: Aims and methods* (pp. 129–161). Bern: Peter Lang.

Bhatia, Vijay. (2011a). Interdiscursive colonisation of arbitration practice. *World Englishes, 30*(1), 76–80.

Bhatia, Vijay. (2011b, August 25). *Contested identities*. Symposium on 'Interdiscursive colonization of arbitration practices: key perspectives'. AILA conference, Beijing.

Ethnologue. (2018). Periodically accessed 1 Oct 2011–22 Jan 2018, from: http://www.ethnologue.com/

Faiza Tamby Chik. (1993). Language and the law: The role of Malay and English in legal education and the practice of law. In K. L. Tee (Ed.), *Legal education in Malaysia Quo Vadis?* (pp. 103–107). Kuala Lumpur: University of Malaya.

Mhd. Ariff Yusof. (1993). Language and the law: The role of Bahasa Malaysia and English in legal education and the practice of law. In Khaw Lake Tee (Ed.), *Legal education in Malaysia Quo Vadis?* (pp. 117–125). Kuala Lumpur: University of Malaya.

Ng Kwai Hang. (2009). *The common law in two voices. Language, law and the postcolonial dilemma in Hong Kong*. Stanford: Stanford University Press.

Nik Ramlah Mahmood. (1993). Language and legal education in Malaysia – past and emerging trends. In K. L. Tee (Ed.), *Legal education in Malaysia Quo Vadis?* (pp. 134–146). Kuala Lumpur: Universiti Malaya.

Nik Safiah Karim, & Faiza Tamby Chik (Eds.). (1994). *Bahasa dan Undang-Undang* [Language and the law]. Kuala Lumpur: Dewan Bahasa dan Pustaka.

Tan, Roger. (2011, February 06). High time for a new Bar. *The Star Online*. Accessed 2014.5.26 from: http://www.thestar.com.my/story.aspx/?file=%2f2011%2f2%2f6%2ffocus%2f8011437&sec=focus

Thiru, Steven. (2011, July–Sept). A first class legal profession. A common bar course to transform the training of new entrants to the Malaysian legal profession. In *Praxis* (pp. 7–10).

Thiru, Steven., & Ang, Kenneth. (2012, Oct–Dec). The Bar Council's Employability Survey: how employable are the new entrants to the bar? In *Praxis* (pp. 16–19).

UM Baseline Study. (2014). *Baseline study on the communication skills of law students*. Kuala Lumpur: Universiti Malaya, 11 June 2013–10 June 2014.

Wan Irham Ishak, Shameem Rafik-Galea & Chan Mei Yuit. (2013). Bilingualism in life insurance sales talk. Paper presented at *17th ESEA (English in Southeast Asia) Conference* , Universiti Malaya, 2013.12. pp. 5–7.

Chapter 9
Bilingual Courtrooms

> *Cakap Bahasa Malaysia, nanti orang marah hakim [Speak Malay or they'll get angry with the judge].*
>
> Sessions Court judge (in David 1993:115)

> *Peering over his spectacles, Abdullah began recounting my life to the audience, braiding sentences in English into his speech, ignoring the sign in the courtroom dictating the use of the Malay language in court.*
>
> Tan Twan Eng (2012:13)

9.1 Analysing Courtroom Discourse

In Malaysia's fused solicitor-advocate profession most practitioners make regular court appearances for at least part of their career, especially in the earlier years. Many younger informants said they began to feel comfortable in the predominantly Malay-medium lower courts within a few months of qualifying, despite having studied law almost entirely in English. But some from the older generation, including former bar president Hendon Mohamed, who had thought of Malay as her mother tongue, discovered through the constraints of courtroom language policy how dependent they were on English, even for non-legal lexis. Mukhtar Abdullah from Terengganu, who had hesitated to enter a profession he saw as dominated by English speakers from big towns, recalled being petrified by the idea of standing up before a judge, yet eventually found his legal feet in the courtroom.

Courtroom discourse has been described as "institutionalised public conversation" (Lo Bianco, p.c. 2014.7.25), "a battle fought not with swords but with words" (Maley 1994:33) and a struggle "in a context of power asymmetry and contestations" (Noraini and Nambiar 2010:73). Courtrooms are key sites for studying language planning as they showcase language in its most authoritative form in public settings where discursive choice between different languages and among different registers is uniquely controlled and controlling. Resistance is not excluded, however, and may be attempted even by lay participants, normally the least empowered

R. Powell, *Language Choice in Postcolonial Law*, Language Policy 22,
https://doi.org/10.1007/978-981-15-1173-8_9

speakers in the room. In the monolingual setting of US trials Atkinson and Drew (1979:178) observed witnesses challenging their interlocutors, while Ng (2009) found Hong Kong witnesses, plaintiffs and defendants more likely to stand up to questioners if proceedings were in Cantonese rather than English. His study focuses on the respective societal roles of the languages in Hong Kong, one a mother tongue for a large majority that indexes informality and solidarity, the other an elite and formal medium there. But as well as sociocultural constraints we should also consider the technical limitations of different languages, such as the availability of legal terminology.

Discursive analyses of the adversarial interactions to be found in common law settings typically focus on formalised features that are rarely found elsewhere, including highly asymmetrical turns (Gibbons 2008:119), questions designed to confirm or refute rather than elicit (Stuckey 2007:154), and answers directed to the court rather than the questioner (Atkinson and Drew 1979:92). For Lakoff (1990:90), the formal structure of adversarial trials sets them apart from other conversational interactions, although attendant features, such as non-reciprocity, may evoke the authoritarianism of other investigative practices, such as psychotherapy (ibid:127–141). Ng's (2009:38) characterisation of courtrooms as sites of "formal-rational legitimacy" is based on how legal facts are produced through formulaic interactions (ibid:40), and he notes that when these formulas give way to spontaneity in the less tried and tested medium of Cantonese, facts become less legal and more "mixed, eclectic, and at times highly moralistic" (ibid:184).

The rules of speaking in courtrooms are underpinned by rules of evidence. The result is intense intertextuality. In constructing competing narratives (Bennet and Fieldman 1981:93), advocates constantly refer to texts such as witness statements (David 2003:14–15) and statutes and cases (Powell 2011a). This can produce speech that is as lexically dense as writing (Gibbons 2003:33). Intertextual practice is important in inquisitorial as well as adversarial courtrooms (D'hondt 2011; van de Houwen 2011), but common law enhances its role by invoking precedent in "a highly institutionalized process of textualization and entextualization" (Ng 2009:41).

A perennial problem for analysts of courtroom discourse is whether and how to link it to conversations beyond the courthouse. Although more usually applied to natural conversation, the discipline of Conversational Analysis has yielded insights into the motivations of courtroom interlocutors by focusing entirely on what happens during proceedings. Philips (1987), for example, uses it productively to explain questioning patterns rarely found elsewhere. However, there are sociocultural and even political elephants in courtrooms that may need to be acknowledged in order to gain a fuller understanding of what is going on there. Goodrich (1984:173) rejects attempts to construct law as "the neutral instrument of purposes peculiar to the internal development of legal regulation" and instead sees it as a "specific, sociolinguistically defined speech community". Conley and O'Barr (1998) go further in drawing on Foucauldian analysis to connect the minutiae of localised communication with macro-discourses and the power dynamics underlying them, reminding us that inasmuch as "power is realized, exercised, abused or challenged in such events, the means are primarily linguistic" (ibid:2). Cotterill (2002:147) has observed advocates indexing societal discourses when pressing home arguments, while Fuller (1993:29–30) and Tiersma (1999:184) note how they employ a range of language registers when doing so.

This investigation assumes that in Malaysia – or at least in the bilingual West Malaysian jurisdiction, where most observations and interviews were conducted – the national language policy, as well as its application to the legal domain, has an influence on courtroom practices that needs to be accounted for. Sometimes it is an explicit influence, as in one of the earliest studies of courtroom code-switching there in which a judge was heard urging a court official to use Malay lest he get criticised for failing to control his courtroom (David 1993:115). Only by referring to the language policy does this speech act make sense as a way of combining national-level authority with local-level solidarity. At other times language policy may play a less self-conscious role, with bilingual interlocutors making choices that index societal associations attached to Malay and English, even when they do this with little deliberation.

Accordingly, the approach toward observations of proceedings here, and toward interviews with advocates, draws more on Critical Discourse Analysis (CDA) than Conversational Analysis, taking into consideration information acquired outside the courtroom such as the institutional background of participants and the way specific courtroom tasks function as components of case-building and even career-building. I nonetheless heeded warnings from CDA researchers themselves about the risk of straying too far from observed conversation (Chouliaraki and Fairclough 1999:152). I also shadow Eades' (2008) coupling of interlocutor-centred interactional sociolinguistics with Giddens' structuration theory (e.g.1979) in acknowledging a need to reference the duality of local/individual agency and social/historical structures when explaining courtroom power dynamics.

The introduction of bilingualism into the adversariality, intertextuality and evidentiary constraints of the Malaysian courtroom has made it an important arena for exploring the nature of legal language as both an instrument of advocacy and also a function of sociolinguistic choice. The first comprehensive account, based on newspaper court reports, comes from Mead (1988), who queried claims that only 18 months after the first practice directions of 1981 90% of lower court cases in Pahang were proceeding in Malay (ibid:41). Overall his textual analysis found application of the policy to be pragmatic, with few attempts to impose Malay where parties were non-Malay (ibid:70) or arguments were complex (ibid:42). In their individual observations of Malaysian cases (David 1993, 2003; Powell 2008) and joint comparison of Malaysia and Kenya (Powell and David 2011), David and Powell concluded that intersentential code-switches and lexical code-mixes were often proficiency-related strategies, thus casting doubt on the assumptions of Malay enthusiasts (e.g. Faiza 1993) that lawyers who resorted to English were taking advantage of judges' leniency toward their poor command of the national language. Language alternation has been tagged to a number of proficiency-oriented functions, including emphasis, shifting between interlocutors, and coercion of witnesses. Rather than add to these analyses of the functional interplay of bilingual speech acts this chapter concentrates on reviewing the wide range of communicative tasks to be found across the full range of Malaysian courtrooms and the degree of bilingual proficiency that those entering the profession need to be prepared for.

While the data presented here is based largely on observations and reports of formal sessions, pre-session conversations revealed how societal multilingualism creeps unchecked into courthouses. Waiting for one delayed case to start in the KL High Court I decided to remain seated at the back of the courtroom, instead of going for a *teh tarek* in the courthouse canteen (a forum of multilingual legal conversations in its own right). For over two hours I heard advocates code-switching intensely as they discussed the case in hand, the state of the profession, the latest business scandals and the football scores. English predominated, but one ebullient Chinese constantly switched into BM to regale his Malay colleague with anecdotes about fake land titles, throwing jokes across to the recorder who responded with cautiously sardonic comments in English. Two older Indian lawyers chatted in English with each other and in Tamil to a client. Two younger Chinese lawyers switched between Cantonese and Mandarin. The Indian clerk spoke a blend of English and BM to the lawyers. As well as reflecting pan-Malaysian multilingualism, the insider references and jousting gave the conversation a theatrical timbre, with the way juniors negotiate ribbing from seniors clearly a part of their professional training.

Pre- and post-session discussions between advocates and judges in chambers is also an important facet of language and register choice, but as these go on out of public earshot they are only mentioned in passing here through the recollections of informants (Fig. 9.1).

[Ex.1]	Extract
(*C.1*)	Case (see Fig. 15)
C	Counsel (PC:Prosecutor; DC: Defence cnsl; Pl.C:Plaintiff cnsl)
Cl	Clerk
CM	Code-mix
CS	Code-switch
CSh	Code-shift
D	Defendant
I	Interpreter
J	Justice (judge, registrar, magistrate)
NonCon	Non-convergence (speakers maintain separate codes)
PP/DPP	Public Prosecutor/Deputy Public Prosecutor
Pl/Pt	Plaintiff/ Petitioner
W	Witness
//	Overlap
Note: All hearings were public but names have been deleted as some cases were ongoing	

Fig. 9.1 Key for courtroom extracts

9.2 Case-Selection and Overall Patterns

Most of the data presented in this chapter comes from direct observations in the Klang Valley (Kuala Lumpur and its satellite cities of Petaling Jaya and Shah Alam), Melaka and Kuala Terengganu, with some additional observations conducted in Temerloh in Pahang. In the course of this research I also spent 3 days in courtrooms in Sarawak (Powell 2011b) but despite reports of bilingualism by some informants, everything I observed there conformed to the monolingual English policy. Observation data has been amplified by the reports of legal practitioners and professional attachment students. My priority was to get a picture of which language seemed to be preferred for which kind of court, case, and legal task. There was less room for detailed analysis of conversational strategies.

Case selection was more complex than for Thekiso (2001), for whom Botswanan Magistrates courts were the only legal sites using Setswana, or for Ng (2009), who confined himself to civil cases in Hong Kong's lower courts in anticipation of finding more Cantonese there. My main interest was in how language planning affects the Malaysian judicial system as a whole and this called for an overview at all court levels. English and Malay intertwine more intricately in Malaysian society than do English and Cantonese in Hong Kong, so it is difficult to talk in terms of 'Malay trials' or 'English trials', even though some subordinate hearings proceed mostly in Malay and some superior hearings entirely in English. This study adds to findings in David (1993, 2003) and Powell (2008) of multilingual societal code-switching being reconstituted in bilingual courtroom discourse.

While this may not be a representative sample, in the three main research sites civil and criminal cases at both subordinate and higher court level were observed. As well as full trials, proceedings included bail extensions and other short applications of the kind that make up a large part of court business, judgments, and sentencing (see Fig. 9.2 for summary of main cases). Like Thekiso (2001) I found schedule changes hampering observation of trials from beginning to end, with three-hour waits and week-long postponements common, and so I sometimes followed her practice of compiling the main trial stages from multiple cases.

In as much as hearings could be described as predominantly monolingual, some 60% were in Malay and 20% in English, with the remainder in a balance. However, quantification is complex: by case count there were certainly more proceedings predominantly in Malay than predominantly in English, but many of them were 10-min applications (e.g. *C35*) whereas some proceedings with extensive bilingualism lasted 3 days (*C10*). Estimates of 90% of provincial lower court trials being in Malay (Mead 1988:41) or 80% of KL High Court proceedings in English (according to Bar Council member Brendan Navin) are impressionistic since no study has gone into word-counts. Were one to be done it would have to overcome a number of methodological difficulties, including how to distinguish lexical loans from code-mixes.

For what it is worth, UM's 2013 batch of attachment students described 30% of the cases they observed as in BM, 20% in English, and 50% in a mixture. Among

Location	Ct level	Case type	Stage	Main Parties	Main lang	Comments
1. KT	Mags	Crim	Application	D:M	BM	Some CM
2. KT	Mags	Crim	Application	D:M	BM	Some CM
3. KT	Mags	Crim	Application	D:M	BM	Some CM
4. KT	Mags	Crim	Application	D:M	BM	Some CM
5. KT	Mags	Crim	Application	D:M	BM	Some CM
6. KT	Mags	Crim	Application	D:M	BM	
7. KT	Mags	Crim	Application	D:M	BM	Extensive CM
8. KT	Mags	Crim	Application	D:M	BM	
9. KT	Mags	Crim	Application	D:M	BM	CM
10.KT	Mags	Civ	Trial	D:M	BM+E	Extensive CM, CS, CSh:
11.KT	Mags	Civ	Application	D:M	BM	Extensive CM
12.KT	Sessions	Crim	Trial	D:M	BM	Extensive CM
13.KT	Sessions	Civ	Application	Pl&D:M	BM	Some CM
14.KT	Sessions	Civ	Application	Pl&D:Ch?	BM	Some CM
15.KT	HC	Crim	Application	D:M	BM	Some CM
16.KT	HC	Crim	Application	App:M	BM	Some CM
17.KT	HC	Crim	Trial	D:M	BM+E	Extensive CM, some CS
18.KT	HC	Civ	Application	Pl&D:M	BM	Extensive CM
19.KT	HC	Civ	Application	Pl:Ch,D:M	BM	Some CM
20.KT	HC	Civ	Application	Pl:Ch,D:M	BM	Some CM
21.KT	HC	Civ	Trial	Pl&D:M	BM+E	Extensive CM,CS&CSh
22. Temerloh	Mags	Crim	Sentencing	D:M	BM	Some CM
23. Temerloh	Mags	Civ	Trial	D:Ind	BM	Some CM
24. Temerloh	HC	Crim	Trial	D:Pakistani	BM	Some CM, some CS
25. Melaka	Sessions	Crim	Application	D:M	BM	
26. Melaka	Sessions	Crim	Judgment	D:M	BM	
27. Melaka	Sessions	Crim	Trial	D:Ind	BM	Some CM & CS W compelled to use BM
28. Melaka	HC	Crim	Trial	D:Ind	BM&E	Balance of 2 langs, extensive CS; some NAc
29. Melaka	HC	Crim	Trial	D:African	E	Some CS into BM
30. Melaka	HC	Crim	Application	D:M	E&BM	Extensive CS, CSh
31. Melaka	HC	Civ			E&BM	
32. Melaka	HC	Civ			E&BM	
33. KL	Mags	Crim	Trial	D:Ch	BM	
34. KL	Mags	Crim	Trial	D:Ch	BM	D used Mandarin interp.
35. KL	Mags	Crim	Application	D:Ch	BM	D used Mandarin interp.
36. KL	Mags	Crim	Application	D:Ch	BM	D used Canton. interp.
37. KL	Mags	Crim	Application	D:Ch	BM	
38. KL	Sessions	Crim	Trial	D:Ch	BM	D used Mandarin interp.
39. KL	Sessions	Civ	Trial	Pl:Ch, D:Ind	E&BM	CM, C.Sh, CS
40. KL	Sessions	Crim	Application	D:M	BM	
41. KL	HC	Crim	Trial	D:M	BM	Some CM; CS by PP
42. KL	HC	Civ	Trial	Pl, D:M	E	
43. KL	HC	Civ	Trial	Pl:Ind, D:M	E	CS for quoting docs
44. KL	HC	Civ	Trial	Pl, D:M	E	CS for quoting docs
45. KL	HC	Fam	Trial	Pl, D: Ind	E	All E. Petitioner fluent
46 KL	HC	Civ	Trial		E	
46. PJ	Mags	Crim	Trial	D:M	BM	Some CM
47. PJ	HC	Family	Trial	R:Ind	E&BM	Extensive CS
48. Shah Alam	HC	Crim	Trial	D:M	BM	Some CM
49. Shah Alam	HC	Family	Trial	R:Ind	BM&E	Extensive CS; J mostly E

Fig. 9.2 Summary of main cases observed

50. Putrajaya	CA	Crim	Appeal		E	DPP CS into BM
51. Putrajaya	CA	Civ	Appeal		E	Preliminaries in BM
52. Putrajaya	CA	Civ	Appeal		E	Preliminaries in BM
53. Putrajaya	CA	Civ	Appeal		E	Preliminaries in BM
54. Putrajaya	CA	Civ	Appeal		E	Preliminaries in BM
55. Putrajaya	FC	Civ	Application		BM	Very brief
56. Putrajaya	FC	Civ	Appeal	App:Ch, R:M	E	Some CM for quotation
57. Putrajaya	FC	Crim	Appeal	App:Ch	E	
58. Putrajaya	FC	Civ	Appeal		E	

Fig. 9.2 (continued)

the minority who categorised cases according to court level in their reports, eight said English was the main language of the High Court and eight said Malay dominated the subordinate courts, with no one reporting the reverse. One stated that all the lower court cases he observed were in Malay whereas most lawyers in the High Court used English. Another referred to frequent use of *bahasa rojak* (mixed language).

9.3 Court Location

Geographical location appears to influence courtroom language without outweighing other factors such as court level. All but eight of the 32 cases observed outside the Klang Valley were in BM except for some English legal lexis, with the only predominantly English session (*C.29*) involving a foreign defendant, whereas a third of cases in the Klang Valley (in addition to appeals in the administrative capital of Putrajaya) were partly or mostly in English. Many informants also reported a KL/outstation[1] divide. One of UM's 2013 attachment students noted that English predominated in KL but BM in Taiping in Perak. A young Melakan lawyer said she filed only in BM in Melaka but bilingually in KL. Most court clerks are bilingual, and many are trilingual, as interpreting is one of their duties, but a Johor Bahru advocate reported that court clerks there tend to stick to Malay in conversations with lawyers even before court is in session. According to a lawyer from the East Coast who moved to KL, most Terengganu cases at all levels were in BM, whereas this was true only of lower court cases in the capital. Further up the East Coast a Kota Bharu lawyer described Malay as *selesa* (comfortable) for everyone.

Melaka and Penang perhaps use more English than other provincial towns. One Melakan lawyer stressed the flexibility of the judges and another reported considerable leeway to use English, especially for witnesses. Ruing what he perceived as a decline in his English since moving back go Terengganu, Zamani Mohammad commented: "It's not as fluent as when I was prosecuting in English in Penang".

[1] The local term for 'provinces'.

Given that several informants felt judges' centralised training and individual preferences attenuated the development of distinct local cultures, it was no surprise that some accounts went against regional trends. A recently qualified practitioner in Johor Bahru said she felt confident about being able to deliver submissions in English when coming before one of the handful of judges there who were originally from KL. A Terengganu advocate noted that a Sessions Court judge who was originally from KL "doesn't mind English if your English is easy to understand", and although it was unclear whether he had the same judge in mind, a lawyer from the same city observed that if the judge used English the local advocates would respond in kind. Mukhtar Abdullah found that lawyers from the capital doing cases in Terengganu preferred to stick to English.

Towns smaller than Johor Bahru or Kuala Terengganu also seem to have their English-friendly judges. One Johor-based lawyer said courts in all the smaller centres, such as Kulai, Muar and Segamat, used Malay and even asked for English testimony to be translated into it. However, when a KL lawyer "used to doing it in English in KL – and if they require BM you just translate it then and there" took the precaution of writing all her submissions out in Malay before attending court in Muar, she found, to her relief: "Lucky for me, they proceeded in English". One Melakan advocate said she and her colleagues tended to call up friends to ask about the situation in towns they were unfamiliar with, and another came to Muar ready to use English because she had done her homework on the local judges. However, her opponent for the day had come unprepared for English.

> So I did help him a little bit by speaking some Malay too but then I thought hey, this is 19.7 million we are talking about, so I'm going to go all out to win the case. Poor you, you are a lawyer. You should pick up your English man!

While reports and interviews confirmed the largely English policy in East Malaysia, a practitioner based in Sabah said that Malay was widely used in lower courts in rural areas, with older participants often conversing in the distinct local Malay. Although it lacked commentary on language policy, an extract from family court proceedings logged by a UM student attached to a firm in Miri, Sarawak suggests that Malay code-mixes are not necessarily interpreted into English:

> DC: *Yang Arif* [Your Honour], I object that the statements to be deleted.
> J: Typist, do not delete the statements. Witness, why are you so confused?
> W: The questions were *berpusing-pusing* [going round in circles].
> DC: *Berpusing-pusing*??!!
> J: It is almost 5pm, DPP, do you have any further questions to question the witness?
> DC:No, *Yang Arif*.

9.4 Area of Law and Type of Proceeding

Accounts of office practice confirm that the rules requiring court documents filing in Malay hardly vary geographically – except in East Malaysia where the rules require English. But in discussions about courtroom advocacy it became clear that these rules are applied to pleadings (the papers in which parties lay out their claims, defences and counterclaims) more strictly than submissions (the arguments, drawing on statute and case law, put forward in support of claims). In general submissions are delivered orally, but written outlines of arguments may be requested in advance of proceedings, and the fact that most Commonwealth judgments, including Malaysian, are in English may conspire with a tendency to cite precedents directly to pull submissions away from Malay. The intricacy of the language of legal argument, as opposed to the language of claims and factual assertions, may be another factor favouring English, the predominant medium of legal education.

Between pleadings and submissions comes evidence, in the form of exhibits and witness statements that in the common law tradition are supposed to be factual rather than argumentative. While the 2012 Rules of Court (O.92 r.1) permit exhibits in English, there is no corresponding provision for witness statements, except for depositions taken outside Malaysia (O.41 r.13), but most practitioners said they felt statements would be accepted in English. It should also be noted that a great deal of court time is spent on simple administrative matters such as bail extensions. These tend to be formulaic and hence perhaps more likely to proceed in Malay.

In addition to the stage of proceedings, the type of case may impact language choice. Of the 58 cases observed, 34 were criminal, of which all but five were predominantly in Malay. As the majority were hearings in subordinate courts, the general preference for BM at lower levels will also have been a factor, but several practitioners, in Johor, Kelantan, Kuala Lumpur and Melaka, as well as a number of students in UM 2012's attachment programme, reported that criminal hearings were likely to be in Malay and civil cases in English, while an advocate who had returned from England to practise in KL went as far as to say civil cases at High Court were "almost exclusively" in English.

But the locality and court level, as well as the preferences of individual judges and trial participants, also come into play. A UiTM student observed extensive citation of authorities in English in a criminal trial and attributed this to the Penal Code being based on Indian models. He also claimed some criminal advocates use English "when they don't want clients to understand". Another student, from UM's 2013 attachment batch, observed a criminal appeal in which the defence used English and the prosecution Malay, and several lawyers remarked on prosecutors using BM more consistently than defence lawyers, the rationale being that they are in government service. This could indicate an awareness of representing the state in court but may also be an extension of government office practices favouring the national language. A Terengganu practitioner felt that the general preference for Malay on the East Coast blurred any difference between criminal and civil law, and in accounting for a Magistrate in Melaka favouring criminal proceedings in Malay while a justice in the next courtroom favoured civil cases in English, a local informant suggested this reflected personal choice as much as the type of proceeding.

Family matters are heard at High Court level. One of the three hearings observed for this study proceeded mainly in English, one was in Malay, and one used both. The preference of parties seemed paramount, confirming the flexibility of judges presiding over family matter that was reported by informants in both Kelantan and

Melaka. The Chinese petitioner in one predominantly English case (*C.44*), from an affluent background judging by discussion of disputed family assets, spoke the language so fluently she sometimes left the judge behind when referring to financial matters. In a mixed-language hearing (*C.47*) the Indian disputants used both English and BM when giving evidence. One attachment student found much less Malay in civil court family cases compared with *Syariah* hearings, but another said the documents her firm filed with the civil court were all in Malay. Practitioners from Ipoh and Penang separately reported wide judicial discretion for English in matters of probate.

Similarly to family law being characterised as English-oriented because of participants being non-Malays, some informants advocating in the Industrial Court felt labour law favoured English because it focuses on private sector disputes; but like the family advocates they reported a need for both languages. A KL practitioner remembered his last two cases, one with a Malay claimant and the second with an Indian, proceeding in Malay and the claim before that, brought by a Malay, proceeding in English. All three cases involved code-switching, typically triggered by a change of witness. A UiTM student remembered most of the cases he observed during his attachment being in Malay, whereas two KL lawyers felt English was more common. One of them remarked that Industrial Court officers tended to use English among themselves, which was my own impression during a visit to the tribunal.

Full trials, from pleadings through witness examinations to submissions and summing up, are the lengthiest procedures in the courts, but they are not the most common. Lawyers are more likely to be appearing for briefer matters such as bail hearings, interlocutory applications, *ex parte* applications, summary judgments and mentions. Even within a trial each stage entails different communicative burdens, with opening statements perhaps the most straightforward and submissions, involving legal arguments related to precedents, the most demanding. The linguistic complexity of witness examination varies according to the nature of the case, with traffic offences toward one end and cases involving financial or scientific evidence toward the other. Observations and interviews revealed a general tendency for more English as the complexity of a communicative task increases.

25 of the cases observed were administrative procedures lasting between 5 and 15 min, such as (*C.1*), (*C.2*) and (*C.3*), which were mentions, (*C.22*), which was a sentencing, and (*C.35*), a bail extension. 23 of these, including an interlocutory in the heavily English Court of Appeal, were predominantly in Malay, with English mostly confined to code-mixes. But among the 24 trials, five were mostly in English and nine mixed. Although observations not extensive enough to generalise, the data collected tallies with the many accounts from informants of English increasing where matters become more contentious or less straightforward. A lawyer in his forties at a large KL firm remembered it taking only a matter of months to feel confident doing routine applications in BM, despite not having used it at all at law school, but even now he prepared detailed notes before attending court on more complex matters heard in Malay. Another KL lawyer of a similar age felt applica-

tions had become briefer and more formulaic, even in the higher courts, because of time constraints.

An experienced Terengganu lawyer and a newly qualified KL lawyer shared the experience of pleadings commonly starting out in Malay, the language in which cause papers are filed, but tending to give way to English when details were disputed. Similarly, the added complexity of oral submissions seems to pull arguments toward English. One Melakan advocate felt she had more impact in English, and Terengganu-based Zamani Mohamad preferred it for submissions because "I can pick up all those authorities in it". Another Melaka lawyer stated that even lower courts would hear arguments in English in complex cases, but a Johor practitioner with limited Malay warned that using English ran the risk of subordinate judges failing to understand properly. While English is often associated more closely with written tasks, in the case of submissions a KL lawyer agreed with another from Melaka that oral discussion often proceeds in English even when based on written submissions drafted in BM. When it comes to appeal cases, an experienced Melaka advocate described submissions as "overwhelmingly" in English, but Zamani Mohamad on the East Coast described them as "often" in it.

9.5 Court Level

As 25 of the 28 subordinate cases, but only seven of the 30 higher court cases, were predominantly in Malay, the evidence from these observations suggests that Malaysia resembles a number of Commonwealth jurisdictions where a language other than English is used extensively at lower level but less so higher up (see Chap. 10). For one Ipoh informant it was clear that the "parties and the type of cases are very much secondary factors. I believe it would be fair to say that Malay is used in the lower courts while English is used in the superior courts". Most informants, however, painted a more nuanced picture and this was largely borne out by observations.

Several practitioners said subordinate courts were strict about Malay, with one from Ipoh commenting "Sometimes the judge makes us go back to BM" and another from KL observing "If you say you want to conduct a case in English because you can't do so in BM the judge may tell you to find someone who can". However, such views were outnumbered by accounts of flexibility. Most informants felt language choice depended ultimately on the judge. For a Penang advocate, judges were "not that 100% strict…they don't penalise you". Her colleague felt switching to English would be tolerated if advocates made an effort in BM before getting stuck, and according to a Melakan, "you can have a third of your sentence in English and it's fine. Every authority, every document you refer to can be in English, so the crux of the matter is in English." A KL advocate felt judges would allow English as long as permission was asked for. Another Melaka-based lawyer, together with one from Penang, even recalled magistrates replying to their Malay utterances in English.

It was clear that English is used considerably more at High Court level than below, even though most cases observed in Terengganu, and several in Melaka and KL, were in Malay. Having conceded that "we have to be prepared for either language", a practitioner who had moved from Kedah to Melaka stressed it was

> very important to be able to converse in English – even Chinglish or Manglish or whatever – unless you are thinking of being a lawyer in the lower court only.

Klang Valley lawyers were the most forthright about English at High Court level: "Asking to use it is a matter of course", commented one civil litigation specialist, while another went as far as to say "The High Court is automatically in English and people tend to ask if they want to use Malay. Some judges really don't want you to use it". Both informants were Malay. Several others spoke of proceedings opening in Malay before moving into English. Elsewhere lawyers talked in terms of the High Court being "more in English" (Penang), "60–40 English-BM" (Melaka) or "English extensively (…) but you can't stop any young practitioner from speaking Bahasa" (Johor Bahru). On the East Coast, however, proceedings were more likely to be described as "more in BM" (Kota Bharu), "mostly BM" (Kuala Terengganu) and even "98% Malay (Zamani Mohammad in Terengganu). A Johor practitioner commented that smaller towns in the state were "more Bahasa" than the state capital.

Regarding the Court of Appeal and Federal Court, informants confirmed the dominance of English. "As for the CA, it's in English – thank God for that!", commented one from Melaka, with lawyers on both coasts and from Penang down to Johor describing the Court of Appeal as "all in English" or "overwhelmingly", "normally" and "mostly" and an advocate from Terengganu elaborated that both written and oral arguments were in English there. A senior Melaka-based lawyer thought the preference for English went across all legal areas, something a KL advocate put down to the appellate court's heavy workload: "They've such a huge number of cases to dispose of that people use the fastest way". This view reinforces the finding that Malaysian lawyers still tend to regard Malay as inadequate or cumbersome for complex cases. A tendency to associate professional efficiency with tried and tested language echoes late medieval support for Law French in England (Fisher 1977; Baker 1979) and the preferences of court stenographers for English in the Philippines today (Powell 2012).

As for the Federal Court, Malaysia's apex court, one Terengganu advocate described proceedings as 99.9% English while another from KL said he had never heard Malay there. However, a Melakan recalled an incidence of Malay being used for the benefit of a death-row appellant, and legal academic Amanda Whiting (p.c., 2012.5.12) has also reported a small amount of BM used by the FC Bench. Among observations for this study one very brief application (*C.55*) was in Malay.

A recent increase in the Sessions Courts' jurisdictions highlighted the close connection between court level and language policy. A KL litigator assumed this "big jump", which put cases with as much as RM1 million at stake under Sessions Court judges, would have him appearing far more often in subordinate courts than before and consequently using more Malay. One Johor Bahru informant came to the interview straight from a Specific Performance, the first time he had had to do anything more complex than traffic cases in the lower courts. For a Kota Bharu lawyer the prospect of subordinate judges handling difficult cases was “very bad” and according to a Melakan there was wide apprehension in the profession, with competency in English as well as law at issue. Some informants passed on anecdotes of colleagues finding ways of adding procedural complexities so that their cases would have to be heard in the High Court.

In a practice that seems to be emerging in Bangladesh too (Chap. 10), the language-specific court hierarchy in Malaysia results in hybrid judgments whereby appellate decisions are generally written in English but incorporate charges, extracts from proceedings and references to authorities in Malay reflecting the passage of cases up from the lower courts (see Chap. 4 for examples).

9.6 Judge Preferences

The language policy gives judges wide discretion to decide which medium better serves the interests of justice in their courtroom. Although this investigation did not include interviews with the Bench because of concerns about getting sufficient reportable answers in the time available,[2] accounts from lawyer and student informants suggest that the stance of individual justices may be paramount, with presumptions based on age, institutional background or ethnicity of only limited value. “Sometimes it’s know your judge”, declared one Melakan family law specialist, while a Terengganu litigator observed that “one may allow you to argue in English, but a strict judge will say we are bound by the Language Act”.

A Johor informant in his 20s, a Penangite in her 30s and a Melakan in his 40s all felt younger judges were more likely to favour Malay and older ones English. This undoubtedly reflects the increased use of BM in general education, but a MMU law lecturer also emphasised the impact of changes in judicial recruitment, singling out the growing intake of graduates from *bumiputera*-only UiTM and Malay-dominant UIA, along with recruitment from the Judicial and Legal Service in preference to the bar. 85% of Federal Court justices now come from the JLS, and a similar percentage of them are Malay (Hafiz 2018.8.15). Over time, judges recruited from the Malay-leaning JLS for the Malay-leaning lower courts are promoted to the higher courts and it can be expected that many will bring their language preferences with them. The MMU lecturer nevertheless maintained that judges who are more comfortable in English, whether educated at UiTM, UIA, UM or overseas, remain influential “at the highest echelons”.

Age, professional seniority and educational background may function independently as indicators of language preference. For one Melakan, judges over 50 from the bar or government service alike were more likely to favour English, whereas

[2] One judge approached early on in the investigation requested his views about language policy be kept off the record.

professional background was a better language predictor among younger judges. Emphasising the role of background, a Penang lawyer mentioned the preference for BM among registrars, who are generally appointed from government service. However, an advocate from the same city remembered many registrars being willing to use English with her when she was starting out, and a young Johor lawyer had been surprised to learn one of his former classmates from UM had become a Senior Assistant Registrar, given that his Malay had been "terrible" as a law student. Another young Johor lawyer thought registrars were apt to be flexible as they mostly deal with matters in chambers, a view tallying with a Melakan advocate's comments about judges being more easygoing in chambers than in open court.

Language preference and disposition toward bilingual discourse thus seem to be connected with individual language proficiency. In northern Italy, Alber and Palermo (2012: 295) found more proceedings being conducted bilingually in Italian and German as the bilingual proficiency of justices and other key personnel themselves increased, and in this study many Malaysian informants associated judges' disposition toward English with their proficiency in it. Several claimed that younger judges weren't using the language because they couldn't: "*Ada judge yang minta* [there are judges who ask you to] translate in bahasa; they don't know the code is in English", remarked one newly qualified advocate from Johor Bahru, and a senior practitioner from the same city noted that when testimony is in English "the judge will sometimes require the assistance of the interpreter" A Kota Bharu informant recalled a fellow advocate objecting to the introduction of evidence "at the eleventh hour", to which the judge responded innocently: "But it's still 10 o'clock". But one Melakan practitioner advised against sneering:

> Magistrates are getting younger (…) and you must put yourself in their shoes. She can't be showing you that she doesn't know what's going on. So for my client I have to come down to her level (…) I will check her reaction and if I notice a blank look I will translate into BM.

Some informants explicitly linked language choice with ethnicity. An ethnic Indian from Johor Bahru said she would "probably speak to Malay counsel in BM but others in English", while another from the same city commented: "If Chinese no problem, I can speak in English". Many others were more circumspect. Another Johor lawyer, for example, described Malay judges who were happier with English for complex arguments. The great majority of judges in the cases observed for this study were Malay, and so there is little basis on which to make ethnic comparisons, but for most lawyers ethnicity, alongside age and professional background, was certainly one factor influencing judges' language preferences.

In contrast to comments on judges, the ethnicity of other lawyers rarely arose in discussions about language preference, although one Johor advocate said he tended to use BM when opposing counsel was Malay. Ethnicity does, however, appear to be an important influence on language policy when it comes to witnesses. The prosecution of an African in Melaka (*C.29*) was observed over a whole day to proceed almost entirely in English, presumably for the defendant's benefit, even though an interpreter stood beside him. Lawyers from KL, Melaka and Terengganu alike said that judges would hear evidence directly in English from non-Malay Malaysians, while two lawyers from Johor and another from Melaka described judges allowing testimony in English but then having it translated. The same courtesy is not always extended to Malays, however. One Kota Bharu advocate recalled an elderly Malay, almost certainly educated mainly in English because of his age, being told he would have to apply to the court in writing if he insisted on testifying in English because "*ramai orang Melayu tak cakap Inggeris* [most Malays don't speak English]".

Pressure to use the national language can sometimes be applied to non-Malay witnesses too. One Sessions Court judge (*C.27*) pressed an ethnic Indian doctor to give his expert testimony in Malay as he was "not a foreigner", which resulted in hesitations and lapses into English. It was unclear whether he was deficient in general Malay or simply unaccustomed to using the language in medical registers, but he had clearly come to court fully expecting to use English. An attachments student from UM recorded a comment on the "sad situation when seeing a Chinese uncle who doesn't speak well in Bahasa Melayu", but did not elaborate on why no interpreter was used. On the balance of evidence from interviews and observations, however, such a rigid attitude to witnesses is unusual among judges.

9.7 Advocates' Discursive Strategies

Although I framed interviews around language choice and bilingual courtroom practice, when I asked advocate informants about strategies for coping with courtroom language difficulties nearly all of them automatically focused on Malay. This was in contrast to the law students, who had a tendency to associate language difficulties at school with English. To a large extent the linkage between language barriers and Malay in lawyers' minds was predicated on their having to switch from predominantly English legal study to predominantly Malay courtroom discourse in the early years of practice.

When the national language was first being phased in, the Bar Council mulled the options available to advocates who couldn't speak it (*The Straits Times* 1967.10.25), concluding that they could either appeal to the judge's discretion or withdraw from a case. One Kelantan lawyer mentioned a colleague down the coast in Terengganu who had quit advocacy after being reprimanded about his Malay. A UM lecturer had also heard of lawyers ceasing to appear in court, but felt that most of the older members of the bar had somehow adjusted. Adjustment doesn't necessarily imply acquiring high proficiency in Malay, however, and indeed when introducing the National Language Act the Tunku acknowledged that there was a generation who never would do so (Chap. 3). Options include making selective appearances according to the nature of the case, and relying on juniors. After several years of confining himself to office work, a senior lawyer from Johor Bahru had started going back to court when anticipating arguments in English would be allowed, while taking the precaution of bringing his junior along in case they weren't. Even in the lower courts advocates with poor Malay may still be found.

Sometimes the clerk-interpreter helps them, according to an informant from Johor. An advocate from Kota Bharu and another from KL were both confident most magistrates would let older counsel use English, but a young Johor Bahru lawyer was startled to witness a young judge there scolding a senior practitioner for poor Malay. Earlier in his career a Melakan lawyer recalled the defiance of an advocate who responded in gibberish made up of Malay words when stopped from using English: enjoined by the judge to speak in a manner that could be understood he retorted: "Your Honour, you asked me to speak in Malay, not in a language you could understand".

Older lawyers offered various accounts of what had motivated them to make the transition to BM. An ethnic Malay practitioner from Shah Alam with a successful career in the English-dominated field of banking behind him had suffered the humiliation of losing arguments in criminal court in his native tongue: "I should be the cock, able to take the fight to the other side, not the hen!" Former bar president Hendon Mohamed, also Malay, had been getting by in court by writing down her questions in advance – until in a straightforward traffic case a magistrate had had to feed her the Malay word for 'drive'. She immediately started reading *Utusan* every night and within 3 months found she was thinking in Malay in court, rather than translating in her head. An English-educated Melakan lawyer described her first court appearance in Malay as "terrifying: I spent the rest of the day sitting in court making notes of the proceedings". A Chinese lawyer from the same town remembered her boss telling her before her first court appearance to say just enough to prevent the case from being struck out. In the event she came away triumphantly after obtaining an order and rapidly gained the confidence to make regular appearances in both Malay and English.

Mukhtar Abdullah, a Terengganu native in his 60s, felt courtroom Malay had come quickly to him because of his general grounding in the language before taking up law, a sentiment also expressed by an ethnic Indian in his 40s from KL and a Chinese in his 30s from Ipoh. Others, however, including two young advocates from Penang, emphasised the necessity of preparation. The Melakan lawyer above who described her first appearance as terrifying still made sure to come to court with a skeleton in Malay, even though she generally gave her submissions in English. Two KL lawyers, both Malay but educated largely in English, described cross-examination of witnesses as one of the more demanding courtroom tasks, although one felt it was easier being a defence counsel as she had the chance to listen through the prosecution case and devise questions accordingly.

Terminology was the most commonly cited problem surrounding the use of Malay in court. One Terengganu lawyer in his 30s thought it had taken him about 6 months to master the language he needed but his colleague, about the same age, still found herself translating in her head from English. A decade into legal practice, one KL advocate said she often had to scour newspapers or ring around friends before appearing in hearings requiring specialised terms. Most practitioners reported using English when the Malay wouldn't come to them and rarely found judges objecting, with a Terengganu lawyer rationalising that "the English terms are common for them so we just use them", while an experienced lawyer from Melaka preferred to mouth the English term and wait for judges to offer the Malay, and a young KL advocate made a point of apologising before using English. In general, permission to use English was asked for perfunctorily and rarely refused. Some advocates simply drift into it, as with the plaintiff counsel observed in case *C.10*. Former bar president Steven Thiru said it was a question of sensing when the moment was right, and another KL lawyer said it was a matter of following the judge. A Melakan pointed out that the judge was often the first person in court to start using English, upon which the advocates could follow suit. Several informants were nevertheless mindful that Malay could be insisted upon at any time, although Hendon Mohamed thought this happened much less now than 20 years ago.

Etiquette emerged from interviews as a soft skill that could bolster linguistic competence. Several younger informants stressed the importance of having court clerks on their side in case they needed help. "When you are close enough you can say *kakak* [sister] but before must say *puan* [madam]", commented a junior lawyer form Johor, while a UM lecturer recalled that overfamiliarity could result in files going 'missing'. Courtesy went down well with judges and one Johor practitioner went as far as to suggest it could even clinch a case in their favour. Conversely, a Melakan lawyer recalled winning over a justice with the desperate spontaneity of inexperience:

> I remember one said *Kalau macam tu* [in that case] – they don't really use formal Malay either – *saya nak batal kes awak* [I'll strike out your case]. I remember I said *Tolong jangan, Yang Arif!* [No, Your Honour, you mustn't!] And he started laughing.

Another soft skill not necessarily dependent on a particular language is ability to argue. However, there was general consensus that successful advocacy was becoming less dependent on complex argument because of time pressure: "It's better to make an argument in simple and easy words", noted a UM student after a period attached to a firm. A Shah Alam practitioner emphasised preparation over eloquence: "You do have to prepare very thoroughly for those cases but they don't depend so much on your powers of advocacy". Although still relatively young, a KL lawyer expressed horror that some appellate judges thought long submissions were against the interests of justice and spoke fondly of an incident when a judge respondent approvingly to a literary reference thrown in by an advocate But another KL practitioner thought literary quotations best avoided: "It's over their heads". Despite her own love of English literature one lawyer advised against rankling the postcolonial generation that had resisted British culture, citing the example of former Chief Justice Zaki, who had told judges to cut down their judgments and lawyers to cut out their Shakespeare. This aspect of cultural decolonisation does not appear to be confined to Malaysia. In the context of Hong Kong, Jones (2010:116) reasons that senior jurists' disappointment at juniors' ignorance of literature reflects their fear of declining Englishness rather than declining English.

9.8 Language Alternation in Court

Language alternation has been reported in several jurisdictions where bilingualism is tolerated (sixteenth–seventeenth-century England: Mellinkoff 1963 and Tiersma 1999; Botswana: Thekiso 2001; New York: Angermeyer 2003, 2008, 2015) or admitted (Hong Kong: Ng 2009 and Leung 2012; Kenya: Powell and David 2011; Philippines: Martin 2012; Tanzania: Rwezaura 1994). In Malaysian studies it is mentioned by Noraini (2006) and explored by David (1993, 2003) and Powell (2008). A number of informants referred to it during interviews, including an Ipoh advocate who concluded "I think switching backwards and forwards has become the norm" and one from Terengganu who noted, despite the predominant use of Malay there, "If we cite a case we just cite in English". A Johor Bahru practitioner even reported that "It can happen one side uses BM and one English". Most cases observed had some lexical code-mixing (insertion of words or phrase, typically from English into BM) and many evinced intersentential code-switching, code-shifting between interlocutors, or non-convergence whereby speakers maintained separate codes. All this is interesting for bilingual research because of the restraints that courtrooms place on discourse, but for this study the main question is how language alternation reflects language planning.

Although Tiersma (1999:157–6) sees alternation as "virtually never random" but related to factors such as topic, proficiency and socioeconomic position, and Myers-Scotton (2000:1259) describes it as rational and intentional, if not always conscious, for Gardner-Chloros (1991:57–8) it can be unmarked or neutral. For Gibbons (1987) it may constitute a code in itself. A great deal of the observed alternation indicated that language policy is flexible enough to accept leakage from societal Malay-English bilingualism, as in Ex.1 from Terengganu and Ex. 2 from Klang Valley, where hybrid speech is especially common.

Ex.1: *(C.17)*
DPP to W: *Kamu* check-out *ke menginap lagi? Atau* stay *lagi dekat bilik itu*?
[Did you check out or extend your stay? Or did you stay in the room?]

Ex.2: *(C.38)*
C: *Berapa gaji* [How much do you earn]*?*
W: *Rata* [about] four thousand.
C: *Ini gaji* basic *atau* sales commission *masuk*?
[This is your basic wage or inclusive of commission?]
W: Commission *masuk* [inclusive].
C: *Ini* payslip. *Gaji dibayar tunai atau cek?*
[Here's your payslip. Are you paid in cash or by cheque?]
W: *Cek.*

Analysis of lexical code-mixing often entails distinguishing mixes from loans. This is especially complex in Malaysia because many speakers alternate constantly, use English with localised phonology, and avoid morphological elaboration. In the case of non-legal lexis the problem can be set to one side by following Angermeyer

(2003:110) in abandoning a monolingual perspective and assuming that many courtroom participants draw upon hybrid lexicons to create cohesive discourse.

Ex.3: (*C.37*)
PC: *Puan, saya* forward *laporan* [I'll forward the report, madam].

With legalese, however, the question of whether hybridity is deficiency- or proficiency-related is relevant to language planning, and if the former, whether it is an individual's lexicon or legal BM itself that is deficient. Although insertion of legal Malay did occur in passages of English (e.g. *pemohon* = applicant, *defendan kedua* = second defendant, *C.56*), the reverse was much more evident, as Powell and David (2011) also found in Kenya. The possibility arises that this is motivated less by proficiency gaps than cultural and discursive stances. Inserting English in the absence of authorised or readily agreed equivalents (e.g. 'judicial review', *C.21*) is one thing; but routine substitutions (e.g. 'mention', *C.1*, *C.2*, 'summary judgment', *C.10*, 'statement of defence', *C.11*), 'appellate jurisdiction', *C.21*) for Malay lexis that exists in *Istilah Undang-undang* or in judgments appear to confirm the positioning of English as the language of legal sources and authority.

Such macro-oriented considerations undoubtedly interact with local-level communicative aims. While motivations are rarely transparent, many of the proficiency-related functions of intersentential code-switching suggested by David (1993) appeared in observations, including clarification (Ex.4.) and indirect quotation (Ex.5).

Ex.4: (*C.28*)
J: *You tanya mana dia punya kad*? [You are asking where his card is?]
C: Yes, I just want to confirm.

Ex.5: (*C.42*)
J: What is the decision on the medical report?
Pl.C: That's my concern, My Lady. It's stated plaintiff *tidak sihat* [unwell].

But later, but when it's the court day, he didn't contact me for instructions.
However he did inform the court. *Beliau kata aku janji akan beri MC*
[He said I promise to bring a medical certificate]

Ex.6 arguably entails coercion as it is a rare switch involving repetition during a cross-examination preceding an accusation that the witness used faulty equipment:

Ex.6: (*C.29*)
DC: May I ask how many weighing machines are in the department in Melaka?

Weighing machine *tu berapa alat punya di jabatan* [how many of those machines do you have in the office]? How many machines?!

I would further suggest contextualisation and textualisation as triggers for switches whereby speakers attempt to structure discourse (Ex.7) or introduce variety through bilingual reiteration (Ex.8).

Ex.7 (*C.17*)
DPP to D:*Lepas check-out kamu pergi mana*
[Where did you go after you checked out]?

D to DPP:*Saya hantar A* [I drove A back].
DPP to J: No further question, *Yang Arif.*

Ex.8 (*C.30*)
J: *Jadi* appeal *lagi. Dan mitigasi. Rayuan dibenarkan*
[So further appeal. Then mitigation. Appeal granted.]

Between macro and local considerations are institutional-level ones. Based on observations, judges seem the court participants most likely to alternate, followed by defence counsel, which might indicate that they are under lower discursive or psychological constraints than witnesses but may also reflect the fact that they speak more. Noraini (2006) found expert witnesses invariably speaking in English even when other witnesses used BM. This investigation observed one adhering to it even though her English was hesitant and she was sometimes questioned in BM (*C.29*), and another constantly reverting to it despite being enjoined to use Malay (*C.27*). Judges were often the ones to initiate alternation. Ex.9 suggests the switch adds to the scolding, while Ex.10 shows counsel following the judge's lead, perhaps hoping accommodation will win favour. But there were also examples of counsel initiating – although with Ex.12 it should be noted that the appellant counsel was not only older and more fluent in English than the judge but also a former judge himself.

Ex.9 (*C.17*)
J to DPP: *Orang kena tuduh kena caj haribulan lapanbelas* [The man was charged on 18th]. How to justify?

Ex.10 (*C.28*)
C to W:*Boleh menjadi kad berbeza tak?*[Mightn't it be a different card?]
J: That's speculation already.
C: But we don't know if he can differentiate.
J: There will be time to debate.

Ex.11 (*C.21*)
J: *Mengapa tidak tanya* [Why didn't they ask…]? //
C: //Burden of explaining is not adduced to me.
J: The land was alienated in 0.5 acres.
C: The reason why because the plaintiff was not aware of it until the government acquired the land.

Alternation is thus bound up with multiple factors operating at different levels: macro (socioculture, language policy); institutional (professional role and task); and local (communicative aims). Observations showed language policy affecting discourse across a broad spectrum of proceedings and supporting various forms of bilingualism at most court levels. Many witnesses have a bilingual choice when giving evidence. Advocates often fall back on English (and are entitled to fall back on Malay) when in difficulty, but they also have some leeway to switch languages to enhance their communicative goals.

If we take a single example (Ex.12), incorporating a recess in proceedings and arguments before the judge when the session reopened, we can see how code and register choices, while apparently local, also have dimensions beyond the courtroom that may be linked to the status, corpus, acquisition and discursive strands of language planning.

Ex. 12 (*C.45*)

C.1 *Bu neng jinxing a?* [Chinese: So you couldn't continue with it then?]

C.2 *Lagipun ada opsyen.* [Malay: There was an option too.] I was dead in the water because of this option. *Tapi saya boleh renang sekit* [But I can swim a bit.] In this case can still settle isn't it.

C.3 [Opposing counsel, breaking off from talking to client in Chinese to address C.2 across the courtroom] Why all these letters? Every day another letter!

C.2 [To C.3] And what's this? Waiting till court to serve notice?

C.3 I'm only responding to all these letters!

C.1 I'm old school. I don't like to serve at court. I usually serve at place of serving...
[Clerk indicates judge is ready to re-enter]

Usher	*Bangun* [rise]. [Judge enters and session resumes]
J.	Mr J?
C.3	*Yang Arif* we are asking indulgence for an additional witness.
J.	*Mengapa...mengapakah tak memberitahu sebelumnya?* [Why didn't you inform before?]
C.3	Because we could not get him earlier. But it is important as he's the contractor who constructed the roof.
C.2	The witness is not in the list. But I leave it to *Yang Arif* how to deal with the matter.
J.	*Saya memang tidak tahu saksi ni akan dipanggil.* [Well I didn't know this witness would be called]
C.3	Because in this case we could not go to the witness then. That was acknowledged. I didn't think we'd be able to obtain him.
J.	All right. *Saya membuat keputusan lepas periksa dokumen yang dikemukakan. Buat masa ni boleh teruskan saksi seterusnya.* [I'll make a decision after looking at the documents filed. Meanwhile let's proceed with the next witness.]
C.3	*Yang* Arif, I apologise. There won't be any more sudden witnesses. I call Mr G.
W.	[Goes to box. Partly audible discussion with clerk in Malay over what language to take oath in. J does not interfere. Takes oath in English.]
J.	[Examining W's identity card] This address is not as appears on your *penyata tuntutan* [statement of claim].
W.	That's my office address. I have my own small business.
J.	And you have amendments to your statement?
W.	Yes. How shall we proceed?
J.	You just need to inform me which the amendments are and I will do them now.
W.	Can I refer to my notes? [J. nods] In part 5 I wish to add "Basically only two options: Miss T keep her word. Or I bring down the roof."
C.2	*Yang Arif* I've been sitting in court for one and a half hours and I've only just been given notice. This is textbook surprise tactics!
C.3	*Yang Arif* this is not a surprise. I already informed the court!
C.2	In the note on the questions and answers I've already informed my friend that I haven't received the statement. [To C.3] Any more surprises?

Status	The extract begins during a recess in a financial case where official language policy is silent. The default medium among the lawyers seems to be English, but Malay is also used, and also some Chinese, reflecting the fact that Malaysian society, including the legal community, is multilingual, even if formal courtroom discourse must be in Malay, with English, or a mix of both generally allowed. The resumption of the session is announced in the national language, whereupon only Malay and English are heard. The latter predominates as a common medium at High Court level and typical of financial cases, but the judge tends to maintain the former, perhaps conscious of his official role, and all counsel use his Malay title.
Corpus	*Opsyen* is a well-established loanword in Malay generally indexing a narrower legalistic or administrative sense than the source. In this case it clearly refers to a financial clause. *Penyata tuntutan* may be an interdiscursive indication that the statement was submitted in Malay, which is the norm for court documents, but the notes the witness refers to are clearly in English and this may be behind his decision to give evidence in that language.
Acq	The Chinese used in pre-session conversation was Mandarin, rather than Cantonese. The latter is the traditional language of wider communication among Chinese Malaysians in KL but is gradually giving way to Mandarin since most younger Chinese have been educated in it. All parties appear competent in both Malay and English, which are taught at primary level and used MOI at secondary level. Clearly counsel on both sides understand the judge's Malay but prefer to respond in English. The pre-session conversation is relatively informal but formality increases as a tool of assertion. At the end of the extract one advocate is bold enough to address his opposing counsel directly, even though formalities dictate he should address himself to the judge.
Disc	While there are no specific references to the language policy, the fact that neither the judge nor clerk gives advice to the witness about which language he should take his oath in suggests a laissez faire approach, as does the judge's tolerance of English from both counsel.

9.9 Practitioners as Language Policy Mediators

This chapter has described the complex of bilingual practices and institutionalised relationships that shape Malaysian courtroom discourse. While failure to use BM more extensively might be cast as contempt for the national language (Abdul Malik 2004.8.20) or as pandering to the 'stylish' and 'classy' trappings of English (Andy Yong Kim Seng, Majlis Peguam website, 2006.6.20), I would suggest that vibrant use of both languages is consistent with the incomplete, vague but pragmatic way in which the language policy has evolved.

It has been argued that some of the flexibility in language-in-law policy comes by default rather than from comprehensive planning. It is in daily practice that its pragmatic potential emerges. It is not so much that lawyers co-construct the policy: as the summary of planning in Chaps. 3, 5, and 6 shows, there has been remarkably little consultation with practitioners, especially in the key practical areas like corpus and acquisition planning. Rather, lawyers, together with lecturers and students, mediate language policy in employing bilingualism to balance a range of institutional interests and professional functions. Pragmatism is evident in the prioritisation of Malay in lower courts and public practice and in the tolerance for English in higher courts, private practice and legal education. As well as the symbolic importance of the national language, authorities recognise its practical value for many of the less complex legal tasks, while accepting the technical and international value of English in jurisprudence and business-related matters. It can nonetheless be concluded that limits to corpus reform, fluctuations in acquisition measures and vagueness in law-related discourses indicate that bilingualism has not been comprehensively planned and has arisen out of necessity more than intention.

Filing court and government documents and doing routine advocacy in Malay, while troublesome for the older generation and not adequately prepared for at law school, is generally accepted as conforming to the public aspects of law, and much of these communicative competencies are felt to be formulaic and easily learnt. Using Malay with clients, on the other hand, is hardly framed as policy orientation at all but rather see as pragmatic orientation to communicative needs. Additional use of Chinese in oral and even some written communication is felt to be similarly pragmatic rather than a deviation from language policy. The need for English is widely accepted as the preference of many clients as well as the professional preference of those working with the texts that make up the bulk of domestic and international jurisprudence.

Inevitably, technical and pragmatic considerations interact with cultural and political stances when it comes to the practical implementation of bilingual policies. In the South Tyrol, proposals to establish a bilingual judiciary in the 1970s had to wait until 1988 to be realised, partly out of technical considerations, such as corpus planning and allowing time for a bilingual generation of recruits to work their way up through the system, but also because of political resistance to bilingualism from Rome (Alber and Palermo 2012: 294–5). In Malaysia, similarly, ideological assumptions tend to influence lawyers resisting the expanded use of Malay or the entrenched use of English, no matter how much their arguments are couched in pragmatism.

Cultural positions also come into play in career paths, intertwining consciously or subconsciously with technical factors. Thus Malay-based work is often considered to be of lower value or intellectual interest than work in English, and proficient English speakers (especially those graduating from overseas law schools) may have an attraction for corporate recruiters that outweighs any edge in legal skills or professional diligence that a weaker English speaker might have. Furthermore this research also confirms that there is sufficient room for bilingualism within official policy to allow some of the code-switching that is endemic in the surrounding society to leak into the more controlled discourse of the courtroom.

References

Abdul Malik Abdul Hakim. (2004, August 20). *Mahkamah abai bahasa Melayu?* [Court neglecting Malay?] *Utusan Online.* http://www.utusan.com.my/utusan/info.asp?y=2004&dt=0820&pub=utusan_malaysia&sec=Rencana&pg=re_07.htm. Accessed 21 Feb 2012.

Alber, Elisabeth, & Palermo, Francesco. (2012). Creating, studying and experimenting with bilingual law in South Tyrol: Lost in interpretation. In X. Arzoz (Ed.), *Bilingual higher education in the legal context. Group rights, state policies and globalisation.* Leiden: Martinus Nijhoff.

Angermeyer, Philipp Sebastian. (2003). Lexical cohesion as a motivation for codeswitching: Evidence from Spanish-English bilingual speech in court testimonies. In L. Sayahi (Ed.), *Selected proceedings of the first workshop on Spanish sociolinguistics* (pp. 112–122). Somerville: Cascadilla Proceedings Project. www.lingref.com.document#1014. Accessed 10 Jan 2005.

Angermeyer, Philipp Sebastian. (2008). Creating monolingualism in the multilingual courtoom. *Sociolinguistic Studies, 2*(3), 385–403.

Angermeyer, Philipp Sebastian. (2015). *Speak English or what? Codeswitching and interpreter use in New York City courts.* New York: Oxford University Press.

Atkinson, J., & Drew, P. (1979). *Order in court. The organization of verbal interaction in judicial settings.* London: Macmillan.

Baker, John. H. (1979). *Manual of Law French.* Amersham: Avebury.

Bennet, W. Lance, & Fieldman, Martha S. (1981). *Reconstructing reality in the courtroom.* London/New York: Tavistock.

Chouliaraki, L., & Fairclough, N. (1999). *Discourse in late modernity: Rethinking critical discourse analysis.* Edinburgh: Edinburgh University Press.

Conley, John, & O'Barr, William. (1998). *Just words. Law, language and power.* Chicago: University of Chicago Press.

Cotterill, Janet. (2002). Just one more time...': Aspects of intertextuality in the trials of O. J. Simpson. In J. Cotterill (Ed.), *Language in the legal process* (pp. 147–161). Basingstoke: Palgrave Macmillan.

David, Maya Khemlani. (1993). Language and law: Communicative strategies in a court of law a Malaysian experience. In K. L. Tee (Ed.), *Legal education in Malaysia Quo Vadis?* Kuala Lumpur: University of Malaya.

David, Maya Khemlani. (2003). Role and functions of code-switching in Malaysian courtrooms. *Multilingua, 22.* http://www.degruyter.de/journals/multilin/2003/pdf/22_5.pdf. Accessed 1 Nov 2003.

D'hondt, Sigurd. (2011, July 2–8). Defending through disaffiliation: Toying with participation frameworks in the criminal courtroom. Paper presented at panel on quoting from the case file: Intertextual practices in courtroom discourse, *12th International Pragmatics Conference*, Manchester.

Eades, Diana. (2008). *Courtroom talk and neocolonial control.* Berlin: Mouton de Gruyter.

Faiza Tamby Chik. (1993). Language and the law: The role of Malay and English in legal education and the practice of law. In K. L. Tee (Ed.), *Legal education in Malaysia Quo Vadis?* (pp. 103–107). Kuala Lumpur: University of Malaya.

Fisher, John H. (1977). Chancery and the emergence of standard written English in the fifteenth century. *Speculum, 52*(4), 870–899.

Fuller, Janet. (1993). Hearing between the lines: Style switching in a courtroom setting. *Pragmatics, 3*(1), 29–43.

Gardner-Chloros, P. (1991). *Language selection and switching in Strasbourg.* Oxford: Clarendon.

Gibbons, John. (1987). *Code mixing and code choice: A Hong Kong case study.* Clevedon: Multilingual Matters.

Gibbons, John. (2003). *Forensic linguistics.* Oxford: Blackwell.

Gibbons, John. (2008). Questioning in common law courtrooms. In Gibbons & Turell (Eds.), *Dimensions of forensic linguistics* (pp. 115–130). Amsterdam: John Benjamins.

Giddens, Anthony. (1979). *Central problems in social theory. Action, structure and contradiction in social analysis*. London: Macmillan.

Goodrich, Peter. (1984). Law and language: An historical and critical introduction. *Journal of Law and Society, 11*(2), 173–195.

Hafiz Yatim. (2018, August 15). More judicial activism today but winter of 88 lingers. *Malaysiakini*. https://www.malaysiakini.com/news/439074. Accessed 15 Aug 2018.

Jones, Carol. (2010). Legal education in Hong Kong. In S. Steele & K. Taylor (Eds.), *Legal education in Asia* (pp. 107–136). Abingdon: Routledge.

Lakoff, R. T. (1990). The limits of politeness: Therapeutic and courtroom discourse. *Multilingua, 8*, 101–129.

Leung, Janny. (2012). Judicial discourse in Cantonese courtrooms in postcolonial Hong Kong: The judge as godfather, scholar, educator and scolding parent. *The International Journal of Speech, Language and the Law, 19*(2), 239–261.

Maley, Yon. (1994). The language of the law. In John Gibbons (Ed.), *Language and the law* (pp. 11–50). London: Longman.

Martin, Isabel Pefianco. (2012). Expanding the role of Philippine languages in the legal system: The dim prospects. *Asian Perspectives in the Arts and Humanities, 2*(1), 1–14.

Mead, Richard. (1988). *Malaysia's National Language Policy and the Legal System*. New Haven: Yale.

Mellinkoff, David. (1963). *The language of the law*. Boston: Little, Brown &.

Myers-Scotton, Carol. (2000). Explaining the role of norms and rationality in codeswitching. *Journal of Pragmatics, 32*(9), 1259–1271.

Ng Kwai Hang. (2009). *The common law in two voices. Language, law and the postcolonial dilemma in Hong Kong*. Stanford: Stanford University Press.

Noraini Ibrahim. (2006). *Courtroom discourse: Expert witness testimony in a criminal case in Malaysia*. PhD thesis. Faculty of Languages and Linguistics, Universiti Malaya. [Viewed at Universiti Malaya].

Noraini Ibrahim., & Radha M. K. Nambiar. (2010). There are many ways of skinning a cat, my lord: Humor in the Malaysian adversarial courtroom. *The Southeast Asian Journal of English Language Studies, 17*(2), 73–89.

Philips, Susan. (1987). The social organisation of questions and answers in courtroom discourse. In L. Kedar (Ed.), *Power through discourse* (pp. 83–113). Norwood: Ablex.

Powell, Richard. (2008). *Motivations for language choice in Malaysian courtrooms and implications for language planning*. Kuala Lumpur: Universiti Malaya.

Powell, Richard. (2011a, July 2–8). *Quotation as a trigger for code-switching in Malaysian courtrooms*. Paper presented at panel on quoting from the case file: Intertextual practices in courtroom discourse, *12th International Pragmatics Conference*, Manchester.

Powell, Richard. (2011b, December 8–11). English or Malay or both? Comparing language policy and practice in the courts of East and West Malaysia. Paper presented at *16th ESEA (English in Southeast Asia) Conference,* Yogyakarta.

Powell, Richard. (2012, July 4–7). Legal vernacularisation and access to justice. Paper presented at the *Asian Regional Conference of the International Association of Forensic Linguists,* Kuala Lumpur.

Powell, Richard, & David, Maya Khemlani. (2011). Language alternation in Kenyan and Malaysian courts. In A. Wagner & L. Cheng (Eds.), *Exploring courtroom discourse: The language of power and control* (pp. 227–250). London: Ashgate.

Rwezaura, Barthazara. (1994). Constraining factors to the adoption of Kiswahili as a language of the law in Tanzania. *Afrikanistische Arbeitspapiere: Schriftenreihe des Kölner Instituts für Afrikanistik, 37*, 109–126.

Stuckey, Roy. et al. (2007). *Best practices for legal education. A vision and a road map*. Clinical Legal Education Association. http://cleaweb.org/. Accessed 12 Dec 2012.

Tan Twan Eng. (2012). *The garden of evening mists*. Edinburgh: Canongate.
The Straits Times. (1967, October 25). *Should counsel quit? – Poser for Bar Council*, p. 2.
Thekiso, Elma. (2001). A sociolinguistic analysis of communication processes in a bilingual court of law in Gaborone, Gaborone. Unpublished PhD thesis, University of Warwick.
Tiersma, Peter. (1999). *Legal language*. Chicago: University of Chicago Press.
van de Houwen, Fleur. (2011, July 2–8). *Reporting writing: Police records in the courtroom*. Paper presented at panel on quoting from the case file: Intertextual practices in courtroom discourse, *12th International Pragmatics Conference*, Manchester.

Chapter 10
Common Law and Vernacularisation: A Global Perspective

Communication was critical to the evolving theory of the Company state, now engaged not only with trade, but with promulgating new laws, understanding court testimony, and communicating with predominantly peasant subjects. Vernacular languages were thought crucial to each of these tasks.

Mir (2006:403) on the East India Company

The source of the law is English. And I don't know any other common law system that abandoned English and yet remained a common law system.

Hong Kong judge Tom Harper (in Ng 2009:230)

10.1 The Value of a Global Perspective

Malaysian law is deeply engaged with global law, not merely though the cross-border agreements that affect any modern polity but also through extensive institutional, personal and discursive links with international common law. Commonwealth enactments are models for many Malaysian statutes. Commonwealth judgments have persuasive authority in Malaysian cases. Australian, British, Irish, New Zealand and Singaporean qualifications satisfy requirements for bar admission in part or in full. Although Malaysian lawyers who studied overseas are now outnumbered by those who studied at home, the former still carry disproportionate weight in the senior ranks of the bar and judiciary. As English is the source language of common law historically, as well as the language in which most common law jurisprudence is constructed, it retains a privileged role in Malaysian legal communication despite decades of bilingual practice. The view of many, perhaps most, practitioners is that the national language is all very well for routine tasks, public hearings and client discussion, but it will be a long time before it replaces English as the main engine of law-making.

While this is not an unreasonable position in present Malaysian circumstances, it overlooks dynamic and socially-grounded aspects of legal language that might

R. Powell, *Language Choice in Postcolonial Law*, Language Policy 22,
https://doi.org/10.1007/978-981-15-1173-8_10

support more comprehensively bilingual law. Moreover the assumption that English predominance is inevitable often ignores the extent to which other languages are used in common law jurisdictions elsewhere. Although many of the professionals interviewed for this book were well informed about monolingual jurisdictions such as Australia, Britain or Singapore, there was little awareness of multilingualism in Canada, Hong Kong or Sri Lanka. Even though different language ecologies and political circumstances present different language planning challenges, making law more accessible and transparent without sacrificing professional integrity is a problem shared by many multilingual postcolonial societies, particularly those inheriting common law its default language is also the default medium of global economics and politics.

Accordingly this penultimate chapter will review instances of multilingual common law from a wider perspective, beginning with the historical spread of English law as it came into contact with other languages, and then exploring how jurisdictions beyond Malaysia balance global pressures with local linguistic and sociopolitical exigencies. While there is no room here for the detailed enquiry applied to Malaysia, evidence from research literature and professional portals is supported by interviews and observations, and the structure of the chapter broadly follows that of the book as a whole, moving from key political and economic factors in the cross-border expansion of common law to a summary of status-, corpus-, acquisition- and discourse-related developments.

10.2 Language Contact and the Expansion of Common Law

10.2.1 From Trilingualism to Monolingualism

Despite the passage of time, the evolution of English law from trilingualism at the Norman Conquest to monolingualism on the eve of its global export invites comparison with modern Malaysia for the way legalese resisted societal linguistic changes and for the various patterns of bilingualism that characterised legal practice.

The rise of postcolonial studies has fed conceptualisations of Norman and Plantagenet Britain as a colony (Madeline 2010:63), bringing new terminology to an old debate about whether key developments constituted imposition or synthesis. While the geographical, economic and religious proximity of eleventh-century France and England precludes direct comparison with later European expansionism, the complex relations between coercion and collaboration unearthed by Memmi (1957), Said (1978, 1993) and others in the colonisation of Africa and Asia suggest there may be parallels between the Norman impact on law and language in England and the British impact on law and language in the empire. English had a long path to travel before becoming the dominant vehicle of law in England, experiencing a digraphic relationship with Latin, a revitalising hybridisation with French, and an expansion through pragmatic administrative policies. Constant interplay between corpus and status planning en route resonates with much of what has happened in Malaysia.

Language evidence offers insights into the hybrid evolution of common law. Lexical items evince the post-Norman survival of elements of Anglo-Saxon law, including 'fee' (from *feh/feoh*), 'deem' (from *dōm*), compound adverbs like 'thereunder' and 'thereof' (Mellinkoff 1963:40–47), along with a significant number of terms used in criminal proceedings that were built on vernacular foundations (Ormrod 2003:770). Repetition (ibid:42–43), alliteration and binomial expressions (Tiersma 1999:13–15) and other rhetoric still evident in texts today echo Saxon legal practices that were predominantly oral (Mellinkoff 1963:42–43) but supported by a tradition of vernacular codification stretching back to the seventh century (Wormald 1999:93). Indeed 1066, while revolutionary for politics and economics, was evolutionary for law. The existing courts were left in charge of litigation (Cantor 1991:68) and most legal innovations came as ad hoc responses to practical problems (Golding 2001:101). The adoption of the Saxon practice of issuing royal writs to enforce laws away from the centre of power demonstrates the Normans' "expertise in using old forms for new ends" (ibid:104).

The new regime did not "slam the door on English" (Mellinkoff 1963:95). Before the invasion the vernacular had been used for legislation, in contrast to the continent's preference for Latin (Wormald 1999:101). Although the latter seems to have been used for all writs after 1070 (ibid:104), Old English remained an administrative medium (ibid:179), and in its transition to Middle English it absorbed elements from Norse, Latin and Greek as well as French, proving itself "a vigorous, flexible tongue, fully capable of adapting itself to new concepts of law" (Mellinkoff 1963:58).

Under Henry II (1154–89) common law emerged as Europe's only viable alternative to Roman law (Cantor 1991:59), but Maitland's exposure of the role of political and economic interest shattered illusions about it having a well-defined ideology (ibid:59). Use of circuit judges, unpaid juries and oral testimony was motivated by expediency rather than justice (ibid:63–64), with the dispatch of itinerant judges a means of reducing the power of local sheriffs (Golding 2001:107). Professional self-interest had important implications for language as jury trials produced a corps of skilled, non-ecclesiastical advocates (Cantor 1991:63) who earned their trade by arguing from cases rather than statutes (ibid:72).

Although the Norman import of Latin record-keeping (Mellinkoff 1963:71) ushered in that language's monopoly of legal writing for two centuries (ibid:81) and its survival in writs for another four (Fisher 1977:877), between the thirteenth and fifteenth centuries it was an English-influenced variety of Norman French (Mellinkoff 1963:96) that emerged as the main medium of advocacy (Ormrod 2003:753), court reports (Fisher 1977:774) and statute (Mellinkoff 1963:81). The rise of Law French went against the grain of societal language shift. The very opposite of legal vernacularisation, it constitutes an important example of how legal language may resist changes in society at large. Hence Malaysian and other modern language planners cannot assume that law will fall into line as society shifts toward a national language. While the gentry populating the Commons and provincial administrations increasingly favoured English (ibid:776), which by the end of the fourteenth century had replaced Latin as the main medium of grammar schools (Mellinkoff 1963:97), the aristocracy in the House of Lords continued to favour their variety of *langue d'ouil*, with the courts developing a hybrid form of Norman French (Ormrod 2003:752). Commercial and administrative oral exchanges, if not records, were mostly in English by the 1360s (Fisher 1996:19) and there was an "outburst of copying and composing" in English after 1400 (ibid:22). Yet French continued to dominate court proceedings and records (Brand 1999:4) right down to county court level (Ormrod 2003:767).

This anachronism is frequently ascribed to professional elitism, with the cultural prestige of French rising in inverse proportion to its popular decline (Mellinkoff 1963:100). The influence of the serjeants-of-law (elite Crown attorneys) and central courts upon local legal culture may have reinforced elitism (Ormrod 2003:766–767). French would have kept out untrained advocates and, in the view of Elizabethan jurist Sir Edward Coke, discouraged "bare reading without understanding" of the law (Tiersma 1999:28). Mellinkoff (1963:101) also speculates about the advantages of retaining a language poorly understood by laymen:

> What better way of preserving a professional monopoly than by locking up your trade secrets in the safe of an unknown tongue?

Similarities with the exclusionary and opaque nature of English legalese often voiced in Malaysia come to mind. However, we should consider the extent to which elitism, both then and now, serves professional needs in addition to sociocultural agendas.

Tiersma (1999:28) sees the movement from Latin toward French from 1200 as a pragmatic choice inasmuch as aristocratic clients understood the latter better. Ormrod (2003:776) suggests French's closer syntactic proximity to English gave it communicative advantages over Latin, hence implying increasing interaction between written and oral argument. And as oral pleading became more complex, attorneys turned to specialised advocates (Brand 1999:4). Law French, once scorned as corrupted, acquired a precision that English would not attain until the 1400s (Fisher 1977:886). Inertia, too, must have helped prolong French (Mellinkoff 1963:100), particularly when statutory punishments for errors in pleadings made innovation hazardous (ibid:114). This brings to mind modern lawyers' reluctance to depart from complex language that has stood the test of time. Efficiency may also have motivated the continuance of set phrases and abbreviations (Baker 1979:11). Legalese became increasingly complex in tandem with growing complexity in law and greater reliance on writing (Tiersma 1999:38–40).

A more technical than conspiratorial explanation of elitism might also be applied to Malaysian law, with the retention of English serving professional expediency rather than the exclusion of non-anglophones. However it is difficult to extricate arguments about the technical superiority of a particular language from the instrumental and integrative advantages it brings to professionals. As Ng (2009:31) comments with regard to Hong Kong, the adequacy of a language for legal representation is ultimately less important than what lawyers believe it capable of. But even if lawyers, whether in medieval England or contemporary Malaysia, appear resistant to language change, it may be unfair to single them out from other professionals.

10.2.2 Extension of English Law to Territories Lacking Written Law

The transatlantic export of English law coincided with the English language's ascendancy in common law. Settlements in Virginia (1607), Massachusetts (1620) and elsewhere were established when the home legal system was already functioning predominantly in English, and the absence of language provisions – apart from a 1683 Pennsylvania law prescribing its use for proceedings (Reinsch 1899:431) – suggests English was simply taken for granted. While time-honoured terms were retained, the principles behind them were often forgotten (Reinsch 1899:436) as proceedings tended to be informal, orientated to unrepresented claimants (ibid:447) and presided over by panels of judges lacking legal training (ibid:446). Yet little came of the plans several states put forward after the Revolution to implement wholesale legal change (Cantor 1991:73). Tiersma (1999:45) offers a linguistic reason: new legal texts entailed the risk of new ambiguities and raised the spectre of chicanery. Similar fears have been voiced by Malaysian lawyers.

In North America and beyond, the unwritten laws of non-European communities were often disregarded, nowhere more flagrantly than in Australia, which was classified as *terra nullius* right down until the 1992 *Mabo* case (Vranken 2012:122). Elsewhere, ancient laws and traditions were 'discovered' by authorities to shore up the legitimacy of colonial practices. In East Africa, for example, administrators favoured local leaders who remembered oral codes conducive to colonial interests (Cain and Hopkins 1993:218).

10.2.3 Contact Between Common Law and European Civil Law

Written law, and above all the law of other European settlers, was taken more seriously by British administrators, not least because of economic and social expediency. Contact with civil law traditions often entailed extended periods of support for legal practices in languages other than English. The proclamation imposing English law that accompanied the 1763 cession of New France flew in the face of established policy (Hogg 1992:34) and the 1774 Quebec Act restored civil law practised in French, while recognising English common law for public administration and criminal law (Laskin & Finkelstein 1986:26). The 1867 Constitution Act, drafted in English, provided for *either* language in national and Québécois parliamentary debates, court proceedings and statutes (Canadian Supreme Court 2012). This was later amended to *both* languages (ibid). In Mauritius, the 1810 *Acte de Capitulation* recognised the 1789 *Code Pénal* and 1804 *Code Napoléon* (Gunputh 2013:58), although English laws and legal practices were also introduced while an 1845 decree removed French as the ordinary language of the court (Mauritius Supreme Court 2013). Malta is another example of this category of Anglo-civilian law incorporating, though not necessarily melding, Italian, Napoleonic and English elements (Andò 2011:240), authorising legislation in Maltese and English versions and admitting both languages in court (Badia i Capdevila 2004:4).

Contact with Roman-Dutch law similarly produced mixed legal systems. In the Cape, laws scarcely modified (Sachs 1973:17; Fagan 1996:40), since Dutch East India Company settlers arrived in 1580 remained in force after British occupation in 1806 (Lenel 2002:5) and elements of Roman-Dutch law were introduced alongside English law in neighbouring territories falling under British administration. But while Dutch remained important in South Africa, laws elsewhere were encoded only in English (ibid), as with the 1891 and 1909 reception clauses for Bechuanaland (Thekiso 2001:13). In Ceylon too, the principle of retaining pre-conquest laws unobjectionable to English law was followed after the island come under East India Company administration in 1796 (Nadaraja 1972:181). In addition to Roman-Dutch law, unwritten Kandyan law was steadily, if not always accurately, recorded and Muslim law retained for relevant communities (ibid: 1972:184–185), but English became the default medium of records.[1]

Meanwhile the Americans retained French civil law in Louisiana (Michaels 2012:78) but promptly translated it. The 1808 *Loix de l'Etat de la Louisianie* were translated and annotated in 1814, just 2 years after the granting of statehood (Louisiana State University 2012). The 1825 Civil Code incorporated French and Spanish customs (Billings 2001:35) and early lawyers, many of them migrants from other states (ibid:29), needed a command of two legal traditions (ibid:25), but they did not require any language other than English (ibid:30). When the Philippines were ceded to the United States in 1898 civil law practised in Spanish was also recognised initially, despite clamours for English from commercial interests (*New York Times* 1899).

However, while we find parallel legal administrations, translation of European and also Asian laws into English, and the retention of civil law in French or Dutch, there is little evidence of the vernacularisation of laws imported from England. Administrations in British India perhaps went furthest in support for vernaculars, but even there they were prioritised for oral communication rather than written records.

[1] Sri Lankan attorney Fathima Marikkar, p.c. 2014.12.12

10.2.4 Vernaculars in Colonial Indian Law and Administration

Language and law were frequently connected in the minds and work of officers of the East India Company (EIC). William Jones hypothesised the common origins of Indian and European languages while serving as an EIC judge (Cohn 1996:75). Inaugural Governor-General Hastings ploughed dead and living languages alike in search of legal traditions to obviate the need to import English law (ibid:61), but while some ancient texts, often selectively or wrongly translated, were drawn on (ibid:28), the concept of Indian law was based mainly on what colonial judges saw as locally appropriate when deciding cases (ibid:147), and to maintain law and order there was instrumental value in learning local languages of command (ibid:31). Hence Madras English judges were required to learn Tamil so they could discuss directly with pleaders (ibid:53). *Vakil* pleaders trained at Hindu or Muslim colleges (Schmitthener 1969:351) and untrained *mukhtar* legal agents (ibid:354) were also appointed. Rahman (1998:62) and Mir (2006:395) concur that, far from foisting English upon India, the EIC exploited the administrative potential of lingua francas.

For the first five decades of British rule English was mainly confined to higher administrative levels, and the retention of Persian in the courts (Mir 2006:398) shows that it is not only European colonisers who leave their legal languages behind. An 1802 Court of Directors' letter to the Governor-General (ibid:399) recommended knowledge of Persian and Hindustani for all officers and Bengali for collectors and civil judges. An 1805 Public Notice in Madras stipulated proficiency in Tamil, Telugu or Kannada for judges and collectors (ibid:400). An 1819 memorial from the Bombay justices to the EIC's Court of Directors complained that lack of vernacular translations of laws was resulting in defendants having no knowledge of the offences they were charged with (ibid:400). Officials were less exercised by the choice between English and Indian languages than choices among Indian languages (ibid:400). Rahman (1998:250) argues that classical tongues were emphasised when conciliating the elites and vernaculars when controlling the masses.

Despite opposition from district commissioners and judges who saw the vernacular as insufficiently standardised (Mir 2006:403), Bengal followed Bombay and Madras in abandoning Persian under Act 29 in 1837 in what Mir (2006:398) calls a triumph for efficiency and justice. A provision for Bengali was incorporated into an all-India Act and thus had influence beyond the Bengal Presidency (ibid:405).

Burma, which had developed an indigenous specialised legal profession (Myint Zan 2004:42), was administered as part of India from 1824 and here too a local language, Burmese, was introduced as a court medium and British administrators required to learn it (*Rangoon Gazette* 1888). But all the appellate decisions that have survived are in English (Myint Zan 2004:386). Even James Mill, an influential historian sceptical of local learning (Rahman 1998:26), felt it improper to exclude vernaculars from court records (ibid, 36, citing Anath Nath Baus), yet we have little evidence from any Indian state of their use in higher courts or jurisprudence.

The initial priority was to translate local laws and customs into English so that judges could bypass interpreters, who were widely distrusted (Cohn 1996:68–70). Despite the Subcontinent's ancient literary traditions, lack of equivalent legal concepts inhibited vernacularisation at higher levels (Cohn 1996:73–75), and Chaklader (1990:90) points out that the substitution of the vernacular for Persian in Bengal's lower courts was not followed up in higher courts or written judgments. Indeed Schmitthener (1969:362) sees this period as the beginning of a process of legal anglicisation. With political control considered more urgent after the 1857 rebellion, English case law was imported and the *vakil* pleaders removed (ibid:75).

The Straits Settlements were under direct EIC administration for several decades, but although Malay was considered the lingua franca, British administrators accorded it less value than Chinese, Hindustani or Tamil (Mills 1960:111–113), possibly because it lacked their depth of literature. Hence Malaya scarcely benefitted even from the limited and largely oral vernacularisation of law that applied in India.

In sum the main evidence we have of vernacularised colonial law is of oral use in lower courts. This seems to have been widespread throughout India, and although we can only speculate about actual practice, the emphasis upon language training for colonial officers suggests that proceedings routinely included discourse unmediated by interpreters. We should not lightly dismiss the importance of oral law: in the context of Hong Kong, Ng (2009:116) has shown how dynamic sociolinguistic practices can disturb the theoretical predictability of written law. But the common law principle of oral law having precedential potential means little in practice since what judges "think or what they say during the proceedings before them is almost entirely irrelevant" (Tiersma 2007:1188) without the force of court records. Lacking written judgments or legislation, the long-term impact of vernacular law remained weak, even though it may have been influential in particular places at particular times.

10.2.5 Vernacularisation as a Largely Postcolonial Phenomenon

From what we can tell from history, then, beyond limited oral use in lower courts, legal vernacularisation is predominantly a postcolonial rather than colonial phenomenon. Indeed we can see this in the contrast in language policy between colonial Malaya and postcolonial Malaysia.

In the rest of this chapter we will review patterns of language planning in global common law today and go on to consider how these affect legal practice. While measures to support the status of vernaculars might imply concomitant activity to modernise their legal corpora or enhance their use in legal education, jurisdictions often apply vernaculars unevenly. A local language may be an official medium of law yet hardly used in practice, or it may have no official status yet play a key role in proceedings. Official status may be undermined by lack of legal corpora or education.

10.3 Status Planning Patterns

In Chap. 3 we saw how language status in Malaysian law is regulated as a subset of national language policy, principally through the constitution, some legislation, a small body of case law, and professional rules. It was further argued that these form a bilingual framework within which there is considerable flexibility for practitioners as long as they remain aware of boundaries: no language other than Malay or English may be used in court proceedings[2] or in dealings with the government, and judges or officials may insist on Malay at any time. The range of positions that we find elsewhere in the common law world suggests that the relationship between language status and language practice is rarely direct. But there is generally some kind of normative connection.

10.3.1 Disparities Between Status and Practice

Exceptionally, status planning may have little to no impact on legal practice. If we entertain the idea of the Norman Conquest as colonisation, for example, with subsequent English wars against France channelling anticolonialist sentiments, the 1362 Statute of Pleading, which required cases in secular courts be "pleaded", "counted", "defended", "answered", "debated" and "judged" in English (Ormrod 2003:772) constituted a strong statement of linguistic nationalism. But what did it achieve in practice? French continued to be used to the confusion of laymen for centuries. For Mellinkoff (1963:111) a major reason for the Statute's sterility was that this "first national outcry against the language of the law was not that it was technical but that it was French". From Ireland (where Irish as the 'first official language' may be used in any proceeding)[3] to the Philippines (where in 2006 the Supreme Court resolved to adapt the language of law to that of the people)[4] declarations about language status sit ill with legal practice in the legal domain, but the rhetorical nature of the 1362 enactment is particularly striking. Ormrod (2003:772) focuses less on weak enforcement than on indications it was intentionally toothless, employing populist nationalism in purporting to abolish a language that privileged its own drafters (ibid:757.) Indeed the document dismissing French as "trop desconue"[5] (Baker 1979:9) was written in that very language. Without evidence of oral practices we cannot know how the enactment affected courtroom discourse, but by allowing continued use of French for documents (Ormrod 2003:755) and providing that "terms and processes be upheld and observed as they are" (ibid:773) it

[2] I once heard a Federal Court judge berate an advocate labouring a point in vain with "Shall I repeat it in Tamil for you?", but the hapless lawyer backed down before the ruse was put to the test.

[3] 2003 Official Languages Act/Acht na dTeangacha Ofigiúla, s.7.

[4] Zuñiga (2006), cited in Martin (2012:2)

[5] insufficiently known

implied the retention of existing practices where advantageous for advocacy. This is not so different from Malaysian legislation allowing English 'in the interests of justice'.

The main intent of status planning in fourteenth-century England seems to have been assertion of national identity at a time of war, just as Malaysian planning has been driven by postcolonial nationalism. Neither agenda prioritised legal transparency, and both stitched in loopholes to cover the lack of vernacular corpus planning. Malaysians have certainly been more enthusiastic about Malay than the Plantagenets were about English, supporting linguistic reforms with economic and administrative measures allowing Malay to become the main medium of the lower courts. But in English they face an obstacle with far greater currency than Law French ever had.

A second ostensible push to transform legal language in England came with the 1730 Proceedings in Courts of Justice Act, which required English for writs, pleadings, indictments and other procedures, but although Fisher (1977:880) described it as ending common law in French, it was a case of status planning following language use rather than leading it. As late as 1650, Parliamentarian measures for "turning the Books of the Law and all the Proces and Proceedings" had been derailed by a profession convinced of the superiority of Latin (Kurzon 2013:118), but by the time of the 1730 bill Latin and French had been largely reduced to terms of art and adages – which could still be called upon after the bill was enactecd because of a 1733 amendment allowing 'Court Hand' (Mellinkoff 1963:135). Rather than through legislation, language practice was changed by the interplay of pragmatism and self-interest and the struggles between a more francophone centre and more anglophone periphery. It is not too much of a stretch to invite comparisons with anglophile Kuala Lumpur and a Malay-dominant periphery.

For modern examples of disparity between language status and legal practice we might consider South Africa, where autochthenous languages play a very minor legal role despite constitutional provisions and even Afrikaans, with a 450-year presence in the region, is disappearing from the legal domain. While the legal system is a blend of English and Roman-Dutch law, legislation is always drafted in English, with each enactment then translated into one of the eleven national languages out of respect for their constitutional parity (s.11) and subject to "usage, practicality, expense and regional circumstances" (s.6(3)). Former Supreme Court judge Louis Harms (2012) considers this "a sop to the constitution" since the translations lack official standing. The Bill of Rights (s.35(3)(k)) grants defendants the right to use their native tongue, but in practice Afrikaans is the only language heard without translation. Exceptionally, isiXhosa was used in *S v Matomela* (1998) as all parties understood it and there was a shortage of interpreters (Hlophe 2004:43), but in *Mthetwa vs De Bruyn* (1998) a magistrate's objection to isiZulu for proceedings was upheld (ibid:43).

In neighbouring Botswana there is also a gap between language status and practice, but in this case it works in favour of an indigenous medium. Part 1, s. 5(1) of the Magistrates Court Act requires English for proceedings and records, but with a profession mostly conversant in Setswana, the national language and spoken by about 80% (Nyati-Ramahobo 2000:253), its oral use without interpreting has become routine at lower court level (Thekiso 2001). Mentions (procedural applications to keep cases in play) are conducted in English but charge sheets usually read out in Setswana (Thekiso 2001:84). Prosecutors, as representatives of the state, are enjoined to speak English more sternly than defence counsel (ibid:201).

10.3.2 Monolingual Law in Multilingual Societies

Whereas Botswana is an example of a formally monolingual jurisdiction that supports bilingualism in practice, of the world's 70 or so systems based on English or American law a majority recognise English alone, even though in many of the surrounding societies it is a minority language. In Malawi, for example, English is known by just 6% (Webb and Kembo-Sure 2000:48) yet used in court even at Magistrates level (Kayambazinthu 1999:53), whereas Chichewa, the language of wider communication (ibid:63) and L1 of over 50% (Ethnologue 2019), lacks any official role. In Fiji, English is the first language of fewer than 3% (Tent 2001:210) yet used in parliamentary debate, legislation and the courts (Mangubhai and Mugler 2003, 372–375). There is a constitutional provision (Art.14) for defendants to be tried in a language they understand, but proceedings are in English, with some witnesses managing without interpreters in the High Court, whose motto is *Dieu et mon droit*, but few able to follow matters in the Magistrates courts (*Rerevaka na Kalou ka doka na Tui* – 'Fear God and honour the Monarch') without constant intervention from clerks interpreting into Fijian or Hindi.[6] In Saint Lucia 95% speak a French-based creole as their first language in addition to standard French, and elements of the *Code Napoléon* have been retained, but legal discourse is thoroughly anglicised (Evans 2005).

Singapore is another example of monolingual law in a highly multilingual society. In many trials most participants are likely to be Mandarin and/or Hokkien speakers, yet any utterance not in English must be interpreted, with translation errors often picked up by multilingual advocates.[7] The authorised texts of the constitution and statutes are in English. As the republic was part of Malaysia until 1965 its monolingual model reinforces the conclusion that the most significant language planning in Malaysia has occurred since then.

With the exception of small claims courts (Sect. 10.3.4, below), the United States enforces monolingual English norms in legal proceedings, to the extent that ability to understand uninterpreted testimony may constitute grounds for juror disqualification (*Hernandez v. New York* 1991).

[6] P.o., Suva, 2014.3.11–14

[7] Siew Kum Hong, Singapore advocate and former parliamentarian, p.c. 2013.10.16.

10.3.3 Largely Symbolic Status Planning

Several common law jurisdictions ascribe a symbolic importance to certain languages out of proportion to their use. The position of Irish certainly goes beyond the symbolic inasmuch as it has been used at all court levels in Ireland, including several apex proceedings (most of them about language itself). Furthermore, the 2003 Official Language Act (s.7) stipulates that legislation be translated into Irish "as soon as may be". Dublin City University's Peadar Ó Flatharta nonetheless concedes that regular use of the language is confined to the lower courts in the sparsely populated *Gaeltacht* area.[8]

Welsh is another example of a language that is widely admissible but, so far, not widely used. While the 1993 Welsh Language Act grants the right to speak it in court, in practice it is usually interpreted. Davies (2012) has analysed the relationship between societal and individual bilingualism in order to explore the cost-benefit feasibility of extending bilingual law there, concluding that the relatively low demand for trials in Welsh means it could be met by the existing pool of balanced bilingual jurors without compromising the principle of random selection.

Despite such hiatuses, however, there does seem to be some correlation between language status and language use, with jurisdictions at one end of the spectrum confining vernaculars to oral use in subordinate proceedings and those at the other using them in the highest courts, legislation and jurisprudence.

10.3.4 Unofficial Oral Use of LOTE in Lower Courts

While the unofficial yet routine use of Setswana in Botswana (Sect. 10.3.2) may be unusual, LOTE (languages other than English) do slip through the interpreter's filter even in overwhelmingly monolingual English systems, especially in less formal proceedings. Angermeyer (2015), for example, found strategic code-switching to be common in New York small claims courts, especially when unrepresented speakers with partial English proficiency strove for discursive cohesion. Elsewhere in the United States, Richland (2008:105–6) observed bilingual participants in tribal courts preferring to give cultural and customary explanations in Hopi.

Untranslated testimony also enters oral proceedings without appearing on the record. Surrounded by Malaysian territory and with close institutional links to Singapore, Brunei officially enforces common law in English within a society that favours a balance between English and Malay, Brunei Malay having the greatest social circulation and standard Malay important in education and administration (Clynes and Deterding 2011:260). In court, English alone is officially admitted, although the 1963 Language of the Supreme Court Act (Art. 5A) allows the giving of evidence in other languages 'in the interests of justice'. In practice, interpreters

[8] Interviewed in Chiangmai, 2013.5.29.

appear to be circumvented frequently, especially where judges (many of whom are expatriates), advocates and witnesses all know Malay.[9] Masmahirah (2016:6~10) found some witnesses being allowed to continue in Malay without interruption, clerks reading out charges in it, and certain judges using it to draw answers from witnesses. It is tempting to speculate that Malay may have crept into Malaysian courts in similar ways long before official vernacularisation, but as Ng (2009:75) reminds us for Cantonese in colonial Hong Kong, any evidence of oral practices has "evaporated into thin air". Comparing Brunei with Singapore we can at least conclude that some 'monolingual jurisdictions' are less monolingual than others.

It should be noted that monolingual proceedings may overlook the importance of language varieties. Forrester (2005), for example, found Jamaican courts at risk of significant misunderstanding by consistently failing to recognise lexicogrammatical distinctions between Standard Jamaican English and the Patois spoken by most witnesses.

10.3.5 Predominantly Oral Use of LOTE in Lower Courts

In Tonga we have an example of a vernacular spoken by nearly everyone[10] and officially sanctioned for the lower courts, yet shut out of higher proceedings. Philips (2000:243) found minor civil matters being heard predominantly in Tongan during proceedings that served as vehicles to assert national cultural values (ibid:243). In the police courts magistrates stick consistently to the language and sometimes admonish defendants for 'foreign' practices such as drinking in the street.[11] But it is not used at all in the courts of record (Supreme Court and Court of Appeal), except through translation. In a "thoroughly English system" barristers wear wigs and gowns over traditional *tupenu* garments and appear before judges, who are mostly drawn from other Commonwealth countries in order to enhance impartiality in a close-knit society of only 100,000.[12] Witness examinations are translated into English for the benefit of the judge (who may be the only non-Tongan speaker in court), yet judge-lawyer interactions in English do not appear to be translated for defendants.[13]

Though not the overwhelming first language in the way that Tongan is, Tagalog-based Filipino is reportedly understood by 85% in the Philippines (2006 census, in Martin 2012:2), yet even in the lower courts its use is sporadic. Under constitutional Article 14 (s.7) Filipino is the national language. English is an official language

[9] Observations conducted in October 2011.

[10] Ethnologue (2019) ranks it at 218 among 246 polities for linguistic diversity.

[11] During observations made in the company of an interpreter in Nuku'alofa in 2014.3.10–13, the only English appeared to be integrated loans such as *polisi*.

[12] Supreme Court advocate interviewed in Nuku'alofa, 2014.3.11.

[13] Nuku'alofa Court of Appeal, p.o. 2014.3.13.

"until otherwise provided by law" and monopolises the legal domain. 70 years ago the acting Secretary of Justice ordered court use of the national language (*The Straits Times* 1950.9.09), but it still takes a back seat to English, with regional languages hardly onboard at all. Benitez (2009) nonetheless notes a rising tendency for judges in Manila to dispense with interpreters when questioning witnesses in Filipino, and Cebuano appears to have currency in some regional courts.[14] Local languages are also used routinely for the minor disputes adjudicated in the *punong barangay* customary courts (Martin 2012:11).

A noteworthy attempt to bring use of the national language in line with its status took place from 2007 to 2012 in Bulacan, a heavily Tagalog-speaking district, where it was admitted in three courts focusing on drugs cases and other matters where few defendants were fluent in English and key legislation was available in Filipino.[15] One judge noted participants and public alike becoming more attentive in court (Reyes 2009.8.20). At one point six regional trial courts were operating in the language, but use in civil cases was short-lived because of heavy reliance on authorities available only in English, while resistance continued from some judges and administrators – including English-trained stenographers who felt they had not been given sufficient support.[16] In 2010 a Supreme Court circular made Filipino optional (Martin 2012:8), and after the 2012 demise of Ma. Resurreccion Ramos-Buhat, one of the judges driving the experiment, all courts reverted to English.[17]

In Mauritius, another mixed law system, testimony in French is directly admissible. Just as Tongan-medium police courts and Philippines customary courts are not really examples of vernacularised English law, however, French is used less to convey common law in Mauritian courts than to convey surviving elements of French law. District Court judges cite precedents from France untranslated, as in *Police v René Louis Josian* (2011). The fact that most lawyers are bilingual obviates the need to translate French law into English – but also the need to translate English enactments into French.[18]

There is better evidence of legally backed use of vernaculars in East Africa, at least at lower court level. In Kenya Kiswahili is the "national language" and understood by some 65% (Webb and Kembo-Sure 2000:48), though the L1 of only 130,000 (Ethnologue 2019), while English is the "official language" (Ajulo 1997:34). Under the 1967 Civil Procedure Act Kiswahili is authorised for the lower courts, where it plays an important role in oral discourse, but records are in English, while English dominates higher courts, a split reflected in courthouse signage (Powell and David 2011:232). In law offices it is common for depositions to be

[14] During a case observed in Cebu in 2009 the local language was used without interpreting for witness examinations and when the recorder, who was filling in for a colleague, struggled to translate this into English for the record she received enthusiastic suggestions from the public gallery.

[15] Judge Herminia Pasamba, interviewed in Bulacan 2009.11.26.

[16] During a visit to Bulacan in 2009 I interviewed officials, mostly native Tagalog speakers, who were on strike and demanding better allowances to retrain in the national language.

[17] Isabel Martin, Ateneo de Manila University, p.c., 2016.3.28.

[18] R.P. Gunputh, University of Mauritius, p.c. 2013.5.29.

heard in African languages but written down in English (ibid, 2011:232). In neighbouring Tanzania Kiswahili is the first official language (Ajulo 1997:32), used for parliamentary proceedings (Rwezaura 1994:112), the Government Gazette and some enactments, including the 2000 Land Act, the Primary Courts Civil and Criminal Procedure Rules, and the Objects and Reasons appendices to legislation (ibid:112–113). Under s.13(1) of the Magistrates Courts Act it is to be used for lower court proceedings (ibid:114). But records, written submissions and judgments in District Courts and above must be in English, the second official language (ibid:114). A 1985 amendment of the Court of Appeal Rules allows Kiswahili for witness examinations in the High Court (ibid:115).

In Hong Kong there has been a steady shift towards Chinese in the lower courts since the first trial in it in 1995 (*Sun Er-Jo v Lo* Ching). While the 1974 Official Languages Ordinance made Chinese an official language after a decade of anticolonial student activity (Cheung 1997:318), the main instigator of language reform was the 1997 handover. In 1989 LegCo started publishing laws bilingually (Sharma 1997.6.06) and in 1995 an amendment to the 1974 Ordinance enabled courts to use either language (Hong Kong e-Legislation 2017). By 2006 Chinese trials outnumbered English (Leung 2012:241). They accounted for 82% of Magistrates Court cases in 2011 (Leung 2013).

It makes communicative sense to use vernaculars in lower courts because defendants, witnesses and the public there tend to be less familiar with elite languages than those attending higher proceedings. Since most cases begin and end at lower levels the use of vernaculars there makes political sense too since it enables the public to see language policy in action. And vernaculars at this level make legal sense inasmuch as there are fewer jurisprudence complexities. From the steady decline of Afrikaans in South African courts we also have evidence that languages may retreat toward oral functions as they get abandoned in jurisprudence.[19]

10.3.6 Local Languages in Higher Courts

Several South Asian jurisdictions give official recognitian to local languages at both lower and higher levels. Under the Indian Constitution (Government of India 2012) the language of the Union is Hindi (Art. 343(1–3)) and states are permitted to use regional languages officially (Art. 345). But communication between states and the Union must be in "the official language" (Art. 346), which may be considered by default to be English as the same article provides additionally for Hindi among states agreeing to its use. English is authorised for the Supreme Court and High Court until parliament provides otherwise, but with presidential approval proceedings in the latter may be in Hindi or an official state language (Art. 348). The Civil

[19] According to former Supreme Ct. judge Louis Harms, apex judgments are no longer made in the language and it is a waste of time to present cases in it except in some lower courts, p.c. 2013.5.27.

Procedure Code (s.137) and Criminal Procedure Code (s.558) allow states to determine the language(s) of the court (Jayaram and Rajyashree 2000:138–139). Calls for Hindi in the Supreme Court typically raise fears outside the Hindi belt about prior proceedings conducted in English needing to be translated before going to appeal (SARI 2000). *High Court of Uttarakhand* (2010) upheld use of Hindi for higher court judgments so long as English translations are supplied, but no obligation was found to translate English court records, notwithstanding obligations implied in the Right to Information Act for public officers to supply information in languages of wider communication. The Law Commission of India (2008) continues to rejected proposals to make Hindi the language of the apex court, referring among other factors to poor proficiency among lawyers in some states (ibid:20), the historical position of legal English (ibid:36), and unfamiliarity with legal Hindi even among Hindi speakers (ibid:36). In 2016 the Chief Justice instructed a District Court judge to use English in the Supreme Court, citing Article 348 read together with Order VIII of the Rules of Court and the Supreme Court of India Handbook on Practice and Procedure and Office Procedure (*Firstpost* 2018.11.02).

In Pakistan, Constitutional Article 251 declares Urdu the "National language", with English retained for official purposes "until arrangements are made for its replacement by Urdu", and provincial assemblies empowered to use regional languages (Government of Pakistan 1973). Supreme Court judgments are also in English (Pakistan Supreme Court 2013) but Supreme Court Rules allow for documentary submissions (Ord. V, 26) or accompanying translations (Ord VII, 2) in Urdu (ibid). As in India the lower courts are the main forum for languages other than English, but Urdu may be used in High Court (Shadab, in Powell 2008:136), especially for submission of evidence, although oral testimony is commonly translated into English for the record.[20] There are reports of the use of Sindhi in Karachi (Rahman 2005.10.08), Urdu in Balochistan (ibid) and Pashto in North West Frontier (Siddique 2012a:21, b), and a survey of District Court litigants found Urdu used in some proceedings in Lahore (Siddique 2010:49–56).

Technically, Sri Lanka demarcates lower court proceedings in local languages (Sinhala or Tamil, depending on the district) from higher court proceedings in English, a policy that emerged from a civil war triggered by nationalism in favour of Sinhala (which was substituted for English by the 1956 Official Language Act and 1961 Language of the Courts Act), and partly rolled back with the inclusion of Tamil (the 1966 Tamil Language (Special Provisions) Regulation and the 1972 Constitution) and retention of English as a "link language" and for records (Art.18, 1978 Constitution) and superior court proceedings. However, by categorising the High Court as a subordinate court the system supports sophisticated legal discourse in Sinhala.[21]

[20] Mhd Arif Sayeed, Pakistani attorney, p.c. 2012.10.10.

[21] Fathima Marikkar, Sri Lankan attorney, interviewed Tokyo, 2014.12.12.

10.3.7 Local Languages at Appeal and Apex Levels

There are at least four common law jurisdictions where official policy supports a language other than English at the highest levels, although in the case of Ireland (Sect. 10.3.3) there is limited implementation of policy in practice.

Myanmar is something of an outlier among common law jursidcitions as it is the only former British territory that never joined the Commonwealth and after 1962 became relatively isolated internationally while undergoing political reforms that included comprehensive intervention in a legal profession that was engaged in civil disobedience.[22] Despite the Union continuing to identify as a member of the common law family (Tun Shin 2013.2.10) and retaining English as an official courtroom medium, Myanmar, an important lingua franca at the heart of a postcolonial centralising agenda, is used for all proceedings.[23] Moreover the need to consult authorities recorded in English has fallen with a decline in the citation of precedents (Cheesman 2011:815).

Neighbouring Bangladesh has closer links with Commonwealth law and when it comes to vernacularisation enjoys certain advantages over the rest of the Subcontinent since the great majority have the same first language (Kabir 2012.2.20). Article 3 of the 1972 Constitution makes Bangla the "state language", and in 1975 the first president executed an order declaring English a foreign language (ibid). However, the 1898 Criminal Procedure Code (s.6) requires charges be in English or "the language of the court" while providing for translation of evidence for an accused who does not understand English (Laws of Bangladesh 2014). Under the 1908 Code of Civil Procedure (s.137) the High Court may require evidence to be recorded in English and the government is empowered to decide what shall be the language of the subordinate courts (ibid). The 1983 Chief Justice Commission came out unequivocally against introducing Bangla at apex level (Kabir 2012.2.20), and no recent legislation clarifies the current position on court medium.[24]

Observations conducted for this study[25] found extensive oral use of Bangla even in the Supreme Court's Appellate Division, with lawyers often beginning submissions in English before being questioned by judges in Bangla and exchanges then proceeding bilingually. In the High Court, Bangla is admissible alongside English (*Hashma Ullah v Azmiri Bibi* (1991), in Ferdousi 2009:66), and in cases observed in Dhaka in 2014 it was used orally rather more frequently than English, especially by the Bench. Bangla has been used extensively in the Magistrates Courts since the late 1980s, when 18 submissions in English were rejected on the grounds that they contravened the Language Implementation Act (Kabir 2012.2.20).

In Canada, bilingualism is enforced officially right up to Supreme Court level with the publication of apex decisions in both English and French (Canadian

---

[22] Myint Zan, Multimedia University, Melaka, interviewed 2013.3.13.

[23] Interviews at Burma Lawyers Council, Bangkok, 2005.10.02.

[24] Interview with practising lawyers at Dhaka International University, 2014.4.08.

[25] Dhaka, p.o. 2014.4.6–9.

Supreme Court 2012). However, neither pressure from the Quebec bar (Gardiner 2011) nor Yvon Godin's 2010 parliamentary bill (Cleroux 2011) has made bilingualism obligatory for judges (Levesque 2012), and in practice bilingualism decreases as distance from Quebec grows, with Federal law literature in French often unavailable in Alberta (ibid). Counsel have argued that cases reported in French cannot be reviewed, and one judgment in French was summarised as merely as "other language spoken (ibid). Even Ontarian courts have been known to classify French as a "foreign language" and to prioritise English translations over original French texts (ibid).

We may conclude that jurisdictions practising English-based law at the highest levels in a language other than English form a rather exclusive club. With the majority opinions in the *Lina Joy* case in Malay, and some use of the language at Court of Appeal and even Federal Court level, Malaysia may now be considered a member.

10.4 Initiatives in Corpus Planning

While few Malaysian informants other than those involved in legal translation referred to syntactical, grammatical or discursive differences between English and Malay when seeking to explain limits to vernacularisation, almost everyone had something to say about legal terminology. Some called Malay terms inaccurate, and many concluded that there were not enough of them. In the case of Subsaharan Africa, Moeketsi (1999) reports terms as basic as 'plead' or 'guilty' to be absent from many vernaculars, and Harms (2012) believes no autochthenous language there possesses adequate legal terminology, the main reason for minimal use in legal discourse.[26] In this section we will look at initiatives to generate vernacular legal terms and also to produce corpora of vernacular legal texts.

10.4.1 Generating Legal Terms

Several Asian polities have pioneered innovation in the legal lexicon of national or regional languages. In Myanmar a Translation Committee for Technical Terms was established in the 1960s.[27] In Sri Lanka the lack of vernacular texts was identified as a brake on national development in the early 1950s (Gunasekera, in Coperahewa 2011:214) and by 1955 43,000 Sinhala and 48,000 Tamil terms and phrases for public sector use had been published (Coperahewa 2011:219). For law, the Ministry of Justice's Legal Drafting Department was tasked with creating a Sinhala, and later

[26] I once asked a court interpreter in Accra how he translated "Do you plead guilty or not guilty?" into some of the nine languages he claimed to handle and he replied: "Did you do it?".

[27] Myint Zan, op.cit.

a Tamil, legal lexicon using neologisms, many based on Sanskrit elements, and modifications of English and Dutch loans.[28]

In India a Language Cell is embedded into each state administration to deal with lexicography, standardisation and publishing, and in some states (e.g. Karnataka, Tamil Nadu and Maharashtra) these cells are in charge of legislative translation and drafting, while others (Kerala and Orissa) leave this task to state legal departments (Jayaram and Rajyashree 2000:67).

One of the most ambitious lexical innovation projects was carried out in Hong Kong. Despite the fact that "[m]any English terms simply do not exist in the Chinese language" (Cheung 1997:330), a 30,000-word corpus of English-Chinese legal terms was published in 1995 (Hong Kong Dept. of Justice, 2007).

Beyond Asia, as early as 1963 Tanzania's Ministry of Justice established a Law Dictionary Committee to produce Kiswahili legal terms (Rwezaura 1994:112). Lack of lexis is considered the biggest hurdle for translators at the Tongan Attorney-General's Chambers, which has to produce texts of new laws in Tongan before they can be ratified.[29] The importance of English as a source language can be seen in the proliferation of modified loans, such as *laiseni* (licence), *kapineti* (cabinet) and *komiti* in the 2002 Aquaculture Act or *konisitutone*, *lesisita* (register) and *minisitā* in the 2014 Education Act, but English loans are not noticeably more prominent than in legal Malay, and high-frequency criminal terms – e.g. *faka'iloa* (defendant), *halaia/tonuhia* (guilty/not guilty), *malu'i* (probation) – of native origin are comprehensive.[30] This may be because Tongan is the official medium of proceedings in the *Fakamaau'anga Polisi* (Police/Magistrates Courts).

10.4.2 Standardising, Authorising and Inculcating Legal Terms

As we have seen with Malaysia, new terminology is of limited effect unless measures are taken to encourage practitioners to use it. Although acquisition planning plays an important role, corpus planners also need to address doubts about disputed meanings and alternative terms.

While the development of French terms for common law has benefited from the establishment of the Centre de Traduction et de Documentation Juridique in 1981 (University of Ottawa 2012), since 2009 Canada has seen collaboration among the Centre, McGill University, Moncton University and Manitoba's Institut Joseph-Dubuc to enhance standardisation (Language Portal of Canada 2013). In India, on the other hand, the funding and time allocated to innovating state languages for legal use has not matched the enormity of the task (Jayaram and Rajyashree

[28] Marikkar, op. cit.

[29] James Lutui, interviewed at Attorney-General's Office, Nuku'alofa, 2014.3.10.

[30] Lutui, op.cit.

2000:132), even though institutional infrastructure has been in place for decades (ibid:27). Moreover the reach of vernacular legal corpora is limited because of problems with distribution (ibid:135–136).

Indian lawyers also express doubts about the quality of texts translated from English (Jayaram and Rajyashree 2000:179), while in Sri Lanka, Perry (2000) has reported confusion among advocates over the meaning of neologisms in Sinhala, even though texts in it are regarded as the authentic versions.[31] In Bangladesh one commercial lawyer reported a lack of basic high-frequency business law terms in the vernacular, such as 'holding over' and 'passing out', but his colleague was quick to point out that it wasn't worth coming up with Bangla alternatives unless they were more transparent than what they replaced.[32] Nahid Ferdousi, a Dhaka academic who sat on the Bench as an assistant judge, concedes that the task of translating terms of art is daunting but urges systematic collaboration between lawyers and linguists so that practitioners are consistent (Ferdousi 2015.2.24). Even when vernacular terms are widely known, advocates may switch to English for professional or pragmatic reasons. During sessions in the lower courts, which generally favour Bangla, Ferdousi found a preference for 'law' over *āina*, 'justice' over *n'yāẏabicāra* and 'court' over *ādalāta*.[33]

10.4.3 Generating Legal Texts

Vernacular legislation, judgments and academics texts offer an opportunity not only to enhance public accessibility but also to take vernacularisation beyond straightforward oral proceedings to more complex jurisprudence. In the case of medieval England the Chancery, which received petitions from around the country and applied equitable principles where the common law proved inadequate, appears to have played a key role in standardising and spreading legal English, and there is evidence that the courts of Equity were using the vernacular as early as the 1420s (Fisher 1977:888). This may, however, have been driven less by a coordinated language policy than a pragmatic approach whereby Chancery clerks responded to the petitions in the language in which they were written (Dodd 2011:263–264). In current postcolonial contexts, however, it is unlikely that vernacular legal corpora will emerge without centralised planning.

In tandem with lexical innovation, Hong Kong produced a large body of legal texts in Chinese before the return of sovereignty, with the Bilingual Laws Advisory Committee translating 600 principle ordinances and 100 pieces of subsidiary legislation between 1988 and 1997 (Candlin and Bhatia 1998:9). Since 1997 there have been over 200 Court of Appeal judgments in Chinese, but all decisions of the Court

[31] Marikkar, op.cit.

[32] Interviewed at Dhaka International University, 2014.4.08.

[33] Interviewed at the University of Malaya, 2013.11.21.

of Final Appeal, which includes 17 non-permanent expatriate judges, are published in English (Hong Kong Judiciary 2013).

In Tonga the impetus for generating vernacular texts – again mainly by translating from English – comes from the status of Tongan as the medium of parliamentary debate. All new laws are gazetted bilingually (Crown Law Tonga 2013), with most Tongan versions 20% longer than the English because of the need to unpack English legal concepts.[34] But vernacularisation doesn't extend to case law. The higher courts function in English and the few lower court decisions that are published (e.g. in the *Annual Report of the Attorney General*) are also in English. Even in Canada, despite all legislation being bilingual, most English-medium judgments remain untranslated.[35]

Myanmar has seen a marked shift to the vernacular for both case law and legislation since independence. In the 1948 *Burma Law Reports* only three of 117 decisions were in Burmese (Myint Zan 2004:405), but the language accounted for 44 of the 47 judgments published by the Chief Court in 1969 and since 1970 it has monopolised apex court judgments (ibid:396). Even the titles of those few English cases that are cited are translated into Burmese.[36] The Burma Codes, dating from the colonial era, have now been extensively translated, and new laws, including those with important international dimensions such as the 2019 Trademark Law, are published in Burmese, but English remains an official medium of law and since 1988 the Attorney General's Office has published English versions of laws (Myanmar Law Library 2001). The 2012 Labour Disputes Settlements Act and 2014 National Education Law, for example, have bilingual texts.

South Asia is generating a growing body of legislation in a number of languages. The Indian Ministry of Law's Official Languages Wing is charged with translating laws into Hindi, and 92 national enactments are also gazetted in Punjabi translation, 91 in Telugu, 70 in Tamil, 33 in Urdu and 16 in Marathi (Government of India 2012). But a researcher for an advocate in the Supreme Court found none of some 200 environmental protection laws to be available in anything except English (Kashyap 2016.8.26). The 1972 constitution of Bangladesh was drafted in Bangla and prevails over any English translation (Art. 153 (3)). The Law Commission is charged with translating English-language enactments,[37] and the 1987 Bangla Promulgation Act requires bilingual drafting. But the current legislative corpus falls far short of being bilingual. The Ministry of Law publishes enactments, orders and extracts going back to 1836 and all are in English until 1980, with fewer than 100 of some 750 English Acts translated into Bangla (Shahiduzzaman, in Kabir 2012.2.20). Full texts of more recent laws are published and since 1986 all are in Bangla (Laws of Bangladesh 2014), but the Ministry's drafting wing does not necessarily produce

[34] James Lutui, op. cit.

[35] Susan Lavender, Hong Kong-based Quebec solicitor, p.c. 2013.7.14.

[36] Myint Zan, op.cit.

[37] Md. Azher Ali Talukder, interviewed at the Development Organisation for the Rural Poor, Dhaka, 2010.11.24.

English versions, so unauthorised translations abound and some, such as the Arbitration Act (regulating a field dominated by English), are described as error-ridden.[38] In Sri Lanka, constitutional Article 23 requires new legislation be published in the two official languages and translated into English, but the majority of older laws remain in English only[39] and the language continues to be used for appeal (Sri Lanka Court of Appeal 2012) and apex (Sri Lanka Supreme Court 2012) decisions.

Through much of the bilingual common law world, vernacular legal corpora are much smaller than their English counterparts and typically focus on laws used most often in the lower courts. Philippines judge Cesar-Peralejo produced Filipino versions of the Civil Code, Penal Code, Family Code, Criminal Rules and Procedures and Rules of Evidence (Gonzalez 1996:230), and the availability of narcotics legislation in the national language supported its use in Bulacan between 2007 and 2012, but the legal corpus remains overwhelmingly in English. Even *Shariah*, which is particularly important in the south of the country, has been encoded in English (Gonzalez 1996: 232). Few judgments are written in Filipino and those that are typically arise during National Language Week (ibid:230) or in politically charged cases, such as a high profile libel appeal drafted in Filipino that brought a 53-page decision in the same language from Jose dela Rama (Reyes 2007.8.22). Pakistan has an Urdu version of the constitution (Pakistan National Assembly 2012), but aside from irregular, unreliable and out-of-date translations, many of them unofficial, enactments are in English (Siddique 2010:48), including those regulating Muslim affairs such as the 1997 Zakat and Ushr (Amendment) Act.

10.4.4 Authenticity and Authority

Bilingual sets of laws inevitably run the risk of semantic and pragmatic disparity. The Law Commission of India (2008: 444) has warned of an increased risk of conflicts as more Hindi texts appear, even though, at least at Union level, laws are supposed to be drafted in it as well as English (Francavilla 2018:436).

To avoid conflict, many jurisdictions apply an *a priori* presumption of the authenticity of one language, as Malaysia does for English texts before 1967 and Malay texts thereafter. In Myanmar, the Burmese text prevails (Myanmar Law Library 2001). In Sri Lanka, constitutional Article 18, which makes Sinhala "The Official Language",[40] and Article 23(1), which requires legislation be in Sinhala and Tamil along with an English "translation", were interpreted in *Thilanga Sumathipala* (2004) as giving the Sinhala wording of the Criminal Procedure Code priority over the English. Under the Kenyan constitution (s.120(20)) differences between English

[38] Md Mashur Rahman, Dhaka advocate, interviewed 2014.4.10.

[39] Faazil Sheriff, Sri Lankan attorney, interviewed Colombo, 2014.4.07.

[40] Tamil is "also (…) an official language" and English "the link language".

and Kiswahili statutes are to be resolved in favour of the text signed by the President – which in practice seems to be the English one[41] since moves to draft legislation in the latter have failed, despite it being a language of parliamentary debate (Mazrui and Mazrui 1995:18). In Tonga, a conflict between Tongan and English legislative texts arose in the case of *Police v Sikuea* (1996, in PacLII, 2012), and to protect the accused the courts have ruled in favour of Tongan for criminal law, while favouring English for civil matters.[42]

While the prioritisation of one language may curtail disputes, as a status-planning stance it is political rather than technical in nature and does not necessarily ensure adherence to legislative intent. One Sri Lankan corporate lawyer[43] found differences between the English and Sinhala versions of the 2007 Companies Act and attributed these to translation errors in the latter, yet advised his client against raising the matter in court as a presumption in favour of Sinhala would apply.

An alternative approach, adopted by Canada and Hong Kong (and also the EU, where laws are published in 24 languages), is to consider all official languages as authentic and resolve textual differences case-by-case. Canada's pursuit of 'shared meaning' tends to favour the text that is plainer and less ambiguous (Solan 2019). Following guidelines in the 1980 Vienna Convention of the Law of Treaties (ibid: 325), Hong Kong requires differences between Chinese and English be resolved by considering context and legislative intent, with ordinary meanings carrying more weight than technical meanings and irreconcilable differences decided in favour of the defendant (Interpretation and General Clauses Ordinance, s.10B). While co-authenticity may disadvantage those who have relied on the dispreferred text, and the search for legislative intent or shared meaning may involve an element of guesswork, it should be noted that between 1960 and 2010 only 246 of 8716 EU judgments were disputed on linguistic grounds (Solan 2019).

Some of the most intense disputes over terminology in bilingual legal systems revolve around commonplace rather than legal lexis. We have already seen how in Malaysia a potential discrepancy between 'parent' and *ibubapa* in the English and Malay versions of the constitution has fomented societal controversy over religious conversion (Chap. 4), and in the heated atmosphere of Hong Kong's transition from British to Chinese sovereignty a difference between 'addition to the plan' and 增建工程 ('additional construction') in the Food Business By-law fuelled allegations of a shopkeeper being guilty in English but innocent in Chinese (Sharma 1997). Overturning a magistrate's conviction, Justice Yeung Chun-kuen ruled in in *R. v Tam Yuk-ha* that placing metal racks outside a shop was acceptable under the Chinese text, which he felt entitled to consult in view of the principle of co-authenticity. However, Yeung's ruling was reversed by Court of Appeal judges, who found insufficient disparity between the English and Chinese to rule in favour of the defendant on the grounds of ambiguity. For Ng (2009: 246), however, the ruling

[41] Thomas Maosa, Kenyan-based Tanzanian advocate, p.c. 2013.6.07.

[42] James Lutui, op.cit.

[43] Interviewed in Colombo, 2014.4.06.

amounted to judges favouring the less specific English text over the more specific Chinese one.

As in Malaysia, Tonga and many other Commonwealth jurisdictions, Hong Kong administrators prefer to draft in English, and so most Chinese texts are translations and often somewhat anglicised (Ng 2009:73). This is indicative of a persistent diglossic relationship between English and other legal languages that is found throughout the common law world and underpinned by legal education.

10.5 Non-English Legal Education

Alber and Palermo (2012:295) see bilingual legal training as the key component supporting German-Italian civil law in South Tyrol, but in the common law world, even where vernacularisation is officially promoted, bilingual practice tends to depend upon the general bilingualism of individual professionals rather than bilingual education. Indeed it is the fact that most lawyers speak at least two languages that leads Francavilla (2018: 444) to describe Indian law as "not really monolingual". In officially monolingual systems practitioners may only need local languages in informal contexts, but in officially bilingual ones where formal argument is required, they often have to make do with incomplete lists of terminology and improvisation. Only in South Asia is there evidence of vernacular education leading to legal qualification, and even there English is in a diglossic relationship with the other media of instruction.

10.5.1 Monolingual Legal Education in Multilingual Societies

Despite its extensive oral use for lower court proceedings and also for some enactments, Kiswahili plays an insignificant part in Tanzanian legal training, and few lawyers are even aware of the vernacular legal terminology that has been developed.[44] Two decades ago Mazrui and Mazrui (1998:111) reported societal alienation from the judicial system in neighbouring Kenya, "based on the assumption that many of the most senior judges might be completely illiterate in Kiswahili". Nowadays the majority of lawyers study locally, rather than in London, but only English is used in the three government universities accredited to teach law.[45]

In the Philippines legal education is similarly monolingual, even though the country had a history of legal bilingualism because of its absorption of both Spanish and American law. According to Gonzalez (1996:232), as recently as the Pacific War most practitioners were bilingual, and the Japanese occupiers seem to have

[44] Maosa, op.cit.

[45] Wycliffe Kutete, Kenyan lawyer, p.c. 2013.11.13.

supported the continued use of Spanish (*The Syonan Times* 1942.9.04). Lawyers no longer need Spanish, and they also have little need of Filipino. The exclusive use of English for bar exams has been blamed for the low pass rate in general and virtual exclusion of candidates from poor and rural backgrounds in particular (Gonzalez 1996:231). In a 2003 Public Opinion Survey 46% of court participants reported difficulty in understanding English proceedings (Martin 2012:6), but calls for compulsory units in Filipino for law students remain unanswered (*Philippine Daily Enquirer* 2009.8.25) and no law school runs courses on Filipino terminology (Reyes 2009.8.20).

In Hong Kong, a Law Society president emphasised the importance of Chinese proficiency – including in Putonghua – a decade ago (Yih 2009), yet despite extensive corpus planning to support Chinese, and despite ethnic Chinese now comprising 82% of the bar (Law Society of Hong Kong 2013), legal education remains entirely in English. Would-be solicitors sitting for the Postgraduate Certificate in Laws (PCLL) must have IELTS band 7 proficiency in English, but there is no requirement for Chinese (Hong Kong University PCLL 2012). For judges, summer schools on the writing of judgments in Chinese have been held at Tsinghua University since 1999 (Ng 2009:248).

In some jurisdictions the problem is not merely that legal education is unavailable in a local language, but that it is not available locally at all. For Tongans the nearest law faculty is at the University of the South Pacific in Vanuatu, with Australia and New Zealand also popular for legal studies.[46] In Brunei, while *Shariah* law is offered at Sultan Sharif Ali Islamic University, the nearest colleges for lawyers wishing to practise common law are in West Malaysia and Singapore, with many preferring to study in the UK or Australia. Qualification in one of these countries is a requirement for admission in Brunei (1983 Legal Profession Act, s.3). Calls for a law faculty at Universiti Brunei Darussalam a decade ago (Tan 2009.9.21) remain unheeded.

10.5.2 Classroom Support for Local Languages

In Chap. 5 we saw how some Malaysian law lecturers required to teach in English employ code-switching as a pedagogical strategy. The language of written texts need not dictate the medium in which they are discussed and classroom code-switching seems to have a long pedigree. At the English medieval Inns of Court, Latin legal texts were explained to pupils through oral French (Baker 2007:11), possibly because it became the default language of pleading in court and perhaps also because it was somewhat closer to English than Latin. The *hospiciae cancellarie*, or Inns where the Chancery trained lawyers and clerks, increasingly taught in English from the fifteenth century, thereby developing a prestigious trilingual sys-

[46] Senior Crown Counsel Sione Sisifa, interviewed Nuku'alofa in 2014.3.12.

tem of education independent of the Latin-based universities and ecclesiastical colleges (Fisher 1996:57–59).

Where code-switching is tolerated within the formal constraints of courtrooms it seems likely that it will also be found in the less formal atmosphere of law classrooms. Several lecturers at Dhaka International University, for example, where teaching and exams are formally in English, commented on the inevitability of extensive oral explanation in Bangla to help students understand legal texts. Some lecturers also allow students to answer exams in Bangla, even though the questions are written in English and most students aim for the English-medium bar exam.[47]

In Myanmar, English plays a significant, if mystifying, role in legal education. The courts operate almost entirely in Burmese, and no overseas-trained lawyer has sat on the Supreme Court since 1998 (Myint Zan 2004:396), but the redistribution of Anglo-Indian statutes to the courts in the 1970s seems to have ushered in the return of law-teaching in English, which had been the medium of all qualifying courses and exams until the mid-1960s. From the 1990s bar admission exams were again set in English (Myint Zan 2008:91). But the extent to which *instruction* is in English is debatable as there are reports of extensive use of oral and even written Burmese as coping mechanisms for students.[48]

In some cases students themselves organise language support. We have already seen that many Malaysian law students form Facebook-based study groups in which discussions may be in Malay as well as English. At Sri Lanka Law College the student union helps coordinate the distribution of lecture notes and these are often in Sinhala, even for courses taught in English.[49]

10.5.3 Partial Study in Languages Other than English

In several common law and mixed law systems students may in theory qualify as lawyers by studying in a local language. In most cases, however, the practical possibilities of doing so are limited.

Bijural courses in Canada date back to the University of Ottawa's establishment of parallel Civil Law and Common Law schools in 1957 (University of Ottawa 2012), with bilingual courses starting in 1977 (ibid). L'Institut Joseph-Dubuc offers common law in French and civil law in English. McGill University in Montreal holds summer schools in bilingual legal drafting (Blais 2009) and has run a bijural and bilingual LLB for several decades, and in Quebec at least, common law can be studied predominantly in French. But because of the preponderance of cases and legal materials available only in English, would-be attorneys cannot bypass the lan-

[47] Interviews in Dhaka, 2014.4.11.

[48] Myint Zan, op. cit.

[49] Faazil Sheriff, op. cit.

guage.[50] Although Canadian apex judgments are published bilingually, failure to require bilingualism of judges and lawyers implies a limit to fully bilingual proceedings.

In South Africa's mixed law system, 'common law' traditionally refers to Dutch-Roman law going back before the arrival of the British. The establishment of Stellenbosch University in 1916 not only saw a more scientific approach to law teaching but also a revival of Afrikaans-medium instruction, and the law faculty set up there in 1921 remains one of five law schools catering primarily to Afrikaans speakers (Kaburise 2001: 364–365). In theory a lawyer could qualify without taking English-medium courses, but former Supreme Court Judge Louis Harms[51] and the University of Pretoria's Koos Malan[52] concur that this is barely plausible, given that little need has been seen to translate English enactments and cases as all lawyers can function in English. Indeed most law faculties require English certification from prospective entrants (Kaburise 2001: 366). As for autochthenous African languages, according to Harms (2012), no South African law school teaches in them, a situation that holds good for the whole continent south of the Sahara.

For a more bilingual model we should consider Mauritius, where the local LLB has entry requirements and compulsory courses in both languages (Gunputh 2013:62) since French-based laws, including the *Code Civil*, *Code de Commerce* and *Droit Pénal*, operate in tandem with newer enactments and procedural common law in English (University of Mauritius 2013). Notaries tend to favour French for private agreements and court proceedings tend to be in English, but the labour division is not clear-cut. However Mauritian legal education constitutes an example of bilingual preparation for a bijural system, rather than provision for studying common law in a language other than English. Indeed one local law academic sees jurists' bilingual training as a reason for not translating English law into French, or French law into English.[53]

In Pakistan it has been possible to obtain a law degree and bar admission by studying in Urdu, but a director of law programmes for one of the country's leading private school networks[54] describes employment prospects for Urdu-educated lawyers as "very limited", and there now seems to be a move back toward English. While provisions about medium of instruction had been deleted from the 1978 Bar Council Legal Education Rules, Rule 9 (as at 2015) clearly states that LLB courses must be taught in English. Since 2018 the Law Admission Test must be passed in order to enter an LLB programme: essays and personal statements may be submitted in either Urdu or English, and there is a set of multiple choice questions in both languages; but the questions in English carry twice as many marks (Higher Education Commission 2018). It is no longer the case, however, that those admitted to the bar

[50] Lavender, op.cit.

[51] Harms, p.c. 2015.3.01.

[52] Malan, p.c. 2014.11.07.

[53] Gunputh, op.cit.

[54] Muneeba Anis, p.c. 2014.8.26.

in England are automatically eligible for the local bar (1973 Legal Practitioners and Bar Councils Act, s. 25, as at 2005). In addition to the medium of instruction and examination, the quality of legal education itself is frequently criticised. One Lahore advocate (Khan 2018.1.20) claims law students merely need memorise 10–15 questions per paper to pass.

10.5.4 Language-Based Class-Division in Legal Education

Elsewhere in South Asia it is still possible for lawyers to qualify through courses and exams in languages other than English, but those who have trained in them face disadvantages compared with those trained in English.

The Indian Bar Council is empowered under the 1961 Advocates Act (s.7) to lay down standards of legal education for the universities, in consultation with state-level bar councils, with 3-year law degrees offered to postgraduates by a large number of universities and 5-year degrees open to candidates without a prior degree at a smaller number of specialised law universities. Three decades ago Chaklader (1990:99) reported that Bangla was permitted as a medium of legal education in West Bengal. While some law departments have their own entrance examinations, since 2008 an increasing number have used the Common Law Admission Test (CLAT), which covers English, general knowledge, mathematics, and legal and logical reasoning (*The Hindu* 2008.1.11). In 2018 a final-year law student filed a petition against Delhi University for holding its law department entrance exam in English only, but sparked discussion about why he stopped short of demanding exams in the regional languages too (Prasad 2018.4.24).

To reduce disparities among states, whose bar councils maintain their own rolls of admitted advocates, from 2010 the Bar Council has obliged those seeking admission to pass the All-India Bar Examination (AIBE), a test that hitherto targeted lawyers aiming to practise in multiple states. It is now offered throughout the country to Indian nationals with a law degree from institutions recognised by the Council and can be sat in eleven languages (Bar Council of India 2010). The careers portal *Sarvgyan* (2019) gives advice in Hindu about the AIBE, but links to guidelines and application forms are in English.

Language policy in Sri Lankan legal education reflects patterns in general schooling there, inasmuch as there has been limited success in encouraging the two main communities to learn each other's language (Lo Bianco 1999:1) or in stemming elite preference for English, which is once again permitted as a state school medium (Gunesekera 2005:16).

Sri Lanka Law College, the profession's gatekeeper, accepts entrants with a 4-year LLB from a recognised Sri Lankan, British or other Commonwealth university for its final examination year, with those lacking an LLB offered 2 years of foundation courses and exams, and in theory all of this is available in Sinhala, Tamil and English.[55] The College also imposes a degree of bilingualism on undergraduate entrants by requiring a general knowledge paper and a language paper be answered in different languages (Sri Lanka Law College 2019). In practice, however, legal study in English is best supported, and some courses may simply be unavailable in Tamil – although one Tamil-speaking graduate conceded that he would have opted for English even if Tamil and Sinhala were better supported as the former would have limited his career geographically and the latter restricted him to subordinate court appearances.[56] Another graduate remembered English being preferred by all those aiming for corporate law or the higher courts.[57] A third, however, recalled seeking out lectures in Sinhala as she felt she already had ample opportunities for English.[58] Even when taking courses in English, some students opt to sit exams in Sinhala as it is generally the language of the lecture notes passed down by seniors.[59] The language of seniors' notes was similarly reported to influence Malaysian students (Chap. 7).

The law institutions that many students pass through before taking their finals at Sri Lanka Law College seem to show a stronger bias toward English. At the University of Colombo, for example, although law courses have been taught in three languages since the 1970s, the university advises that "it is vital students be proficient in English as approximately all legal materials – cases, legislation, textbooks and journals – are available only in English" and obliges LLB students deemed deficient in it to enrol in a language programme (University of Colombo 2019). In 2008 Sri Lanka Law College itself tried to reinstate English as the compulsory medium of exams (*The Island* 2008). It backed down in the wake of student union protests, but renewed its efforts to reinstate it in 2014.[60] For the present at least there is a generation of lawyers who function largely in Sinhala. Many lack proficiency in English and most appear to work in very small practices.[61]

In Bangladesh, eight national universities teach and examine LLB courses bilingually while leaning toward English, with a growing number of private universities teaching[62] and examining[63] in English only. English-medium twinning programmes with overseas institutions are booming, but there are also 46 private law colleges offering 2-year bridging courses in Bangla.[64]

[55] Marikkar, op.cit.

[56] Faazil, op. cit.

[57] Buwaneka Basnayake, Sri Lankan attorney, interviewed Colombo, 2014.4.07.

[58] Marikkar, op.cit.

[59] Basnayake, op.cit.

[60] Basnayake, op.cit.

[61] Personal observations and interviews in Colombo and Negombo, 2014.4.6–12.

[62] Ferdousi, op.cit.

[63] Shameem Haider Patwary, interviewed at Dhaka International University, 2014.4.09.

[64] Patwary, op.cit.

In general, those from the Bangla stream are seen as second-class advocates with few chances to work in superior courts.[65] Exams for subordinate court advocates and magistrates may be sat in either language but those for the High Court are in English only, and steeper bar fees for superior court advocates reinforce this class division.[66]

While the ability of some Asian societies to support vernacular legal education may suggest that Malaysia, with relatively more resources, is falling behind, evidence of language-based class division in South Asian legal professions sheds some light on the reluctance of some Malaysian institutions to abandon English, even where students struggle in it. Although graduates weak in English may have few chances of entering the lucrative corporate world, many lecturers feel the language should be its use enforced to maintain the prestige of the institution and motivate students.

10.6 Common Discourses Surrounding Vernacularisation

We saw in Chap. 6 how the main discourses driving and disseminating language planning in Malaysian law are political and cultural rather than professional or academic, with debates typically revolving around constructions of justice in general and linguistic justice in particular, and with little analysis of communicative needs. Although broader in scope, in this section it will also be shown that politics and culture shape the key discourses on legal vernacularisation in other common law-based systems. While rhetoric and policy may align neatly, many of the discourses within which Malaysian language-in-law policy has been framed have their counterparts further afield.

10.6.1 Common Law and English Language as Inextricably Linked

As in Malaysia, there are sections of the legal profession elsewhere for whom English is crucial to common law reasoning processes. Tom Harper, a Hong Kong expatriate judge, has emphasised English's position as the *source* of the law (in Ng 2009: 230). In opposing an expanded role for Hindi in Indian law, former Karnataka Chief Justice focuses on how English has affected judicial *thinking* there after centuries of use (Law Commission of India 2008:36). As with most arguments about language choice, however, it is difficult to separate technical from cultural motivations. Those who develop high-level skills in a particular language may find it hard to conceive acquiring the same acumen in another, not least when they have few opportunities to witness equivalent reasoning in vernaculars newly introduced into

[65] Interviews at Dhaka International University, 2014.4.09–10.

[66] Patwary, op.cit.

law. The strongest supporters of legal English in Malaysia, Hong Kong, India and elsewhere are typically in senior positions and many write judgments or devise legal arguments in no other language, so what has always been done best in English gets blurred with what can only be done well in English. Even if the next generation have better vernacular skills, many may continue to see English as the quintessential medium of jurisprudence in deference to their anglophone role models.

Going beyond personal limitations, it is of course also entirely possible that English – or rather English legalese, with its wealth of Latin and French expressions – has acquired more efficiency in replicating the relatively context-independent arguments common law strives for than do languages more firmly anchored in local culture, but whether this will continue to be the case depends largely on the extent to which English-educated lawyers are prepared to push against the boundaries of their communicative comfort zones.

Conflating common law with English-medium law may also have political dimensions. Where legal traditions appear threatened, vernacularisation is often distrusted as an instrument of legal transplant, and typically cast as an attack on integrity. While Malaysia's Karpal Singh feared alien legal ideas slipping in with the expansion of legal Malay (Chap. 1), the founder of the Burma Law Council, a body monitoring Myanmar judicial affairs from exile, goes much further in alleging that English was replaced there to undermine a predominantly anglophone and politically hostile legal profession.[67] He also cites examples of the mere use of English implicating those suspected of civil disobedience (Aung Htoo 2011:36). In postcolonial Hong Kong, one reason that Harper, and many of the anglophiles interviewed by Ng (2009), remain defensive of English is a conviction that replacing the language of the law means replacing the legal system itself, and while Ng focuses mainly on senior lawyers who distrust the informality of Cantonese trials from a culturally elitist position, English is also discursively constructed as a symbol of local independence and integrity in contrast to the sociolegal uncertainties of China. Conversely, the lawyers best disposed to the expansion of Chinese are the ones most open to the phasing out of common law, leading Ng (2009:266) to conclude wryly: "If there is one thing that counsel for and against the continued dominance of English agree on it is that the common law in Hong Kong requires English to authenticate its identity".

10.6.2 English as Indispensable for Jurisprudence and Research

We have seen how legal education is the strongest bastion of English in the common law world, dominating public as well as private Malaysian institutions, maintaining a prestige in South Asia that other languages of law cannot compete with, and holding sway even in law schools in Myanmar, where every other legal sector operates

[67] Aung Htoo, p.c. 2013.5.13.

in Burmese. A major reason for this situation is a lack of vernacular jurisprudence or educational materials, but it is reinforced discursively by a widespread assumption that English is a superior medium for argument and research because of its rigour, impartiality or international status.

In the early days of vernacularisation in Hong Kong, Chief Justice Andrew Li slipped references to "vigour" and "respect" into an assertion about the international accessibility of English (in Ng 2009: 267). Press reports supporting the Sri Lankan Chief Justice's call for law exams to be in English linked his remarks to the need for "high standards" (*The Island* 2008). The University of Colombo's law faculty website precedes a statement about the importance of being able to read English materials with one emphasising independent and critical thinking (University of Colombo 2019).

The chair of Lahore's University of Management and Technology, taking a more pragmatic view despite prioritising English himself, warns that the language is no guarantee of rational and systematic thinking, particularly when proficiency in it is in question (Rashid 2016.3.06). This evokes a wider debate about the medium of general education in multilingual societies, where proponents of English argue for its international outreach and opponents doubt its value if students do not fully understand it. In fact debates on the medium of legal education to a large extent track those on general education. Nyati-Ramahobo (2000: 252), for example, begins her description of the dominance of English in Botswanan law by pointing out how it dominates schooling there. Chaklader's (1990: 90–96) account of West Bengal, where Bangla has had a legal presence since the 1830s, shows how its inferior status in law mirrors its consignment to the first 6 years of school before English takes over.

This discursive construction of English as the language of education, and the educated, can be exploited cynically as well as benignly. In Kenya, while Kiswahili is routinely used in court to communicate with those from rural areas or with less schooling, advocates may switch to English to gain advantage over hapless police witnesses who feel they *should* be able to speak it.[68]

10.6.3 Language-Based Labour Division

In many jurisdictions where two or more languages are employed, discussions revolve around their respective roles, rather than around the merits of one displacing, or resisting, the other, and are often framed pragmatically. Thekiso (2001:84), for example, characterises Setswana as "the language of the defendant" and English as "the language of the court" when describing the former's use on charge sheets and the latter's dominance in procedural applications. However, she taps into a more

[68] Wycliffe Kutete, Kenyan lawyer, p.c. 2013.11.13.

ideological dimension when attributing the heavier onus on prosecutors to stick to English to their position as representatives of the state (ibid: 201). A similar linguistic division between professional and lay participants has been reported in Kenya, where advocates routinely break off from questioning witnesses in Kiswahili to discuss legal points with the judge in English (Powell and David 2011). Informants at Tonga's Justice Department also blend pragmatism with ideology in ascribing the prioritisation of the national language when interpreting criminal (though not civil) law texts as a measure to protect weaker participants in the judicial process.[69]

Two pervasive discourses that feed a diglossic relationship between English and other languages are their respective associations with formal and international, or informal and local, functions. Ng (2009) devotes a large part of his thesis on Hong Kong bilingualism to the idea that English and Cantonese occupy different habituses, with the result that trials under the same rules of procedure take very different discursive tacks. Tanzanian court rules more or less allocate Kiswahili to the lower courts and English to higher, but this is somewhat blurred by a broader tendency for advocates to favour Kiswahili in chambers and corridors and English in more formal submissions.[70] Such a formal/informal distinction may be a discursive oversimplification of language use on the ground, however. While Malaysia may go further than many societies in the extent to which it integrates and mixes English across a range of registers, in many common law societies English has been indigenised too much and for too long to characterise it as exonormative or academic.

As for the role of English as a language of international jurisprudence, this is often accepted without reservation or reflection. Rashid (2016.3.06), for example, insists the language be retained for legal education in Pakistan because of the referencing of foreign sources, despite condemning the poor proficiency of students. However Ferdousi (2015.2.24), while also drawing attention to variability in English proficiency, argues that the unavoidable retention of English for international legal communication too easily becomes an excuse to overuse it domestically. She argues that countries smaller than Bangladesh have no difficulty maintaining international communications while using a local language for law. It should be pointed out, however, that none of her examples is a common law jurisdiction.

10.6.4 Enhancing Access to Justice Through Local Languages

Enhancing access to justice in jurisdictions where law has hitherto been decided in a minority language is prima facie a powerful argument for vernacularisation. Resting on the presumption that defendants, litigants and indeed the public ought to be able to understand proceedings, this view is typically woven into pragmatic dis-

[69] Interviews in Nuku'alofa, 2014.3.10.

[70] Maosa, op cit.

courses but punctuated by moral indignation. Hence Martin (2012) questions the overwhelming use of English in Philippines courts, given that nearly half of trial participants report difficulty understanding proceedings, before going on to say how language policy reinforces the marginalisation of the poor. Ferdousi (2015.2.24) highlights the injustice of death penalty Bangladeshi defendants who cannot understand the verdicts of High Court judges without paying for translations, while elsewhere[71] accusing judges of favouring English because they are more interested in impressing their superiors than being understood by those with most at stake. Kashyap (2016.8.26) speculates that the dearth of Indian legislation available in Hindi, let alone regional languages, may be a ploy to limit access to the very people most in need of legal protection. And linking injustice to flawed legal training, Kamal (2015.11.05) contends that poor teaching and the unreliability of law exams in Pakistan are compounded by students' inadequate English.

As in Malaysia, there are also numerous examples of pragmatism being invoked on the side of English. One Quezon City attorney (Monsanto 2009.10.05) argues that since Tagalog is as foreign as English to many Filipinos outside the Tagalog belt, real linguistic reform would involve wading through a cacophony of court records in different dialects. This view was largely shared by the attorneys Martin (2012) surveyed, most foreseeing insurmountable difficulties in using local languages since judges are often from other provinces and if cases go to appeal they will be heard outside the region. Like Malaysian leaders who promote the idealism of law in Malay while accepting the practicality of retaining an important role for English, many language nationalists elsewhere have been prepared to compromise. Bandaranaike, prime mover of the pro-Sinhala policy in the 1950s, is on record warning parliament that the national language was not to be "thrust down the throats of everybody for every purpose" (in Coperahewa 2011:208). Even the Myanmar regime, according to Cheesman (2011:824), showed pragmatism in redistributing Anglo-Indian statutes to the courts in the 1970s.

A somewhat more ideological discourse in favour of English invokes impartiality. This typically does not refer directly to any qualities in the language per se but inevitably entails the use of English through recourse to overseas precedents and expatriate judges. A strong case for the latter is made by the Tongan Attorney-General's Chambers in view of the country's small size. In keeping with his emphasis on maintaining international respect, Hong Kong's Chief Justice Li also supports the retention of foreign judges, while conceding that most of the Bench needs to be bilingual nowadays (Ng 2017.6.1).

In several jurisdictions there is dialogue focused specifically on legal transparency that sees language as only part of the problem. This is well articulated by Siddique 2012a:28, b), who relates an encounter with a litigant unfazed at being told to wait outside the court by her lawyer as she couldn't follow proceedings in either

[71] Nahid Ferdousi, p.c., op. cit.

English or Urdu.[72] While he doesn't dismiss linguistic issues, Siddique (2010.56) lays greater blame on the complexity, corruption and egoism of the legal and judicial profession.

10.6.5 National Language for Postcolonial Restitution, Unity and Dignity

Never easily reduced to pragmatic agendas, language planning is important to any jurisdiction, be it in largely monolingual societies where the priority is translation or in systems where different language speakers routinely appear in court. But vernacularisation as a solution to language disadvantage is essentially a concern for postcolonial societies, where the discourses of restitution, unity and dignity often outweigh practical arguments. Overcoming language disadvantage on the ground may come down to pragmatic day-to-day decisions, but arguments in favour of one language or another frequently brim with rhetoric.

We have seen how the restoration of precolonial sovereignty is a recurrent theme among Malaysian critics of English-medium – and indeed English-based – law. Whether this comes a director of DBP harking back to the Melaka Sultanate (Awang Sariyan 2013) or Islamic NGO ISMA calling for *Syariah* to take over all functions of the law (Zurairi Ar 2013.10.19), the reduction or removal of English is envisaged. We can find this idea of restoring precolonial law through precolonial languages echoed in Ferdousi's (2009:55–60) historical account of judicial use of Bangla, alongside Farsi and later English, but it seems to have more currency in Malaysia than elsewhere.

A discourse more commonly drawn on is postcolonial unity. Martin (2012:5) comments wryly on the minor and mostly oral role the national language plays in Philippines law nearly 25 years after President Cory Aquino described Filipino as an "instrument of unity and peace for national progress". Alongside efficiency, legitimacy, and due process Rwezaura urges Kiswahili, the "the unifying language" (1993:31), to be used more widely in law as part of Tanzanian nation-building. Conversely, in pointing out that Bangla is effectively the medium of the executive and legislative functions of the Bangladeshi state Ferdousi (2015.2.24) impugns the judiciary's sense of national solidarity for failing to follow suit.

Morales-Gálvez's (2017) contention that unequal recognition of languages amounts to a violation of dignity is instantiated in perennial references to respect by Malay language nationalists. Similarly for Bangladesh, where linguistic identity was at the centre of the struggle for independence from Pakistan, Ferdousi (2015.2.24) describes the urgency for using Bangla at all court levels as a matter of

[72] In my own visits to courts in Dhaka I observed that there was very little public seating, reinforcing an assumption that the public were not expected to take part.

not only of equitable justice but also of showing "respect to the martyrs of the Language Movement". We should note that dignity and respect may also be invoked on behalf of English. As we saw in Chap. 5, the possibility, however small, of sending graduates to respected corporate firms is an important motivation for less prestigious Malaysian law schools insisting on English. Along with academic standards, press reports supporting the Sri Lankan Chief Justice's call for law exams in English (*The Island* 2008) refer to restoring "the dignity" of the legal profession (Senaratne 2008.3.30). One corporate law informant there advocates a return to compulsory English in order to rescue non-anglophone, but otherwise capable, lawyers from a life of poorly paid low-prestige work.[73] Turning again to Hong Kong, Ng (2009:267) feels the emphasis by anglophiles like Chief Justice Li on English as a key to international respect is tied up with the SAR's desire to avoid becoming a legal backwater. Respect can also be a money-earner: Hong Kong has successfully marketed itself as a major international arbitral centre (HKIAC 2017), a legal field increasingly dominated by English and common law principles (Bhatia 2011).

10.7 Summary

While systematically planned vernacularisation in common law seems largely to be a postcolonial phenomenon, many of the theoretical and practical issues it entails have recurred historically. These include the framing of legal measures to assuage nationalistic aspirations without undermining political or professional elites; the use of code-mixing and code-switching to compensate for lexical deficits but also to perpetuate cultural advantages; and the relative difficulty of producing written jurisprudence in comparison with lower-court oral discourse.

Far from exhaustive, this review of language policy in common law systems today reveals nearly 20 of them routinely using a language other than English in courtroom discourse, legislation or legal education, with the most widespread practice being oral arguments in subordinate courts and the rarest being legal education and apex level jurisprudence (Fig. 10.1). Significantly, none has entirely abandoned English, and in most it retains a more important role than any vernacular.

Jurisdictions that are more active in using vernaculars in the courts also tend to have taken them further in legislation or education, but there are many discrepancies, such as Myanmar's use of Burmese everywhere except in law exams. Mixed legal systems are difficult to categorise since legal bricolage, and translation of civil law into English, seem more significant than the development of common law in languages other than English. Cautiously, however, it can be said that Malaysia places at the more active end of the vernacularisation spectrum, and may accordingly offer lessons for other jurisdictions.

---

[73] Basnayake, op.cit.

Courtrooms		**Legislation**		**Legal education**	
Routinely in apex ct. & below	Canada Malta Myanmar	All new enactments. Comprehensive translation of English acts	Canada Hong Kong	Qualifying courses & exams in languages other than English.	Bangladesh India Pakistan Sri Lanka
Occasionally in apex ct., routinely in those below.	Bangladesh *Malaysia*	All new enactments. Extensive translation of English acts	Bangladesh *Malaysia* Malta Myanmar Sri Lanka Tonga	Bilingual schooling	Malta Mauritius
Rarely in apex ct., occasionally in higher cts., routinely below.	Ireland S. Africa	Most new enactments. Many English acts translated	India Ireland S. Africa	Law courses in other languages but heavy dependence on English sources	Canada S. Africa
Extensively in High Ct. & below	Sri Lanka	A few enactments translated	Pakistan Philippines Tanzania	Some subjects taught in other languages	*Malaysia*
Some oral & documentary use in higher cts., more extensive use below	Hong Kong India Pakistan	French civil codes, but language hardly used for new enactments	Mauritius	All qualifying courses and exams in English.	Botswana Hong Kong Ireland Kenya Myanmar Philippines Tanzania Wales
Some oral use in higher cts., routine documentary & oral use below	Tanzania	Some legislation but not used for records	Kenya Wales	Law studied in English overseas.	Brunei Tonga
Routine oral use in many lower cts	Philippines Botswana Kenya Mauritius Tonga Wales	No legislation or ct. records.	Botswana		

Fig. 10.1 Non-English proceedings, legislation and education

Cases Cited

Mabo and Others v. Queensland (1992) 175 CLR
S v. Matomela 1998 (1) BCLR 339 (Ck)
Mthetwa vs De Bruyn NO and Another 1998 (1) BCLR 366 (N)
Hernandez v. New York, 500 U.S. 352 (1991)
R v Tam Yuk-ha [1996] HKCFI 445
HKSAR v. Tam Yuk Ha [1997] HKCA 711
Thilanga Sumathipala v. Inspector of Police [2004] 1 Sri L.R

References

Alber, Elisabeth, & Palermo, Francesco. (2012). Creating, studying and experimenting with bilingual law in South Tyrol: Lost in interpretation? In Xabier Arzoz (Ed.), *Bilingual higher education in the legal context* (pp. 287–309). Leiden: Martinus Nijhoff.

Andò, Biagio. (2011). The role of judges in the development of mixed legal systems. The case of Malta. *Journal of Civil Law Studies, 4*(2), 237–260.

Ajulo, Sunday Babalola. (1997). Myth and reality of law, language and international organization in Africa: The case of African economic community. *Journal of African Law, 41*(1), 27–42.

Angermeyer, Philipp Sebastian. (2015). *Speak English or what? Codeswitching and interpreter use in New York City courts*. New York: Oxford University Press.

Aung Htoo. (2011, October). Seeking judicial power: With a special focus on Burma's judiciary. *Centre for comparative and public law occasional paper No. 20*. Faculty of Law, The University of Hong Kong.

Awang bin Sariyan [Direct-General, Dewan Bahasa]. (2013, November 30). *Memperkasa Sistem Perundangan Negara melalui Bahasa Melayu* [Empowering the legal system through Malay]. Keynote paper presented at *Ceramah Memperkasa Sistem Perundangan Negara melalui Bahasa Melayu* [Forum on empowering the legal system through Malay]. Malaysian Bar Council, Kuala Lumpur.

Badia i Capdevila, Ignasi. (2004). A view of the linguistic situation in Malta. *Noves SL. Revista de Sociolingüística* Spring-Summer 2004. Accessed on 6 June 2011 from http://www.gencat.cat/llengua/noves. Spring-summer 2004.

Baker, John. H. (1979). *Manual of law French*. Amersham: Avebury.

Baker, John. H. (2007). *Legal education in London 1250–1850*. Selden Society Lecture Delivered at University College London, July 4th, 2005. London: Selden Society.

Bar Council of India. (2010). Portal accessed10 Mar 2014 from http://www.barcouncilofindia.org/all-india-bar-examination-rules-2010-notified/

Benitez, Irene. (2009, November 26–28). The relevance of English in Philippine Courtrooms. Paper presented at 14th *English in Southeast Asia Conference*, Ateneo de Manila University.

Bhatia, Vijay. (2011, August 25). Contested identities. Symposium on 'Interdiscursive colonization of arbitration practices: Key perspectives'. *AILA Conference*, Beijing.

Billings, Warren M. (2001). A course of legal studies. Books that shaped Louisiana law. In Fernandez & Billings (Eds.), *A law unto itself? Essays in Louisiana legal history* (pp. 25–39). Baton Rouge: Louisiana State University Press.

Blais, François. [Director Centre for Legal Translation and Documentation, University of Ottawa] (2009). *Canada's jurilinguistic centres* (Language Portal of Canada, 2009.10.08). Accessed on 12 Jan 2013 from http://www.noslangues-ourlanguages.gc.ca/collaborateurs-contributors/articles/jurilinguistique-eng.html

Brand, Paul. (1999). *Observing and recording the Medieval Bar and Bench at work. The origins of law reporting in England*. Selden Society lecture delivered at Lincoln's Inn, London, July 6th, 1998. London: Selden Society.

Cain, P. J., & Hopkins, A. G. (1993). *British imperialism (Crisis and Deconstruction)* (Vol. 2). Harlow: Longman.

Canadian Supreme Court. (2012). Official portal accessed 14 Nov 2012 from http://www.scc-csc.gc.ca/decisions/index-eng.asp

Candlin, Christopher., & Bhatia, Vijay. (1998). *Strategies and competencies in legal communication. A study to investigate the communicative needs of legal professionals*. Hong Kong: The Law Society of Hong Kong.

Cantor, Norman F. (1991). *Inventing the middle ages: The lives, works and ideas of the great medievalists of the twentieth century*. New York: Morrow.

Chaklader, Snehamoy. (1990). Language and reformation of India's Federal Structure: The case of West Bengal. In B. Weinstein (Ed.), *Language policy and political development* (pp. 87–107). Norwood: Ablex.

Cheesman, Nick. (2011). How an authoritarian regime in Burma used special courts to defeat judicial Independence. *Law and Society Review, 45*(4), 801–830.

Cheung, Anne S. Y. (1997). Towards a bilingual legal system – The development of Chinese legal language. *Loyola of Los Angeles International and Comparative Law Review, 19*(2), 315–336.

Cleroux, Richard. (2011, September 19). The Hill: Solution to bilingual judges falls short. *Law Times*. Accessed 20 Jan 2013 from http://www.lawtimesnews.com/201109192514/commentary/the-hill-solution-to-bililngual-judges-issue-falls-short

Clynes, Adrian, & Deterding, David. (2011). Standard Malay (Brunei). *Journal of the International Phonetic Association, 41*(2), 259–268.

Cohn, Bernard. S. (1996). *Colonialism and its forms of knowledge: The British in India*. Princeton University Press: Princeton.

Coperahewa, Sandagomi. (2011). The language situation in Sri Lanka. In Kaplan & Baldauf (Eds.), *Language planning in the Asia Pacific: Hong Kong, Timor-Leste and Sri Lanka* (pp. 160–241). Abingdon: Routledge.

Crown Law Tonga. (2013). Official portal of Tongan Justice Department accessed 12 Dec 2013 from www.crownlaw.gov.to/

Davies, Rachel. (2012). Hyrwyddo system Gyfreithiol Ddwyieithog yng Nghymru [Facilitating a bilingual legal system in Wales.] Unpublished doctoral thesis, University of Swansea. [English summary supplied by author.]

Dodd, Gwilym. (2011). The spread of English in the records of central government, 1400–1430. In E. Salter & H. Wicker (Eds.), *Vernacularity in England and Wales, c.1300–1550* (Utrecht studies in medieval literacy) (pp. 225–266). Turnhout: Brepols.

Evans, Sandra. (2005, July 2–4). The use of court clerks as "Makeshift" legal interpreters in St. Lucian courts. Paper presented at 7th *International Forensic Linguistics Conference*, University of Cardiff.

Ethnologue. (2019). Accessed 2011.10.1~2019.1.22 from http://www.ethnologue.com/

Fagan, Eduard. (1996). Roman-Dutch law in its South African historical context. In R. Zimmerman & D. Visser (Eds.), *Southern cross: Civil and common law in South Africa* (pp. 33–64). Oxford: Clarendon.

Ferdousi, Nahid. (2009). *Bangladesher bichar bebosthae Bangla vasha – poristhiti* [Bangla language in the judiciary of Bangladesh – The state]. *The Dhaka University Journal of Linguistics, 2*(3): 53–68. [Summarised by Mahmud Hasan, University of Liberal Arts, Dhaka].

Ferdousi, Nahid. (2015, February 24). Status of Bangla in the legal arena. *The Daily Star*. Text supplied by author, 2016.9.23.

Firstpost. (2018, November 02). In Supreme Ct you must speak in English. Accessed 20 Nov 2018 from https://www.firstpost.com/india/in-supreme-court-you-must-speak-in-english-cji-ranjan-gogoi-tells-judge-after-hearing-him-argue-in-court-in-hindi-5491101

Fisher, John H. (1977). Chancery and the emergence of standard written English in the fifteenth century. *Speculum, 52*(4), 870–899.

Fisher, John H. (1996). *The emergence of standard English*. Lexington: University of Kentucky Press.

Forrester, Clive. (2005). The Discourse of Time in the Jamaican Courtroom: Creole speaking witness meets English speaking counsel. Paper presented at *7th Conference of the International Association of Forensic Linguists*, University of Cardiff, July 2–4.
Francavilla, Domenico. (2018). Law, language and communication in the Indian context. In J. Visconti (Ed.), *Handbook of communication in the legal sphere* (pp. 434–449). Berlin: De Gruyter.
Gardiner, Heather. (2011, August 25). Barreau du Québec insist SCC judges be bilingual. *Legal Feeds* (Weblog of *Canadian Lawyer* and *Law Times*). Accessed 20 Jan 2013 from http://www.canadianlawyermag.com/legalfeeds/423/Barreau-du-Quebec-insists-SCC-judges-be-bilingual.html
Golding, Brian. (2001). *Conquest and colonisation. The Normans in Britain, 1066–1100.* Basingstoke: Palgrave.
Gonzalez, Andrew. (1996, July). Incongruity between the language of law and the language of court proceedings: The Philippine experience. *Language & Communication, 16*(3), 229–234.
Government of India. (2012). Ministry of law and justice portal accessed 15 Dec 2012 from http://lawmin.nic.in/
Government of Pakistan. (1973). *The constitution of the Islamic Republic of Pakistan, 1973.* Lahore: Nadeem Law Book House.
Gunesekera, Manique. (2005). *The postcolonial identity of Sri Lankan English.* Colombo: Katha Publishers.
Gunputh, Rajendra Parsad. (2013). The professional and vocational training of lawyers according to the Anglo-Saxon model in a mixed legal system – The case of the Republic of Mauritius. In I. Kraśnicka & M. Perkowska (Eds.), *How to become a lawyer* (pp. 57–74). Berne: Peter Lang.
Harms, Louis [Former Deputy President, Supreme Court of South Africa]. (2012). Language and law in a multilingual society. *Potchefstroom Electronic Law Journal, 2012*: 15. Accessed 20 Dec 2012 from http://www.saflii.org/za/journals/PER/2012/15.html
Higher Education Commission (Pakistan). (2018). Accessed 20 Oct 2018 from http://hec.gov.pk/english/HECAnnouncements/Pages/LAW-LAT.aspx
Hlophe, J. M. [Judge President Cape HC]. (2004). Receiving justice in your own language – the need for effective court interpreting in our multilingual society. *Advocate* April 2004, 42–47. Accessed 1 Dec 2012 from http://www.sabar.co.za/law-journals/2004/april/2004-april-vol017-no1-pp42-47.pdf
HKIAC. (2017). Portal of Hong Kong International Arbitration Centre. Accessed 20 Feb 2017 from http://www.hkiac.org/
Hogg, Peter W. (1992). *Constitutional law of Canada.* Toronto: Carswell.
Hong Kong e-Legislation. (2017). Portal accessed 2017.6.21 from www.elegislation.gov.hk
Hong Kong Judiciary. (2013). Official portal accessed 2013.3.30~31 from http://www.judiciary.gov.hk/en/legal_ref/judgments.htm
Hong Kong University PCLL. (2012). Website for Hong Kong University postgraduate certificate in Laws. Accessed 15 Dec 2012 from http://www.ple.hku.hk/pcll/
Jayaram, B. D., & Rajyashree, K. S. (2000). *State official language policy implementation.* Mysore: Central Institute of Indian Languages.
Kabir, Nurul. (2012, February 20). Bangla still ignored in Bangladesh Sixty years of Ekushey. *New Age* (Online Edition). Accessed 20 Mar 2013 from http://newagebd.com/newspaper1/archive_details.php?date=2012-02-20&nid=50994
Kaburise, John. B. (2001). The structure of legal education in South Africa. *Journal of Legal Education, 51*(3), 363–371.
Kamal, Natalya. (2015, November 05). *Courting the law.* Accessed 27 Sept 2018 from http://courtingthelaw.com/2015/11/05/faqs/english-urdu-legal-terms-w/
Kashyap, Praavita. (2016, August 26). Can I have some laws in Hindi? *The Hindu.* Accessed 20 Feb 2018 from https://www.thehindu.com/features/magazine/'Can-I-have-some-laws-in-Hindi'/article14591190.ece

Kayambazinthu, Edrinnie. (1999). The language planning situation in Malawi. *Current Issues in Language Planning, 1*, 15–85.
Khan, Ahmed Hasan. (2018, January 20). The Bar licensing system — an empty show. Accessed 20 June 2018 from https://dailytimes.com.pk/184569/bar-licensing-system-empty-show/
Kurzon, Dennis. (2013). Foreign and archaic phrases in legal texts. *The International Journal of Speech, Language and the Law, 20*(1), 117–142.
Language Portal of Canada. (2013). Accessed 18 Mar 2013 from http://www.noslangues-ourlanguages.gc.ca/manchettes-headlines/lcumf-eng.html
Laskin, Bora, & Finkelstein, Neil. (1986). *Laskin's Canadian constitutional law* (5th ed.). Toronto: Carswell.
Law Commission of India. (2008). Non-feasibility of introduction of Hindi as compulsory language in the supreme court of India. (216th report).
Laws of Bangladesh. (2014). Government of Bangladesh legislative and parliamentary affairs division portal. Accessed 20 Jan 2014 from http://bdlaws.minlaw.gov.bd/
Law Society of Hong Kong. (2013). Official portal accessed 20 Apr 2013 from http://www.hklawsoc.org.hk/pub_e/about/#profileprofession
Lenel, Beat. (2002). The history of South African law and its Roman-Dutch roots. Accessed 03 Mar 2013 from http://www.lenel.ch/docs/history-of-sa-law-en.pdf
Leung, Janny. (2012). Judicial discourse in Cantonese courtrooms in postcolonial Hong Kong: the judge as godfather, scholar, educator and scolding parent. *The International Journal of Speech, Language and the Law, 19*(2), 239–261.
Leung, Janny. (2013). As good as it gets? Unrepresented litigant and courtroom dynamics: A case study. Paper presented at *11th Biennial Conference on Forensic Linguistics* (IAFL), Mexico City, 2013.6.
Levesque, Gérard. (2012). L'exercise des droits linguistiques devant les tribunaux d'Alberta. Paper presented at *XIII AIDL-IALL International Conference*, Chiangmai, 2012.12.
Lo Bianco, Joseph. (1999). A syntax of peace. Pragmatic constraints of language teaching and pragmatics in language learning. In J. Lo Bianco, A. Liddicoat, & C. Crozet (Eds.), *Striving for the third place: Intercultural competence through language* education (pp. 51–63).
Louisiana State University. (2012). LSU Law Center website accessed 12 Dec 2012 from https://www.law.lsu.edu/index.cfm?geaux=clo.maindigest
Madeline, Fanny. (2010). Les processus d'identification et les sentiments d'appartenance politique aux frontières de l'empire Plantagenêt. *Cahiers de recherches médiévales et humanistes* [en ligne]19. Accessed 10 Dec 2012 from http://crm.revues.org/11985
Mangubhai, Francis & Mugler, France. (2003). The language situation in Fiji. *Current Issues in Language Planning, 4*(3), 367–454.
Martin, Isabel Pefianco. (2012). Expanding the role of Philippine Languages in the legal system: The dim prospects. *Asian Perspectives in the Arts and Humanities, 2*(1), 1–14.
Masmahirah Hj Mohd Tali, Hjh. (2016). Courtroom discourse: A case study of the linguistic strategies in Brunei courtrooms. In N. A. Haji-Othman, J. McLellan, & D. Deterding (Eds.), *The use and status of Language in Brunei Darussalam: A kingdom of unexpected linguistic diversity* (pp. 135–163). Dordrecht: Springer.
Mauritius Supreme Court. (2013). Official portal accessed 3 Mar 2013 from http://www1.gov.mu/scourt/home/welcome.do
Mazrui, Ali, & Mazrui, Alamin. M. (1995). *Swahili state and society - The political economy of an African language*. Nairobi: EAEP.
Mazrui, Ali, & Mazrui, Alamin. M. (1998). *The power of babel: Language and governance in the African experience*. Nairobi: EAEP.
Mellinkoff, David. (1963). *The language of the law*. Boston: Little, Brown & Co.
Memmi, Albert. (1957) (1965 Trans.). *The coloniser and the colonised*. New York: Orion.
Michaels, Ralf. (2012). American law (United States). In J. M. Smits (Ed.), *Elgar encyclopedia of comparative law* (pp. 66–77). Cheltenham: Edward Elgar.

Mills, L. A. (1960). British Malaya, 1824–1867. *Journal of the Malayan Branch of the Royal Asiatic Society,* vol. XXXIII. Reprinted 2003 by MBRAS, Singapore.

Mir, Farina. (2006). Imperial policy, provincial practices: Colonial language policy in nineteenth-century India. *Indian Economic Social History Review, 2006*(43), 395–427.

Moeketsi, R. H. (1999). Redefining the role of the South African court interpreter. *Newsletter of the National Association of Judiciary Interpreters and Translators, 8*: 3–4. Accessed 20 Apr 2013 from http://www.najit.org/membersonly/library/Proteus/HTML%20Versions/v8n3-4/moekesti_v8n3-4.htm

Monsanto, Stephen L. (2009, October 05). But Tagalog is Greek in Visayas, Mindanao. *Inquirer.net.* Accessed 21 June 2017 from http://opinion.inquirer.net/inquireropinion/letterstotheeditor/view/20091005-228430/But-Tagalog-is-Greek-in-Visayas-Mindanao

Morales-Gálvez, Sergi. (2017). Living together as equals: Linguistic justice and sharing the public sphere in multilingual settings. *Ethnicities, 17*(5), 646–666.

Myanmar Law Library. (2001). Accessed 20 Apr 2016 from http://www.myanmar-law-library.org/law-library/laws-and-regulations/burma-codes/burma-code-volume-1.html

Myint Zan. (2004). A comparison of the first and fiftieth year of independent Burma's law reports. *Victoria University of Wellington Law Review, 35*(2), 385–426.

Myint Zan. (2008). Legal education in Burma since the mid-1960s. *Journal of Burmese Studies, 12*, 63–107.

Nadaraja, T. (1972). *The legal system of Ceylon in its historical setting*. Leiden: Brill.

New York Times. (1899, May 30). Philippine Courts Opened. Accessed 12 Sept 2007 from http://query.nytimes.com/mem/archive-free/pdf?_r=1&res=9D0DE4D71F3DE433A25753C3A9639C94689ED7CF&oref=slogin

Nyati-Ramahobo, Lydia. (2000). The language situation in Botswana. *Current Issues in Language Planning, 1*(2), 243–300.

Ng, Joyce. (2017, June 01). Foreign judges must be retained in Hong Kong, former chief justice insists. *South China Morning Post.* Accessed 21 June 2017 from http://www.scmp.com/news/hong-kong/politics/article/2096355/foreign-judges-must-be-retained-hong-kong-former-chief

Ng Kwai Hang. (2009). *The common law in two voices. Language, Law and the Postcolonial Dilemma in Hong Kong*. Stanford University Press.

Ormrod, W. M. (2003). The use of English: Language, law, and political culture in fourteenth-century England. *Speculum, 78*(3): 750–787.

Pakistan National Assembly. (2012). Official portal accessed 12 Nov 2012 from http://www.na.gov.pk/en/report_detail.php?id=8

Pakistan Supreme Court. (2013). Portal accessed 01 May 2013 from http://www.supremecourt.gov.pk/

Perry, Amanda. J. (2000). Is legal globalisation an impossible dream? National Implementation of international standards. *CEPMLP Internet Journal* (Centre for Energy, petroleum and mineral law policy). Accessed 10 May 2011 from http://www.dundee.ac.uk/cepmlp/journal/html/vol3/article3-4.html

Philippine Daily Inquirer. (2009, August 25). Filipino in court. (Editorial). Accessed 30 Mar 2011 from http://opinion.inquirer.net/inquireropinion/editorial/view/20090825-221861/Filipino-in-court

Philips, Susan. (2000). Constructing a Tongan nation through language ideology in the courtroom. In P. Kroskrity (Ed.), *Regimes of language* (pp. 229–258). Santa Fe: School of American Research Press.

Powell, Richard. (2008). Bilingual courtrooms: In the interests of justice? In J. Gibbons & M. T. Turrell (Eds.), *Dimensions of Forensic linguistics* (pp. 131–159). Amsterdam: John Benjamins.

Powell, Richard., & David, Maya Khemlani. (2011). Language alternation in Kenyan and Malaysian courts. In A. Wagner & L. Cheng (Eds.), *Exploring courtroom discourse: The language of power and control* (pp. 227–250). London: Ashgate.

Prasad, Vivek. (2018, April 24). DU law exam in Hindi: it's impossible to satisfy everybody. *Newslaundry*. Accessed 28 Feb 2018 from https://www.newslaundry.com/2018/04/24/du-law-exam-in-hindi-regional-languages-pmt-upsc-mains

Rahman, Tariq. (1998). *Language and politics in Pakistan*. Karachi: Oxford University Press.

Rahman, Hafizur. (2005, October 08). Poor national language. *The News* [Internet Edition]. Accessed 2006.8.08 from http://www.jang.com.pk/thenews/oct2005-daily/08-102005/oped/o3.htm

Rangoon Gazette and Weekly Budget. (1888). Report on lecture by Reverend Dr. J.N. Cushing. Reprinted in *SOAS Bulletin of Burma Research, 1*(2), Autumn 2003.

Rashid, Umar. (2016, March 6). Problems With Legal Education In Pakistan: Are Pakistan Bar Council Legal Education Rules 2015 Enough? Accessed 20 Jan 2018 from http://courtingthelaw.com/2016/03/16/commentary/problems-with-legal-education-in-pakistan-are-pakistan-bar-council-legal-education-rules-2015-enough/

Reinsch, Paul Samuel. (1899). English common law in the early American colonies. *Bulletin of the University of Wisconsin 1899*, 396–456. Madison, WS.

Reyes, Carmela. (2007, August 22). 3 Bulacan courts to use Filipino in judicial proceedings. Inquirer.net. Accessed 30 Mar 2011 from http://globalnation.inquirer.net/news/news/view_article_id=84080

Reyes, Carmela. (2009, August 20). Bulacan uses Filipino in court trials. *Inquirer.net*. Accessed 30 Mar 2011 from http://article.wn.com/view/2009/08/20/Bulacan_uses_Filipino_in_court_trials/section=TopStories&template=cheetah-photo-search%2Findex.txt

Richland, Justin. (2008). *Arguing with tradition. The language of law in Hopi Tribal Court*. Chicago: University of Chicago Press.

Rwezaura, Barthazara. (1994). Constraining factors to the adoption of Kiswahili as a language of the law in Tanzania. *Afrikanistische Arbeitspapiere: Schriftenreihe des Kölner Instituts für Afrikanistik, 37*, 109–126.

Sachs, Albie. (1973). *Justice in South Africa. Berkeley:* University of California Press. Accessed 3 Mar 2013 from http://ark.cdlib.org/ark:/13030/ft3489n8p6/

Said, Edward. (1978). *Orientalism*. New York: Pantheon Books.

Said, Edward. (1993). *Culture and imperialism*. New York: Random House.

Sarvgyan. (2019). https://www.sarvgyan.com/articles/aibe-2019-hindi

SARI [South Asia Research Institute]. (2000) The right to our language: Some aspects of how the problem poses itself. *Second World Punjabi Conference*, Prince George, B.C., August 2000. Republished in *Shunpiking* 8(44). Accessed 21 June 2006 from http://www.shunpiking.com/shun0844/ind-lang.htm

Senaratne, Madhushala. (2008, March 30). Law College to switch to English medium: CJ. *The Sunday Times Online* [Sri Lanka]. Accessed 2011.4.12 from http://www.sundaytimes.lk/080330/News/news0020.html

Schmitthener, Samue. (1969). A sketch of the development of the legal profession in India. *Law & Society Review, 3*, 337–382.

Sharma, Yojana. (1997, May 06). *International Press Service Agency*. Accessed 20 Nov 2011 from http://ipsnews2.wpengine.com/1997/05/hong-kong-jury-still-out-on-bilingual-legal-system/

Siddique, Osama. (2010). Law in practice – The Lahore District courts litigants survey (2010–2011) *DPRC Working Papers*, Development Policy Research Centre, Lahore University of Management Sciences.

Siddique, Osama. (2012a). The other Pakistan: Special Laws, diminished citizenship and the gathering storm (December 5, 2012). *Social Science Research Network*. Accessed 30 Aug 2013 from http://ssrn.com/abstract=2185535

Siddique, Osama. (2012b, February 28). The language of justice. *The Express Tribune*. Accessed 03 Mar 2012 from http://tribune.com.pk/story/342487/the-language-of-justice/

Solan, Lawrence. (2019, March 07). The promise of the Europe's multilingual legal order: Has it been fulfilled? Paper presented at the *Conference on Legal Communication in a Multilingual and Multicultural Context*. Bergische Universität Wuppertal.

Sri Lanka Court of Appeal. (2012). Sri Lanka Court of Appeal (2012) Official portal accessed 11 Nov 2012 from http://www.commonlii.org/lk/cases/LKCA/
Sri Lanka Law College. (2019). Portal accessed 20 Jan 2019 from http://www.sllc.ac.lk
Sri Lanka Supreme Court. (2012). Official portal accessed 11 Nov 2012 from http://www.supremecourt.lk/
Tan, Genevieve. (2009, September 21). Aspiring advocates call for law courses at UBD. *Brunei Times*. http://www.bt.com.bn/home-news/2009/09/21/aspiring-advocates-call-law-courses-ubd
Tent, Jan. (2001). A profile of the Fiji English lexis: An account of how the lexis of Fiji English is being recorded. *English World-Wide, 22*(2), 209–245.
Thekiso, Elma. (2001). A sociolinguistic analysis of communication processes in a bilingual court of law in Gaborone, Botswana. Unpublished PhD thesis, University of Warwick.
The Straits Times. (1950, September 09). 'Use Tagalog'. p. 3.
The Syonan Times. (1942, September 04). Spanish language to be used in Philippines law courts. p. 3.
Tiersma, Peter. (1999). *Legal Language*. University of Chicago Press.
Tiersma, Peter. (2007). The textualization of precedent. *Notre Dame Law Review, 82*, 1187–1278.
The Hindu. (2008, January 11). Common Law Admission Test to be held in May. Accessed 21 Jan 2011 from https://www.thehindu.com/todays-paper/Common-Law-Admission-Test-to-be-held-in-May/article15141636.ece
The Island. (2008, March 30). Law College to switch to English medium: Chief Justice. p. 6.
Tun Shin [Attorney-General of Myanmar]. (2013, February 10). The rule of law in Myanmar; perspectives and prospects. *New Light of Myanmar, X*(6): 1. Accessed 3 Mar 2013 from http://www.burmalibrary.org/docsMA2013/NLM2013-02-10.pdf
University of Colombo. (2019). Portal accessed 20 Feb 2019 from https://law.cmb.ac.lk/?page_id=127
University of Mauritius. (2013). Official portal accessed 2 Feb 2013 from www.uom.ac.mu/programmes/Courses/FLM/YR0910/.../LM310E.rtf
University of Ottawa. (2012). Official portal accessed 1 Dec 2012 from http://www.uottawa.ca/academic/info/regist/crs/0103/clEN/cl-eng3.htm
Vranken, Martin. (2012). Australia. In J. M. Smits (Ed.), *Elgar encyclopedia of comparative law* (pp. 120–125). Edward Elgar: Cheltenham.
Webb, Vic., & Kembo-Sure. (2000). The languages of Africa. In Webb & Kembo-Sure (Eds.), *African voices. An introduction to the languages and linguistics of Africa* (pp. 26–54). Cape Town: Oxford University Press.
Wormald, Patrick. (1999). *The making of English law: From king Alfred to the twelfth century*. Oxford: Blackwell.
Yih, Dieter [former president of Law Society Hong Kong]. (2009, September 07). *Becoming a lawyer in Hong Kong*. Presentation to law Society of Hong Kong. Text accessed through personal communication with author, 2013.7.15.
Zurairi Ar. (2013, October 19). Make syariah Malaysia's only law, urges ISMA. *The Malay Mail Online*. Accessed 19 Oct 2013 from http://www.themalaymailonline.com/malaysia/article/make-syariah-malaysias-only-law-urges-isma

Chapter 11
Malaysian Bilingualism as a Model for Postcolonial Law

> *...each jurisdiction is embedded in its own historical, political, cultural and economic circumstances ...globalization and diversity can and do co-exist.*
>
> Steele and Taylor (2010:5)

> *Sociolinguistics can benefit from law and society's focus on who gets what and when, whereas law and society can turn to sociolinguistics for a deeper understanding of how they get it.*
>
> Conley and O'Barr (1998:14)

11.1 Reflection and Reappraisal

Emerging from curiosity about bilingualism as a means of enhancing legal accessibility in postcolonial settings, this investigation has focused on the processes and issues involved in making Malay a viable medium of modern law and explored how language policy influences communicative and vocational choices in legal practice. Given the global position of English, as well as its importance to Malaysia as the former administrative medium and current business lingua franca, law might well have continued in English alone if not for specific measures to facilitate the use of Malay, the national language and most important vernacular. The study was framed accordingly as a problem of planned vernacularisation involving the interaction of status, corpus, acquisition and discourse planning.

Within a framework prioritising the role of political and structural factors while allowing for a degree of agency on the part of legal practitioners, orientations and attitudes toward language policy in law schools, offices and courtrooms were also examined. While complete shift to Malay may be envisaged by some planners, legal vernacularisation for now and the foreseeable future accommodates both Malay and English at institutional and individual levels, with lawyers playing a key role as mediators between speakers of different languages and between legal and lay discourse.

R. Powell, *Language Choice in Postcolonial Law*, Language Policy 22,
https://doi.org/10.1007/978-981-15-1173-8_11

With ethnic and religious conflicts pervading national identity and political polarisation permeating public discourse, Malaysia is a complex setting for the study of language planning. But as a developing economy and multilingual society it is far from alone in seeking to reconcile promotion of an indigenous language in the service of national independence and unity with support for an international language in the service of global engagement and material development. And as a polity whose main system of law is a colonial legacy it is not the only country in which tensions between nationism and nationalism complicate the challenge of making legal discourse more accessible without compromising professional standards. The third strand of this investigation therefore incorporated international comparison, moving from colonial language contact to postcolonial language planning. Malaysia is a potential model for bilingual law, not only as an exemplar of what can be achieved and what should be avoided, but also as a research construct for planning analysis. While the 60 lawyers interviewed are mere drops in an ocean of 16,000 practitioners, and judiciary perspectives have mostly been gleaned secondhand, many of the patterns that emerged seem to hold good for Malaysian law as a whole and may also help to inform investigations into other jurisdictions.

In this concluding chapter we begin (Sect. 11.2) by reviewing the key characteristics of Malaysian language-in-law policy, bringing together strands explored within the frameworks of status, corpus, acquisition and discourse planning. We will then (Sect. 11.3) discuss the role of practitioners in policy implementation before going on (Sect. 11.4) to consider the strengths and weaknesses of Malaysian bilingual law and what it might offer other postcolonial jurisdictions. The following section (Sect. 11.5) evaluates status, corpus, acquisition and discourse planning as necessary but insufficient instruments of vernacularisation and evaluates the role of political and employment incentives. We will then move on to the more speculative questions of what is likely to change when legal language changes, (Sect. 11.6) whether law is particularly resistant to language reform (Sect. 11.7), and how bilingualism might help postcolonial polities make law more accessible and equitable.

11.2 Characteristics of Malaysian Language-in-Law Policy

Malay was not promoted by British colonisers in the way they had promoted vernaculars in India, although it was an administrative medium in the Unfederated States, reportedly employed in a "slipshod" form as a result of contact with English (Det 1949.4.24). A provision in Article 152 of the 1957 constitution for Malay testimony to be heard and recorded without translation may explain sporadic reports of its use in courtrooms as early as 1960 (*The Straits Times* 1960.6.24), but Choo Mun Sou, one of the country's longest-serving practitioners, remembered no Malay in any court when starting out in practice in the 1960s. The key status planning measure was, and remains, the 1967 National Language Act, which provided a framework for the use of Malay alongside English and gave it a symbolic priority that could be reinforced by more extensive or specific directives.

Early planning, and discourse about planning, centred on practical issues such as the need for terminology. In the year of the Language Act the AGC produced a Malay version of the Penal Code, perhaps the most frequently cited legislation in the courts, and in 1970 Dewan Bahasa published *Istilah Undang-undang*, the first Malay legal terminology. Few informants for this study had clear recollections of when Malayanisation started affecting their legal practice, but former bar president Hendon Mohamed recalled turning to the newly published terminology when finding her Malay wanting, which indicates that courts were requiring the language as early as 1970. Many of *Istilah*'s 3000 entries were studied innovations, while others fell back on modifications of English that prioritised legal accuracy over linguistic purism. However, corpus planning later ran out of steam and the main complaint about Malay legal terms even today is that there are not enough of them. Consequently there are also uncertainties about the use of unauthorised lexis. Despite the 1979 establishment of a special unit to translate existing laws, Malay corpus development pales in comparison with Hong Kong's support for Chinese. Several administrators and academics confirm that most new laws are still drafted in English, even if these drafts are officially regarded as translations.

The 1970s were crucial for the expansion of Malay in education and parliamentary debate, but there were few significant reforms in the legal domain until the early 1980s, when a spate of judicial circulars and directions called for greater use of BM in lower courts and a 1983 statutory amendment required those entering the profession to show proficiency in Malay. In the same year UM started teaching law bilingually, with remedial classes for students in their weaker language, which for most of them was Malay. Around this time the Bar Council organised 'crash courses' in Malay for the state bars. Press accounts soon after the 1981 judicial circulars report proceedings partially in Malay, and one 1983 report claims it was being used for 90% of lower court proceedings in Pahang, but we have no data on how observers arrived at this figure or how they accounted for code-switching.

There was some consensus among informants for this study that pressure to use Malay was strongest in the early 1990s following a third (and so far final) round of status reforms requiring it for all court proceedings and for the filing of court documents. With no evidence of an acceleration of communicative problems at the time it is likely that politics was the main factor behind these reforms. The removal of the Lord President and other leading judges in 1988 was an unprecedented act of political interference in the judiciary, and the language reforms that came in their wake may be seen as a push to extend the symbolic power of the Malays in the face of political instability within UMNO, just as the language reforms of the 1980s were, according to Mead (1988), a cultural strategy to assuage economic frustration among UMNO supporters.

It should nonetheless be emphasised that this study uncovered few accounts of politicians riding roughshod over the complexities of legal practice. No practitioner recalled needing to respond directly to a direction on language. Rather, Malayanisation was felt as a series of waves of judicial pressure, mitigated by variations in the preferences of individual judges and an understanding that English would be tolerated in higher courts and for complex arguments. It should also be remembered that status policy itself retains provisions for English, including for urgent applications (Rules of High Court) or judges' opinions (*Dato' Seri Anwar*, 2010). Policy implementation has been more pragmatic than the politicised rhetoric surrounding it, and former bar president Steven Thiru's appraisal still holds good: "Most lawyers nowadays understand the unwritten rules that allow English to continue as long as Malay is not criticised or neglected, since this would have political ramifications".[1]

Lack of further status reform after 1990 may indicate recognition that a framework was already in place by then that promoted Malay while leaving room for English. But lack of corpus and acquisition planning, each crucial for realising the potential of status planning, is harder to explain. The 2003 *Istilah Undang-undang* is essentially the same as the 1986 edition, which itself added little to earlier versions. Terms developed elsewhere certainly circulate, but evidence of academics having to improvise, and of practitioners resorting to Google Translate, indicate that much more might have been done in a field where it is vital not only to disseminate terms but also to achieve consensus on their authority.

Beyond lexical gaps, jurisprudence in Malay is handicapped by a lack of legal texts. The AGC's production of bilingual legislation has added to the Malay corpus, but despite the constitutional primacy of Malay versions of enactments English is still regarded as the more important language inasmuch as it remains the source of most Malay texts. By 2004 *Malayan Law Journal* had published only 12 appellate judgments in Malay. When Chief Justice Zaki Azmi (Koshy 2013.9.15) estimated that only a fraction of what lawyers need to read is available in BM, he was including domestic, as well as international, jurisprudence. The first apex judgment partially in Malay did not come until 2007. In academia, international university rankings add to the pressure on lecturers and researchers to publish in English rather than Malay.

As for education, Dewan Bahasa started organising seminars on the legal application of Malay as early as the 1980. Yet the lectures and workshops that were observed for this study were longer on rhetoric than practicalities. Interviews conducted with DBP officers a decade ago (Powell 2008) revealed an assumption that the universities should take the lead, and not much seems to have changed since. The officer in charge of legal Malay for the bar admitted that there were no comprehensive training programmes and suggested it was DBP that should take the initiative. The Bar Council continues to play an educational role through its Bahasa Melayu Committee, but the annual workshop I attended focused on lexicogrammatical and orthographical aspects of general rather than legal Malay. Most of the participants were clerks or administrators rather than lawyers. There appears to have been no collaboration with the bars of other bilingual jurisdictions such as Hong Kong, whose Law Society has a Bilingualism Committee.

Among university law departments, UKM and to a lesser extent UM still have some lectures in BM, while UiTM has a final year class on legal Malay, but from

[1] Interviewed in Kuala Lumpur, 2013.8.

entering law school until graduation the emphasis is on English. It is the only MOI of private schools and of the overseas institutions that many Malaysians attend, and the only MOI until the final year at UiTM and UIA. Drafting is taught in English at UM, even though court documents must be submitted in Malay. One reason for the dominance of English in legal education is the lack of Malay legal corpora and lexis referred to above. But this study also found educators, lawyers and students compelled by the premise of English being the more authentic medium of legal argument. Moreover general proficiency in English is widely assumed to be lower than in Malay, while the legal tasks likely to be done in English are thought more complex, more lucrative and more prestigious.

It would be unfair to single out law departments for bias toward English, however. UM was still adhering to its bilingual policy in the late 1990s even after prime minister Mahathir had ordered a swing back toward English in tertiary education, and the language is emphasised in many other disciplines. UKM, an institution established to promote the national language, teaches all its dentistry courses in English (Universiti Kebangsaan Malaysia 2013).

Lack of Malay legal education derives mainly from the assignment of different roles for Malay and English in law, with the former assumed to be less demanding academically and less crucial professionally and hence best left to the general education that precedes law school and the professional training that follows it. While the Bar Council proposes taking more control of training, and includes a role for both languages in its proposals, the universities largely assume that legal Malay will be acquired through professional experience. Indeed, UM students reported learning more about Malay terminology, writing style and politeness strategies during their professional attachments than at school.

The increasingly nationalistic tone adopted by organs such as *Utusan* from the 1990s may be seen as reflecting disappointment with the slow pace of Malayanisation. Government negligence or hypocrisy features prominently in critical discourses, and many lawyers, even those happy to retain English, express surprise that legal Malay has not developed further. The language's capacity to influence legal practice seems to be undermined by planners' fixation on the dignity of the nation rather than on practical strategies to improve access to justice. As long as Chief Justices and Attorneys-General continue to see no reason to push for faster change, discourse on the side of Malay will be further debilitated by the public's low concern for language-in-law in comparison with education, most of them having less contact with lawyers than with teachers and being content to leave the details of legal procedure to the professionals. Educational policy involves several languages and invokes cultural and religious issues, ethnically based affirmative action, gatekeeping for employment, and the possibility of trilingual burdens on children. Law is more remote, most discussants accept some balance between Malay and English, and discourse tends to be broadly cast. There are no equivalents to the detailed and hotly debated blueprints on education issued periodically by the government.

11.3 Practitioner Orientations

Malaysia's language-in-law policy is less a static body of prescriptions for professionals to obey (or subvert) than a relationship between written and unwritten rules on the one hand and practical orientation to these rules on the other. While this is not a multilaterally negotiated relationship, the ambivalent agendas of policymakers and the prestige of the profession leave lawyers considerable space to manoeuvre. Malaysian law hence lends support to Heller's (2008, 249) conceptualisation of bilingualism as a set of practices to be described and interpreted rather than a fixed object to be discovered. Legal practitioners enjoy less agency than professionals in other domains as they are restricted not only by the authoritarian nature of law but also by strict procedural rules. Yet this study shows that many find enough flexibility in the language policy to turn bilingualism to their advantage when performing communicative tasks, and also when planning their careers.

Malaysian language policy in general constructs national unity upon a platform that prioritises Malay for symbolic, domestic and high-frequency activities while incorporating Chinese and Tamil and other languages for domestic multiculturalism and English for global outreach and economic expansion. After reinforcement through six decades of one-party rule, this model appears to be fairly resistant to radical reform. With a new government under Mahathir Mohamad, long an advocate of the practical importance of English within the symbolic priority of Malay, there are some signs that the constant seesawing between Malay and English may be coming down more heavily on the side of the latter, but UMNO, which was not expected to lose the 2018 elections and remains remarkably resilient through its rapprochement with PAS, is quick to pounce on any signs of Malay being marginalised, especially when this seems to involve greater use of Chinese.

The capacity of legal practitioners to openly challenge the official position of Malay as the medium of law is restricted by the institutionally and epistemologically hierarchical nature of the profession. Few lawyers want to be seen as subverting the constitution. The bar has a long record of upholding its constitutional interpretations against what it sees as political encroachment, but it is vulnerable to accusations of being political itself. Even calling for the repeal of the Sedition Act, a colonial hangover used to arrest 91 people in 2015 alone (Amnesty International, cited in *Malaysiakini* 2016.4.15), can be seen as politicking now that the Act has been declared constitutional by the Federal Court (Hafiz 2015.10.06).

Hence lawyers obey formal requirements for Malay even if it means having documents translated or sending juniors to present cases. No informant thought the indomitable Karpal Singh's filing of appeal documents in English (*Dato' Seri Anwar*, 2010) was a deliberate attempt to subvert a policy that allows room for pragmatism, as long as formalities are adhered to. It should further be noted that this flexibility has generally been upheld by key figures in pivotal positions that straddle policy and practice. Chief Justices may be defenders of national language policy but they also received their legal education in English. Even the more staunchly pro-Malay among them like Ahmad Fairuz, who initiated the first apex judgments in the language, have changed language use far less than other aspects of legal culture such as the independence of *Syariah* courts.

Proficient bilingualism, along with legal acumen, increases the agency of individual practitioners. Most informants agreed on the importance of being prepared to present arguments in either language and understood the need to comply with rules and rituals. Scope for communicative and discursive preference is then to be found in the Bakhtinian liminality between official Malay and discretionary English, between cultural conformity and rhetorical adversariality, and between time-honoured discourses and spontaneous responses. A code-switch in the courtroom, or an extemporaneous argument, is more powerful when it emerges from proficiency than from deficiency.

Proficient bilingualism not only helps win cases but is also important in career-building. As one Ipoh-based lawyer put it: "Speaking Malay in a government department or to civil servants in the courts can help get you better treatment than if you spoke English. And speaking good English to a prospective employer can help you in your job application". Moreover it is a vital tool for mediating between the legal and lay worlds. Even monolingual lawyers are bicultural in the way they acquire specialised communicative competencies and forms of thinking (McCaul 2011: 13) and interpret law for clients (Maley et al. 1994). Interviews with lawyers and reports by students showed most practitioners using at least two languages to perform legal tasks. For most, this was unconscious and unremarkable.

Not surprisingly, law students exercise less agency than qualified lawyers. Many feel they lack a genuine language choice, even when offered one on paper. Although English suggests greater career instrumentality to many, its preference as a medium of study rests mainly on immediate pragmatic considerations such as the availability of educational resources, considerations that may even outweigh personal proficiency levels. That said, language orientation emerged from this study as a key factor in career choices, and although Malaysian law does not exhibit the kind of language-linked class division evident in South Asian jurisdictions, there is little doubt which language attracts the money and prestige.

Lecturers have more freedom about language choice, at least within their own classroom, with many using Malay orally to reinforce understanding of English materials. Bilingualism as a pedagogical practice in law dates back at least to England's medieval Inns of Court, and observations showed that it is alive and well in Malaysia today, not merely to help students understand legal language but also to connect them with legal discourses.

11.4 Lessons From Malaysia

Malaysian bilingual law is not an elegant model. Language status is ambiguous. Malay legal corpora are inadequate. Legal education depends on predominantly English-medium instruction sandwiched between general schooling that leans toward English at its higher end and bilingual training that leans toward Malay in the early years of legal practice. Discourse about language policy is vague and shallow, quicker to criticise perceived injustices than to offer solutions. However, models elsewhere have their defects too.

None of the jurisdictions surveyed in this study is comprehensively bilingual in the sense of presenting a balanced choice between two or more languages at all court levels and in all legal fields. Hong Kong and Canada grant two languages equal authority, but in the former Chinese is seldom used in jurisprudence and hardly at all in law school, while in the latter French is unevenly supported outside francophone-majority provinces. Sri Lanka has generated a large body of vernacular law terms and uses vernaculars extensively up to high court level, but it virtually shuts them out of the superior courts and, like Bangladesh, risks evolving into a two-tier system in which the best spoils go to anglophones.

If balanced bilingualism is rare, comprehensive language shift is rarer still, and at least as far as English-derived law is concerned it seems to require legal disruption. Myanmar's shift to Burmese, for example, cannot be disassociated from its politicisation of law, debasement of legal education and abandonment of *stare decisis*.

With Malay and English used in tandem in most courts and offices and a considerable degree of legal continuity, Malaysia offers one of the better models of bilingual law available today. Yet it is the product of relatively little planning. And little of what has been planned is based on analysis of legal communication. Status planning is encapsulated in a small number of Acts and rules and even fewer judgments, but in combining authority with flexibility it is the foundation of a policy that manages to meet the needs of the courts that deal with the bulk of cases while allowing higher courts and corporate law extensive cross-border interdiscursivity. To move an overwhelmingly anglophone profession toward Malay and assuage cultural nationalists, the prioritisation of Malay was enshrined constitutionally but modified crucially by making English admissible in the interests of justice at the discretion of judges. To deter pro-English practitioners from exploiting loopholes, practice rules obligate the use of Malay more precisely while still leaving a formal role for English. The practitioners most likely to prefer English work in superior courts or on commercial matters, and as long as the documents they file include Malay versions their chances of arguing cases in English are good. Magistrates and Sessions Court judges are less flexible, and while there are increasing signs of their own weak proficiency in English being a factor behind this, their insistence on Malay is justifiable when considering the kind of cases they typically adjudicate. Moreover lawyers in lower courts are generally younger and better acquainted with Malay than their seniors, and inadequacies in corpus and acquisition planning are attenuated by the fact the tasks they perform there rarely depend on technical lexis or complex argument. If language shift, whether or not it occurs within a bilingual framework, is to emerge from legal practice rather than from political fiat then an initial focus on the lower courts makes sense.

Ambiguities in status planning are undeniably open to politicised manipulation. When pushed, the judiciary may reaffirms its right to insist lawyers use Malay, especially when the parties doing the pushing are opposition politicians. When seeking the attention of an audience that might otherwise pay little attention to apex court judgments the judiciary may write opinions in Malay, as in the *Lina Joy* conversion case. But far from being a particular feature of Malaysian law, the political nature of language planning applies to most polities and most domains. Language planning seems generally to be most effective when there is alignment, or at least compromise, between political agendas and communicative practice. For Kaplan and Baldauf (1997: 11), no amount of planning will bring sustained change without the cooperation of the communities involved. In spite of the political conflict running through Malaysian society, in law the complexities of language policy are worked out through habitual accommodations. Lawyers rarely try to force the hand of the judiciary on language matters as, irrespective of politics, the judges' say is what counts. On the other hand, hardline linguistic nationalists such as Faiza Tamby Chik are rarely promoted to the highest levels of the judiciary.

The weakest components of Malaysian policy are corpus and acquisition planning, inasmuch as they attenuate the growth of legal Malay while doing little to reassure those who fear that English standards are falling, and legal standards with them. Yet here too Malaysia may have something to offer other jurisdictions. Dewan Bahasa's early innovations in the Malay legal lexicon demonstrate a pragmatic balance between neologisms, many of them more transparent than their English counterparts, and retentions or modifications of English where translations might be cumbersome or ambiguous. Granted, some practitioners voice frustration with continued reliance on English (or English-like) lexis, though less with French or Latin. One Shah Alam practitioner encountered in 2013 at a DBP event about legal language criticised the language planners for failing to be serious about raising legal Malay to the level of English legalese, and many feel coinages like *aset, litigasi* and *underait* to be mere window-dressing. But there are also those who feel an accepted and widely understood English term might as well be retained if the alternative is an ambiguous or little known Malay one. Others conceded that reliance on English lexis is common to many professions, not just the law. What all this shows is that the development of a new legal lexicon involves cultural as well as semantic issues. It cannot be hurried, but it need not be so laissez-faire as to allow pragmatic code-mixes to slide into wholesale shifts into English discourse, as often appears to be the case in Malaysian courts.

Lack of Malay terms constitutes a bigger barrier than their quality. Hong Kong's ability to translate more legislation over a shorter period, and Sri Lanka's production of terminology with fewer financial resources, cast doubts on Malaysia's commitment to corpus planning. Given that all new Malaysian legislation is bilingual, it is likely that many more terms are being generated than the average practitioner is aware of, and coordination and education may be bigger problems that productivity. Planners may nevertheless need to break the vicious circle of lexical gaps inhibiting legal writing and insufficient texts inhibiting lexical innovation. Lack of terms and texts further undermine legal study in Malay, and this educational imbalance produces lawyers and judges reluctant or unable to use the language for jurisprudence. Notwithstanding half a century of bilingual legislation, the intertranslatability identified by Sibayan (in Martin 2012: 9) as crucial for bilingualisation is still in doubt, leaving the above-mentioned Shah Alam critic of DBP to lament:

> Malay could be respected if there was more effort. But there is more talking than effort. It's all politics and an absurd waste of time.

As long as Malay remains confined to simpler cases, the main effect of a deficient legal corpus is entrenchment of the status quo. However, the increase in the financial limits for cases within the jurisdiction of the lower courts is bringing more complex matters before justices who function better in Malay. Maintaining legal standards will either require falling back more on English or redoubling efforts to expand and promote Malay's legal lexicon.

11.5 Considerations when Implementing Language Change in Law

If the Malaysian case is anything to go by, reasonably effective language shift within a context of legal continuity involves a wide range of factors that may compete with each other for the attention of planners, including political needs; flexible but enforceable status measures; comprehensive corpus planning; regulation of general as well as legal education; pragmatic alignment of public and professional discourses; and employment planning.

11.5.1 Political Needs

While communicative needs analysis, corpus development and acquisition policies might be expected to be linchpins of successful language planning, Malaysia's current legal bilingualism more clearly reflects a set of status planning measures that frames broad political goals without stifling professional practice. Conducting law in a minority language, and above all in a colonial one, has been constructed discursively as an insult to national dignity or a brake on cultural independence more consistently than as a barrier to justice, and in some ways this stance evokes the prioritisation of political and ideological factors that surrounded medieval England's passage of the Statute of Pleadings or postcolonial Myanmar's promotion of Burmese as a means to contain bar hostility. Sri Lanka's Language of the Courts Acts (1956, 1962) and Hong Kong's Official Languages Ordinance (1974) also emerged from political pressure to raise the status of local languages, while the capacity of English legalese to survive linguistic nationalism evinces private preferences for the language among political elites.

With notable counterexamples such as Myanmar, enough lawyers go into politics, and enough politicians come from legal backgrounds, to maintain personal links that cut across many of the official institutional stances that divide the two domains. Dezalay and Garth (2010, 9), for example, emphasise how local Asian elites were coopted by colonisers, who themselves learned to use the colonisers for their own ends. The conduit for this relationship of strategic collaboration was typically the law, and has remained so in postcolonial times:

> It is relatively easy to see that lawyers invest in politics. The colonial origins of legal professions in Asia through the co-option of elites already possessing political power ensure that law and politics will mix. (Dezalay and Garth 2010: 3)

A number of the lawyers interviewed for this study in Malaysia and beyond were involved in politics. Many others showed a keen understanding of local and national political affairs. Law, and perhaps adversarial law in particular, lends itself to strategic role-playing, and so it is likely lawyers maximise their own professional space by learning which political games to play.

In Malaysia, the importance of Commonwealth case law is undeniably a reason for retaining a role for English in legal education and jurisprudence. Indeed it resembles Hong Kong and Singapore in relying on overseas citation to a greater extent than either England or the United States (Ng and Jacobson 2017). But political considerations also support the language's wider use. The continued tolerance of English in domestic commercial law and property conveyancing, for example, is indicative of the government's desire to be seen as international, open to business, and a model of moderate and modern Islam.

11.5.2 Necessary but Insufficient Role of Status Measures

The frail effect of the Philippines' Constitution and Executive Order 335, or the confinement of most of South Africa's constitutional languages to token legislation, show that status planning is an insufficient condition for vernacularisation. It is nevertheless a necessary one. While the example of Botswana shows that extended oral use of a vernacular may emerge without any enabling legislation, it is difficult to imagine comprehensive lexical innovation or the admissibility of vernacular legal qualifications without measures granting legal status to the language in question. Hence the driving force behind the generation of legal lexis and texts in Tongan is its status as the language of parliamentary debate, rather than its oral use in the police courts. Malaysia's 1967 legislation engendered widespread expectations of change and was the justification for the professional reforms that eventually came in the 1980s and 1990s.

The degree of clarity in status policy may also have a bearing on the nature of practice. Where policy equivocates, by reserving the right to decide the language of the court to the government in Bangladesh, for example, or by deferring to the discretion of judges in Malaysia, there may be greater scope for spontaneity. Sri Lankan legislation is clearer about assigning vernaculars to the lower courts and English to superior courts, and although diversions into English are common in the former they do not seem to trigger language shifts for the entirety of proceedings of the sort that occur in Malaysia. Despite its potential significance, however, status planning need not be detailed or extensive. A sentence in a constitution or enactment declaring a language the medium of law may be enough. Malaysia's National Language Act, including the preamble and amendments, is nine pages long with a mere handful of paragraphs referring to legal practice. Subsequent case law reaffirms this legislation but very little of it elaborates upon it.

11.5.3 Corpus Support for Vernacular Practice

This investigation confirmed the heavier use of local languages in lower courts and in oral mode than in higher courts or texts, indicating that vernacularisation is easier to implement where cases are straightforward and detailed records unnecessary. Vernaculars were used orally in lower courts in British India, but not above. They may continue to be used at that level for decades without infiltrating higher courts, as in Kenya, Tanzania. The fact that the most widespread instantiation of legal vernacularisation is to be found in oral lower court proceedings undoubtedly reflects the lower burden of corpus planning entailed there, although other factors such as the typical socioeconomic, educational and cultural background of subordinate court participants cannot be overlooked.

Wherever there is regular use of vernaculars at high court level, as in Sri Lanka, the Indian states and Malaysia, there is a large body of vernacular legislation, even if it has been generated largely by translation from English. Lower courts may be able to manage with a small number of frequently cited enactments, such as criminal codes or traffic laws. The one court in the Philippines that sustained proceedings in Filipino for several years specialised in drug cases for which key legislation had been translated.

As with status planning, however, corpus measures are a necessary but insufficient condition for vernacularisation. Tonga, as we have seen, publishes all legislation bilingually but Tongan is excluded from the superior courts. There is a long history of Afrikaans jurisprudence in South Africa, but its use in higher courts is declining and increasingly confined to questions of fact.

The general conception of legal lexis as complex, difficult to acquire and hard to translate has been a major factor in the retention of English, just as it was a factor in the continuance of French and Latin in England into the eighteenth century, but it should be remembered that legal disputes may turn on ambiguity in quite ordinary words. In *Tam Yuk-ha* (1996) in Hong Kong a by-law banning the use of pavement space for 'additions' to shops ruled out the metal racks set out by a fishmonger when the English text was used, but allowed them when the Chinese text was referred to. The change from *ibubapa* (arguably, 'both parents') to *ibu atau bapa* ('either parent') in Malay translations of a constitutional provision has fomented debate about the legality of religious conversions. One Malaysian attachment student observed how even the simplest of traffic cases can get bogged down in discussions about the meaning of 'slowly' or 'turn left'. Such disputes inevitably stoke the flames of legal conservatism and put doubts into the path of vernacularisation. But we should not forget that the necessity for translation that bilingual law brings provides opportunities to expose and resolve ambiguities that may have lain hidden. *Tam Yuk-ha* eventually led to an amendment to remove the ambiguity. Ambiguities surrounding *ibubapa* remain, but the reasons for leaving them reflect ambiguities in legal policy itself.

While this study shows lack of terminology to be the most commonly voiced complaint about vernacular law, or most common excuse for resisting it, even where language cells are embedded in administrative institutions as they are throughout India, it is also clear that corpus planners need to go beyond developing lexis to persuading practitioners to use it. Tanzania has had Kiswahili legal terms since 1963, yet even today few lawyers seem to have heard of them. Technical arguments about the suitability of terms are intertwined with cultural and institutional stances, and in a profession that depends not only on precision but also on persuasion, inculcating confidence in the right term may require more than the memorisation that is reportedly the major component of classes in legal Malay.

Encouraging the drafting – rather than translation – of legislation, jurisprudence and law books would help increase the acceptability of innovations inasmuch as writing entails longer reflection than speaking, greater attention to context, and more elegant syntactical, morphological and orthographical integration. Even where translation is the more efficient option, there could be greater attention to the illocutionary effect of target texts. Candlin and Bhatia (1998: 11) highlight the problems of arcane expressions, translation equivalence, and (echoing Šarčević 1997: 70–71), the context of the surrounding legal system – although the latter should not be a major concern where vernacularisation without legal shift is envisaged. In the Malaysian case it is also clear that the development of Malay suffers from being used less in judgments, textbooks or contracts than in legislation, all of which have distinct generic features.

11.5.4 Role of Both Legal and General Education

The lack of law teaching and learning in Malay has been identified as a significant impediment to the expansion of the language in jurisprudence. The survey of other jurisdictions contextualising this investigation found little evidence of vernacular law classes except in the Subcontinent, where they are associated with less lucrative employment. French is important in Canadian legal education, and Afrikaans retains a role in some South African law schools, but these are languages that have long been used for complex legal argument. When it comes to introducing a language hitherto hardly used in law, law schools seem to be even more conservative than the courts.

While the continued use of English in legal education is understandable in most of the common law world (though less readily in Myanmar, which left the

Commonwealth and largely abandoned the citation of cases decades ago), failure to make more use of vernaculars alongside English is more questionable. Soon after its return to Chinese sovereignty, Candlin and Bhatia (1998: 4) conducted a survey of the communicative needs of the legal profession in Hong Kong and recommended training in "legal Putonghua and Chinese", and a decade later Chinese was being emphasised by the Vice President of the Law Society (Yih 2009). But Chinese proficiency is still not required. Even in Sri Lanka, where in theory lawyers may qualify by taking exams in Sinhala or Tamil, courses in those languages rarely cover all obligatory subjects.

There appears be linkage between *general* education and courtroom language. Languages heard orally in lower courts normally have some role in primary education. Setswana, for example, which is used unofficially but routinely in Botswanan Magistrates hearings, is an official MOI in schools. Secondary schooling in Bangla, Cantonese and Malay are more common than in Filipino, Kiswahili or Tongan and may help to explain how vernaculars are found at higher court level in Bangladesh, Hong Kong and Malaysia but not in the Philippines, Tanzania or Tonga. Indeed most Hong Kong secondary schools shifted to Chinese medium around the same time as the lower courts began shifting toward it. But tertiary education in English, or predominantly in English, is the norm for much of the Commonwealth, and this puts its dominance of higher courts and legal education into perspective.

11.5.5 Public Discourse and Professional Compromise

While this investigation lacks extended analysis of discourse planning beyond Malaysia, interviews, academic literature and news reports reveal perennial concerns about the use of English restricting access to justice. Colonial authorities across India seem to have been wary of replacing elite Persian with elite English except at higher levels, citing defendants unable to understand charges. Ferdousi (2009) found the use of English for judgments in Bangladesh disadvantaging lower court advocates as well as lay participants. Elitism is not specific to English: long after French had disappeared from popular use English lawyers continued to use a form of the language impenetrable to laymen, while Persian survived for five decades into the British occupation of India.

Criticism of the impenetrability of elite languages rarely gathers the same momentum as criticism of their foreignness, however. As Mellinkoff (1963: 111) argues for medieval England, it was the Frenchness of law rather than its lack of transparency that provoked the first ambiguous attempts at vernacularisation there. Discourse supporting legal Malay in both media reports and judgments focuses on political and cultural rights more than on communicative accessibility.

But cultural preferences can be difficult to untangle from technical preferences. Whether resistance to language reform comes from Law French-using pleaders in England, English-trained stenographers in the Philippines, or even Indian police clerks perpetuating Urduised jargon (Siwach and Rohatki 2012.2.05), what looks like elitism to outsiders may represent professional pride to insiders. While many reformers point to evidence of vernacularisation making hearings more transparent for the majority (e.g. in Bulacan's Filipino hearings or the Tongan police courts), many practitioners, including the lecturers interviewed at Dhaka International University, see little benefit in vernacularisation per se without a concomitant effort to reduce archaic terminology or elitist professional attitudes. There are also critics of English-medium law (e.g. Siddique 2010: 56; 92) who doubt linguistic reform will do much good without cultural reform. This allows those who fear the legal repercussions of language reform to wield considerable influence in arguing that English remains the best medium to ensure just processes and outcomes. To recap an assertion made in the first chapter of this book, short of extended and complex simulations of controlled hearings in two or more languages it is impossible to predict trial outcomes from language choice. The merits and demerits of different languages thus rest heavily on perceptual, cultural, macro-legal and non-legal considerations, all of which leave scope for competing discourses. All of this suggests that one of the reasons that so little language-in-law planning is based on communicative needs analysis is that there is no consensus about how to carry out such analysis.

11.5.6 Employment Policy

In addition to language policies, this investigation sought to shed light on the potential of employment policies to influence language behaviour. The Malaysian government is the country's larger employer, expanding notably after the 1969 race riots (Kuan 2015: 230). In 2012, only 16% of civil service applications were from non-Malays in East Malaysia (where they form a majority), and just 5.6% in West Malaysia, fuelling accusations of a bloated civil service being used to prop up pro-Malay affirmative action (*Malaysiakini*, 2012.9.04). But there are also those who feel Malays are discriminated against in the private sector (Koon 2012.11.10), sometimes through language requirements (Haspaizi and Kow 2019.6.03), the fact remains that Malaysia's public sector, proportionately one of the largest in Asia (Kuan 2015: 232), is dominated by Malays.

This imbalance extends to the law. A mere 1.87% of the police force are Chinese (*Malaysiakini* 2014.3.01). In 2008 Ong Ka Tin, then president of the MCA, called for a more multiracial judiciary in order to "correct any perception that our judges will not be able to adjudicate fairly and impartially on sensitive issues" (*The Star* 2008.5.01). One private law school lecturer interviewed for this study commented that the overwhelmingly Malay institutions of UIA and UiTM are the largest suppliers of graduates for the judiciary and AGC, and a lecturer from UM added that the AGC, in turn, is the largest employer of law graduates.

As argued throughout this study, the connection between ethnicity and language preference is indirect at best, and both UIA and UiTM emphasise English in their law departments. The bulk of informants with experience of the AGC or judicial service nevertheless attested to an emphasis on the Malay language there.

Malaysian-type affirmative action, while unavailable to many polities, demonstrates how market forces favouring colonial or international languages may be offset by manipulation of the public sector. Introducing a new medium of law can open up legal professions to new socioeconomic and ethnic groups with new sets of language preferences. Where bilingual law amounts to no more than "shallow equality" (Leung 2019) among languages, however, government intervention carries the risk of opening cultural gaps between the judiciary and the bar, as well as widening language-based class divisions. In this light, the Malaysian East Coast lecturer who insisted on English to give students a chance of entering prestigious firms (Chap. 5), or the Sri Lankan lawyer who called for the reinstatement of compulsory English exams (Chap. 10), may represent an alternative orientation toward equity. But this stance too is flawed if access to English remains far from equal.

11.5.7 International Positioning

Malaysia presents us with a telling tale of how the traditional dominance of English in common law is compounded by its increasing dominance in international economics. For numerous informants one of the more compelling reasons for retaining English was its role in business, which in the context of postcolonial developing economies generally has its eye on attracting foreign investment even when all the enterprises involved are local. Ongoing plans to facilitate the involvement of foreign law firms are primarily driven by promotion of the country as a reliable and just environment for business. Government promotion of arbitration, a dispute resolution system dominated by English, is also largely motivated by business concerns (Azirah and Powell 2011). Malaysia is currently ranked 15th on the Ease of Doing Business Index, behind Singapore, Hong Kong, Korea and Taiwan but well ahead of other economies in the region (World Bank 2019), and managed to attract record foreign direct investment in 2018 despite political disruption (Kana 2019.3.15), and with the new government struggling to pay off debts inherited from its predecessor it is unlikely to favour language policies that might be perceived as inward-looking.

Hence vernacularisation in postcolonial common law is doubly constrained: by continued reliance on English-medium case law, both domestic and international, and by global business practices. Postcolonial polities with civil law heritages also face the challenge of global English, but they appear to have certain advantages when it comes to vernacularisation. Indonesia and Vietnam, for example, have managed to abandon colonial languages in law, and their lack of dependence on historical or cross-border case law, together with the lower vehicularity of languages like Dutch or French in comparison with English, may have facilitated this. Although relatively free of the constraints of *stare decisis*, many civil law systems do share sets of similar legal codes, but these may be more amenable to translation than common law precedents: Timorese lawyers with minimal Portuguese have been observed managing to work with codes written in the language because of their similarity to the Indonesian codes they had used before independence (Powell 2011a).

However, the prospects of comparing common law and civil law jurisdictions are bedevilled by political and historical differences. While sharing similar national languages, Indonesia's legal system differs from Malaysia's not only in its civil law roots but also in the legal and political disruptions that accompanied its violent decolonisation. In Vietnam French law, which had developed in parallel with precolonial laws and traditions and influenced the structure of postcolonial law, was not simply transferred into the vernacular but transformed by socialism and antilegalism (Rose 1998). Moreover there is ample evidence beyond Asia of postcolonial civil law failing to introduce local languages. Most former French and Portuguese colonies in Africa continue to rely on the colonial legal medium, even where it has limited social currency (Mabasso 2013).

11.6 What Changes when the Language of Law Changes?

Changing the language of the law may entail intervening in language in other domains, such as education and administration, and manipulating non-linguistic factors such as employment policy or the financial jurisdictions of the courts. Key questions for planners, then, include not only what is needed to change legal language, but also whether proposed reforms are likely to produce adequate returns in access to justice or language rights, and what else is likely to change when the medium of law is changed. The complexity of language ecology is not necessarily a reason to refrain from legal vernacularisation: if law isn't broken there is certainly a case for advising against fixing it, but reports from many postcolonial jurisdictions of alienation and inaccessibility suggest that it is often in a poor state of repair. Successful language reform does, however, call for a breadth of vision that goes beyond the creation of terminologies or revision of court rules to an awareness of its potential ramifications within and beyond the legal domain.

11.6.1 Perception and Perpetuation of Legal Culture

Given that perceived elitism or foreignness is often cited to justify language reforms, one of the more foreseeable outcomes of language shift is a change in societal perceptions of legal culture, whether or not this reflects changes in legal practice itself. An increasingly Malayanised judiciary's obligations toward the national language and the propensity of the senior ranks of the Bar to work in English inevitably reinforce cultural tensions between the respective institutions in the minds of the public. The association of the Malay language with a particular ethnicity and religion further invites speculation about motivations for language choice in legal affairs, with discussion of the use of Malay for an apex opinion on religious conversion or the appointment of an anglophone non-Malay Attorney General straying beyond technical issues.

In Hong Kong, legal culture has been at the heart of struggles over the meaning of One Country, Two Systems, with language typically playing a symbolic role. Candlin and Bhatia (1998: 16) found barristers struggling to disassociate the introduction of Mandarin from the introduction of Mainland values, and a decade later Ng (2009) concluded that those barristers least favourable toward the Chinese language were also the ones most concerned about the erosion of links with Commonwealth law.

Attempts by Beijing to increase its say in Hong Kong's legal system continue to trigger popular resistance. In turn, PRC-supporters accuse its critics of a necolonialist agenda in the name of judicial independence. When condemning the jailing of police officers convicted of assaulting Umbrella Revolution demonstrators, for example, Beijing supporters focused on the British-born judge who had handed down the sentence, with Beihang University Law School's Tian Feilong claiming expatriate judges failed to understand the importance of public order or the nature of the Basic Law, Beijing University's Rao Geping questioning their disproportionate representation in the apex court, and LegCo member Peter Wong going as far as to accuse them of foreign allegiance (Lee 2017.3.09). On the other side, Simon Young Ngai-man of Hong Kong University's law faculty defended non-local judges as contributing to judicial independence and a Department of Justice spokesman argued that they broadened legal perspectives in the SAR, while *South China Morning Post* downplayed the 'foreign' nature of Hong Kong law in claiming that 89% of the judiciary were bilingual (ibid). In a ruling that found favour with Beijing, Justice Thomas Au Ching-heung referred both to the PRC's controversial interpretation of the Basic Law and to common law principles in upholding the dismissal of LegCo members who had amended their oaths[2] during the Council's 2016 swearing-in as a protest against PRC interference (Lau and Chung 2017.7.14). Tian Feilang accused the ruling's critics of failing to accept the 'nationalisation' of the legal system (Tian 2017.7.25).

The idea of nationalising common law, voiced also in the Malaysian context by Hickling (2001:37), an expatriate who advocated greater use of Malay, is far from antithetical to the traditions of common law, which emerged from the systematisation of local precedents, partially incorporated pre-existing laws when expanding overseas, and developed independent bodies of case law in England, the United States and elsewhere. As well as this localising orientation, however, the international dimension of common law has to be taken into account. But what looks like adherence to international standards or a guarantee of impartiality to some may appear to be foreign interference or neocolonialism to others. The very notion of judicial impartiality is controversial since the Bench's willingness to stand up to

[2] Exercising their right to take the oath in English, the dismissed councilors added words or adopted ambiguous pronunciations and were accused of lacking sincerity.

pressure from one side (e.g. Beijing, or *Syariah* rulings) is likely to be interpreted by some as a tendency to align itself with other interests (e.g. London, or non-Muslims). All of this underlines the difficulty of presenting language choice as a neutral or technical matter.

As for the role of language in perpetuating legal culture itself, given the wealth of studies (e.g. Hoffman 1991) on how bilinguals adjust their behaviour when switching languages, bilingualism adds an interesting dimension to the biculturalism all practitioners display in switching among legal and lay registers (McCaul 2011: 13). Hong Kong brings us compelling evidence of linkage between professional preferences and wider ideologies. Despite admitting that the very first Chinese trial there had gone smoothly enough, one member of the Legislative Council suggested that the judge's final comments had "turned the adversarial system of the common law into some court of reconciliation and togetherness" (cited in Candlin and Bhatia 1998: 14). Leung (2012) has noted how judges are more likely to assume the stance of educators or scolding parents when using Cantonese. Although the influence of changes in professional practice will likely be less dramatic and more nuanced in societies such as Malaysia where multilingualism and code-switching are endemic, there too we see differences between metropolitan and regional courts that have distinct linguistic components.

It has already been emphasised that it is difficult to link language choice to immediate legal outcomes. Where there is a choice of medium for proceedings it is nonetheless probable that calculations about which one is more likely to bring a favourable verdict will influence considerations about individual proficiency and the availability of relevant jurisprudence.

In practice, English is intricately woven into the fabric of everyday life in Malaysia, where Malay nationalists code-switch into it without thinking and competent speakers are encountered even in rural areas. This suggests that English has an important part to play in legal indigenisation, and in time the influx of ethnically Malay lawyers and of non-Malay lawyers fluent in the national language should help break down linguistic stereotypes, especially if the judiciary can ensure that the younger generation of justices do not abandon English before its time. Speculatively, the highly multilingual environment of the Philippines should also be able to support increased use of local languages alongside English without necessarily entailing a marked change in legal culture. Conversely, in societies where English is confined to an elite, such as Bangladesh, any shift away from English toward the national language in law might be expected to have significant repercussions for legal culture.

11.6.2 Career Paths

In addition to association with particular languages, law is commonly associated with particular socioeconomic groups who may bring their own language preferenes to the profession. Anglophone Indians long dominated Malaysia's Bar Council

(*Insaf*, 1968~2013). Lack of familiarity with English compounds financial disadvantage to keep rural Filipinos out of legal practice. Introducing a new language into the law therefore has the potential to change the sociology of the profession.

Typically, the Malaysian picture is muddied by fragmented correspondence between language and ethnicity and clouded by affirmative action to increase *bumiputra* participation in higher education, but it is reasonable to conclude that the raised status and use of Malay is linked to the increase in Malay lawyers, who at 41% now form the largest ethnic group (*Majlis Peguam* 2017), while still punching somewhat below their demographic weight. Malaysia has not opened up career paths for those lacking proficiency in English, with even the lower court judges having passed exams involving English, but interview evidence about language practices and career preferences confirms links between Malay and the government sector and English and commercial law.

As noted in the previous chapter, on the Subcontinent language-career linkage is more explicit, resulting in a class of lawyers who may qualify and work in a vernacular while being largely limited to less lucrative areas of legal practice.

11.6.3 Accessibility and Transparency

Unless there are reasonable prospects for enhancing access to justice it may be difficult to justify the time, resources and potential disruption of vernacularisation, whatever the symbolic or ideological incentives to do so. The minimal requirement would be the availability of an established language that is better understood by a sufficient number of people than the existing legal medium, which suggests Kenya, Tanzania, Bangladesh, Pakistan and the Indian states may be ripe for further vernacularisation, while limiting the potential of Tagalog or Hindi to become the main media of law at national level. Where a new legal medium can be agreed on, planners need to ensure that lawyers, judges and administrators are themselves proficient in it and its lexical and legislative corpus is up to the demands of modern legal practice.

This still leaves the matter of whether lay participants will find local legalese any more accessible than exonormative legalese. But the idea that legal language is too remote for most people to make it worth vernacularising overlooks the important role of less specialised communicative legal tasks such as witness examinations. It also suggests, implausibly, that legal jargon embedded in a familiar lexicogrammatical matrix is no more intelligible than when embedded in an unfamiliar one. In many cases vernacularisation is a step in the right direction, even if it will not in itself close the distance between lay participants and a highly specialised discursive culture. While LegCo member Margaret Ng was right to warn that the use of Chinese in post-1997 Hong Kong law would not be a "panacea for solving all legal disputes surrounding problems of interpretation of law" (in Candlin and Bhatia 1998: 10), evidence from the Philippines suggests discretionary use of Tagalog can shed light on cases that participants feel shut out of by their lack of English (Martin 2012), and more extended use in the regional courts shows how language reform may enhance public engagement. From observations of US claims courts (Angermeyer 2015) and Hong Kong lower courts (Ng 2013), and from the accounts of Malaysian advocates comparing work with interpreters in Sarawak and without them in Malaya (Powell 2011b), we also have evidence of how interpreting affects legal discourse.

11.6.4 Professional Standards and Procedural Efficiency

Admission of more than one legal language not only offers the possibility of faster trials and more transparent discourse, but may also produce more accurate court records, given that the speech of witnesses using admissible languages may be preserved without translation. However, the benefits of introducing vernaculars need to be weighed up against possible disruptions to professionalism or efficiency, at least in the minds of the practitioners who policymakers ignore at their peril. As with the efficacy and acceptability of lexical innovations, however, it is difficult to make assessments until new practices have a chance to establish themselves.

The requirement to file in Malay may have actually increased paperwork in Malaysia as many firms now produce two sets of documents, knowing that judges or clients may rely on the English translation. Expectations that Filipino trials would be more efficient because of dispensing with the need for translators were confounded in Bulacan (Chap. 10), although to a large extent this was because court recorders were given insufficient training and legal corpora were lacking.

Bilingual trials in languages non-professional participants understand may avoid time spent tracking down interpreters, although this may be less significant in Malaysia where there have long been court-based clerk-interpreters for the main languages. Ng (2013) has suggested that the time and resources saved by having more trials in Chinese could allow better support for other languages in Hong Kong, where the increasingly multilingual background of court participants, especially in the New Territories, seems to have been overlooked in the postcolonial focus on Cantonese-English interpreting (Powell 2017).

The idea, expressed by a Solicitor-General in pre-bilingual Hong Kong (in Candlin and Bhatia 1998: 14) that common law cannot adequately be conveyed in new languages is hard to support in light of the dozen or so common law jurisdictions that do use other languages while maintaining discursive and institutional links with each other, but it is important to remember that the burden for successful language shift within legal continuity falls heavily on the shoulders of bilingual individual professionals. Yet neither Malaysia nor any other vernacularising jurisdiction has paid much attention to the challenges of bilingual legal communication.

11.7 In Support of Bilingual Law

Discursive and cultural connotations make choosing among languages a much more complex and significant affair than merely deciding which ones communicate propositional content more effectively, and choices are all the more loaded when one option is a symbol of postcolonial identity and another is a vehicle of international economics and politics. Communicative and technical questions about which language better allows justice to be done, and to be seen to be done, run up against issues about which language more authentically represents the cultural and socio-economic outlook of the people using the justice system. Although not feasible or appropriate everywhere, bilingualism offers a bridge between the competing orientations of law, and while a functional bilingual community does not require every member of it to be functionally bilingual, bilingual lawyers constitute a valuable human resource deserving of support because it is largely through their linguistic proficiency and associated cultural pragmatism that tensions in the legal system among national identity, international engagement, cultural diversity and legal integrity are resolved, or at least circumvented.

Malaysian legal practitioners interact with a language policy that serves multiple practical and ideological interests, and receive little training for this. Planners, who are usually politicians, sometimes lawyers, but rarely linguists, often assume it is a small step from speaking two languages in daily life to using them professionally in legal contexts. Yet older lawyers wince at the English grammar of their juniors while young lawyers have low expectations about their seniors' Malay. Most practitioners learn how to be bilingual professionals only when they start representing clients in the office and in court. In Hong Kong and elsewhere there may be even less bilingual training for practitioners being asked to perform legal tasks in more than one language. The status, and then the corpus, of legal languages are routinely prioritised over the needs of the people who use them.

As far as access to justice is concerned, while legal language is never likely to be fully accessible to non-lawyers, and legal transparency involves cultural practices and professional integrity as well as language, bilingualism as a mainstay of biculturalism is an important factor. The pragmatic code-switching of Malaysian lawyers and lecturers that was observed in this study holds potential for creating a system that embraces constant interplay between two languages. But it needs to be supported by a more integrative approach to corpus development and legal education based on long-term collaboration between lawyers and linguists and, if possible, allowing politicians to take a backseat.

Even if bilingual law can only replace legal interpreting and translating in specific circumstances, there is a strong case for expanding its role. Moreover the legal ambiguities that opponents of bilingualism fear should be approached as paths toward greater transparency rather than crossroads of confusion.

Cases Cited

Dato' Seri Anwar Ibrahim v Tun Dr Mahathir Mohamad [2010] 3CLJ 444 CA [Malaysia]
R. v Tam Yuk-ha MA1385/1996 [Hong Kong]

References

Angermeyer, Philipp Sebastian. (2015). *Speak English or what? Codeswitching and interpreter use in New York City courts*. New York: Oxford University Press.
Azirah Hashim, & Powell, Richard. (2011). Exploring language choice in Malaysian trials and arbitrations: Common aims, complementary methods. In M. Petersen & J. Engberg (Eds.), *Current trends in LSP research: Aims and methods* (pp. 129–161). Bern: Peter Lang.
Candlin, Christopher, & Bhatia, Vijay. (1998). *Strategies and competencies in legal communication. A study to investigate the communicative needs of legal professionals*. Hong Kong: The Law Society of Hong Kong.
Conley, John, & O'Barr, William. (1998). *Just words. Law, language and power*. Chicago: University of Chicago Press.
Det, C. H. E. (1949.4.24). Malay – "modern" and standard. *The Straits Times*, p. 6.
Dezalay, Yves, & Garth, Bryant. (2010). *Asian legal revivals – lawyers in the shadow of empire*. Chicago: University of Chicago Press.
Ferdousi, Nahid. (2009). *Bangladesher bichar bebosthae Bangla vasha – poristhiti* [Bangla language in the judiciary of Bangladesh – The state]. *The Dhaka University Journal of Linguistics, 2*(3), 53–68 [English summary by Dr Mahmud Hasan, University of Liberal Arts, Dhaka].
Hafiz Yatim. (2015.10.06). 1948 Sedition Act is valid, Federal Court rules. *Malaysiakini*. Accessed 7 Oct 2015, from: http://www.malaysiakini.com/news/314666
Haspaizi Zain & Kow Gah Chiei. (2019.6.03) *Job discrimination – Malay and Chinese firms' different perspective*. Accessed 10 June 2019 from: https://www.malaysiakini.com/news/478458
Heller, Monica. (2008). Doing ethnography. In W. Li & M. Moyer (Eds.), *The Blackwell guide to research methods in bilingualism and multilingualism* (pp. 249–262). Malden: Blackwell.
Hickling, Reginald Hugh. (2001). *Malaysian Law*. Kuala Lumpur: Pelanduk.
Hoffman, Charlotte. (1991). *An introduction to bilingualism*. London: Longman.
Kana, Ganeshwaran. (2019.3.15). M'sia FDI at record high. *The Star Online*. Accessed 16 Mar 2019, from: https://www.thestar.com.my/business/business-news/2019/03/15/msia-fdi-at-record-high/
Kaplan, Robert., & Baldauf, Richard. (1997). *Language planning from practice to theory*. Clevedon: Multilingual Matters.
Koon, Kew Yin. (2012.11.10). Hiring discrimination study a half-finished product. *Malaysiakini*. Accessed 20 Nov 2012, from: http://www.malaysiakini.com/news/213938
Koshy, Shaila. (2013.9.15). Language makes the law. *The Star* (online edition). Accessed 15 Sept 2013 from: http://www.thestar.com.my/News/Nation/2013/09/15/Education-Tun-Zaki-English-Medium-Schools.aspx
Kuan Heong Woo. (2015). Recruitment practices in the Malaysian public sector: Innovations or political responses? *Journal of Public Affairs Education, 21*(2), 229–246. https://doi.org/10.1080/15236803.2015.12001830.
Lau, Chris, & Chung, Kimmy. (2017.7.14). Court ruling disqualifying Hong Kong lawmakers over oath-taking controversy 'a declaration of war'. *South Morning China Post*. Accessed 15 July 2017 from https://www.scmp.com/news/hong-kong/politics/article/2102609/four-more-hong-kong-lawmakers-disqualified-over-oath-taking

Lee, Eddie. (2017.3.09). Beijing throws the book at Hong Kong's foreign judges. *South Morning China Post*. Accessed 15 July 2017 from: https://www.scmp.com/news/hong-kong/law-crime/article/2077521/experts-line-throw-book-hong-kongs-foreign-judges

Leung, Janny. (2012). Judicial discourse in Cantonese courtrooms in postcolonial Hong Kong: The judge as godfather, scholar, educator and scolding parent. *The International Journal of Speech, Language and the Law, 19*(2), 239–261.

Leung, Janny. (2019). *Shallow equality and symbolic jurisprudence in multilingual legal orders*. New York: Oxford University Press.

Mabasso, Eliseu. (2013). *Official language, written and customary laws in Mozambican police stations*. Paper presented at 11th Biennial conference on forensic linguistics, Mexico City, 2013.6.

Majlis Peguam. (2017) *Bar Council Annual Report 2016/17*.

Malaysiakini. (2012.9.04). *PSC: More non-Malays applying to join civil service*. Bernama. Accessed 6 Sept 2012, from http://www.malaysiakini.com/news/207899

Malaysiakini. (2014.3.01). *PDRM seeks more Chinese to join force*. Accessed 1 Mar 2014, from: http://www.malaysiakini.com/news/255767

Malaysiakini. (2016.4.15). *Amnesty calls conviction of Haris Ibrahim for sedition a 'travesty'*. Accessed 16 Apr 2016, from: https://www.malaysiakini.com/news/337912

Maley, Yon, Candlin, Christopher, Crichton, John, & Koster, Pieter (1994). *Orientations in lawyer-client interviews* (Working Papers no. 3). Centre for Language in Social Life, Department of Linguistics, Macquarie University.

Martin, Isabel Pefianco. (2012). Expanding the role of Philippine languages in the legal system. *Asian Perspectives in the Arts and Humanities, 2*(1), 1–14.

McCaul, Kim (2011) Understanding courtroom communication through cultural scripts. In A. Wagner & Le Cheng (Eds.), (pp. 11–28).

Mead, Richard. (1988). Malaysia's National Language Policy and the Legal System. New Haven: Yale.

Mellinkoff, David. (1963). *The language of the law*. Boston: Little, Brown & Co..

Ng, Eva. (2013). Power and control in interpreter-mediated trials. Paper presented at *11th biennial conference on forensic linguistics*, Mexico City, 2013.6.

Ng Kwai Hang. (2009). *The common law in two voices. Language, law and the postcolonial dilemma in Hong Kong*. Stanford: Stanford University Press.

Ng Kwai Hang & Jacobson, Brynna (2017). How global is the common law? A comparative study of Asian common law systems – Hong Kong, Malaysia, and Singapore. *Asian Journal of Comparative Law, 12*(2), 209–232.

Powell, Richard. (2008). *Motivations for language choice in Malaysian courtrooms and implications for language planning*. Kuala Lumpur: Universiti Malaya.

Powell, Richard. (2011a). *Challenges facing the construction of a vernacular legal system in Timor Leste/Timor Lorosae*. Paper presented at panel on 'Language shift in postcolonial law: comparing East Asian policies and practices. *Law and Society Annual Conference*, San Francisco, June, 2011.

Powell, Richard. (2011b, December 8–11). Language policy and practice in the courts of East and West Malaysia. *16th ESEA (English in Southeast Asia) Conference*, Yogyakarta.

Powell, Richard. (2017, July). *Ideology and pragmatism in bilingual law*. Paper presented at 13th Biennial conference of the International Association of Forensic Linguists (IAFL), University of Porto.

Rose, Carol. (1998). The "new" law development movement in the post-cold war era: A Vietnam case study. *Law & Society Review, 32*(1), 93–140.

Šarćevič, Susan. (1997). *New approach to legal translation*. The Hague: Kluwer Law International.

Siddique, Osama. (2010). *Law in practice – The Lahore district courts litigants survey (2010–2011)* (DPRC working papers). Development Policy Research Centre, Lahore University of Management Sciences.

Siwach, Sukhbir, & Rohatki, Hina. (2012.2.25). Use of Urdu In FIRs Baffles courts, commoners. *Times of India* (Haryana Edition). Accesed 18 Dec 2012, from: https://timesofindia.indiatimes.com/city/chandigarh/Use-of-Urdu-In-FIRs-Baffles-Courts-commoners/articleshow/11766436.cms

Steele, Stacey, & Taylor, Katheryn. (2010). Introduction: Globalization, change and contexts. In Steele & Taylor (Eds.), *Legal education in Asia* (pp. 3–19). Abingdon: Routledge.

The Star. (2008.5.01). *Multi-ethnic judiciary needed*, p. N8.

The Straits Times. (1960.6.24). *Malay is not accurate enough for all courts, says Leong*. p. 2.

Tian, Feilong. (2017.7.25). Hong Kong's legal system is undergoing 'nationalisation', and the opposition must realise this. *South Morning China Post*. Accessed 15 July 2017, from https://www.scmp.com/comment/insight-opinion/article/2103971/hong-kongs-legal-system-undergoing-nationalisation-and

Universiti Kebangsaan Malaysia. (2013). *Portal of UKM*. Accessed 20 Nov 2013 from: http://www.ukm.my

World Bank. (2019). *Portal*. Accessed 10 May 2019, from: https://data.worldbank.org/indicator/ic.bus.ease.xq

Yih, Dieter. [former president of Law Society Hong Long]. (2009.9.07). *Becoming a lawyer in Hong Kong*. Presentation to Law Society of Hong Kong. Accessed through personal communication with author, 2013.7.15.

Index

R. Powell, *Language Choice in Postcolonial Law*, Language Policy 22,
https://doi.org/10.1007/978-981-15-1173-8

The manufacturer's authorised representative in the EU is Springer Nature Customer Service Centre GmbH, Europaplatz 3, 69115 Heidelberg, Germany. If you have any concerns regarding our products, please contact ProductSafety@springernature.com

Printed and bound by CPI Group (UK) Ltd, Croydon, CR0 4YY
30/09/2026
02225447-0008